Cavalier and Yankee

CAVALIER AND YANKEE

The Old South and American National Character

BY

WILLIAM R. TAYLOR

Harvard University Press
Cambridge, Massachusetts
and London, England

PRINTED IN THE UNITED STATES OF AMERICA

Library of Congress Catalog Card Number: 79–91066

ISBN 0–674–10440–4

10 9 8 7 6 5 4 3 2

FOR ELLEN

Acknowledgments

IN THE COURSE of completing this book, which has now consumed perhaps too many years, I have accumulated a great many obligations, more than I could hope to acknowledge adequately or even list. Furthermore, the life of the mind being what it is, there are still other debts, I am sure, which will be obvious to some of my readers but of which I am not myself fully conscious. Some of these debts will be apparent from my footnotes and from references in the text. Some minds, however, have contributed so extensively and compellingly to our cultural self-awareness that their ideas have become absorbed into our intellectual "public domain" and are subject to pre-emption by all who travel their way. I hope they will forgive my trespassing.

I can only hope at this point to pay a few private debts, first to those who helped me when I was completing parts of this study as a doctoral dissertation, and finally to those who have encouraged me and guided me through the intricacies, the endless labors and the discouragements of book-making. I am grateful for the criticism and suggestions of Kenneth B. Murdock and Perry Miller, both of whom read my thesis. A stimulating discussion of Southern thought in Louis Hartz's seminar in the Fall of 1951 probably determined me to write about the South. I still remember with gratitude the encouragement and help I received from Kenneth Lynn, whose interest in some of these ideas goes back to our days in graduate school. I recall with equal nostalgia what it meant to me to know and converse with Donald B. Meyer at the time when I was conceiving this study.

Acknowledgments

More recently I profited from a year spent in the city of Washington, and from many courtesies extended to me by the staff of the Library of Congress, especially by Colonel Willard J. Webb. Among the historians working there for the year three friends deserve special mention. J. Merton England, Joseph H. Harrison, Jr., and Christopher Lasch read my entire manuscript chapter by chapter, parts of it more than once, and offered many valuable and face-saving criticisms. William Abrahams first interested himself in this book some years ago, and has recently combed through it with a writer's sure eye for clarity, detail and arrangement. To Oscar Handlin, whose faithful support and generous help has been extended to me at every phase of this study, I owe perhaps most of all. His encouragement and his criticism have been indispensable to me, and I doubt that I could —or would—have written the book without him. The help of Donna Spies Taylor through all this defies enumeration, and her work on certain parts of the manuscript has been so extensive as to earn her the title of co-author. Finally, every historian needs an editor who believes in him and makes the fateful decision to put him in print. I am fortunate in having found such an editor in Edwin Seaver.

Portions of the chapter titled "From Natural Aristocrat to Country Squire" appeared in the *William and Mary Quarterly*. I wish to thank the editors of this journal for permission to reprint material from their pages. Two grants from the Harvard Foundation for Advanced Study provided me with funds for travel and research, and a grant from the History Department of Harvard University aided me in preparing the manuscript for publication.

Preface to the *1979* Edition

The first copy of *Cavalier and Yankee* reached me in New Hampshire toward the end of August, 1961. Rereading it during the dog days of July almost eighteen years later, I have been forcibly reminded of some of the circumstances surrounding its writing and publication. The ensuing years have brought with them many changes — to the historical temper of the country, to the state of the art in history, and to my own perspective — enough changes, certainly, to make any revision or updating of the text unthinkable. I am therefore reprinting it without modifying in any way what I originally wrote. Books, like people, should probably be allowed the dignity of assuming their place in history without excessive tampering with their appearance.

I have been struck in going back through the book these past weeks by how much, in both tone and spirit, it belongs to the period in which it was written. It is not an accident that most of it was written in Washington, much of it in an attic of the Library of Congress during the winter and spring of 1959–60. There was all that year a sense of imminent change about the city and a feeling that the nation was on the point of confronting some of its serious social problems. There was, accordingly, a sober hopefulness about the efficaciousness of the federal government, perhaps best summed up in a series of articles written by Walter Lippmann for the *Washington Post*, as the Eisenhower administration was winding down and the Kennedy campaign was tuning up. There was also a feeling that great changes were about to occur in race relations in the wake of *Brown* v. *Board of Education*. I remember shuttling back and forth between the room where I worked and the gallery of the Senate or the chamber of the Supreme Court when a bill or case pertaining to civil rights was being discussed. And there was, finally, a belief that the historical isolation of the South was about to end. With it, we were assured, would go a whole catalog of myths and presuppositions that had conditioned relations between North and South for over a century. The expectation for a new kind of biracial society — perhaps best expressed in Martin Luther King's dream — was shared by many whites. I was unable to share fully in those hopes and expectations, alluring though they were, and no doubt the book reflects my sense that these complex historical relationships were not about to yield to legislative or judicial action.

The mood among historians was encapsulated in *The Southerner as American*, a volume of essays edited by Charles Grier Sellers, Jr., and published in 1960. These essays make the point over and over that the South experienced in good measure the historical forces that were rapidly shaping and transforming the Northern states. In the most important of these studies Sellers argued that it was precisely this similarity with the North in values and perspective that had created such a problem with Southerners over slavery and had finally goaded and tormented the South into civil war. *Cavalier and Yankee* makes a similar kind of point by showing how certain historical ideas of the North and South, of Yankee and cavalier, played dialectically through the thinking of all Americans during the antebellum years.

At the time it first appeared, *Cavalier and Yankee* was widely, even indulgently, reviewed, yet I have found myself puzzling over some aspects of its reception. It was seen as a study of Southern culture, as an examination of the formative process through which historical myths are created. Its relationship to other recent studies of American character by Henry Nash Smith, John William Ward, and Leo Marx was frequently, and plausibly, mentioned, but few reviewers bothered to note the many differences between my work and the work of these other scholars. At least two other peculiarities about these generous reviews stand out as I read them today. No one challenged the validity of reaching conclusions about a society by analyzing the types of characters found in its imaginative literature, nor did anyone seem to sense how little historical work seemed to derive its insights from literature. No one noticed my attempts to correlate my analysis of the literature with psychoanalytical theory, although I cited the work of Erik Erikson.

Generous though the response to *Cavalier and Yankee* was, it produced few disciples. There was as little discussion of my methods as of my conclusions. I remember at one point considering the inclusion of a methodological chapter similar to the one that H. Stuart Hughes had included in *Consciousness and Society*. As time went on, I began to regret that I had not done so. To many readers, historians among them, work in intellectual or cultural history has often seemed like social mind reading, sometimes justifiably. The Hughes chapter on method had the virtue of being explicit about assumptions, procedures, and evidence. For example, to show that canons of evidence apply to cultural sources as well as to others is important. The text can only show what a historian has concluded. It can rarely indicate how a conclusion was reached, nor with what degree of assurance, nor can it show what other possible inferences were rejected and why. A good discussion of how a historian reasons from intellectual and literary materials, I came to feel, might serve to point out the significance of my analysis in the text. At odd moments I imagined a dialogue between myself and my critics, and the opportunity to write a new preface has allowed me to perfect this dialogue now. It goes something like this:

Reviewer: Your preoccupation with national character seems to be part of a fashionable movement of postwar social science, most evident in the work of certain anthropologists like Geoffrey Gorer and psychoanalysts like Erik Erikson. Isn't there a danger in trying to apply such insights to the nineteenth century where the same kind of evidence is not available and the method might not be applicable?

Author: You are right, of course, about the concern with national character as a fashionable movement. A glance at the *Reader's Guide* confirms that new work on national character virtually disappeared after the early sixties. But *Cavalier and Yankee* owes less to such a trend than it does to the language of the period it was trying to analyze. The eighteen thirties and forties produced its own literature on national character, as I try to show, one that emphasized the moral temper of the genus *Americanus* and worried over its capacity to withstand the shock waves of antebellum social and economic change. In this sense, the term national character, as I use it, is a historical pun, since it only indirectly refers to the modern anthropological sense of the term.

Reviewer: How do you justify generalizing about Southern character from examining the thinking of only a handful of writers and publicists? What can be learned about the historical experience of a whole region by analyzing the lives and intellectual gropings of a few individuals?

Author: Quite a lot, I believe. As I wrote to Clement Eaton in 1964, "We watch one man (or woman) draw conclusions, conceive of ideas, change his (or her) mind, develop inconsistencies, struggle to resolve them, lose hope, etc. We see the process of historical change from the *inside out*, and our understanding of group behavior is increased in accordance. We see the range of difference between individuals who hold the same general views, and we come to appreciate the complexity of human motivation."

Reviewer: I can understand your interest in the South's publicists and propagandists, but why such attention to its novelists, especially since their work was derivative and without much literary merit? If you add that these novelists reached only a small number of readers in either the North or South, how do you justify attributing historical significance to their work?

[4]

Author: Damaging as the questions may seem, there are, I think, convincing answers. A novelist, even an indifferent and derivative one, is compelled first of all to create or evoke a little social world in which to place his (or her) characters. The novelist must try to make this imaginary world believed by his contemporary world. Nineteenth-century sentimental novels tended to focus on the domestic circle with its radiating concerns with the plantation, the town, and the larger social community. Relations between children and parents, between family and servants, were its stock in trade. Any novel that attempted to do this perforce introduced elements of the historical reality of its time. The very form of the nineteenth-century novel, which itself evolved historically, restricted the capacity of the novelist to find expression for the purely idiosyncratic and eccentric. To the extent that these novelists drew on the conventions of the novel, they were tapping a literary form that had developed hand in glove with the Western bourgeoisie. The nineteenth-century novel was social and ideological history in microcosm. When Southerners attempted to write versions of the English novel, therefore, they were forced by the evolution of the genre to see Southern life against a backdrop provided by countless fictional precedents. English country houses became plantations, landed gentry became gentleman planters, dialect-speaking rural retainers became Negro slaves, etc. It is precisely this juxtaposition of Southern life and English cultural heritage that makes such an inquiry historically revealing.

Moreover, the ineptitude of many of these writers attracts our attention to the difficulty they had fitting English convention to Southern circumstance. Sometimes the more skillful of these writers would have a little fun with a deliberate parody of English conventions in the light of Southern customs. In any event, the historicity of antebellum Southern fiction lies not in the size of the reading audience or in the reputation of the authors, but rather in the way it relates Southern life to a long tradition of genteel manners locked within the conventions of the novel. Novels like

Harriet Beecher Stowe's *Uncle Tom's Cabin,* of course, become historical in still other ways. *Uncle Tom,* for example, coming as it did at the end of a period of sentimental domestic fiction, capitalized on the experience of both Southern and Northern writers who had tried to write about slavery and the plantation South. It thus became a refinement of a developing indigenous literary tradition. It also incited countless Southerners to attempt "answers" to its sentimental logic and in doing so exerted a historical force of its own.

Reviewer: What does all this "literary sociology," as you call it, tell us about the larger questions of antebellum history? What insight does it give into the debate over slavery, the sectional conflict, and the coming of war?

Author: I thought no one would ever ask. Reviewers seemed to take the importance of examining Southern culture for granted and did not probe further. Despite my own evident interest in the matter, moreover, scant attention was paid to insights plantation fiction provides into Southern feelings about Negro slavery, especially my treatment of this issue in chapter IX, "Whistling in the Dark."

The sentimental domestic novel, as it turned out, proved to be a real Pandora's box. To portray slavery in a favorable light (once the slave had been given a central place in this fiction) required acknowledging the slave's humanity. Once one accepted that the slave had feelings like anyone else, that he loved his children, longed for his wife, felt love and loyalty for his master, and experienced some of the same dependence as a child, he awakened in readers the same sentimental indulgence as the women and children of this fiction. He became, as it were, a full-fledged member of the sentimental family and was entitled to his share of tears and flapdoodle. Making such a concession unleashed an endless stream of problems for those who in fiction argued for the rightness of slavery. The only other option was both morally unthinkable and stylistically difficult to manage within the conventions of the sentimental novel: to deny the humanity of the slave and to treat him as some kind of subhuman creature. To do this was to suggest that the slave was incapable of loyalty, kindness, happiness — or pity. He thus became an embodiment of those Southern nightmares about slave insurrection, a creature who might rise in the night and murder his master and his master's family without compassion or feeling. Only rarely and fleetingly did writers of this fiction allow themselves to explore such an option. It is not surprising, therefore, that most writers of plantation fiction, trying to be humane, elected to play up the humanity of the slave and, in doing so, they bought a pack of future troubles.

The slaveholder was under enormous pressure by the middle of the century to acknowledge that holding men and women in bondage was unjust and inhumane. This pressure was only increased by the existence of an imaginative literature — capped off by *Uncle Tom's Cabin* — that perceived the slave as human and childishly dependent. For the planter to deny this inhumanity, all while acknowledging that the slave was human, required suppressing some of the century's most powerful moral feelings: those for the pitiful and the helplessly dependent. There was, of course, another contradiction confronting the Southerner that required painful if more abstract suppression: to proclaim his belief in Liberty and to deny the same liberty to his slaves, as Charles Sellers has shown. *Cavalier and Yankee* argues that the sentimental logic that emerged from this fictional scrutiny of the plantation was a key factor in creating these contradictions and hence in producing the tinderbox of 1861. The problem was not that those who owned slaves or defended the institution expressed guilt, as Eugene Genovese appears to feel in his critique of this argument in *The World the Slaveholders Made*. The situation became explosive because these feelings of guilt could *not* be expressed without undermining the institution and could not be denied without denying one's own humanity. The effect of guilt on a group as large as those concerned with slavery is far from clear, but it seems plausible to argue, as I do in the book's

Epilogue, that suppressed feelings as powerful as those awakened by the slavery issue must have found hostile expression somewhere.

Reviewer: One last question. As you know, the New Social History pretty much dominates the current historical scene. How do you see the usefulness of older studies such as yours in the present historical setting? What kind of connections can you make between *Cavalier and Yankee* and more recent work of an analogous kind?

Author: I agree, of course, about the recent predominance of social history, but there has been a remarkable change in the last few years. I myself, for example, am more interested than I was even five years ago in cultural studies from the period of *Cavalier and Yankee*. There is considerable evidence to suggest, moreover, that I am far from alone. New kinds of historical questions have been prompting many of us to re-examine older work to determine the "state of the art" in deciphering literary and iconographic sources that embody these new interests.

After a prolonged period of positivism, studies that stress the mental outlook or perspective of social groups, that conceive of historical change in intellectual and psychological terms, are suddenly much in evidence. Of particular significance has been a virtual eruption of new work on public, visual culture; studies based on city plans, old engravings, artifacts, and, more recently, photographs have probed the significance of religious ritual, public ceremony, fraternal orders, street life, and family style. This new work differs both in scale and in preoccupation. It also ranges beyond thinking to touch upon a whole spectrum of human response, of a sensory and passionate experience.

Some new term seems to be needed that stresses, among other things, the functional, day-to-day character of human response as a dimension of historical change. It is tempting to think of adopting from French historians like Le Roy Ladurie the concept of *mentalité* as a way of describing the collective conceptualization of historical groupings. The concept of *mentalité*, however, presents problems for historians of modern times because it appears to have been devised to illustrate the changelessness of collective belief in earlier times. The *mentalité* of Ladurie's fourteenth-century shepherd is structured to resist change and filter out novelty; it is a brake on the kind of responsiveness that is of greatest interest to historians of the modern period. What seems most needed is a term that will prove descriptive of the arrows that penetrate this medieval armor with increasing frequency after Ladurie's shepherd is laid to rest, those eruptions into consciousness and passion that define and give shape to societal change.

A history of *perception* captures these newer, emerging tendencies in historiography. Perception has the virtue of referring to a whole range of environmental responses, of thinking, feeling, and seeing. Environmental theorists employ the term *perturbation* to refer to environmental disruption of all magnitudes. When the concept of perturbation is translated into historical terms, it becomes clear that the clocking of the impact of such perturbations is central to the work of modern historians. It would be utopian to suggest that a history of perception in any complete sense will ever be written, but we are beginning to discover that certain strains of perceptual change can be traced, some of it directly through graphic evidence of one kind or another, some of it as in Ladurie's reconstruction of fourteenth-century Montaillou from sources spun off from the Inquisition, some of it by inference as in the brilliant hypotheses of Walter Benjamin on early nineteenth-century Paris. Certainly, writing a history of perception will remain exacting, difficult, even exasperating, work, but it does help to know what you are looking for. The attempt to arrive at a history of perception is, in any event, best viewed as an attempt to clarify and objectify, rather than resolve, certain problems that have characteristically bedeviled those seeking an understanding of historical change.

W. R. T.

August 1979

Contents

Introduction   15

PROLOGUE—Two Aristocracies: A Dialogue   23

PART ONE: BEGINNINGS

I Crisis in the Old Order   37
    Innocence Abroad
    The New Provincialism
    The Southern Planter as Doomed Aristocrat
    Southern Mugwumps

II From Natural Aristocrat to Country Squire   67
    Thomas Jefferson Confronts the Legend
    A New Man
    The Legend Grows
    The Natural Aristocrat Takes to the Woods
    The Legendary Planter Gains Civilized Restraints

III Point Counterpoint: The Growth of the Southern
    Legend in the North   95
    The Age of Anxiety
    The Yankee Takes Cover
    The Transcendent Yankee and Society
    Daniel Webster and the Transcendence of Sectionalism

[11]

Contents

The Yankee at Home and Abroad
The Yankee Ethos in Limbo
From Yankee to Southern Cavalier
The Problem of American Gentility
A Division of Labor

PART TWO: THE SUSTAINING ILLUSION

IV   Holding the Wolf by the Ears: The Plantation Set-
     ting and the Social Order   145
     The Plantation Legend and Southern Introspection
     From Hotspur to Hamlet
     The Plantation Becomes a Matriarchy
     The Origins of Southern Chivalry
     Women and Negroes: One and Inseparable

V   A Squire of Change Alley: The Plantation Legend
     and the Aristocratic Impulse   177
     The Literary Origin of the Plantation Legend
     From Jest to Sentiment
     The Mythmaking Ethos
     The Cult of Chivalry and the New Imagination
     Literature and Aspiration

VI   The Promised Land   203
     A Scotch-Irishman Takes Stock
     Whigs and Harmony
     Yankee and Cavalier
     From Whig Harmony to Cavalier Insurgency

VII A Northern Man of Southern Principles   225
     From Provincial to Citizen of the World
     A Southern Exposure
     Westward Ho!
     From Jackson to Randolph
     The Route to Insurgency

Contents

VIII   Revolution in South Carolina   261
    The Spirit of '76
    Toward Insurgency
    Thermidor
    The Vanishing Patriot
    From Falstaff to Hamlet

IX   Whistling in the Dark   299
    Slavery and the Sentimental Revolution

X   The Rage for Order   315
    The Virginia Frontiersman

EPILOGUE—And the War Came   325
    The Southern Cavalier Redivivus
    Coda

References   343

Index   375

I do not wish to be a prophet of evil but you as a people, have conflicting interests and ambitions and unappeasable jealousies. You have the Puritans in the North and the Cavaliers in the South, Democracy with its leveling rod, and Aristocracy with slavery raising its haughty head in the other section and creating a social elegance, a superiority of breeding, and race. . . .

LOUIS PHILIPPE TO CHARLES GAYARRÉ, 1835

The Creator has beautified the face of this Union with sectional features. Absorbing all minor subdivisions, He has made the North and the South; the one the region of frost, ribbed with ice and granite; the other baring its generous bosom to the sun and ever smiling under its influence. The climate, soil and productions of these two grand divisions of the land, have made the character of their inhabitants. Those who occupy the one are cool, calculating, enterprising, selfish and grasping; the inhabitants of the other are ardent, brave and magnanimous, more disposed to give than to accumulate, to enjoy ease rather than to labor.

WILLIAM LOWNDES YANCEY at Columbus, Georgia, 1855

Introduction

By 1860 MOST Americans had come to look upon their society and culture as divided between a North and a South, a democratic, commercial civilization and an aristocratic, agrarian one. Each section of the country, so it was believed, possessed its own ethic, its own historical traditions and even, by common agreement, a distinctive racial heritage. Each was governed by different values and animated by a different spirit. According to a theory then in vogue the North had been settled by one party to the English Civil War, the Roundheads, and the South by the other, the royal party or the Cavaliers. The Yankee was a direct descendant of the Puritan Roundhead and the Southern gentleman of the English Cavalier, and the difference between the two was at least partly a matter of blood. The terminology sometimes varied, but contemporaries generally settled upon some such distinction as "Saxon" or "Anglo-Saxon" for the North and "Norman" for the South. Under the stimulus of this divided heritage the North had developed a leveling, go-getting utilitarian society and the South had developed a society based on the values of the English country gentry. It was commonly felt, furthermore, that these two ways of life had been steadily diverging since colonial times, and there were many after 1861 who believed that these characteristic differences between North and South had brought on the Civil War.

This idea of a divided culture has died a slow death. It certainly long outlasted the Civil War. As recently as 1927 Charles Beard could trace the war to two distinctive civilizations, one dominated by the "capitalists, laborers, and farmers of the North and West," the other by the "planting aristocracy of the South." It has been my purpose in this study to show how this idea grew and developed in the first half of the nineteenth century, what social problems produced the need for this kind of historical rationalization, what kind of worries and anxieties attended its development, and what kind of men and women contributed to its growth and dissemination—what sort of mentality, in other words, created this legendary past and this fictional sociology, and what sort of needs it satisfied.

My own concern has been principally with the South, both as represented in the North and as Southerners themselves have conceived of it. My sources, furthermore, have been chiefly literary. There are many things about the history of an era that cannot be learned from its literature, but historians, it seems to me, have been too timid about searching out the things that can. Stories and novels, even bad and unskillful ones, possess an element of free fantasy which is sometimes very revealing, as Henry Nash Smith demonstrated so well ten years ago in his *Virgin Land: the American West as Symbol and Myth.*

While there is a certain basis to the belief that the North and South were distinctly different during the antebellum period, few historians would any longer contend for the idea of a divided culture as this idea was formerly advanced. It is rather that the nature of the distinction must be re-examined and redefined. Recent scholarship has tended to narrow the range of differences between life in the North and in the South and to stress the essential similarity rather than the divergence.[1] No one has gone so far as to claim that anything like a consensus existed, but we now know that the South experienced in some measure all of the historical forces which were fast changing the face of society in the North. The Southern states after 1830 underwent a political upheaval of the kind which was occurring elsewhere in the country. New states in the Southwest entered the Union with white manhood suffrage and other provisions for popular government and many of the older Southern states modified their constitutions in response to the growing opposition to minority "aristocratic" rule. It is also clear that during the resettlement of the Southwest, the South suffered much the same kind of social dismemberment and atomization—the breaking up of families and kinship groups—which had been occurring in the North, and that it participated with almost equal enthusiasm in the growth of liberal capitalism which characterized the Jacksonian period. The South after 1800 also experienced a prolonged religious awakening which preceded and paralleled in its effects the revival of evangelical religion in the North. Societies devoted to Christian benevolence appeared and certain reforms like the temperance movement attracted for a time Southern advocates. A sentimental revolution, probably in response to the revivals, swept the whole country in the thirties and forties, and both North and South contributed to the growing popularity of sentimental literature concerned with the home and family. In the workaday world they traded profitably with each other and collaborated in the founding of the two major parties which ruled the country until the fifties.

At the same time certain important differences persisted. The economy of the South was less diversified, its population was more dispersed, its wealth more concentrated, its democracy less complete, and its cultural attainments by comparison were negligible. Most important of all, close to a third of its population lived in a condition of chattel slavery, a fact which exposed it to a growing wave of criticism not only from the North but from the whole Western world.

The problem for the South was not that it lived by an entirely different set of values and civic ideals but rather that it was forced either to live with the values of the nation at large or—as a desperate solution—to invent others, others which had even less relevance to the Southern situation. Even in areas of outright conflict the South had to reckon with the preoccupying concerns of the rest of the country and these preoccupations were always to some extent its own. As a result, Southerners carried on a peculiar kind of dialogue with the nation, sometimes constructive and harmonious, sometimes carping and critical. Through it all they persisted in seeing themselves as different and, increasingly, they tended to reshape this acknowledged difference into a claim of superiority. More and more it became difficult for Southerners to live in peace with themselves: to accept the aspirations and the ideals of the nation and, at the same time, accept the claims and rationalizations produced by the South's special pleaders. Almost invariably they found themselves confronted with contradictions of the most troubling and disquieting kind.

The North was simultaneously engaged in a similar kind of introspection. Northerners had early begun to express reservations and exhibit worries about the materialistic civilization which they saw developing around them, and they too had begun to take stock of the weaknesses and deficiencies of their culture. If swift change and social mobility of an unprecedented kind produced glowing optimism and expectations of a secular millennium, they also produced nostalgia and disquietude. Northerners soon found much to criticize in the grasping, soulless world of business and in the kind of man—the style of life—which this world seemed to be generating. Was all stability to give way to flux? Was an absorption in money-making and material things to replace the intellectual and spiritual heritage with which Americans had begun their national life? Questions such as these led a great many Northerners to see in the culture of the South many of the things which they felt the North lacked: the vestiges of an old-world aristocracy, a promise of stability and an assurance that gentility—a high sense of honor, a belief in public service and a maintenance of domestic decorum—could be preserved under republican institutions. The dialogue carried on by the South was thus part of a larger mood of introspection and self-criticism, and in this new literature which examined the national character, the Yankee with all his thousand faces and the Southern Cavalier play central parts.

Few things are more characteristic of the eighteen twenties, thirties and forties than the absorption with what was called the national character. Everywhere, but especially in states with a long colonial history, Americans exhibited an intense curiosity about themselves—what they had become and how they appeared to others. Travelers noted the dogged persistence with which they were cross-examined about their impressions of the country and the people, and it is a matter of record that Americans hungrily and indiscriminately consumed the sometimes hostile, sometimes sympathetic descriptions of America which appeared in such books as Mrs. Frances Trollope's *Domestic Manners of the Americans* (1832). American writers, too, quickly followed suit and works such as Cooper's *Notions of the Americans* (1828) and *The American Democrat* (1838) swelled the volume of writing which purported to characterize the new nation. For the first time, really, Americans in large numbers were able to read about themselves in works of fiction. Popular magazines like *Godey's Lady's Book* and illustrated anthologies known as "gift books" introduced Americans to the moral tale with a familiar, local setting. Beginning with *The Spy* in 1821, a novel about the Revolution, Cooper's novels one by one fancifully illuminated some patch of the American past. William Gilmore Simms in South Carolina began to weave his intricate fictional history of the Revolution in his native state. George Bancroft in 1834 published the first volume of a history which portrayed the unfolding of America's democratic character from its colonial origins. All over the country orators turned to the theme of national character as they addressed the local citizenry on the Fourth of July. At Harvard, at Yale or far off in the hills of Georgia, speakers stood before literary societies and addressed themselves prophetically to the question of a native American culture. At the bicentennial festivities at Plymouth in 1820, and in the solemn addresses which commemorated Jefferson and Adams after their deaths in 1826, the strong character of the Founding Fathers was examined and held up for emulation.

In the sea of words which enveloped the reading and listening publics, the words "national character"—or their equivalent—occur with startling frequency. Probably not until the rise of cultural anthropology in the twentieth century were Americans to be quite so interested in the characteristics of their group behavior. Within a few years the editor of *Godey's Lady's Book*, Sarah Josepha Hale, published two collections of stories: *Sketches of American Character* (1829) and *Traits of American Life* (1835). A concern with American character did not mean an investigation simply to determine what traits Americans happened to share. It meant searching about among American types for human ingredients which were sufficiently strong and elastic not only to withstand the strain and the temptations of American life but to exploit its possibilities most effectively. It meant searching out the points of weakness in American habits and manners. Scarcely any distinctive trait escaped the glass which was turned upon the social scene. New England life and history were carefully reviewed and the traditional symbol of New England, the legendary Yankee, became a resonant figure in the writings of Irving, Cooper, Hawthorne and countless minor writers. Similarly, the Southern planter began to assume his legendary character as a New World aristocrat in works of popular fiction.

Slowly there emerged from this body of literature certain clusters of traits which were thought to be characteristically Southern or Northern—or indeed Western, since Americans in this same period became familiar with the wild Westerner in plays such as James Kirke Paulding's *Lion of the West* and in the various books about David Crockett. In 1822 one writer for *The North American Review*, in a discussion of Cooper's *The Spy*, concluded that nowhere was there "greater variety of specific character, than is at this moment developed in these United States of America." He then listed the general types which he took to be distinctly American: "the highminded, vainglorious Virginian, living on his plantation in baronial state," "the active, enterprizing, moneygetting merchant of the East," "the Connecticut pedlar, who travels over mountain and moor . . . vending his '*notions*' at the very ends of the earth," and "the long shaggy boatmen '*clear from Kentuck.*' " In the old Dutch settlements of New York and in the clean and efficient farms of the Pennsylvania Germans there still existed the distinctive remnants of old and admirable ways of life, and as for New England he asked, "Are all the remnants of her ancient puritanism swept out of the corners?"[2]

The result of the search for a national character was the creation of a Decalogue for nineteenth-century Americans, a set of commandments directed at what were thought to be the flaws and failings of the society. In parables and cautionary tales Americans were instructed in the traits which would weaken them as individuals and as a nation, and in those which would make them strong. No region escaped this scrutiny of social virtues and vices, and a certain ambiguity played over the identifying characteristics of each section of the country. The West was thought of as enterprising and independent, but, on the other hand, it was often portrayed as wild and unruly. The Yankee in his thrift, his industriousness and his asceticism was a praiseworthy figure in American popular culture; yet story after story dwelt as well on the mercenary, hypocritical and Philistine aspects of New England character. Similarly, the gay, pleasure-loving and generous-hearted Southerner won admiration for his indifference to pecuniary drives and his reputedly greater familiarity with polite culture and genteel ways, yet he, too, early became a cautionary figure in tales which revealed him as weak, vacillating and self-indulgent, or wild, vindictive and self-destructive. Northern fantasies about the promiscuity of the slaveowner and the highly publicized behavior of such eccentric and outspoken Southerners as John Randolph stimulated writers of fiction and political moralists to comment on the liabilities of the type.

The chapters which follow attempt to isolate the conditions in America which stimulated this kind of introspection and myth-making, especially in the South. My concern has been primarily with the dynamics of the legends rather than with their literary origins or the degree of their historical authenticity, which are subjects in themselves. It is the mythmaking frame of mind, the social imagination of the mythmakers and the circumstances which have molded their lives that have interested me most, and I have dealt with these other matters only when they have seemed to me necessary to illuminate the thinking of the men who were principally concerned with compounding and publicizing popular beliefs about the American past. I have assumed that the writings of these men were less determined by idiosyncrasy and by literary convention than by the intellectual and social ferment which surrounded them. If Sir Walter Scott provided many of them with the flexible form of the historical romance, it was they who did the casting and adjusted the plot to American circumstances. Literary historians may quarrel with my tendency to interpret works of fiction and other similar sources rather freely as social fantasy, but I believe they will finally concede that the fiction I have examined, for all its apparent reliance on convention, does in fact embody a considerable quantity of troubled speculation about the historical predicament of the South within the nation.

PROLOGUE

TWO ARISTOCRACIES: A DIALOGUE

Whatever parties may exist in a country, and under whatever names they may go, there are always two aristocracies —the aristocracy of wealth and the aristocracy of talent. . . . You belong to one and I to the other.

THOMAS HEYWARD TO JAMES LOUIS PETIGRU[1]

For I agree with you that there is a natural aristocracy among men.

JEFFERSON TO JOHN ADAMS, October 28, 1813

THE SOCIAL AND political changes of the early nineteenth century were sufficiently extensive to shake the composure of members of the Revolutionary generation who survived into the national period. In particular, these changes raised important questions concerning the kind of social mobility which republican institutions were producing in America. What class of men would replace the ruling aristocracies of Europe? Would merit alone govern advancement, or would men be put forward on the basis of such accidental qualities as wealth, good family and popular manners? Was there a danger that the opportunism of an Aaron Burr or the reputed materialism of a Hamilton would finally characterize America's spokesmen, or could America's exceptional situation be counted upon to produce a class of leaders possessing exceptional civic virtues?

"Is the Nineteenth Century to be a Contrast to the Eighteenth?" John Adams asked Jefferson in 1815. "Is it to extinguish all the Lights of its Predecessor?"[2] Adams had enlarged upon this worry two years before at the opening of the extraordinary exchange of views with which these two men closed their lives. In the course of it they discussed a whole range of subjects—the Revolution, political leadership, the permanence of the Union, the state of the world and the immortality of the soul. Through it all Jefferson was imperturbably hopeful and perhaps just a touch grandiose—"I steer my bark with Hope in the head, leaving Fear astern"—and Adams was skeptical but somehow tender in his dissent—"I admire your Navigation and should like to sail with you."[3] It was always Adams who called Jefferson's optimism into question and doggedly insisted that they re-examine their postulates in the light of more recent experience.

Let me now ask you, very seriously my Friend, Where are now in 1813, the Perfection and perfectability of human Nature? Where is now, the progress of the human Mind? Where is the Amelioration of Society? Where the Augmentations of human Comforts? Where the diminutions of human Pains and Miseries . . . ?

When? Where? and how? is the present Chaos to be arranged into Order?[4]

Adams himself concluded that the French Revolution and its aftermath had not only arrested progress but had set the human race back "at least a Century, if not many Centuries."[5] Jefferson, despite his declared contempt for "gloomy and hypocondriac minds" was forced to agree that the world had been "thrown back again to the age of the Borgias, to the point from which it had departed 300. years before."[6]

From the perspective of their retirement from active politics they viewed events taking place at home with considerable distrust and uneasiness, especially the Hartford Convention and the bitter squabbling a few years later over the admission of Missouri as a state. Jefferson felt that he saw in the New England of 1813 the makings of "a civil War, a La Vendée," and he concluded by asking Adams how they could "conjure down this damnable Rivalry between Virginia, and Massachusetts."[7] Both Adams and Jefferson from time to time expressed doubts about the capacity of the Union to endure. Speaking of the Missouri question, Adams remarked to Jefferson that he was "sometimes Cassandra enough to dream that another Hamilton, another Burr might rend this mighty Fabric in twain," and he went on to observe that "a few more choice Spirits of the same Stamp, might produce as many Nations in North America as there are in Europe."[8]

Despite statements such as these, however, there is a strong strain of assurance running through their utterances, a tacit conviction that they had seen the nation into being and could now afford to indulge themselves in speculations, and even fears and uncertainties, which long lives of action had restricted or discouraged. Neither man played Cassandra for very long, and Adams, when he allowed his thought to play calmly over the most likely prospects for the future, generally revealed how deeply he believed in the capacities of the republic to survive. "I have no doubt," he wrote to Jefferson in 1814, "that the horrors We have experienced for the last forty Years, will ultimately terminate in the Advancement of civil and religious Liberty, and Ameliorations, in the condition of Mankind."⁹ Both men had been schooled in the complexities and the intractability of republican government, and in their assessments they were realistic enough to confront the serious risk and dangers which they knew almost certainly lay ahead. American Liberty, Jefferson felt, had not been gravely threatened by the retrograde course of the democratic revolution abroad. "Old Europe," he wrote to Adams in 1816, "will have to lean on our shoulders, and to hobble along by our side."¹⁰ Between them they found at home many changes taking place which they viewed as significant advances. In particular, Jefferson had become convinced that in America, in contrast to Europe, men were beginning to succeed on the basis of solid merit—"talents and enterprise" and political freedom and economic opportunity seemed to indicate that the old criteria of "rank, and birth, and tinsel-aristocracy will finally shrink into insignificance."¹¹ Adams was less certain that this would happen, but he showed himself willing to explore the idea which has probably made their exchanges most memorable: the concept of a natural aristocracy.

Both Jefferson and Adams were anxious to disclaim any attachment to the traditional idea of an aristocracy, except for the name itself which, they reminded each other, meant "rule by the best." Both of them believed that it would be necessary for America to produce more qualified leaders and leaders of a different kind from those who had presided over the affairs of other nations. America, rather than depend upon those pushed forward by the accident of birth or good fortune, must seek its leaders from among men of superior character and superior intelligence, the real "aristoi" rather than "pseudo-aristoi" of the kind which had dominated European politics since the Middle Ages.

Having agreed so far, however, their characteristic differences of temperament began to show themselves as they sought to specify what exactly they meant by a natural aristocracy and what role such a group was to play in American life. Jefferson's temperament led him to smooth over certain problems which Adams foresaw. Adams, who was fond of playing the sage— "When I was your Age, Young Man," the letter began—edged his reservations with irony. "But who are these 'Aristoi'?" he asked Jefferson. "Who shall judge? Who shall select these choice Spirits from the rest of the Congregation? Themselves? . . . Shall the Congregation choose?" To this Jefferson replied unhesitatingly: "*I* think the best remedy is exactly that provided by all our constitutions, to leave to the citizens the free election and separation of the aristoi from the pseudo-aristoi, of the wheat from the chaff." And then he added by way of assurance, "In general they will elect the real good and wise."[12]

When they came to discuss the reliability of a natural aristocracy, they disagreed again. Adams quickly picked Jeffereson up on his rather simplistic moral distinction between "natural" and "artificial." By "natural" Jefferson clearly meant to imply a kind of inherent moral quality, an indigenous imperviousness to power and corruption. Adams saw no difference in the moral capacities of the two types. "I would trust one as soon as the other with unlimited Power,"[13] he wrote back, and he reminded Jefferson that intelligence was not the only "talent" to be considered. Wasn't beauty a talent, too? What were the qualities, he wondered, which historically had swayed men's minds and won their allegiance? Hadn't the rich and the well-born always won out over the men of intelligence and good will, even in the ancient republics? What reason was there to suppose that circumstances had now changed? "What chance," he asked, "have Talents and Virtues in competition, with Wealth and Birth? and Beauty?" Then, groping for the secret elixir which explained the mystery of power, he stumbled onto an idea which closely resembles Max Weber's concept of charisma: the irrational and indefinable quality which men historically have looked for in their leaders. "Beauty, Grace, Figure, Attitude, Movement," he told Jefferson, "have in innumerable Instances prevailed over Wealth, Birth, Talent Virtues and every thing else."[14]

They reached a similar impasse when they came to discuss the kind of society which they expected to see develop in the United States. Neither seemed to have a very sure sense of the way in which Americans as individuals would get ahead. Jefferson was more interested in the hurdles than the race. He was most concerned with eliminating the vestiges of colonial aristocracy, with removing every obstacle which he felt would hamper the extension of the republican ideal and check the advance of men of real talent. Once such embarrassments were cleared away he assumed that men of ability could be expected somehow to get recognition. Meanwhile, traditional leadership by certain distinguished families presented itself as a major problem. "From what I have seen of Massachusetts and Connecticut," he wrote to Adams, "there seems to be in those two states a traditionary reverence for certain families." Members of these families, he reasoned, had probably once possessed qualities which won them deserved respect, and this respect had been passed along to their sons and grandsons, more or less independently of their individual worth. "In Virginia," he remarked, "we have nothing of this." Certain families had accumulated large fortunes before the Revolution and these fortunes had been passed along from generation to generation, but there was no political magic in the names of old Virginia families. "A Randolph, a Carter, or a Burwell must have great personal superiority over a common competitor to be elected by the people, even at this day."[15] Adams, in so far as he allowed himself to speculate, seemed to anticipate a new social world which differed very little from the old. His secularized Calvinism prompted him to attribute the source of social evils to human nature itself, and he consequently told Jefferson that he would expect to find a "White Rose and a Red Rose" in "every Village in the World." The old families which remained prominent— "Our Winthrops, Winslows, Bradfords, Saltonstalls, Quincys, Chandlers, Leonards, Hutchinsons, Olivers, Sewalls etc."[16]—would continue to monopolize political power as long as they succeeded in flattering the people into supporting them. New wealth, however, would also quickly make itself felt, and he cited a popular Greek saying to the effect that "the meanest blooded Puppy, in the world, if he gets a little money, is as good a man as the best of them."[17]

There was never any prospect, both men quickly sensed, that they would reach agreement in matters on which they differed. As Jefferson once put it, their objective had been to explain themselves to each other, not to arrive at any kind of consensus. "We are both too old," he conceded, "to change opinions which are the result of a long life of inquiry and reflection."[18] They had, of course, agreed that certain distinctions naturally occurred among the people of any society and that the naturally superior, if properly trained, were best fitted to hold positions of leadership; yet at times they appeared to have in common nothing but the word "natural." What each of them meant by it was left somewhat uncertain. By the time the nineteenth century had finished with the concept of nature the idea of a natural aristocracy had lost any crispness and clarity it may once have possessed. John Adams might have asked, but did not, one question that Emerson certainly would have asked: What is Nature?

When Jefferson used the word he generally had in mind a mechanistic process of some kind through which the business of the universe was accomplished. Although he came to an appreciation of the concept of the sublime in nature, he did not, characteristically, refer to nature either as a wild and unruly force or as a source of intuitive truth, and he would probably have found Emerson's transcendental view of nature as alien to his thinking as he found Plato. For much the same reason he scoffed at those who said that "The information of books is no longer necessary" and who recommended "rejecting the knoledge acquired in past ages, and starting on the new ground of intuition."[19] In referring to men as natural aristocrats he did not for a moment wish to suggest that they would take their coloration from "unhandselled savage nature" like the true American Scholar whom Emerson was to call for a few years later. He saw neither the natural world of violence and struggle which the evolutionists later revealed nor the universe of darkness and mystery and occluded meaning which yawned before Hawthorne and Melville. His temperament was "sanguine," as he once told Adams, and he possessed to the end the soul of an agriculturalist who regarded human nature, like wild nature, as useless without cultivation, improvement and careful husbandry.

Thus when he turned to Virginia he found his most promising materials in the very class of men who were most intimately associated with agriculture. He expected that natural aristocrats almost as a matter of course would be recruited from the yeoman class where the republican spirit was strongest. Jefferson's educational schemes were designed to select from this class of men those most qualified to rule. In order to implement his belief that ability and character alone should govern advancement, Jefferson worked out a complicated educational system in which, through a process of gradual elimination, only the very best students would be filtered out and given university training.[20] Through this somewhat mechanistic strategy he expected to bring the real aristoi into prominent positions in the political and intellectual life of Virginia and the nation.

The process through which men actually rose to positions of power and influence and the nature of the aspirations which drove them on were matters which Jefferson discussed with some uncertainty and some distaste. Writing in 1782 he conceded that the public spirit which had characterized the country during the Revolution was probably temporary and that, once the fighting had stopped, the people would again devote themselves exclusively to making money. "From the conclusion of this war," he predicted, "we shall be going down hill. . . ."[21] But, in balance, Jefferson's view of the people's preoccupation was more charitable, or at least more euphemistic. "The pursuit of happiness"—was this not another way of phrasing the freedom to devote oneself to private ends, whatever they might be? He was clearly uncomfortable discussing the aristocratic emulation which had been so prominent a force in colonial Virginia, and he was equally discomfited by Adams' assertion that the people were easily duped by aristocratic pretensions and susceptible to flattery and cajolery. He would have had very little use for the democratic speculation and the competitive swirl of Jacksonian America or for the high-pitched stump oratory and bidding for votes which characterized its politics. He continued to believe that most men would be satisfied with a decent competence and that through some sort of calculus the best men would be chosen for office, at least most of the time. At the same time he was occasionally forced to admit the existence of a drive for power and money, a straining upward of society, although his very words conveyed his disapproval.

Early in the century he had been asked to comment on the characteristics of society in Virginia before the Revolution. In reply he had sketched the picture of a society which had settled into "several *strata*, separated by no marked lines, but shading off imperceptibly from top to bottom, nothing disturbing the order of their repose." There was in this society no very great mobility of any kind. Emigration to the west had not yet begun on any scale, and there was comparatively little vertical mobility. Those families which had earlier accumulated wealth passed it along from generation to generation "under the law of entails." "Families in general," he concluded, "had remained *stationary* on the grounds of their forefathers," but his description nonetheless conveyed the impression of a much more restless and shifting social scene than he cared to admit to in his generalizations. At the top were the "aristocrats," whom he defined as "the great landholders who had seated themselves below the tide water on the main rivers, and lived in a style of luxury and extravagance, insupportable by the other inhabitants." Directly below the aristocrats were their descendants and relatives—"half breeds," Jefferson called them—who aspired to aristocratic status without possessing the necessary wealth to bring it off. Next came still another aspiring group without even family to recommend them, whom Jefferson referred to somewhat scornfully as "pretenders." These were men "who from vanity, or the impulse of growing wealth, or from that enterprize which is natural to talents, sought to detach themselves from the plebeian ranks." Finally, there came the group which Jefferson obviously considered the principal stabilizing force in the society: the "solid and independent yeomanry," who, more or less content with their station, possessed no aristocratic yearnings of any kind. Although they looked "askance at those above," Jefferson commented, they did not venture to "jostle" them. The only other group mentioned—and mentioned only to deride— was that "*feculum* of beings called overseers," who as subservient lackeys were a further buttress to aristocracy. Of Negro slaves and their part in encouraging aristocratic pretensions he said not a word.[22]

It was Jefferson's hope that by removing the top layer of society, he might be able to eliminate both the "half breeds" and the "pretenders" from the scene as well. With the downgrading of these groups from the prominent place they once held it might then be possible to anticipate a social world in which aristocratic aspirations would play little or no part. Of course, in the end, events proved him terribly wrong, but Jefferson's forecast was scarcely more mistaken than Tocqueville's reckonings twenty years later. It was the Southern planter and not the yeoman farmer whom the nineteenth century was to place in the center of the legend it soon created about the South.

PART ONE

BEGINNINGS

CHAPTER I

Crisis in the Old Order

When the Southern Gentleman has fully completed his labors—has honorably gone through the University Curriculum—if his means be ample he seldom studies a profession, but gives education a finishing polish by making a tour of Europe.

DANIEL R. HUNDLEY[1]

THE GROWING PROVINCIALISM of the South had an important bearing on the legends which developed around the figure of the Southerner in the first half of the nineteenth century. This provincialism, furthermore, differed in certain important respects from the provincialism of the country at large. During the colonial period Virginia and South Carolina had retained much closer cultural contact with the Old World than had the colonies to the North. During the first half century of national experience this situation was reversed. The South gradually lost touch with Europe at the very time that intellectual leaders in the North, and especially in New England, were establishing new cultural contacts abroad. This reorientation within American culture had significant consequences for the South. The cosmopolitan outlook of the Revolutionary generation was communicated to a bare handful of Southerners who attempted to carry on the older traditions of the coastal South in the face of growing obstacles. Talents of a different kind were called for and men of a different stripe were soon receiving the recognition which had once gone to gentlemen of the old school. The result was the alienation of a generation of highly educated Southerners who tended to view changes taking place within the South—and the nation—with mounting alarm, and to take a tragic view of their own displacement.

Innocence Abroad

On the sixteenth of April, 1815, an ambitious and well-organized young Bostonian by the name of George Ticknor set sail from Boston on the Liverpool packet. Europe was soon to learn about the energies and the charm of this one-man task force which approached its shores. Before he returned four years later, he probably managed to see as much of Europe as any other American of his generation. He made the acquaintance of Mme. de Staël, Byron, Goethe, Wordsworth, Scott, Chateaubriand, August von Schlegel and many others. Scarcely a celebrated man escaped his carefully arranged itinerary as he worked his way deliberately from England to France and on to Germany, where he paused for almost two years to study at the University at Göttingen before passing on to Italy and Spain.[2] Out of this journey were to come certain enduring effects for American culture; for Ticknor himself it was to result in a distinguished academic career at Harvard College and in his authoritative three-volume *History of Spanish Literature*.[3] For the country as a whole, Ticknor's experience— and that of the Americans who accompanied or soon followed him to Göttingen—was to lead not only to a rediscovery and reappraisal of Old Europe but also to the recognition that there was a New Europe growing up in Germany.

The Europe which Ticknor saw was only in part the Old World of monuments and ruins which had ornamented an eighteenth-century gentleman's Grand Tour. Much that he saw impressed him with its youth and vigor, qualities which Americans had generally appropriated to themselves. It was a mistake, he was soon writing home, for Americans to assume that the "real" Europe was to be found in the South "amidst the ruins of national independence," any more than it was to be found in a France which had fallen victim to both court and revolution, or in England with its "ancient prejudices against everything continental." Knowing Europe only through the French and the British, he concluded, had encouraged Americans to neglect Germany, where "all is still new & young" and where "the work ings of its untried spirit" were beginning to transform the face of Europe. Not only was German scholarship the best in the world but everything about German culture, its "free, & philosophical spirit," "the contempt of all ancient forms" and "the unwearied activity with which they [the Germans] push forward" suggested Germany's kinship to America and left Ticknor with the conviction that it would soon "leave all the rest of the world very *far* behind."[4]

Almost exactly two years after George Ticknor's departure, a young Virginian set out on a somewhat different kind of excursion. For William Campbell Preston this was a gay and unforgettable journey, and he was inclined in later life to look upon these years more as his *Wanderjahre* than his *Lehrjahre*. Thirty days out of New York on the *Amité* he was seized by excitement at the sight of land, jumped ship off the Irish port of Cork and made his way overland to Dublin, crossed the Irish Channel and journeyed through Wales to London. In six months' time he had traveled through France, Switzerland and Italy as far south as Rome, and was settled in Edinburgh studying civil law. Forty years later he was able to set down in a memoir for his family a detailed itinerary —where he had gone, what he had seen, what had impressed him most. He recalled his first glimpse of an original sculpture at Wrexham in Wales, a journey with Washington Irving through the Highlands, his delight in the Louvre and the broad, tree-lined boulevards of Paris, and the fountain-filled piazzas of Rome. He wrote only of his travels and omitted any mention of his student life in Edinburgh. Preston's European education ended abruptly in 1819, the same year as Ticknor's, when he journeyed home to enter a distinguished career in politics and law in his adopted state of South Carolina.[5]

With the Napoleonic wars ended and peace established in Europe, trips such as these were to become more common and, especially from the North, young Americans in annually increasing number began visiting England and the countries of Western Europe. These "visits," however, were far from the same, as the examples of Ticknor and Preston suggest. Ticknor, the Northerner, was in a sense beginning something new, while Preston, the Southerner, in 1817 was helping to bring an old tradition to a close. Before 1815 very few New Englanders had lived or studied abroad, and direct contact with English and European culture had been slight. Ticknor himself found it necessary to journey south to collect letters of introduction and recent information about conditions of travel. He was a member of the first group of Americans to undertake a course of study in a German university. He traveled with a determination and intensity of spirit which were not characteristic of the Southerners who visited Europe. "The whole tour in Europe," Ticknor wrote to a friend, "I consider a sacrifice of enjoyment to improvement."[6] Ticknor made his own decision to go abroad, without any substantial encouragement from anyone. There was nothing in Ticknor's family background—he was the son of a former schoolteacher and a wholesale grocer—which prompted European study. Since he had abandoned the law, he had no firm expectations concerning a career to smooth his way. In all these respects he was representative of the kind of man of good hope who ventured into Europe in this period from New England. He was, like Hawthorne's Miles Coverdale, a perfect example of the transcendental Yankee—or, to designate his type more precisely, a transcending or transcendent Yankee.

Preston's journey, on the other hand, while resembling Ticknor's in certain obvious ways, had much about it that was characteristically Southern. For him Europe had little to do with the real business of life. One could almost say he was predestined to law and politics. Born in the nation's capital, the eldest son of a prominent Virginia Congressman, he had been steeped in politics since childhood. President Washington had even called to bestow his blessing on him as an infant. Long practice, furthermore, established the successive steps which would bring young Southerners like him to their life's work—college, reading law under some prominent lawyer and, for the fortunate, a period of travel and study in Europe. When Preston went to Europe he went as a student of law, lightheartedly and at his father's urging. "I knew that my father's plan of education for me," he later recalled, "was that I should go thro' some Southern College, then to Yale or Princeton and complete my course in Europe."[7] His *Reminiscences,* set down at the end of his life, suggest that his flying trip through Europe with a group of friends was much more of a pleasure jaunt than anything George Ticknor experienced, part of a conventional pattern set long before when young Englishmen first undertook the Grand Tour. It is characteristic, for example, that Preston in his travels eschewed Germany, which was off the beaten track for Southerners until much later in the century. As the experience of Ticknor indicates, a different kind of contact with Europe became identified with the North.

This new cultural relationship between New England and Europe is suggested by a pattern which developed early in the century. It became the practice, more and more after 1815, for young men to begin intellectual careers by a period of study in a European, usually a German, university. Göttingen and Berlin became for the Northern states "cities of light," and the cultural interchange which was begun in 1815 helped give the romantic movement in the North its distinctive intellectual tone, perhaps best characterized by the reflective intensity of New England transcendentalism. Those New Englanders who studied in Europe, furthermore, generally found easy access to the world of scholarship. Trained scholars were everywhere in short supply, and the experience of Edward Everett, who was appointed to a chair in Greek at Harvard even before he went abroad to study, was by no means unusual. Longfellow in 1825 received a similar offer from Bowdoin College. George Ticknor received notice of his appointment to the Smith professorship of French and Spanish at Harvard while he was still at Göttingen, and prolonged his stay in Europe in order to equip himself to fill it.[8] Similarly, Benjamin Silliman had held a chair of chemistry and natural history at Yale for three years before he went abroad in 1805 to receive advanced training. Both Longfellow and Lowell, who succeeded Ticknor in the Smith professorship, set off for Europe to receive further training after they had received their appointments. George Bancroft went to Göttingen after graduation from Harvard on the understanding that he might return to teach, as in fact he did.[9]

The experience of Europe proved to be far more than a preparation for college teaching, even for those New Englanders who went specifically for such training. Very few members of this first elite group of student pilgrims actually remained in college teaching for any significant time. Those like George Bancroft who had felt the attractions of European universities most strongly sometimes proved the most impatient with the American college, where the faculty, one historian has commented, "were not there to teach, but to see that boys got their lessons."[10] The effort to transplant German educational standards met with discouraging resistance, and even George Ticknor, who succeeded in introducing the idea of departments and specialization at Harvard, finally retired with a conviction that it was futile to attempt more. He probably spoke for most of the European-trained when he observed of Harvard in 1823, "we are neither an University—which we call ourselves—nor a respectable high school, —which we ought to be."[11] Those who left the college fanned out into activities of so many kinds that one is tempted to say that the most important effect of Europe was the general stimulus given to intellectual pursuits. This stimulus had in turn an almost revolutionary effect on the choice of careers by this generation and those which followed.

The significant thing about New England when compared to the South was the variety of intellectual careers which became available to the prewar generations. The threefold choice of the law, medicine and the ministry was greatly widened after about 1820, and many of the men who attained intellectual distinction before 1860 groped their way toward careers which did not exist for their fathers. The New England clergy in particular, reared a generation of wide-ranging scholars and thinkers, most of whom, like Everett, Emerson and Bancroft, had found the ministry limiting and uncongenial. Unlike Southerners of the same age, they tended to travel more, to be more sophisticated and worldly-wise—in short, less provincial—than their fathers. The law, too, exerted far less of a hold on the next few generations of New Englanders than it did on their Southern contemporaries. Ticknor and Prescott and Joseph Cogswell, all trained for the law and for a brief time at least practicing attorneys, switched to intellectual pursuits which brought them international prominence—Ticknor in Hispanic literary scholarship, Prescott in history and Cogswell as a pioneer of American library science. The group of intellectuals whom Dr. Holmes called "Boston Brahmins"—and whom he so well represented—were not, with one or two exceptions, born members of a social elite. They owed their prestige to a subtle combination of good manners and scholarly or literary attainments. It is clear that these new careers, far from involving them in sacrifices, opened the way to social advancement. George Ticknor married a daughter of Samuel Eliot, Edward Everett married a daughter of Peter Brooks and Longfellow's second wife was an Appleton. Intellectual attainment, furthermore, was in New England no bar to a political career, as it tended to be in the South. George Bancroft while a schoolmaster married into the merchant aristocracy of Springfield. He later became Secretary of the Navy under Van Buren and subsequently served as Minister to Great Britain and Germany. Everett's career, in particular, suggests the continuity of intellectual and political achievement in New England. He was successively professor of Greek literature, Congressman, Governor of Massachusetts for four terms, Minister to Great Britain, president of Harvard, Secretary of State, United States Senator and, in 1860, candidate for the vice-presidency of the Constitutional Union party.

These New Englanders played a cultural role similar to that of a significant group of Southerners in the previous century. Preston, who went to the Senate in 1833, was unusual among his contemporaries in having received some of his education in Europe —a striking contrast to the late eighteenth century when Southern leaders almost characteristically had read law in one of the Inns of Court in London. The practice of sending young men to study law in England became after 1760 an entrenched tradition in the South. For more than a century prominent Southern families had sent their sons to the Inns of Court in order to prepare them for careers in the colonies. Here, in one of the four ancient legal societies—Lincoln's Inn, Gray's Inn, the Inner Temple and the Middle Temple—these Americans, along with their English contemporaries, were trained for the law under an old and rather relaxed system of apprenticeship which dated back at least to the fourteenth century. While those who entered the Inns of Court were by no means all of the Americans who studied in Europe, they provide as a group some revealing statistics. Of a total of 236 American-born colonials in the records of the Inns, 123 were from South Carolina and Virginia alone, as opposed to 19 from Massachusetts, 21 from New York and 23 from Pennsylvania. The number from South Carolina—74—is greater than the total from all the Northern colonies. Enrolled on the records of the various Inns are the names of practically all of the great historical families in the South, from the second William Byrd, who entered Middle Temple in 1692, to men like John Julian Pringle of South Carolina, who was studying there at the outbreak of the Revolution. The Middletons, Rutledges, Pinckneys and Gaillards of South Carolina, and the Harrisons, Lees and Randolphs of Virginia are all present in number. Such training was almost a sure index of political prominence.[12]

Judged by any standards these were superior men, probably as influential a group as any in the colonies. It included many men who held high positions under the Crown, including one Lord High Chancellor of England. Even more impressive, however, was the crucial part played by members of this group during the Revolution and the early years of the Republic. Among its celebrities were such men as John Dickinson, "Penman of the Revolution," governor of Delaware and Pennsylvania, and John Rutledge, president of the Continental Congress and later Chief Justice of the United States Supreme Court, and Charles Pinckney, governor of South Carolina, United States Senator and Minister to Spain. Among the Southerners in the group were five signers of the Declaration of Independence, twenty delegates to the Continental Congress, five members of the Constitutional Convention, seven in the diplomatic service, seven members of the United States Congress, two Justices of the Supreme Court, several state governors and Chief Justices of state supreme courts, and innumerable lesser officers.[13] This invasion of the Inns of Court by prominent Southern colonials had immense consequences for Southern culture more generally. Not only did these men set standards of political and legal knowledge, they also played a significant part in implanting in the South an image of English culture in the late eighteenth century—its oratory, its literature and its manners —which, unchallenged by fresh experience, continued to dominate Southern life into the nineteenth century.

With the coming of the Revolution, the flow of American colonials into the Inns of Court fell off sharply and, despite the fact that certain families continued to send their sons abroad, only a few Americans studied or traveled in Europe before 1815 when the new invasion began from the North.

The New Provincialism

The circumstances under which this generation of young Americans visited Europe posed them all with a similar set of problems and drew from Northerners and Southerners alike, at least initially, somewhat similar responses. Some of these problems were simply slight intensifications of what traveling Americans had always encountered. Others were entirely new. The ocean voyage itself, long and dangerous until late in the century, continued to emphasize the distance which separated the two continents, and most of those who traveled dwelt on the significance of the crossing. Since 1776 the Atlantic had widened; instead of a highway joining province to metropolis, it was now a barrier of isolation and growing estrangement. Emerson appears to have had something of this kind in mind when he commented, in *English Traits*, that "the roar of the ocean is silencing our traditions."[14] Americans, when they arrived in England, seem to have felt less assurance than English colonials in the previous century, many of whom were almost returning home. Washington Irving described himself as a "stranger in the land" when he returned to England in 1815,[15] and a slight sense of inferiority, a certain discomfort pursued all of the others wherever they went. They were unprepared for many of the experiences they had, and much that they saw was unfamiliar to them. "I gazed a little at first," commented a young Virginian in 1829, "whenever I saw a distinguished person."[16] Customs, manners and, on the Continent, language stood formidably between them and a ready comprehension of the countries they visited. Everywhere they hungered for and sought out the familiar: the family birthplace, literary or historical landmarks about which they had read or been told.

As provincials they had experienced almost nothing which prepared them for polite society as it existed in the capital cities of Europe. Even more than American colonials in the previous century, they were inclined to be distrustful of the more social aspects of culture—the salon, the comic theater, decorative arts, all of which to them smacked of the superficial. Most of them found something slightly immoral in the emphasis on physical beauty and pleasure which they everywhere detected. Perhaps their greatest worry was themselves.[17] Serious and morally earnest, they worried considerably about the danger of succumbing to the enticements of European society; as professed republicans and patriotic Americans, they were sometimes distressed to discover how much they were awed by titles and impressed and intimidated by celebrities and by the rituals of Church and Court. When Joseph Carrington Cabell was on the point of departure in 1802, he was warned by his brother "not to suffer anything to shake his attachment for his own country, or to render him dissatisfied with the American state of society, manners, and customs." His brother then added, "The moment you feel any disposition of the kind, fly back to America."[18]

These worries were part of the general problem thrown up, at least in part, by the new status of citizen of the United States. It was one thing to travel as an English Colonial, sure of his place in an Atlantic community, and quite another to move about in a world which had rarely set eyes on "an American." Everywhere these travelers went they encountered intense curiosity. The novelty of being an American in Europe was brought home to them through countless incidents which they recorded with surprise and amusement. George Ticknor commented that at Göttingen Americans "were taken in as a kind of raree-show . . . with much the same curiosity that a tame monkey or a dancing bear would be."[19] In England Ticknor was annoyed by compliments about his "excellent" English, and Southerners, in particular, bristled at the assumption that all Americans were the same. When Preston insisted to an English lady he met in Dublin that he was a Virginian, not a Yankee, he was met with the reply, "Aye, a proud Virginian. To us you are all Yankees, rascals who cheat the whole world."[20]

Perhaps the most stubborn and deeply troubling idea about

America which this generation encountered was summed up in the term Yankee. The word itself, of uncertain origin, quickly came to stand for the traits of character which were thought to be most characteristically American. In America the term was associated most frequently with New Englanders, but in England and on the Continent it was generally loosely applied to all Americans. It carried with it the implication of crass commercial dealings, shrewd bargaining and even a hint of sharp practices. Thanks to English reviews and a handful of articulate English travelers, the word Yankee by 1815 clearly invoked for Englishmen the image of a society of monotonous uniformity composed of uncouth and curious rustics whose energies were exclusively given over to the pursuit of the main chance. American society was portrayed as lacking refinement and its cultural pretensions were scoffed at.[21] Emerson, visiting England in 1833, heard what was by then an old refrain when Wordsworth remarked to him that Americans "lack a class of men of leisure,—in short, of gentlemen,—to give a tone of honor to the community."[22]

It was not, of course, what Wordsworth, or anyone else, *said* which proved most disturbing to these men. They were troubled by what they themselves discovered to be the case. Their response, furthermore, was by no means a simple one. The complicated nature of their feelings becomes intelligible only in the light of their sense of urgency, their mission, in coming to Europe when they did. Those from the North especially came to Europe for many expressed reasons, but few of them came as tourists in any ordinary sense. Some of them were artists or writers, a few like the Irvings had originally gone on business, but most of them were students who, having finished college, had come to avail themselves of a kind of advanced training which America could not easily provide. All of them were young, and there was something a little special about each of them—a precociousness, perhaps—which had led to his selection for a cultural venture of this kind. They were also men of unusual adventurousness and all of them, almost without exception, were very ambitious.

It is not possible to read their letters and journals without feeling that something further than training, or greater usefulness to their country—the reasons generally given—lay behind their coming. The suppressed premise behind the undertaking was a kind of quest which all of them were somewhat aware of but few of them would have been able to define. As the sensory antennae of their class and culture, they sought in some sense to probe the limits of social experience, to see—in William James's phrase—how much civilization, how much history they could *stand*.[23] Behind them lay a kind of provincial life—a world limited both socially and intellectually to which they were deeply committed and to which they expected to return. All of them commented that they came to know America better, but few of them more than hinted at the force of the shock waves which battered their provincial loyalties while they remained abroad. To learn too much, to admit too much, might make a return to America difficult or even impossible; yet almost without exception they returned home, if not eagerly, at least with the readiness with which all men are finally drawn back to the familiar.

Those who went felt without exception called upon to defend themselves from the imputation that they had gone for enjoyment or leisure or anything which smacked of self-indulgence. The letters which they sent home are full of work schedules and lists of achievements, and generally play down the social activities and recreation which formed a substantial part of every American's first experience of Europe. "Wherever I establish myself," Ticknor wrote to a friend, "it will be only with a view of labor; and wherever I stay,—even if it be but a week,—I shall, I hope, devote myself to some study, many more hours in the day than I do at home."[24] On one occasion when he had apparently outdone himself in the scenic descriptions he sent home, Ticknor was warned by his father to heed the purpose of his visit. "You have not left your home," wrote the elder Ticknor, "for the sole purpose of describing the lawns, the hills, the valleys, the tops of mountains, the columns of smoke, the villages. . . . But you have left your father to grow wiser and better, to learn to be more useful to yourself, your friends, and your country." He concluded with the admonition to "Shun everything that does not lead to improvement."[25]

Pressures of this kind coupled with an uncertainty about their social status produced the intense self-consciousness which characterized nearly all those who went abroad in these years. Conflict almost inevitably developed between two opposing sets of commitments which most Americans felt. One commitment, an obligation *to* Europe, as it were, urged them to savor foreignness most fully in order to make it more comprehensible; a conflicting —and, in general, a stronger—obligation insisted that they surrender not a particle of their republican outlook and sternly resist the attractions of Europe, as if they were the wiles of Circe. It was almost impossible to live up to expectations such as those of Ticknor's father without closing one's eyes altogether to European society; it was equally difficult to accept Europe on its own terms, since most of those who traveled carried their parochialism with them wherever they went. One of the most sophisticated of them—and an excellent and enthusiastic dancer—Jesse Burton Harrison, reported that the German practice of giving balls on Sunday night aroused his "Prince Edward Presbyterian principles."[26] They were fascinated by society and yet they were not really comfortable in it. Most of them were glad to flee from the social whirl of large capital cities to provincial centers like Geneva and Edinburgh, where they felt more at home. It was finally for many of them an even greater relief to return to America.

The experience of Europe forced the visitors to see America in a new perspective. "When I went away," Ticknor observed of the library at Harvard, "I thought it was a large library; when I came back, it seemed a closetful of books."[27] "What a mortifying distance there is," he went on to exclaim, "between a European and an American scholar!"[28] They acquired, most of all, a new sense of history, an awareness of the endurance of human society through the ages and the related conviction that continuity and traditions matter in the development of culture. The fact that

America lacked such continuity and traditions was brought home to them, often rather sharply. This was the experience of Richard Henry Wilde, a cultivated Georgia politician who retired from Congress in 1835 in order to go to Italy and devote himself to poetry and scholarship. "Never, most assuredly," he recalled, "since I bivouacked in my boyhood amid a wilderness lately in the possession of the Indians . . . did so deep a sense of my own insignificance and the enduring solitude of ages come over me as in my first visit to the Florentine archives."[29]

The Southern Planter as Doomed Aristocrat

Despite many similarities, the image of Europe which became popular in the South during the early nineteenth century was a significant variant of the new national image. In the North, and especially in New England, this new consciousness of European culture was readily assimilated. The open-mindedness of the Unitarian outlook, a respect for learning and high, if somewhat rigid, standards of literary excellence, and especially a desire to learn about contemporary intellectual and literary developments abroad, distinguished the Boston gentleman from the gentleman planter. All of these factors conspired to create a responsive and congenial atmosphere where culture flourished and intellectuals thrived. Intellectual novelty, of course, did not go unchallenged in Boston, any more than in London or Berlin, but in this period Boston in its provincial setting provided the best which the new world had to offer.

Southerners too looked upon Europe with respect and acknowledged their provincial limitations but, on the whole, they were more dispirited in their response to this new knowledge. Throughout the North there were groups of men like Ticknor who proudly sounded the note of youth and looked upon the unformed state of American culture as an opportunity and a challenge: programs of action were proposed, magazines were founded as men solemnly dedicated their lives to creating a distinctive American culture. For such men Emerson's *American Scholar* address in 1837 was both a call to action and a resonant summing up of a deep strain of already existing feeling.

After 1830 few Southerners shared more than halfheartedly in the drive for cultural self-sufficiency and in the sentiment of cultural nationalism which characterized the North. This impulse was increasingly checked by the growing intensity of sectional feeling. The drive for the cultural autonomy of the South—a paper revolution which did not proceed beyond a few manifestoes —was even more short-lived and unproductive than the impulse which it replaced. It was kin to the movement for the economic independence of the South which found expression in *De Bow's Review* and in the proceedings of the Commercial Conventions of the forties and fifties. Long before this, however, educated Southerners had begun to recognize that there were in the South no foundations on which to build a distinct regional culture, no beachhead, even, where such a momentous operation might begin. In the absence of any other recourse, any program of action, educated Southerners were inclined to despair and turn this new awareness against themselves, like a gun to the temple. Europe was, for these men, a mirror which threw back a distorted image of what was happening to the South, an image which threatened revolution, class warfare and the extinction of polite culture. As the century progressed, moreover, this image of degeneration was intensified and the South saw itself as experiencing in a few years a historic decline which in Europe had spread over centuries—the old colonial capital of Williamsburg was compared to a ruined Rome and the neglected port of Charleston to contemporary Venice. The idea of the gentleman underwent an equally abrupt change, and Jefferson's conception of a natural aristocracy made up of men of superior virtue and superior talent tended to be replaced by an image drawn from Revolutionary Europe of the gentleman as a doomed aristocrat. Among Southern intellectuals, tragic exaggeration was all the rage. One young Southerner recorded the chills of premonition he felt as he watched an execution by guillotine in Paris in 1829. To his family in Virginia he also sent a carefully drawn sketch of this historical mechanism.[30]

The experience of Europe which had made George Ticknor into a gentleman-scholar, productive and almost complacently satisfied with the social atmosphere of literary Boston, had the reverse effect upon such a Charleston littérateur as Hugh Legaré, who found himself progressively alienated from South Carolina and, indeed, from America. Two years spent studying law at Edinburgh proved only indifferently useful to a young Southerner like Legaré, whose most serious challenge when he returned was the low intellectual level of the state legislature and the stubborn soil of a family plantation. Criticized as an ornate and pretentious lawyer and orator throughout his career, Legaré was inclined in later life to lay the blame for his failure to achieve his ambitions on his European experience. In 1841, he wrote advising a young friend then in Europe to return home and not prolong his stay. "I have found my *studies in Europe* impede me at every step of my progress. They have hung round my neck like a dead weight, —and do so to this very day."[31]

Unsuccessful as a planter, undistinguished as a practicing lawyer and a legislator, Legaré gained a certain reputation in the South as an authority on civil law and a scholar of some pretensions in the field of Greek and Roman history. He became well known (but in all likelihood not well read) as an editor of the *Southern Review*. He ended his life as Attorney General and Secretary of State *ad interim* in President Tyler's ill-starred cabinet.[32]

The career of Legaré is perhaps worth detailing since it illustrates in an extreme form the effect which the experience of Europe could have on a young Southerner of great ability. Despite the success which seemed to characterize the end of his life, his disenchantment with South Carolina began early. Legaré, who had served one term without distinction in Congress and had been attorney general for the state, was eager in 1832 to leave South Carolina. The growing crisis over nullification seems only to have hastened his decision. When an opportunity was offered him in 1832 to serve as American chargé d'affaires in Brussels he quickly accepted.[33]

His journal and letters sent from abroad indicate very clearly what was happening to him. He had at first supposed that by returning to Europe he might somehow return to scholarship as well. He wrote in his journal that at the end of a year he had found his old appetite for learning once again awakening:

The spirit of philosophical research,—the thirst for permanent & *great* renown among those who have done something for the dignity of human nature and the happiness of their fellow men,—have, I know not how, sprung up afresh in my mind within a few weeks past, and their inspiring impulses are, I am sure, about to triumph completely (as they have before) over my *evil genius*, the soft epicurean "indolentia" that so easily besets me.

Despite his good intentions, however, these four years were not to recall Legaré to scholarship. Society was his study, almost his obsession, during his stay in Brussels, and a few months after he had made the entry quoted above, he scribbled beside it in the margin, "Never was confidence so ill bestowed."[34]

"My ambition is dead," he wrote to a friend, "and I think only of *repose* and social enjoyment. . . ."[35] A certain note of silliness creeps into his jottings about the social goings-on in and about the legations of Brussels. He devotes pages of his journal to the question of whether or not to give a ball, or to the seating arrangements at formal dinners. "I find my existence a very pleasant thing indeed," he wrote to his sister. "With means of living like a gentleman, well received . . . time has passed so pleasantly of late that I have hardly remarked its flight."[36] The English colony in Brussels especially attracted him, and he mentions constantly, but with what degree of seriousness it is hard to tell, the possibility of marrying into the English aristocracy. "I am just beginning to think of passing a longer time in Europe," Legaré wrote to his sister Mary in 1833. "What should I do in Charleston, for heaven's sake? Or in New York in a sort of society which never did suit me entirely altogether, and would hereafter be insupportable, I fear. . . . The *ton bourgeoisie* [sic] is so odious."[37]

Legaré's newly acquired identification with the aristocratic classes of Europe, aided perhaps by his enraptured reading of De Maistre, led him to the gloomiest of political reflections. Jefferson became for him, as he had become for John Randolph, the "Arminius of our institutions, St. Thomas of *Cantingbury*."[38] Comparisons between the planter class and the *ancien régime* rushed to his mind. Everywhere he went he encountered the effects of revolution, the premonition of further revolutions which would sweep away the aristocratic classes from the face of Europe. In his own mind the nullification crisis, which developed rapidly during his first year abroad, became another revolution in which the canaille were rising to overturn the old planter leadership. As a member, along with Petigru, William Elliott and others, of the stanchly Unionist old guard, he looked upon insurgents such as Rhett as social upstarts and opportunists. The term "Jacobin," which they all used to describe the Nullifiers, suggests the revolutionary metaphor they had in mind.[39] In the end he came to accept the fact that he and what he represented were destined to go down to defeat. A visit paid to Versailles provoked him to wonder why it was that "a society so charming and so accomplished, [as our lowland aristocracy]—be doomed to end so soon, and, perhaps, so terribly."[40] "We are (I am quite sure) the *last* of the *race* of South-Carolina," he wrote in October, 1832. "I see nothing before us but decay and downfall."[41]

Southern Mugwumps

To understand the feelings of men like Legaré it is helpful to know something about the kind of Southerner who was apt to study in Europe at this time. These student-travelers were themselves members of a larger and more coherent group of historically displaced persons of the classical Mugwump type.[42] Like their historical cousins in New England fifty years later, these Southern Mugwumps were generally of good family, highly educated— often in Europe or at Harvard or Yale—and well traveled. Born in the seventeen eighties or nineties, their lives usually spanned the first half of the nineteenth century. They were children of the Enlightenment—men of broad experience and tempered provincialism. They were apt to be conservative both in politics and in their personal lives, relying heavily on the precept and example of the Founding Fathers. They were inclined to look upon their lives as a never-ending procession of duties and responsibilities which were to be undertaken as a public service and discharged in a spirit of *noblesse oblige*. Even in their manners and tastes they were throwbacks to the ethos of a previous generation. Joseph Carrington Cabell of Virginia is said to have adopted Washington as his model and to have followed his example, even in matters of dress.[43] In his approach to intellectual problems, this kind of man was characteristically a rationalist—logical, objective and precise —and he was apt to distrust emotion of any kind, especially religious emotion. His belief in the essential rationality of man led him to place great emphasis on education. His point of view was, in general, cosmopolitan rather than local and his intellectual interests were apt to range wide.[44] He not infrequently took a special interest in one of the natural sciences or in classical literature. He was often at least a dabbler in literature, a writer of elegiac verse or essays modeled on Addison or Goldsmith, and he was almost always a connoisseur of oratory and an admirer of the Roman Republic.

Despite the range of his interests, however, nothing seems to be more characteristic of this kind of man than his isolation from the culture of his own time. Although he lived most of his life in the so-called Romantic Age, his literary tastes, like almost everything else about him, were apt to reflect the fashions of the previous century. The published catalogue of Legaré's large library, for example, lists works of literature by only six roughly contemporary writers—Coleridge, Channing, Goethe, Schiller, Thomas Moore and Herder. Despite his long residence in Brussels and his excellent knowledge of French, not a single modern French author is listed.[45] Legaré's friend, William Grayson, in 1854 wrote his famous proslavery treatise, "The Hireling and the Slave," in heroic couplets. Grayson's *Autobiography*, written at the end of his life, contains a neat formulation of the Mugwump literary credo:

I believe in Dryden and Pope. . . . I have faith in the ancient classical models. . . . My taste is too antiquated to fall into raptures over the metaphysical sentiment of Shelley, or the renovated pagan deities of Keats.[46]

It is not surprising that men holding such views as these experienced some difficulty in adjusting to the changes which swept the South after 1820, and although comparatively few of them were driven to Legaré's feelings of bitter alienation, almost all of them felt ill equipped for the struggles which accompanied the rapid growth of the nation. Born into a predominantly coastal society at about the time that a federal government was established, they were still young men when Louisiana was purchased; they were close to thirty at the time of the Missouri Compromise and close to forty when Andrew Jackson became President and the issue of nullification arose. Many of them lived on to see California become the thirty-first state. These changes, furthermore, far from adding to the wealth and prominence of the South, appeared to have had the reverse effect. Those who survived into the fifties saw the power and the influence of the South slowly decline as events issued in a new world which seemed both foreign and hostile. The Virginians especially, all of whom had grown up under Virginia Presidents, felt the altered circumstances most keenly. "And thus we, who once swayed the councils of the Union," commented one of them in 1852, "find our power gone, and our influence on the wane. . . . As other States accumulate the means of material greatness, and glide past us on the road to wealth and empire, we slight the warnings of dull statistics, and drive lazily along the fields of ancient customs."[47]

Within the South itself, changes of a similar kind made men of this older stamp feel isolated and ineffective. They tended to discover that the ideals on which they had been reared were rapidly being replaced by the values of a new generation whose approach to politics and culture was at once more ruthlessly pragmatic and opportunistic than their own. These new men who invaded the relatively stable social world of the South were shrewd and energetic, and they brought to both politics and law a new set of sanctions, new tactics and an atmosphere of intense competition— all of which were novel and frightening to men brought up within the older ethos. While many of the Mugwumps were lawyers, they had been trained in an older, more oratorical tradition which looked upon the law, not as a lucrative business, but as a preparation for statesmanship and high-minded public service. "The profession of law in this country," one of them commented, "involves the cultivation of eloquence, and leads to political advancement and public honors. In this respect we nearly resemble the Roman Republic."[48] To men of such convictions, the appearance of "vigorous newcomers from the county courts" who shared neither their ideals nor their scruples threatened the moral tone of the whole society and especially the ideal of the Roman Republic. This new man was, accordingly, a subject of intense speculation among men of the older type. As Grayson sketched him, the newcomer

was an able speaker and good lawyer; bold, ready, regardless of respect to opposing counsel, witnesses, or clients, and unscrupulous as to the language in which he expressed his contempt; skilled in cajoling the jury and bullying the judge; little sensitive as to his own feelings, and utterly without regard to the feelings of others. One purpose only seemed to govern him—the purpose to gain his case at all hazards. He was a formidable adversary, and the lawyers of the old school were reluctant to encounter his rude assault.[49]

Under more crowded conditions neither a law practice nor political office were any longer to be had without active solicitation. Those who came to politics with the belief that "it is the temper of the people to give their suffrages to those who come to it with a reputation of talents and learning,"[50] lost out to men whom they looked upon as their inferiors. With some bitterness they began to conclude that they had survived into an age where, as one of them put it, "Right, justice, truth are secondary considerations or rather no considerations at all."[51] Like Henry Adams, they came to feel that history in some sense had passed them by. Legaré, especially, invokes comparison with Adams as Grayson describes him at Petigru's Broad Street house, where, ". . . in a sulky fit of surly discontent with Nature or society," he noted, "he would sit brooding over the shortcomings of both in reference to his particular claims and merits."[52]

When it came to politics, men of this stripe adopted a widely varying set of postures. Mostly, they seemed to represent the residual Federalist sentiment existing in the South. During the nullification crisis in South Carolina, for example, they characteristically held strong Unionist views; in Virginia during the thirties they were apt to be among those who opposed Jackson and participated in the formation of the Whig party. Representative of this kind of man was Charles Fenton Mercer, whose father had been a prominent Revolutionary leader in Virginia and a justice of the Court of Appeals. Mercer was educated at Princeton, and after his graduation traveled for two years in Europe before returning home to study law. He entered Congress in 1817 and remained until his resignation in 1839 a vigorous proponent of national measures and a stanch Whig. Like Mercer, these men, however, do not owe their greatest importance to their active participation in politics. During the thirties many of them, either through outright resignation or through failure to win re-election, began to leave active politics and to seek other means of making themselves felt, often as propagandists and agitators.[53] Several years after he left politics, Mercer, for example, published anonymously his gloomy assessment of the state of the nation in a volume as prolix as its title: *An Exposition of the Weakness and*

Inefficiency of the Government of the United States of North America. In this book Mercer lashed out at universal manhood suffrage, Andrew Jackson and the spoils system, Jefferson and states' rights, intemperance and Negro slavery—which he called the "blackest of all blots, and foulest of all deformities." Only a miracle, he felt, could save the nation from mob rule, and the Union from dissolution and civil war. "How long," he asked, "will it require to work this ruin? I believe some twenty years, not more. . . ." Mercer for a few years after his retirement moved restlessly between Florida, Texas and Kentucky. Ill and suffering, first from neuralgia and later from a painful cancer of the lip, he crossed the ocean a seventh time at the age of seventy-six and devoted the last years of his life to traveling about Europe from St. Petersburg to Berlin and Paris in the hope of forcing general agreement on ending the international traffic in slaves.[54]

The names of those who left politics at this time compose a *Who's Who* of Southern intellectual life. Legaré was defeated for re-election to Congress in 1838. Edmund Ruffin resigned from the Virginia senate in 1826 in protest over the methods employed by his enemies, and William Elliott in 1832, weary of pettifogging lawyers, resigned the seat in the South Carolina legislature once held by his father rather than accept the mandate of his constituency on nullification. William Grayson, who had abandoned his law practice with disgust in 1822, left politics in 1837 when he failed through an unwillingness to solicit votes to win re-election to Congress. Joel R. Poinsett retired[55] from active politics at the end of the nullification crisis, and William Drayton, another leader of the Union party in South Carolina, not only left politics but moved himself permanently to Philadelphia. Throughout the South the controversy over the instruction of legislators brought more resignations of a similar kind before the end of the decade. Richard Henry Wilde, who had served Georgia with distinction in Congress and in 1834 was almost elected Speaker of the House, failed to win re-election after breaking with Jackson in 1835 and thereafter devoted his energies primarily to travel, scholarship and poetry.[56]

What is most interesting and characteristic in the careers of all of these men was not the particular expression which this new impulse took but rather the alienation from the blood and soil which tended to precede it. Even Tucker and Ruffin, who would seem to be exceptions to much of the preceding, were bitterly alienated men before they were secessionists, and both of them were inclined to use the Palmetto flag of their adopted state of South Carolina as a rod to chasten Virginia.[57] It would be misleading, furthermore, to argue that their malaise was fundamentally the result of disappointed opportunism or that it came exclusively from a consciousness of diminished personal status, although this was undoubtedly an important factor. Much of the fury with which they turned upon the South, or some aspect or part of it, came from their futile effort to shut out or translate into Southern terms the currents of popular sentiment which were flowing freely in the North. It is evident that in a period of awakening religious consciousness and evangelical humanitarianism many Southerners were unable to find an adequate moral basis for their lives within the official Southern credo. The South Carolina jurist and militant Unionist James Louis Petigru had the patience and moral fortitude—and saintlike immunity—to wage his fight against what he considered mindless Southernism while remaining in South Carolina. Others were forced to emigrate. Edward Coles, a highly educated young neighbor of Jefferson who had served for a time as President Madison's private secretary, left Virginia in 1819 because of his "objections and abhorence to slavery." He subsequently became the first governor of Illinois and successfully led the fight to keep the state free of slavery. After his defeat for Congress in 1831, he retired from politics and left Illinois to spend the last thirty years of his life as a private citizen in Philadelphia.[58] What happened to the children of John Faucheraud Grimké of South Carolina, distinguished patriot and jurist, is also symptomatic of what was occurring within the old judicial aristocracy. The elder Grimké was educated at Trinity College, Cambridge, and at the Middle Temple, and later served as a member of the ratifying convention, and became successively senior associate justice of the state and speaker of the state house of representatives. One of his sons, Frederick Grimké, left South Carolina and became a supreme court justice in Ohio. Another son, Thomas Smith Grimké, a distinguished member of the Charleston bar, who had been educated at Yale and had read law under Langdon Cheves, was an ardent Unionist in 1832 and became a crusader in the peace and temperance movements. His two famous sisters, Sarah Moore Grimké and Angelina Emily Grimké, left "the ungentle, uncongenial air" of Charleston and Episcopalianism in the eighteen thirties for Philadelphia and the Society of Friends and, finally, for Garrison and abolition. The violent revolution in the lives of these shy, retiring women which uprooted them from their father's house and made them stump speakers in the North a few years later—and Angelina the wife of abolitionist Theodore Weld—illustrates the force of the shock waves which were playing over the old style of life.[59]

Perhaps most characteristic of the Mugwump was a penchant for the apocalyptic. Frustrated in his ideals and disappointed in his expectations, he was inclined to cast aside his rational approach to human problems and adopt ever more strident means of expressing his feelings of bitterness and alienation. Behind the sense of urgency which overtook these Southerners in the eighteen thirties was the new historical consciousness which grew out of a reassessment of historical changes taking place in Europe.[60] Europe, according to this new view, was no longer the cultural playground it had been for Preston. Instead, it had become a center of revolutionary ferment, an Armageddon where the forces of light locked with the forces of darkness; and the American South no longer possessed the immunity it had for Preston in 1819. As the center of aristocratic culture, it now seemed to have a peculiar vulnerability to revolution. The imminent eruption of social chaos drove men to what even they considered desperation tactics. Edmund Ruffin, who almost singlehandedly revolutionized Virginia agriculture through his scientific experiments with calcareous manures, disowned Virginia for its neglect and became in later life an agitator and propagandist for Southern rights. Similarly, St. George Tucker's son and John Randolph's half brother, Nathaniel Beverley Tucker, a distinguished judge and teacher of law but an unsuccessful lawyer, carried on during the last half of his life an impassioned campaign to free the South from oppressive Northern domination.[61] All of them were inclined to see disaster awaiting the South at every turn, and it seems apparent that many of them, like the Grimké sisters, felt driven to employ means which they had once scorned to use, or had thought unnecessary.

During the heated controversy in Virginia over Jackson's war on the Bank, one Virginian exclaimed with characteristic impatience: "Instead of argument, we hear nothing but scurrilous epithets, impotent threats, and low abuse, such as men of decency and sense should scorn to use. Our society is no longer what it was—partisan heat and violence are to be seen everywhere."[62] In South Carolina, during the same year, the vision of chaos and anarchy was even more widespread, as Unionists, men like Petigru, Elliott and Legaré, despairingly predicted bloody revolution and the dissolution of civilized society. At the base of these anxieties was the disappearance of rational appeal as an instrument of persuasion. Political considerations, although obviously of great importance, formed only a part of the growing apprehensiveness in the South. The Southerner's awareness of his cultural limitations and the failing light of rationality fed his pessimism and incited him to gloomy prophecy. "The day . . . has really come," Petigru wrote to Elliott in 1831, "when passion is openly preferred to reason. . . ."[63]

There is in the experience of these men, nonetheless, just a suggestion, but a revealing suggestion, of what was to come—the successive waves of alienation which were to sap the vitality and morale of the South. It was one thing for men in the North, who had on the whole less to lose, to fret at the decreasing emphasis on rationality and to decry the partisan political tactics of the Jacksonian era. It was quite another matter for Southerners. Even by 1820 it was becoming increasingly clear that the South could not continue to hold to the ideals of the nation at large nor share for long its democratic aspirations. The wave of egalitarian sentiment which swept the country in the eighteen thirties left many Southerners feeling that they were sitting on top of a potential volcano. "Whoever has looked at the actual condition of society," Preston told the Senate in 1836, "must have perceived that the public mind is not in its accustomed state of repose, but active, and stirred up, and agitated beyond all former example. The bosom of society heaves with new and violent emotions. The general pulse beats stronger and quicker than at any period since the access of the French Revolution." Ominously he saw lights going out across the continent of Europe, and for Preston Europe was a portent.

In Germany, in France, and in England, there is a great movement party organized upon the spirit of the times, whose tendency is to overturn established institutions, and remodel the organic forms of society—for whose purposes the process of experiment is too slow, and the action of reason too cold. . . .[64]

Men like Preston became convinced that the position of the South within the nation was at best one of delicate equilibrium, which almost any outbreak of emotionalism might upset. They therefore responded to the drift of opinion about slavery with exaggerated defensiveness. The Missouri Compromise and the English Emancipation Act of 1833 left them with the conviction that history was operating to isolate them further and that their time was running out. After a slave insurrection in Charleston was uncovered in 1822, the dread name of "Santo Domingo" was invoked with increasing frequency to call forth an image of bloody revolution—"the black terror"—of a kind Southerners most feared.[65] "Our Negroes," observed one Charlestonian, "are truely the *Jacobins* of the country."[66]

The existence of feelings of this kind among a small but significant group of Southerners must, of course, be seen in perspective. As a group these men had less coherence and probably less influence than the Mugwumps at the end of the century. Many of the sentiments which motivated them, furthermore, and the characteristics which distinguished them from their contemporaries were shared by Americans of a similar kind in other parts of the country, as for example by John Quincy Adams. They should not be confused, moreover, with certain other influential groups in the antebellum South who superficially resembled them. While some of them, like Grayson and Preston, contributed to intersectional hostility, and two of them, Ruffin and Tucker, were outspoken secessionists, they were men of a very different stamp from the young Hotspurs like Rhett and Yancey, who became active agitators in the thirties and forties. Similarly, men like William Elliott and Grayson produced a disciplined elegiac literature in praise of the old style of life, which they saw as a golden age, yet they played a relatively minor part in creating the literary legends which are popularly associated with the Old South. They had little taste for the flamboyant in character or for the historically sentimental. The creation of the impetuous Southern Cavalier and the nostalgic portrayal of plantation life were to be largely the work of men of a different social background.

CHAPTER II

From Natural Aristocrat
to Country Squire

Not out of those on whom systems of education have exhausted their culture, comes the helpful giant to destroy
the old or to build the new, but out of unhandselled savage
nature, out of terrible Druids and Berserkers, come at last
Alfred and Shakespeare.

EMERSON, *The American Scholar*[1]

ALTHOUGH THE MOST active period of Southern mythmaking began
only in the eighteen thirties, the plantation legend was interestingly foreshadowed in some of the patriotic writing which appeared after the War of 1812. The planter-aristocrat of Southern
fiction was a recognizable descendant of the Revolutionary hero
of this earlier writing, a combination of natural aristocrat and
European gentleman, nature and civilization, freedom and restraint. Those who labored to develop such a hero were aspiring
men seeking to understand the values of the society in which they
made their way. They were rarely members of the planter class,
seldom of English ancestry and sometimes not even Southerners.
They were—to use the term current at the time—from among the
New Men.

Thomas Jefferson Confronts the Legend

When Daniel Webster and Mr. and Mrs. George Ticknor visited Jefferson at Monticello in December, 1824, Jefferson proudly showed them through the still-unoccupied classical buildings of the new university—his "future bulwark of the human mind in this hemisphere"[2]—in which the natural aristocracy was to receive the last formal phase of its education. "Mr. Jefferson is entirely absorbed in it," Ticknor commented, "and its success would make a *beau finale* indeed to his life."[3] There was time for other things as well—general conversation, politics and reminiscence—and in particular Jefferson had not forgotten his irritation with a book published some seven years before. He talked of it at some length. The book, which had first appeared in 1817, was William Wirt's immensely popular biography of Jefferson's old Revolutionary associate, Patrick Henry. Jefferson had known about Wirt's project from its inception, had supplied him with materials and had read the final work in batches of manuscript which Wirt had sent to him. He had even suggested revisions. Nevertheless, his judgment of the book as it had finally appeared was summary and unqualified. "It is a poor book," he told his guests, "written in bad taste, and gives an imperfect idea of Patrick Henry. It seems written less to show Mr. Henry than Mr. Wirt."[4]

The social world in which Wirt had placed his hero belonged, Jefferson seemed to feel, in the pages of a romance rather than in those of a history book. Jefferson looked upon Henry as the most popular American who ever lived[5] and as a crucially important figure in the history of the Revolution—he was "the man who gave the first impulse to the ball of revolution," he told Wirt —but he had many, many faults. His apostasy at the end of his life when he went over to the Federalists had not raised Jefferson's estimation of him. His knowledge of the law, he had written Wirt, was "not worth a copper: He was avaritious & rotten hearted. his two great passions were the love of money and fame."[6] When it came to the practical business of drawing a bill, Henry had proved hopelessly inefficient. Even his oratory was not without its faults. "His pronunciation was vulgar and vicious, but it was forgotten while he was speaking."[7] His chief gift lay in his ability to incite and move men to action. "He said the strongest things in the finest language, but without logic, without arrangement."[8] In his discussion with Webster and the Ticknors it was perfectly clear that Jefferson was not only annoyed that Wirt had whitewashed Henry's faults but puzzled that Wirt, in his effort to portray Henry as a self-made man, should wish to construe some of his more evident limitations—his indolence and his lack of formal education—as virtues. In William Wirt's eyes, on the other hand, Patrick Henry had obviously emerged as a kind of romantic hero, a natural leader very different from anything Jefferson could conceive of as admirable. The reactions of other Southerners varied somewhat but emphasized the same general point. John Taylor of Caroline called it "a splendid novel," and John Randolph, who was Wirt's exact contemporary and a great admirer of Henry, referred to it as "a wretched piece of fustian."[9]

John Adams expressed himself to Wirt in similar terms but with a slightly different emphasis. Wirt had sent Adams a copy of the book when it appeared and asked him for his opinion. Adams replied in a letter written from Quincy early in January, 1818. He, too, felt that Wirt had made rather free with the facts of Revolutionary history, although he confessed that he had been moved by Wirt's narrative. He also clearly sensed in what he read the appearance of a new mode of historical writing which smacked of fiction. About the same time he wrote to a fellow New Englander, "I have read it with more delight than Scott's Romances in verse and prose, or Miss Porter's *Scottish Chiefs* and other novels."[10] To Wirt he humorously threw out a challenge. "If I could go back to the age of thirty five, I would endeavour to become your rival,—not in elegance of composition, but in a simple narration of facts, supported by records, histories, and testimonies of irrefragable authority."

Had Mr. Wirt, he wondered, forgotten Massachusetts in 1761

when he dated the Revolution from 1765 and located its beginning in Virginia? Did this not represent some unfounded puffing of the sectional issue? "I envy none of the well-merited glories of Virginia, or any of her sages or heroes, but I am jealous, very jealous, of the honour of Massachusetts." Adams himself believed that no adequate account of the Revolution could be written around the life of any single individual, and he told Wirt that if he were to undertake the job he would "introduce portraits of a long catalogue of illustrious men, who were agents in the Revolution."[11] To the editor of the *North American Review* he confided his judgment: "Is it not an affront to common sense, an insult to truth, virtue and patriotism, to represent Patrick Henry,—though he was my friend as much as Otis,—as the father of the American Revolution, and the founder of American independence? . . . The gentleman who has done this is of yesterday, and knows nothing of the real origin of the American Revolution."[12]

A New Man

Wirt, who was forty-six in 1818, was not exactly "of yesterday," but by any standards which Adams or Jefferson might have applied to him he was an outsider, and by proper Virginian standards he was a man from nowhere. A Virginian by neither birth nor rearing, he was the orphan child of a German mother and a Bladensburg, Maryland, tavern keeper of Swiss origin who had come to the colonies as an indentured servant. Almost without formal preparation Wirt had risen rapidly to a position of eminence at the Virginia bar. He had been elected a chancery judge at the age of twenty-nine, and a few years later he became attorney general of the state. In 1818 he was appointed Attorney General of the United States in Monroe's cabinet, a position he was to occupy with distinction for almost ten years. In 1832 he became the first American to receive the nomination for the Presidency from a national convention. By the time of his death in 1834 he was an almost legendary figure in and around Washington, where along with Webster he had been one of the two or three most effective advocates pleading cases before the Supreme Court. In 1826, following the death of Jefferson and Adams, Wirt had been invited by Congress to deliver an address on their lives in the House of Representatives. Perhaps his greatest distinction, although he did not so regard it, came the same year when Jefferson, a few weeks before his death, offered Wirt, who had never attended college, the presidency of his new university, an office which had been specially created in the hope of luring Wirt into accepting a professorship of law.[13]

In a state which—despite Jefferson's claim—continued to pride itself on the pedigree of its prominent men, Wirt seemed to have done the impossible. He had repeatedly been offered, and as steadfastly had refused, opportunities to run for purely political office. Only twice had he weakened: once as a young man when he had consented to serve a term in the Virginia House of Delegates, and again in 1832 when he allowed himself in a pathetic relapse to be flattered into accepting the Presidential nomination of the Antimasonic party. For a considerable portion of his life he must have been regarded as one of the most promising and able men in the state of Virginia. Like Benjamin Franklin, with whom he was sometimes compared, William Wirt became a success story. John Pendleton Kennedy, a fellow Baltimorean who edited his letters, described him in 1849 as a man "who, springing from an humble origin, was enabled to attain to high distinction amongst his countrymen,"[14] and the following year it was possible to purchase in New York an inexpensive little book entitled *Success in Life. The Lawyer*, which was principally concerned with the story of Wirt's life and placed him in the distinguished company of John Jay, John Marshall and other famous men of the bench and bar.

The personal legend greatly exaggerated Wirt's achievements and his ability. Wirt was an ornamental figure in the intellectual and social life of the early republic, but he was not essentially a very complicated person or a very penetrating or original intelligence. Fluent, handsome—he was thought to resemble Goethe—and a brilliant mimic, he possessed perhaps most of all a ready capacity to adapt himself like a weather vane to shifting fashions of opinion. In politics he was the proverbial rubber man whose elasticity would finally have carried him, had he lived a few years longer, into the Whig party. As a lawyer his greatest triumphs were achieved through briefs aimed primarily at juries and courtroom audiences rather than at the bench. As a thinker he had a tendency to light upon the commonplace with the excitement of discovery. Undaunted by irreconcilables and untroubled by inconsistencies, he skated along the surface of his times. His twistings and turnings reveal, nonetheless, contradictions which were much more deeply embedded in the thinking of his more reflective elders and contemporaries. As a self-made man and self-help hero, furthermore, he was the forerunner of a kind of man who was to become increasingly important in the cultural life of the South. Not least of all, he was one of the South's most energetic mythmakers.

Unlike Jefferson or Adams, Wirt had been early cast upon his own and impressed with the urgency of making his way in the world. He later recalled how as a child he had stood on a pier in Baltimore and watched an elder brother sail out to sea to make his fortune. His mind had been teeming with dreams of success long before the day in 1790 when he packed up his Blackstone, his *Don Quixote* and his *Tristram Shandy* and set off for Virginia to become a lawyer. In his unpublished autobiography he tells of a recurrent fantasy with which, at about the age of ten, he used to while away the long, cold walk to school on winter mornings.

I imagined myself the owner of a beautiful black horse, fleet as the winds. My pleasure consisted in imagining the admiration of the immense throngs on the race-field, brought there chiefly to witness the exploits of my prodigy of a horse. I could see them following and admiring him as he walked along the course, and could hear their bursts of applause as he shot by, first one competitor, and then another, in the race.[15]

In his first book, *The Letters of the British Spy* (1803), Wirt has his aristocratic English narrator comment òn the rapid rise of Southern families from humble origins. There were in Virginia "a venerable groupe of *novi homines,* as the Romans called them; men, who, from the lowest depths of obscurity and want, and without even the influence of a patron, have risen to the first honors of their country, and founded their own families anew."[16] Throughout most of his life Wirt regarded himself as one of these "new men" whom he had done so much to publicize. He never thought of himself as rooted in the city or state in which he lived —he once referred to himself humorously as a "wandering Arab," and his whole life was a restless pilgrimage in pursuit of fame and fortune. He was fond of pointing out to friends, especially those who wished him to run for political office, the differences between himself and men of inherited wealth. Rich men might enter politics and still not leave their children impoverished; a man who had his fortune to make could not. The threat of insolvency seems to have overshadowed Wirt during most of his life, and the indebtedness of Jefferson, whose private attorney Wirt became, was a sober warning of the price of a political career. "They have been pressing me here to become a politician," he wrote to his son-in-law in 1830, "but I think of Monticello and Oakhill [Monroe's plantation], and shake my head."[17]

In his private scale of values Wirt placed his profession before everything else, and to it he made great and repeated sacrifices. In order to advance his reputation as an advocate he abandoned his literary enterprises, refused political office, gave over his evenings almost exclusively to the preparation of briefs, resigned as a justice of chancery, lived many, many months of his life away from his wife and children and finally destroyed his health by overwork. His lifelong ambition was to join the planter class. His retirement to a plantation on the James, a project he had fondly nursed from young manhood, never took place, however, and he remained active in his profession until a few days before his death. The one high office he did accept, that of Attorney General, he accepted after cautiously observing that his predecessor, William Pinkney, who had continued his private practice, had found the office an easy means of enhancing his reputation and attracting new and lucrative clients. "My single motive for accepting the office," Wirt wrote to his friend Dabney Carr, "was the calculation of being able to pursue my profession on a more advantageous ground— *i.e.* more money for less work."[18]

No one took greater pleasure than Wirt in advising the young on how to succeed. To Francis Walker Gilmer, Ninian Edwards, his daughter Laura and his sons-in-law, he freely dispensed wisdom which was a curious combination of Franklin and Chesterfield, utility and expediency. It was Wirt who told Gilmer that he would be better off not studying in Europe. A young lawyer, he wrote to him, must *seem* busy, orderly and common-sensical. A witty or humorous man is generally not taken seriously; it was therefore better to keep one's humorous fancies to oneself or reserve them for intimate friends. In public all should be sober earnestness. There was nothing more important for a lawyer's reputation than to be known for "solidity" and to possess the kind of logical and analytic skill which had characterized John Marshall's legal career.[19] A showy man was bound to be lost to fame as a lawyer. "The age of ornament is over," he wrote to a young law student in 1833, "that of utility has succeeded."[20] Meanwhile, he was writing to others that a lawyer must learn to cultivate all kinds of people, fools, criminals included, and his success was dependent on learning the secret of winning their confidence and esteem. "I want to tell you a secret," he wrote to Laura Wirt in 1820. "The way to make yourself pleasing to others is to show that you care for them."[21] To Gilmer he wrote admonishingly: "Above all, never make a man feel *ridiculous*. It is an injury which it is not in human nature to *forget*, much less to forgive."[22]

Advise what and how he would, however, Wirt himself seems

finally to have been somewhat baffled by his own success. He frequently commented that he had received more recognition than he deserved. He also made no effort to conceal the fact that his own life scarcely resembled the sober affair he was recommending to the young. When he returned to Bladensburg on a visit in 1819 he was amused to find himself pointed to as an example of a poor boy who had made his way through self-discipline and hard work. "Good conduct and an industrious application to business!! What a satire do I feel it!" he wrote to Dabney Carr. "God only knows how and why I have been thus shoved and pushed along in life."[23] A man of whims who advocated prudence and steady application, an ornamental preacher against ornament, and the most fanciful imaginable foe of fancy, Wirt often seems merely a figure of contradiction, pathetic both in his pretensions and his self-contempt. Yet his rapid rise and wide reputation highlight certain forces that were at work in his society. The course which his career took sheds considerable light, furthermore, on his interpretation of Patrick Henry, some of his other attempts to understand Virginia's past and the evolving legends of the Old South.

Wirt's confusion about himself seems to have derived in part from the fact that his own success had come while he steadfastly disregarded most of the advice which he recommended to others. In fact, in writing to young men he often, like Franklin, pointed a moral by referring to "mistakes" which he himself had made. Far from appearing the serious young lawyer, Wirt, when he moved to Richmond in 1799, lived for a number of years what he afterward regarded, apparently with good reason, as a very dissipated life. On one occasion his future father-in-law, Colonel Robert Gamble, found him in his office quite drunk after an all-night party. In the course of these same years, he embarked on several literary projects, among them his satirical *Letters of the British Spy*, which gained him a wide reputation as a wit and a man of sentiment and fancy but also wounded a certain number of sensitive feelings. All of these irregularities, far from retarding his career, seemed to have advanced it, and Wirt soon gained the reputation of a young man of "genius" (although in Justice Marshall's circle he was frequently referred to as a "Whip Sylla-bub Genius").[24] Virginians, like Americans in general, hungered for literary distinction and were only too willing to see genius in a young man who possessed a rhetorical flair for the sentimental and the nostalgic. Wirt himself began to speculate at about this time that it was not so much talent as *publicized* talent which brought recognition—"great talents thrown fairly into the point of public observation," as he expressed it in the *British Spy*.[25] In his more cynical Chesterfieldian moments, he seems thoroughly to have understood the importance of stage-managing his life and directing the formation of a favorable public image of himself, but he never comprehended how much he owed to the romantic concept of genius which he himself did so much to publicize in his *Patrick Henry*. His willingness to undertake politically sensitive legal work which Jefferson and other ranking Republicans urged upon him, as in the prosecution of Aaron Burr in 1807, early established him as a party regular and a man of "correct views," but it was the sentimental romance and nature idyll which he spun around the figure of Burr's co-conspirator, Harman Blenner-hassett, that first made him famous.

Harman Blennerhassett was the wealthy Anglo-Irishman on whose island in the Ohio River Burr assembled his forces. Since Burr himself had not been present when the conspiracy was dis-covered, the defense held that he was not guilty of treason. The case, which was tried in the circuit court in Richmond before Chief Justice Marshall in the fall of 1807, eventually led to the acquittal of both Burr and Blennerhassett. The part of Wirt's long speech which was most widely reprinted in the newspaper press was his portrayal of the latter. It was Wirt's objective to get at Burr through creating sympathy for Blennerhassett, whom he characterized as an innocent, a sort of natural aristocrat, duped and misled by the scheming and insidiously persuasive Burr. Blen-nerhassett became a New Adam in Wirt's drama, living in pastoral tranquillity apart from society among books, music and scientific lore. "Such was the state of Eden," Wirt commented, "when the serpent entered its bowers."[26] Wirt's attack on Burr as the snake in the Republican garden cleverly introduced the democratic myth of the West into the proceedings and enlarged the imaginative range and popular appeal of the trial through its sentimental portrayal of Blennerhassett's home and family life, which was cast in the image of the later plantation legend. Jefferson himself was apparently impressed since he wrote to Wirt early the following year urging him to enter Congress and assume leadership of the party. "With your reputation, talents and correct views," Jefferson told him, "you will at once be placed at the head of the republican body in the House of Representatives."[27]

By the time of the Burr trial Wirt had begun to be more self-conscious about the impression he was making upon his contemporaries, and his activities thereafter were characterized by greater caution. When war with England seemed imminent in 1807, for example, Wirt briefly flirted with an ambitious plan to raise a "legion" of four regiments with himself as commanding general, but when his idea stirred up jealousy and criticism from militia officers—and met with discouragement from Jefferson—Wirt contented himself with the prosecution of Burr as a means of exhibiting his patriotism and party loyalty. In view of what he took to be the adverse effect of the *British Spy*, he was especially careful about the literary projects he embarked upon. When in 1813 he completed a play, he cautiously solicited the opinions of his friends about the advisability of producing it. "I want to know your opinion now," he wrote to St. George Tucker, "whether . . . a play is likely to do me any injury with the world, either as a man of business or as a man pretending to any dignity of character?" How, he wondered, would the writing of a play have affected the reputation of Jefferson, Madison, Monroe or Marshall?[28] More and more Wirt seemed impressed with the necessity of maintaining a dignified public presence. "I lost the best part of my life indulging the frolics of fancy," he wrote to Francis

Gilmer in 1818, "— and the consequence is, that it will take me all the rest of it to convince the world that I have common sense."[29]

The Legend Grows

Wirt's study of Patrick Henry was undertaken as part of his reformation of character and of his deliberate campaign to alter the public image of himself. Scarcely a year after the appearance of the *British Spy* Wirt had written to Dabney Carr that he had been reading Samuel Johnson's *The Lives of the Poets* and had developed an "itch for biography." What he had in mind, he told Carr, was a sober study "of some *departed* Virginia worthy. I meddle no more with *the living*." Eventually he hoped to compile a portrait gallery of such exemplary lives and publish a volume modeled on Plutarch.[30] About the same time he addressed his first letter to the President in Washington announcing his purpose and soliciting his recollections of Henry. His full purpose was defined only six years later in a second letter when he wrote to Jefferson that there seemed to him a crying need for patriotic literature. For a number of years Wirt had been outdoing the Mugwumps in his solemn denunciation of the times in which he lived. Napoleon's betrayal of the ideals of the French Revolution by the Franco-Russian alliance, the Burr conspiracy and the Hartford Convention had all brought forth ornamental jeremiads which prophesied the disappearance of liberty and the dissolution of the Republic.[31] Now, he wrote to Jefferson, it seemed increasingly apparent that "the times require a little discipline" and that this discipline might best be imposed through didactic writings which instructed the young in the ways of the Revolutionary fathers. What better choice could there be than the man who was known as "the trumpet of the Revolution"? "Mr. Henry," Wirt concluded, "seems to me a good text for a discourse on rhetoric, patriotism and morals."[32]

Wirt was not long in learning, however, that his task was more complicated than he had supposed. By 1810 he had discovered that it was almost impossible to reconstruct exactly what Patrick Henry had said on certain occasions, and even the events of his life proved difficult to fix with any certainty. Patrick Henry seemed to exist almost exclusively as a memory—and memories, he soon learned, varied a good deal. By conducting a wide correspondence with men like Jefferson and St. George Tucker who had known Henry, Wirt began to make some progress in compiling materials for the book, but in the course of doing so he encountered still other problems of a much more perplexing kind. He discovered first of all that Henry was not the nonpartisan Revolutionary hero which he had at first taken him to be. The events at the end of Henry's life had scarred his reputation in orthodox Republican circles and earned him the unflattering title of "the great Apostate." It became increasingly clear to Wirt that he would be unable to discuss Henry's life candidly without involving himself in a kind of political controversy which he sought above all things to avoid. "I despair of the subject," he wrote to Jefferson in 1813. "The truth, perhaps, cannot be prudently published by me during my life."[33] Perhaps most troubling of all, he had developed some reservations of his own about his hero. "There are some ugly traits in H.'s character," he told Carr, "and some pretty nearly as ugly blanks. He was a blank military commander, a blank governor, and a blank politician. . . . In short, it is, verily, as hopeless a subject as man could well desire."[34]

Nonetheless, having applied to Henry's flaws all the "plaster of Paris" he could command, Wirt went ahead with the book and by August, 1815, he reported that he had written 107 pages of manuscript—"up-hill all the way, and heavy work, I promise you."[35] The process of writing brought still another set of problems to the fore: Wirt began to worry his correspondents with his uncertainties concerning style and presentation. St. George Tucker had warned him two years before that American biographical writing was almost bound to be dull, since American lives were characteristically uneventful,[36] and Wirt himself was soon protesting that Henry's life was "extremely monotonous." "It is all speaking, speaking, speaking."[37] In order to pad the slender data which he possessed concerning Henry, Wirt was forced to retell in full the story of the Revolution in Virginia. To do so he used long unwieldy quotations from documentary sources, and in other ways employed the short-cuts of the contemporary memorialist. To compensate for the deadness which he sensed in the book, Wirt colored the narrative with fanciful and hyperbolic metaphors, suggestive of those used in Homer, which sometimes ran on for half a page.

This was the style of writing which had gained him such notoriety at the Burr trial and on other public occasions, but Wirt, grown more cautious, now experienced terrible uncertainty when it came to committing this kind of rhetoric to paper. As his uncertainty mounted, he sent portions of his manuscript again and again to friends and asked for their comments. When their recommendations did not agree, he attempted to arbitrate the differences between their views by still further correspondence. It soon became apparent that there was to be no consensus in the matter of style either. The most controversial passage described Henry at the Virginia ratifying convention in 1788, and compared him successively to a mountain stream, a river, a cataract and finally to the ocean beating against the shore. Wirt sent this particular passage to five different friends—to one or two of them several times—before he decided to include it unchanged in the final draft. Jefferson wrote to Wirt that the differences of opinion he was encountering were probably a matter of age. He himself found parts of the book "too flowery" for his taste, but he added that these same passages would probably "please younger readers in [their] present form." Wirt was thus forced to choose the generation to which he wished to appeal, and he finally, and with great misgivings, beamed his historical image at the present and future rather than at the past. His decision made, Wirt left in the "excrescenses" which Jefferson had recommended he "prune" and sent the manuscript to the printer in September, 1817.[38]

The Natural Aristocrat Takes to the Woods

The book which was finally published the following November has three important characteristics. It is a success story, it is social panegyric and it is a nature idyll. The conjunction of these characteristics at first seems curious and unpromising, yet all three relate directly to Wirt's problem and become integral parts of what he needed to say. Take away any one of them and the "solution" which he contrived would have been inadequate. Although the book was seriously criticized in the reviews and is now conceded little authority in what it says of Henry's life and times, it was enduringly popular—there were twenty-five editions by 1871—and it initiated a kind of historical writing which was almost wholly new.[39] Neither Wirt's critics nor his admirers could even find a word to describe it; they thought the book unique even when, like Adams and Jefferson, they were unreceptive.

Unlike Mason Locke Weems's popular didactic biography of Washington, to which one critic of Wirt has recently compared it,[40] Wirt's book was generally more accurate and restrained, did not invent or even employ dialogue, and unlike Weems's treatment dealt with its subject's personal life only in the most general terms. Weems, furthermore, though he too recounted the events of the Revolution, had almost no interest in larger social questions and did not indulge himself in a nostalgic portrayal of Virginia's past. Weems was after all a book peddler who composed chapbooks for those Americans who verged on illiteracy, while Wirt aimed his *Patrick Henry* primarily at educated Virginians of roughly his own degree of sophistication. "Panegyric," the word Wirt's contemporaries most often came up with, was misleading, since he was not simply writing in praise of a single man. What Wirt wished to say involved him in writing a eulogy of a whole society. It was a utopia set in the past. It resembled in many ways the kind of writing about the past which would become characteristic of the later nineteenth century. It mattered less where in the past one located the Good Society than what values such a society was made to stand for. Wirt's *Patrick Henry* stands in the same relation to the Virginia past as Webster's Plymouth oration of 1820 does to the Puritan past of New England. Wirt wrote of Revolutionary times in Virginia as a golden age, an age of heroes. "*Those* were the times," he seemed to be repeating, "and those were the giants such times produced."

Wirt wished to show that during the early stages of the Revolution an epic struggle for pre-eminence had taken place between the old ideal of an aristocracy of birth and wealth and a new ideal of natural leadership. Involved in the conflict were two opposing sets of values, a classical ideal and an idea of natural vitality. Wirt felt the classical ideal was fading out of American life along with an aristocracy of birth, while Nature, he appeared to believe, was about to emerge as a dominant cultural force. In a period of twenty years he changed his estimate—in fact, reversed himself—concerning the relative merits of these two value systems, but at the time that he wrote his *Henry* they were more in equilibrium than they had been before or were to be again.

The classical ideal is perhaps best represented in what Southerners like the Mugwumps meant when they referred, as they constantly did, to the Roman republic. Although Greek culture and political life were by no means forgotten, many of Wirt's contemporaries thought they saw in Roman politics under the Republic the perfection of civil government. Then more than at any time in history, they felt, the affairs of men rested in the hands of high-minded and decorous patricians who conducted their business and settled their differences rationally and with eloquence. Of all Romans Cicero, though himself something of a self-made man, best exemplified to Southerners the legalism, the highly developed oratorical technique and the aristocratic qualities elicited by the idea of Rome.[41] In Wirt's eyes this classical ideal was especially associated with the Tidewater aristocrats—Jefferson's "pseudo-aristoi"—while the other idea was associated with Henry personally, the yeoman class from which he arose, and with American nature. For William Wirt, Patrick Henry became the embodiment of the idea of a natural aristocracy.

It was Wirt's purpose to show how the Ciceronian rhetoric of the classical ideal, which he greatly admired, came to be superseded by the more vigorous kind of oratory and leadership represented by Henry. Thus an important part of the book is Henry's rise from a simple rustic to his eminence as governor of Virginia in 1776, when he becomes for Wirt a new and indigenous kind of aristocrat "with a dignity and even majesty, that would have done honour to the most polished courtier in Europe."[42] To achieve his purpose Wirt was forced to rebuild the social world of eighteenth-century Virginia from both ends, so to speak. In the Tidewater counties, and especially at Williamsburg, he portrayed an aristocracy as practiced and cultivated as any similar group in London or Paris. In Wirt's eyes Williamsburg became a metropolis of empire, "the *focus* of fashion and high life."[48] This and other similar claims drew a protest from St. George Tucker, who had been sent the early chapters of the book in manuscript. "I think the picture both of Governors, & Councillors' stile of living rather exaggerated. . . . Their *hospitality* was without Bounds: but there was not much pomp; & less of it, by far, than may be seen in Richm[on]d at this day. . . ."[44] In the political life of the capital the ideal of the Roman Republic was best exemplified for Wirt in the person of Richard Henry Lee, who, though Henry's associate in the cause of independence, was an aristocrat educated in Europe whom contemporaries had called "the Cicero" of Virginia. The Augustan note in the characterization of Lee is struck heavily. "His face itself," Wirt comments, "was on the Roman model; his nose Caesarian; the port and carriage of his head, leaning persuasively and gracefully forward; and the whole contour noble and fine." These "two models of eloquence," Henry and Lee, are continually compared and contrasted as the events of the Revolution move toward their climax.[45]

At the same time, Wirt manipulated the circumstances of Henry's early life so as to place him at the other end of the social scale and to make his rise more dramatic than it really was. Despite the mention which Wirt made of Henry's respectable family, his emphasis was of another sort. Jefferson had written to Wirt complaining of Henry's ignorance, his laziness and his lack of cultivation. Wirt wove these same characteristics into a legend of a very different kind. For him Henry's limitations became his strengths. Instead of receiving the classical education bestowed upon his future confederates, Henry was permitted to spend his time roaming the forests like an Indian, hunting and fishing, and absorbing the very essence of American nature—its wildness, its capacity for mercurial change, its strengths and its "languor." The emphasis placed on the languor and "indolence" of Henry is really quite extraordinary in a book of this date and is suggestive of the Lincoln legend half a century later and certain passages in *Huckleberry Finn*. According to this view, the greatness of Henry lay not in his deliberate ambitions but in his capacity to bide his time and to wait for the historic moment. Then it was destiny, not personal ambition which summoned him forward to be the man of the hour. Napoleon's opportunism and quenchless lust for power, Wirt felt, had destroyed the meaning of the French Revolution and, like most Americans, he seemed to fear terribly the kind of naked ambition which he saw revealed in Americans like Burr. Henry is thus brought forward as a solution to the problem of opportunism, a natural man, ignorant of his own strength and wanting, needing almost nothing.[46]

Wirt lays heavy dramatic emphasis on the moment of awakening when Henry discovers his powers. The occasion is the famous Parson's Cause in 1763 when he first rose to attack privilege—in this instance the privilege of the clergy. As he stood awkwardly before sniggering spectators, his genius was fired and the aspect of the clown dropped suddenly away:

The spirit of his genius awakened all his features. His countenance shone with a nobleness and grandeur which it had never before exhibited. There was a lightning in his eyes which seemed to rive the spectator. His action became graceful, bold, and commanding; and in the tones of his voice . . . there was a peculiar charm, a magic . . . of which no one can give any adequate description.[47]

In Henry, Wirt declared, Americans discovered a new kind of eloquence which achieved its effect, not by convincing the reason, but by overwhelming the sensibilities of the listener. Henry spoke directly to the heart "with a force that almost petrified it." One witness told Wirt that on this occasion "he made their blood run cold, and their hair rise on end," and Wirt himself added that all those there seem to have been "bereft of their senses."[48] Wirt's vocabulary for expressing Henry's effectiveness suggests the kind of novelty he was attempting to define. As early as the *British Spy* he had tried to put into words his wonder and admiration at the preaching of the blind evangelist James Waddell, whom he had heard as a young man. While he had not himself heard Henry, he had feasted on the reports of actual witnesses. This was a kind of oratory which aimed at an almost physiological effect. Henry appeared to "worm his way through the whole body, and to insinuate his influence into every mind."[49] Suddenly, seemingly from nowhere, the electrifying image or phrase came forth. His performance was more than mortal; it was as though the deity spoke through him. "It was so unexampled, so unexpected, so instantaneous, and so transcendent in its character, that it had, to the people, very much the appearance of supernatural inspiration."[50]

The underscoring given to Henry's indolence and his untutored greatness of mind was quite as necessary for Wirt's case as the emphasis given to his unpretentious social background. Henry could not have been portrayed as an ambitious young lawyer making his way up by shrewdness and guile. This was the aspect of Henry's life which Wirt was most anxious to play down. To have laid stress on Henry's ambition and his all-too-evident love of money and power would have led to portraying him as a kind of Yankee. Rather, it was Wirt's objective to suggest that Henry succeeded almost in spite of himself, that his speeches and court-room performances were spontaneous and owed their greatness to the inspiration of the moment. He was a large-spirited and disinterested man, a man who placed his love of country and his sense of duty above his own interest and pleasure. It was, of course, still a fact that Henry rose to high place, a fact which Wirt had no wish to conceal. Wirt's problem was to show that this rise had nothing about it of pecuniary ambition; he tried to suggest by constant repetition that Patrick Henry followed Wordsworth's divine "impulse from the vernal wood" rather than the main chance. It thus becomes clear that Wirt's natural aristo-crat was not the carefully selected and highly trained scholar-statesman whom Jefferson had in mind when he spoke of a natural aristocracy. Rather he was a man steeped in American nature, guided by the elemental forces which direct it and sharing their capacity for moral grandeur. According to Wirt, Henry became at the height of his powers both a natural genius and the kind of natural gentleman which Americans were soon to admire in Andrew Jackson.

The Henry that emerges from these particular pages is the forerunner of several other American types which soon became important, and it is in this elusive quest for an indigenous Ameri-can character and the suggestive ambiguity and fluidity of the figure he finally sketched that Wirt is most interesting. As a speaker Henry is portrayed as aggressive, provocative, turbulent —the prototype of later fire-eaters like Rhett and Yancey. "His was a spirit fitted to raise the whirlwind," Wirt concluded, "as well as to ride in it."[51] Throughout the narrative he is also spoken of in terms which, in their emphasis on the prodigious, anticipate the Western hero of the folktale and the Crockett legends. It was only a step from the natural giant described by Wirt to the comic exaggeration of Western humor. Henry was compared to "A cataract, like that of Niagara, crowned with overhanging rocks and mountains, in all the rude and awful grandeur of nature."[52] He was compared to Samson shaking the pillars of the temple, to Hannibal crossing the Alps, to Demosthenes, to Francis the First, and to Charles the Fifth.[53] The qualities stressed were natural strength, natural endurance, natural eloquence and natural courage. Patrick Henry was characterized, Wirt added, by "strong natural sense." "In short," he concluded, "he was the Orator of Nature: and such a one as nature might not blush to avow." "In a word, he was one of those perfect prodigies of nature, of whom very few have been produced since the foundations of the earth were laid."[54]

Wirt's greatest problem of organization was presented by the anticlimactic quality of Henry's career after 1776. Once the trumpet call to Revolution had sounded and the business of incitement was at an end, the most distinguished phase of his career was over and nothing he subsequently did, according to Wirt's own estimate, enhanced his earlier reputation. Yet he remained in public life for fifteen years. By 1775, Wirt is forced to comment halfway through the book, "The spirit of resistance was sufficiently excited; and nothing remained but to organize that resistance, and to plan and execute the details. . . . In business of this nature, Mr. Henry, as we have seen, was not efficient."[55]

Nothing was left, that is, except fighting and winning a war and organizing a government! Having portrayed Henry as a fire-eater and insurgent whose special skill was incitement and provocation, Wirt was thus left with a rebel without a cause. Only in his fight to prevent ratification of the Constitution in 1788, a fight with which Wirt was personally out of sympathy, does the old Henry replace Henry the wooden paragon about whom most of the book revolves. And yet this very circumstance prompted reflections which clearly worried Wirt. It was in connection with Henry's speech at the ratifying convention that he had employed the cataclysmic metaphor which had provoked so much discussion and criticism. Did nature prompt only to rebellion? His cherished chain of crescendoing metaphors, which finally compared Henry's voice to the ocean pounding the shore, strongly suggests some awareness of the potential destructiveness of the natural man when his powers are unleashed.

Wirt, pushed to this extremity, could bring himself to explore this implication no further and changed the subject in obvious discomfort. Thereafter, he clothed his hero in the conventional garb of high civilization. He often, in fact, makes Henry sound a good deal like the George Washington of the contemporary legend. He dwelt at length on Henry's vision of America's future, of her destiny to become a great and powerful empire; he spoke of "her golden harvests waving over fields of immeasurable extent— her commerce penetrating the most distant seas, and her cannon silencing the vain boasts of those, who now proudly affect to rule the waves."[56] What emerges most clearly is not Patrick Henry, nature's rebel, but Patrick Henry as a symbol of American aspirations and an example of moral perfection.

The aspect of Henry's character which Wirt held up for emulation was not his indolence or his provocativeness but his selfless devotion to his country. In dedicating his book as he did, "To the young men of Virginia," he meant to read these young men a lesson in disinterestedness and patriotism, not simply a lesson in how to succeed. Henry's success could be explained, Wirt felt, by his genius. His moral character could not. On the occasion of Henry's retirement from public life in 1789, Wirt in an incredible instance of self-deception observed that, "No man had ever passed through so long a life of public service, with a reputation more perfectly unspotted."[57] Few young men could hope to emulate a man who could sound like a cataract or a raging sea, but Henry's love of domesticity and his self-discipline and high moral character were the very qualities which, Wirt felt, his own times required.

The difficulties which Wirt encountered in completing his narrative were only partly due to deficiencies in his subject, although these were numerous enough. While he was forced to explain away Henry's love of power, to concede—at the risk of inconsistency—that his love of money was a fault, and to suppress certain events which took place at the end of Henry's life, his difficulty lay mostly in determining a standard of judgment. Where in 1817 was one to find the sanction for personal ambition, for striving for eminence? What justifiable motive free of the taint of rank opportunism could be found for self-advancement? In a society in which selfless devotion to God was no longer an ideal which found wide acceptance, patriotism—selfless devotion to a national destiny—provided an outlet for American apirations. A man was asked to transcend his private ambitions and to aspire for his country rather than for himself. If his genius had predestined him for greatness, he then might safely follow his natural destiny, as America was to follow hers. This appears to have been Wirt's message, although he never put it in precisely this way.

Opportunism was such a prominent feature of Wirt's own life that he could scarcely bring himself to talk about it sensibly, let alone analytically. Like Webster and other eminent contemporaries, he sensed a disturbing gap between his ideal of disinterested service and his mundane success and mounting ambition. Like these others, he found no satisfactory solution to the problem posed by personal power in a democratic society, a problem which has bedeviled Americans to the present day. Any further explorations of a like sort which he may have contemplated were, in any event, abandoned with his appointment to Monroe's cabinet a few weeks after the publication of his book. He had "done" Virginia, he must have felt, and could now let his imagination wander over wider fields.

The Legendary Planter Gains Civilized Restraints

Wirt addressed himself publicly to the questions raised in the *Henry* only once during the rest of his life, although his letters continued to worry over the problems of reason and fancy, civilization and nature, which were meanwhile preoccupying growing numbers of Americans. Wirt's most conspicuous leap forward into the psychology of the Southern legend, however, did not come until 1826, when he registered his increasing distrust of the natural man. In 1803, at the time he wrote the *British Spy*, Wirt believed that the highest forms of the imagination were possible only in a "state of nature." "Civilization," he wrote, "deters the fancy from every bold enterprise, and buries nature under a load of hypocritical ceremonies."[58] Only the simple man and the primitive man possessed that capacity to touch the heart which is the essence of eloquence, and he scoffed at the oratorical claims of Cicero and at all formal traditions of oratory. In his *Patrick Henry*, as we have seen, he expressed a much fuller appreciation of civilization in his many tributes to the Augustan ideal and its embodiment in the life and politics of colonial Williamsburg.

In 1826, in his discourse on the lives of Jefferson and Adams, he modified his previous views still more radically. On this occasion genius, fancy, imagination were mentioned only to be set aside as essentially dangerous and disruptive forces in human character. Jefferson and Adams were *not* geniuses, Wirt began by declaring. They were not "great and eccentric minds 'shot madly from their spheres' [the "blazing comet" had been Wirt's favorite metaphor in describing Henry] to affright the world and scatter pestilence in their course." Rather they were "minds whose strong and steady light . . . came to cheer and to gladden a world."[59] They were calm and reasonable men, possessed of common sense, who had been chosen by Providence to guide America to independence. What Providence had given, Providence now, in an instance of unsurpassable "moral sublimity," had simultaneously taken away —and on the fiftieth anniversary of American independence. Clearly, he continued, Providence, in ending both lives dramatically on the Fourth of July, must have wished to instruct, to point a moral.

What could be learned about American nationality from the lives of these two men? Both, first of all, were highly cultivated men, the products of regional cultures. Together they symbolized the civilization of the North and of the South. Each was the product and the spokesman of his "hemisphere." The thought and character of each of them had been shaped and disciplined by the experience of his ancestors. Adams represented the Puritanical spirit of a New England which was inured to physical hardship, characterized by self-discipline and schooled in political contention—the Sparta of the colonies. Jefferson was the product of an aristocratic and chivalric Virginia, America's Athens, over which the "spirit of Raleigh" had presided since its founding. As Wirt went on it became clearer that his comparison was meant neither to offend nor to flatter. Both types of American were admirable because both possessed the capacity to maintain civilized life in the tumultuous social environment of the new world.

The modern New Englander was thus a product of the past. "The robust character of the fathers descended upon their children." Like their forefathers they were skilled in the arts of verbal as well as physical combat. "Violations of their charters, unconstitutional restraints upon their trade, and perpetual collisions with the royal Governors . . . had converted that province into an *arena*, in which the strength of mind had been tried against mind, for a century, before the tug of the Revolution came." Virginia, meanwhile, "resting on a halcyon sea, had been cultivating the graces of science, and literature, and the genial elegancies of social life."[60] Out of these contrasting circumstances had come two American types at once preferable to and more useful than the wild men who adhered to neither ethos and who took their impulses from an ungovernable nature.

In other ways, too, Wirt had closed the door on the social ideas with which he had begun his own ascent. In 1810 he had looked upon colonial society as characterized by the kind of mobility which Jefferson had ascribed to it. He had printed Jefferson's letter without alteration in the text of the *Henry*.[61] In 1826—

ironically, in view of the occasion—he had greatly simplified the contents of Jefferson's letter. In Jefferson's youth, said Wirt, there were three social classes in Virginia, the aristocracy, the yeomanry and "a *fæculum* of beings, as they were called by Mr. Jefferson, corresponding with the mass of the English plebeians."[62] Jefferson had restricted this "fæculum" to overseers alone, and he had of course inserted his "half-breeds" and "pretenders" in order to suggest the absence of precisely the kind of rigidly stratified society which Wirt was now nostalgically sketching. Where now were the new men, the "*novi homines*" of only twenty years before? In the South especially, memories were short and Wirt had now constructed for himself exactly the kind of legendary Southern past into which successive generations of Southerners were to retreat in full flight from the problems of the present. What, in heaven's name, had Jefferson to do with Sir Walter Raleigh, or, for that matter, Raleigh with Wirt?

As the idea of nature changed meaning, so did the conception of —and tolerance for—the natural man. In the legend that grew up around the Southern planter he was always portrayed as a product of benign and salubrious country life—a horseman, hunter and fisherman. He embodied many of the traits of Wirt's natural aristocrat, including the absence of driving personal am- bition, but his instinctual proclivities were held in check by a massive set of restraints. His natural impulses were disciplined by his concern for family and racial traditions, by rigid standards of decorum and a complicated code of honor, which all but paralyzed him as an effective man of action. The explanation for this legend lay in the experience of the men like Wirt who created it, their growing awareness of the amorality of nature and its consequent inability to monitor the conditions under which men advanced themselves in American society. The means through which men succeeded offered no assurance that only good men would prosper, and success itself often seemed almost an act of deception rather than the reward of virtue which Jefferson had nobly anticipated.

In the careers of these men who made their way in Southern life, the last act was almost invariably the same: disillusionment and self-contempt. The very men who had mastered the techniques of self-advancement and who best exhibited the cultural pluralism that at least potentially characterized the South almost from the beginning were the first to reaffirm—or, in the case of Wirt, invent—the legend once they themselves had arrived. Once at the top, they quickly disowned their own cultural roots and pretended to a heritage they neither possessed nor understood. Meanwhile, they turned upon the parvenu and the qualities of mind that had made them what they were. In these men America awakened expectations which it could never have satisfied and anxieties it could never have stilled, and most of them died disappointed and unforgiving. "Common sense," Wirt told his daughter Elizabeth in 1826, "is a much rarer quality than genius." And to this sober observation he added the bitterest fancy he had ever entertained. With a peculiar aptness, he chose the conventional fireworks display on the Fourth of July as his vehicle for expressing his growing distrust both of genius and the democratic process:

Genius, what is it? a fever of the brain—sparkling with delirious brilliancy; a nocturnal exhibition of fire-works in a state of rapid metamorphosis:—now it is a horizontal hoop, turning and whizzing, and cracking and shooting off its lateral spouts of fire; and then, with a louder *crack*, it becomes a fountain, a *jet d'eau*, pouring up a roaring flood of fire, which parts at the top and falls off on every side, like a weeping willow composed of pencils of descending sparks; then, crack! it becomes a vertical wheel, and way it goes, round, round, round, whiz, whiz, crack, whiz, whiz, crack, crash, crack—and then the foolish mob laugh, and clap their hands, and huzza! huzza! and the heart of the foolish exhibitor is proud. Such is genius![63]

In 1832, just two years before his death, Wirt wrote to his friend Dabney Carr that he was "a disappointed man." He was not, he said, personally neglected but rather "disappointed in my country and the glory that I thought awaited her;—disappointed, most sadly, in the intelligence and virtue which I had attributed to our countrymen;—disappointed in life itself, which is, indeed, all vanity and vexation of spirit."[64] The Antimasonic fiasco and the subsequent collapse of a speculative venture in which he tried to settle a colony of Württemberg Germans on his Florida estate—"Wirtlands"—only embittered him the more.

The end of his life followed hard upon the collapse of this undertaking. In the early months of 1834 Wirt was again in Washington for the sessions of the Supreme Court. During the first week in February he took to his bed with what appeared to be a bad cold. The infection, however, quickly developed into a virulent case of erysipelas and he died a few days later, toward noon, on February 18. Shortly before he died, he overheard the members of his family praying that he might recover. Somebody caught his audible dissent as he muttered, "No, no!"[65]

Hearing of his death the same day, the members of the Supreme Court adjourned and reassembled in the courtroom to listen to brief extemporaneous addresses by Daniel Webster and Chief Justice Marshall. Two days later both Houses of Congress adjourned, in an unprecedented gesture to a nonmember, to attend Wirt's funeral. Andrew Jackson and Martin Van Buren, followed by the Diplomatic Corps, the Bench and the Bar of the Supreme Court, and a great body of Senators and Congressmen led a long procession to the spot in the National Cemetery where Wirt was to be buried. It was a small world. In addition to those named, Daniel Webster, John Calhoun, John Quincy Adams, Henry Clay, Roger B. Taney and Edward Everett stood witnesses to William Wirt's last moments of public attention.[66]

CHAPTER III

Point Counterpoint: The Growth of the Southern Legend in the North

> It is a commonplace to state that whatever one may come to consider a truly American trait can be shown to have its equally characteristic opposite. This, one suspects, is true of all "national characters". . . . so true, in fact, that one may begin rather than end with the proposition that a nation's identity is derived from the ways in which history has, as it were, counterpointed certain opposite potentialities; the ways in which it lifts this counterpoint to a unique style of civilization, or lets it disintegrate into mere contradiction.
>
> ERIK ERIKSON, *Childhood and Society*[1]

THE IDEA OF the Yankee, despite its New England derivation, was no more acceptable in the North than in the South. The conclusion that America had produced a race of acquisitive, uncultivated and amoral men was resisted with all of the imaginative resources which intellectuals in the North could muster. Some sought to show that beyond the materialism and opportunism of the Northerner lay certain transcending concerns which gave his individualism dignity and civic value. The Yankee's proverbial curiosity, his asceticism and his single-mindedness by these calculations became aspects of a higher idealism. Still others sought to counterpoint the limitations of the Yankee ethos by summoning before their Northern contemporaries the legendary Southern gentleman, who seemed to possess every quality which the Yankee lacked: honor and integrity, indifference to money and business, a decorous concern for the amenities, and a high sense of civic and social responsibility. Neither line of investigation succeeded in quieting the uneasy speculation which focused upon the nature of civilization in the North. The Yankee was still very much alive when the period ended, and the Southern gentleman had developed certain apparent deficiencies. Among the significant and enduring results of this search for values was the new authority granted to American women, who assumed in this period a new role as moral guardians of the home and spiritual regulators of the acquisitive society.

The Age of Anxiety

One of the strangest, and most ironic, developments of the egalitarian thirties was the resurgence in the North of an aristocratic ideal based on the popular conception of plantation society. It is important to determine why this essentially antidemocratic and static ideal of a Good Society, with its obvious source in the literature which celebrated the English squirearchy, should have had such wide appeal during a period characterized by the extension of democracy and by the dynamic expansion of American society into the West and Southwest. There is no question about the fact that it did. Francis J. Grund, a perceptive German traveler who spent almost the whole decade observing American life, devoted his *Aristocracy in America* to descriptions of the kind of blatant aristocratic emulation which he had found among the genteel classes in the cities of the eastern seaboard. A recent study of American writers and the Northern magazine press, furthermore, has shown to what a large degree this hankering after aristocracy in the North took the form of eulogizing the social system in the South.[2] In 1860 Daniel Hundley, a Southerner with long experience of the North, conceded that "one portion" of the North believed:

that the citizens of our Southern States are so many Chevalier Bayards, *sans peur et sans reproche;* living upon their broad estates in all baronial splendor and hospitality, but being, nevertheless—like the slave-holding Catos and Brutuses of republican Rome, and the equally slave-holding Solons and Leonidases of democratic Greece— still true to the Constitution, the Commonwealth, and the Laws.[3]

James Fenimore Cooper, writing in 1828, struck the note which was to characterize the thinking of Americans for almost thirty years when he pointed to the South as the last best hope of the cultivated gentleman:

I am of the opinion, that in proportion to the population, there are more men who belong to what is termed the class of gentlemen, in the old southern States of America than in any other country of the world. So far as pride in themselves, a courteous air, and a general intelligence, are concerned, they are, perhaps, quite on a level with the gentry of any other country, though their intelligence must necessarily be chiefly of that sort which is obtained by the use of books, rather than of extensive familiarity with the world. In respect to conventional manners, they are not so generally finished as the upper classes of other countries, or even of some classes in their own; though I do not know where to find gentlemen of better air or better breeding throughout, than most of those I have met in the southern *Atlantic* States.[4]

Feelings of this kind clearly indicate the kind of reservations which Americans were beginning to have about their developing democracy. Such praise of the gentleman planter, coming as it did from Americans who were "good" democrats, seems to have masked a whole complex of fears and anxieties about the consequences of changes then taking place in American life. Prominent among them, certainly, was the uneasiness about the natural man which William Wirt had finally come to feel. Figures like Ishmael Bush, Cooper's brutal soulless squatter in *The Prairie*, underlined one of the threats which these men saw in the process of westward settlement. If men were naturally self-centered and rapacious, bent on pursuing their own private ends, and nature was an amoral or a neutral force, then what was there in the classless and open society of America to prevent its becoming a social jungle the equal of which the civilized world had never seen? What was to preserve the sanctity of the home and family, upon which it was felt depended the stability of society, from the forces which were daily tearing it apart? What, finally, was to provide the nation at large with a coherent set of common aims which would prevent its breaking up into a number of armed bands and hostile factions each bent upon satisfying its wants at the expense of the society as a whole?

It is difficult now to recapture the sense of the time, and to uncover the vein of uncertainty and pessimism which underlay the more evident buoyancy and expansiveness of the eighteen twenties and thirties, but these darker feelings were very much part of the scene in the North as well as in the South. The assertions of orators might point to a bountiful future, but locked in the syntax of their sentences lurked the lingering doubt, the scarcely noticed qualifier, the parenthetical "if." Speaking in 1843 at a ceremony to commemorate the completion of Bunker Hill Monument, Daniel Webster proclaimed that the memory of the Revolution would remain bright, that the monument itself would endure—but he hedged his boast about with characteristic qualifications, the apocalyptic kind of afterthought which marked the age: ". . . If the civilization of the present race of men . . . be not destined to destruction."[5] America, it was thought, would become a great empire comparable to Rome. Yet what, after all, had finally happened to Rome and to all other great historical empires? In the eighteen thirties a young English-American artist named Thomas Cole painted a series of tableaux which he entitled *The Course of Empire*.[6] These tableaux portrayed the successive stages in the rise and fall of an imaginary classical city. In the most melodramatic of these paintings, the city, having reached a state of great wealth and splendor, falls in a single afternoon to the barbarian invader. The implications of Cole's series, one can be sure, were not lost upon his viewers, as Perry Miller has suggested. A recent study has uncovered something like an epidemic of catastrophic fiction which swept the country in the eighteen thirties. "Even in the bright optimistic morning of Transcendentalist America," it concludes, there "ran this black current of terror."[7] The same kind of uncertainty as to whether Utopia or cataclysm lay ahead characterized the millennial religions which were so prominent a part of the same decade.

Of course, it may be objected that, if the truth were fully known, every age would probably appear to be an Age of Anxiety, yet it is difficult to escape the feeling that these haunting fantasies are an especially important part of this particular time—a part which we now too readily forget. The rapidity with which every aspect of national life was changing produced both sets of response: the optimism and the despair. Some of the alarm appears to have sprung from the very fact that American institutions were free and men were free to change them—for better or for worse. It was precisely because the Union had grown and changed so rapidly, for example, that people began to wonder whether it could survive. Another anecdote concerning Webster makes the point. Suddenly, in the midst of an earlier speech he gave at Bunker Hill in 1825, some of the temporary seats along the hill had collapsed with a roar and a small riot had broken out. "It is impossible, sir, to restore order," someone told him. Webster's booming reply characterized the mood of the day, "Nothing is impossible, sir; let it be done."[8]

It was a little difficult, in view of the vagueness of the threat, to prescribe a course of action to meet it. Nonetheless, it is possible to trace in the pulpit and platform oratory of the time a definite pattern of response. Over and over, speakers stressed the fact that the situation was one which called for individual initiative rather than external coercion in the form of legislation or the manipulation of institutions. In the face of such an indefinite but continuing crisis, individuals were warned that they must find within themselves the sense of dedication and the strength of purpose to see the country through. "Thus, gentlemen," William Wirt in 1830 told an audience at Rutgers, "you perceive that your lot has been cast in stormy times: and every political indication warns you that the quality which, above all others, you should seek to cultivate, is *strength of character: strength of character*, as displayed in *firmness of decision*, and *vigor of action*." In better times, he added, the easy graces of a gentleman might assume priority in any scheme of education and it might be possible to introduce young men in college to the proper enjoyment of rational pleasures, but these were times of storm and stress when, to use his own metaphor, the ship of state needed deck hands and not cabin passengers:

If, gentlemen, you were about to embark in the voyage of life, on a summer's sea, in a barge like that of Cleopatra . . . I might recommend it to you to give yourselves up entirely to the culture of those bland and gentle accomplishments which contribute to cheer and sweeten social intercourse. But I foresee, distinctly, that you will have to double Cape Horn in the winter season, and to grapple with the gigantic spirit of the storm which guards that Cape. . . .[9]

What America needed most, Wirt concluded, was another generation of men with the self-control and the "character of decision" possessed by Washington's generation. A similar point had been made by Webster a few years earlier when he addressed himself to the virtues of Adams and Jefferson after their death in 1826. In Webster's eyes selfishness and mercenary greed were the forces which most threatened the harmonious operation of society and these worthy men were particularly deserving of emulation because "no men . . . ever served their country with more entire exemption from every imputation of selfish and mercenary motives."[10]

When Americans discussed the needs of their society as a whole, they simply extrapolated from these simple prescriptions concerning individual character. In 1831, following his victory over Robert Hayne and nullification, Webster was asked to address a group of Whiggishly inclined merchants at a dinner in New York. On this occasion he carefully defined the kind of threat to the Union which he saw growing up in the South. He let his hearers peep into a chamber of social horrors. To speak of nullification or "state veto" was to speak of "commercial ruin, of abandoned wharfs, of vacated houses, of diminished and dispersing population, of bankrupt merchants, of mechanics without employment, and laborers without bread." He provided his hosts with his prescription for an ordered and prosperous society. As one would expect, he listed "public credit," "systematic finance" and "uniformity of commercial laws." More surprising was the item he placed first on his list: "national character." Without national character, by which he appears to have meant a combination of national self-knowledge and self-discipline, there could be no enduring social order.[11]

Few things were accordingly more representative of the twenties and thirties than this growing concern with the national character. Few figures reveal more about the nature of this concern than the legendary Yankee who begins to make his appearance in works of American fiction.

The Yankee Takes Cover

In 1821, a few months after the settlement of the Missouri question, Cooper published *The Spy*, a novel set in Westchester County, New York, in the final months of the Revolution. This immensely—and enduringly—popular book which launched Cooper's literary career is perhaps the first important novel about

American character. Into his New York countryside Cooper imported an ingenious Yankee peddler, a troop of Virginia dragoons under a dashing Southern officer and a large assortment of genteel Virginians, including General George Washington. Out of this curious and improbable assortment of types he managed to contrive both a successful conventional yarn and an extraordinarily revealing account of conflicting American loyalties.

In the opening scene of the novel, Washington, on a secret mission in Westchester, is forced to take shelter during a storm at "The Locusts," the estate of a prominent loyalist named Henry Wharton. During Washington's visit Wharton's son, who is serving with the British garrison in New York City, arrives for a visit, after passing the Continental pickets in disguise. A short while later young Wharton, still in disguise, is captured by the Virginians and taken prisoner as a suspected spy. The plot is principally concerned with attempts to save Wharton from being hanged like Major André, with whom he is compared. The successful rescue of Wharton is accomplished by the patriot-peddler, Harvey Birch, acting on instructions from Washington, who *knows* that Wharton is not a spy and who had pledged himself before leaving to be of service to his hosts.

Into these complicated circumstances are interjected a great many observations which explore more generally certain themes suggested by the novel, such as the distinction Cooper is interested in making between narrow partisanship, which he distrusts, and American loyalty, which he admires but experiences some difficulty in defining. The subtitle, "A tale of the neutral ground," is peculiarly apt, since to its obvious military meaning can be added another more central to the novel. Cooper's Westchester is also a neutral ground between the regions, a contrivance for assembling and examining all the character types which make up the *genus Americanus:* loyalist gentleman, patriot gentleman, Yankee commoner, officer, soldier, planter, belle, Negro retainer and Irish servant.

The spectrum of characters which Cooper exhibits is most colorless in the middle ranges. The elder Wharton, a Europeanized American gentleman, collapses into immobility and madness soon after his son's capture. The captured "hero," Henry Wharton, is little more than a pawn. The genteel Dunwoodie, who is one of many Virginians in the novel, is almost as ineffective. At every turn, even in the case of Washington, the gentlemanly code of honor is weighed, measured and found wanting.

While taking the measure of the American gentleman, Cooper had the happy sense to introduce Harvey Birch. Harvey possesses all the traits which characterized the Yankee in folklore. He is shrewd, acquisitive and mysterious in his movements. He always travels alone, pack on back. He is thought to be in league with the devil. His superior intelligence, Cooper hints, might mean that his family "had known better fortunes in the land of their nativity," but he arrives on the scene devoid of gentility. He spits tobacco juice into the fireplace, talks straight and bargains hard, even with his "friends" the Whartons. He has "the common manners of the country."[12] In particular, he is characterized by his overt and unabashed love of money. He receives payment for a sale of tobacco in a fetishistic ritual:

Harvey's eyes twinkled as he contemplated the reward; and rolling over in his mouth a large quantity of the article in question, coolly stretched forth his hand, into which the dollars fell with a most agreeable sound; but not satisfied with the transient music of their fall, the pedler gave each piece in succession a ring on the stepping-stone of the piazza, before he consigned it to the safe keeping of a huge deer-skin purse, which vanished from the sight of the spectators so dexterously, that not one of them could have told about what part of his person it was secreted.[13]

"I am afraid," Mr. Wharton commented sadly, "[Harvey's] love of money is a stronger passion than love of his kin."[14]

An atmosphere of illegality and guile hovers about Harvey, who is generally thought to be an English spy, perhaps a double agent. He has been many times jailed and has as many times escaped. While the proper American gentleman like Wharton is ineffective and unable to disguise his gentility, Harvey is something of a chameleon. When he goes to rescue Henry Wharton from the troop of Virginians, his disguise is brilliantly successful. He appears as a Puritan zealot, that second face of the Yankee, as though he had been summoned in to prepare Henry for his approaching execution. His disguise exceeds by a good deal the requirements of the situation. Dressed in sober black, he arrives, beetle-browed and forbidding, at the place of Henry's imprisonment. "All was fanaticism, uncharitableness, and denunciation." At one point Harvey hums a psalm in "the full richness of the twang that distinguishes the Eastern psalmody," and Cooper commented in a footnote that "By 'Eastern' is meant the States of New England, which, being originally settled by Puritans, still retain many distinct shades of character."[15] Wishing to be alone with Henry and provide him with a disguise, he treats those present to a display of religious jargon—of Providence, Grace and Eternal Damnation—that soon drives them all from the room. A few minutes later Harvey emerges with the genteel Henry ironically disguised as the Negro retainer Caesar. They successfully make their escape. As they disappear down the road, a young Virginian shouts after them, "Off with you, for a hypocritical, psalm-singing, canting rogue in disguise. . . . If I had you on a Virginia plantation for a quarter of an hour, I'd teach you to worm the tobacco, with the turkeys."[16]

Although a range of character traits exists among the Virginians, all of them put service to their country before their own interests. Washington himself personifies the idea of service. He is the fearless leader of the rebel forces. In his disguise as "Mr. Harper," he is the model of the republican gentleman, simply and unostentatiously dressed, dignified and decorous in his bearing. The plot of the story, nonetheless, involves him in curiously contradictory behavior. As Washington he is charged with defeating the enemy and, one would think, preserving his own safety. Yet as "Mr. Harper," he ventures among the enemy, accepts hospitality from a Loyalist and secretly arranges for the escape of a valuable prisoner. He lives in an uneasy truce with himself, as he is many times made to remember. His allegiance to the Whartons is that of a gentleman; his allegiance to the Continentals is that of an American.

Cooper never resolved the dilemma with which he confronted his major characters: of being both gentlemen and rebels. The fiery sense of honor of Captain Jack Lawton, the Virginian in command of the dragoons, leads to his heroic death—rather needlessly, it is implied. Major Dunwoodie is immobilized by his honorable bearing toward his enemy kin. Washington, on the other hand, manages to divide his gentility and his Americanism into more or less separate personalities and therefore succeeds in remaining somewhat above the battle. He hires the Yankee, Harvey Birch, to do his undercover work for him, his furtive spying, and to arrange for the rescue of his young Loyalist friend. Toward the end of the novel he attempts to pay Harvey for his services, but Harvey refuses the money without hesitation. "Does your excellency think," he asks, "that I have exposed my life, and blasted my character, for money?" Mr. Harper expresses amazement. "If not for money," he asks the acquisitive Yankee, "what then?" Harvey terminates their conversation with another question. "What has brought your excellency into the field?"[17]

While Washington is surprised at Harvey's display of disinterested patriotism, the reader has all along been carefully tutored in Harvey's virtues. He knows long before the final chapter that the peddler is as selfless a patriot as General Washington. When Harvey is robbed of his gold by the Continental partisans, the "Skinners," he shows no attachment to his earnings. "Here, take the trash," he shouts as he tosses them his purse.[18]

Cooper had made Harvey Birch his most important character and not, as the model of Scott might have prompted, young Henry Wharton. He had called his book *The Spy*, not *Wharton*. Most important of all, he had discovered that the most "heroic" thing an American could do was to give up money, a kind of renunciation deemed almost more praiseworthy than the sacrifice of one's life. The more conventional heroic death of the Virginian, Captain Jack Lawton, pales to nothing beside the momentous act of self-denial performed by Harvey Birch in his final interview with Washington. Harvey's own "heroic" death at the Battle of Niagara in 1813, described in the final chapter, is anticlimactic and unnecessary after this transcendent act, which is the real ending of Cooper's romance. This final chapter, it is interesting to note, was printed and paged under pressure from Cooper's publisher several weeks before the novel itself was finished.[19] It shows how radically—and rapidly—Cooper's imagination had outgrown more conventional expectations. In denying himself the money, Harvey becomes a hero of a more indigenous kind. Washington is made to sense this, and his behavior toward Harvey on this occasion betrays his confusion.

The Transcendent Yankee and Society

Neat as Cooper's solution to the problem of American acquisitiveness might seem, his transcendent Yankee represented no real solution to America's social problem. The first commitment of the gentleman, the novel suggests, is to the society of gentlemen; the transcendent Yankee like Harvey remains and must remain outside of society. As Harvey's dying father had told him, he must be "a Pilgrim through life. The bruised reed may endure, but it will never rise." The chapter which contains the interview with Washington opens—as does the book—with General Washington mounted on a horse, "a noble animal, of a deep bay; and a group of young men, in gayer attire, evidently awaited his pleasure, and did his bidding." Harvey is as little at home with the general and his court as his successor in Cooper's fiction, Natty Bumppo, is at home in a settled society. Harvey's real home is his solitary mountain-top hideout, which with all its homely comforts becomes a symbol of his self-sufficiency and his transcendence of society. As he tells Washington. "It is little that I need in this life. . . . I can never want in this country."[20] The need is the other way around. The gentleman in American fiction is often portrayed as helpless and ineffective without a Harvey Birch, a Natty Bumppo or a Horse-Shoe Robinson at his side. This was to be particularly true of the fictional Southern gentleman, whose numerous retainers of one sort or another suggest the degree of his social dependency.

The romance by convention begins and ends *in* the everyday world of organized society. In a certain kind of romance the central figure sets out from society, has his adventure and returns to the everyday world at the end. The adventure is measured against the values of society, seen in relation to them. No matter how far afield the romancer might take his hero, whether he is made to move from Nantucket to the South Seas or from a nineteenth-century customhouse into the Puritan past, the action of romance begins and terminates in a familiar social world where the gentleman has his place. Cooper's various gentlemen, like Mr. Harper, Mr. Wharton and Judge Temple, stand for a kind of social order which the romancer could not dispense with. They stand for the fixed values of an older culture with which Cooper and other romancers wished to remain in touch. They stood for Europe and for continuity with the past. In a sense, only the gentleman *believed* in society, and only Harvey believed in America. Yet you could not make up a society of Birches and Bumppos, because their very function in fiction was to interpret wilderness to civilization, novelty to tradition. They were pathfinders. Once removed from their mediating lookout on the periphery of civilization, they become comic boors, a source of comedy. Besides, they are so far from being acquisitive and predatory, appearances to the contrary, that they end in having no aggressions at all. They seldom marry or make love. They are incapable of reproducing themselves, because they are both sexless and sterile.[21]

This, of course, was the ideal, the ideal that a Yankee nation wanted, in fact needed, to believe in—and to convince others to believe in. This was the transcendent Yankee who chased the White Whale of the sea or White Stallion of the plains—it hardly mattered which—while his alter ego, alas, turned sperm oil into bullion, and rich Indian lands into prosperous real-estate holdings, and shipped ice from Walden to the Ganges.[22]

The real Yankee, whose appearance only is given to Harvey Birch, is an unpleasant type: hypocrite, chiseler, fiend. He rarely shows his undisguised face in good company. He is an outcast of a sort, an Ishmael, whose grasping hand is turned against everyone. If the transcendent Yankee is kept in the woods or at sea, the real Yankee is kept in the cellar or locked in the woodshed like an idiot kinsman. He is always apt to break out. His footfall haunts the family household like an ancestral ghost. Occasionally he does break out. When he does, the American family is his first target of destruction, as Americans were to learn with shocked surprise when they encountered Simon Legree from Vermont. Meanwhile, all ingenuity is devoted to barring the door against his threatened irruptions. He is to the benign, transcendent Yankee what the fire-eater is to the selfless gentleman, the Lawton to the Dunwoodie, the Randolph to the Washington.

Between the transcendent Yankee and his hellish twin lay a whole spectrum of motivation. The transcendent Yankee only seemed to be self-interested and acquisitive. Like Harvey Birch, he had to seem acquisitive in order to "pass" in American society. He had to remain above suspicion, and to create an air of *vraisemblance*. The admirable quality about the transcendent Yankee was his real aloofness from the competitive swirl. He believed neither in success nor in progress. Rather than go up, he preferred to go out, to go back. Like Thoreau at Walden, he cultivated the primitive. By reducing his material needs to a minimum, he could attain a degree of self-sufficiency which provided him with a fresh perspective on an acquisitive society. He could be as the gentleman could only pretend to be: disinterested.

Harvey, whose virtues remain disguised, sets the pattern for a familiar kind of American hero, the man whose real motives are cloaked by a mask of toughness and practicality, the man who is so much less selfish, so much more generous, than he seems. The real Yankee, the man who values the dollar above everything else, has provided us with most of our legendary villains. These are the men who do not bother to conceal their depredations behind a front of virtue and genteel honor. Both were types of the Yankee, because both were defined by their relation to money. Both types fascinated Americans because the problem of acquisitiveness bulked so large in American consciousness. A man bent upon pursuing his own ends in a time of national crisis was indeed a cautionary figure in the eyes of most Americans, and yet an ordinary man without self-interest, without ambition, was not believable, as one critic reminded Cooper.[23] It is a little difficult to see precisely what form of patriotism Cooper was recommending. What in *fact* makes Harvey run? Is he anything more than a paradox, an ingenious and masterful evasion? What motives could be offered to Americans for acting collectively, rather than selfishly? This question preoccupied the twenties and thirties with an intensity which scarcely slackened. A strong sense of mutuality was clearly lacking in an age characterized by social atomism and high mobility. The conception of a federal Union embodied in the Constitution was too legalistic, too abstract and too ambiguous to fire many imaginations. On what basis, then, were men of different sections and often conflicting interests to collaborate?

Daniel Webster and the Transcendence of Sectionalism

Americans were still reading *The Spy* ten years later when another best seller appeared in the form of a speech made in the United States Senate. At least one hundred thousand Americans bought and read the famous answer by Daniel Webster to Robert Y. Hayne, in which the virtues of New England life and character were pitted against those of the South. Seldom had the complexities of the national character been so interestingly and so publicly expressed. Each of these two men, Hayne and Webster, became the personification of his region and adopted a suitable role. Hayne cast himself as a passionate Cavalier and slipped frequently into a military terminology of defense and attack. Webster was the transcendent Yankee, peaceable, cool and deliberate. All the while, the presiding officer of the Senate, Vice-President John C. Calhoun, sat scowling down upon them like the Great God of Faction himself.

A Senator from Connecticut had risen to propose that surveys and the sale of public lands be stopped for a period. Soon afterward Thomas Hart Benton, a Senator from Missouri, was on his feet. The Yankees were at it again. This was a conspiratorial proposal to keep New England's workers from going west and to keep wages down. Hayne rose to join the attack on the East. An alliance between South and West, he hinted, might strengthen the voice of each. Daniel Webster, busy with a case before the Supreme Court, happened to drop by. He listened. The East, Hayne asserted, was ever the enemy of the West. The East was Yankeeland. In the course of the debate he ascribed to New England every legendary Yankee trait. She was greedy, selfish, hypocritical and conspiratorial.[24]

The man who had entered the lists for Carolina and the South was as little the born aristocrat as his Northern opponent. In many ways they had much in common. Both came from old English stock. The Webster family was descended from Thomas Webster, who had arrived in Ipswich, Massachusetts, about 1635. Hayne was descended from John Hayne, who had come to Colleton District, South Carolina, about 1700. Neither family had reached any particular eminence until the two men in question appeared. Both were large farming families, and neither of the men found an education easy to finance. Webster had to quit Exeter to ease the burden on his family. At one point he was forced to teach school. Hayne had been unable to go to college at all. Each had read law with a famous lawyer of his region, Webster with Christopher Gore in Boston, Hayne with Langdon Cheves in Charleston. Each made his way up through a successful law practice and through marriage. Hayne had the good fortune to marry successively a Pinckney and an Alston. Like Webster, he early entered politics, but had served primarily in state offices. He had been a member of the state legislature, speaker of the House, and had served two years as the attorney general of his state. In another alliance, Hayne was just as fortunate. He soon became a political lieutenant of John C. Calhoun, through whose good offices he was elected to the Senate in 1822. He was now serving his second term. He would finish his political career as governor of his state during the nullification crisis of 1832 and, afterward, as mayor of Charleston.

On the second day of the debate, Webster asked for the floor. "Sir, I rise to defend the East." The bidding had begun; Yankee and Cavalier were casting their eyes west. Webster made two speeches. The first was factual and at points rather technical. It had to do with the sale and survey of lands. Without fireworks, he made his point. New England had settled Ohio and Ohio thrived. It was filled with peaceful Christian homes. He asked his audience to look across the river to Kentucky and then decide which system of land settlement was most advantageous to the Westerner. In Ohio there was none of the chaos of speculation and litigation found elsewhere. On the whole, he was gentle. He made no mention of slavery and his invidious comparison was passed over in few sentences. It was a lawyer's clever hint to the jury.[25]

Hayne in reply wore the mask of a Randolph. With indignation he seized on Webster's comparison and made it appear what it certainly was not, an attack on Southern life in general and the system of domestic slavery in particular. Webster was the Yankee invader and Hayne a knight in shining armor.

He has crossed the border, he has invaded the state of South Carolina, is making war upon her citizens, and endeavoring to overthrow her principles and institutions. Sir, when the gentleman provokes me to such a conflict, I meet him at the threshold—I will struggle while I have life, for our altars and our firesides; and, if God gives me strength, I will drive back the invader discomfited. Nor shall I stop there. If the gentleman provokes the war, he shall have war. Sir, I will not stop at the border—I will carry the war into the enemy's territory, and not consent to lay down my arms, until I shall have obtained "indemnity for the past, and security for the future."[26]

Hayne went on to portray the South as honorable, benevolent and disinterested. The South, and especially the Old Dominion, had produced America's greatest statesmen. The slave was not a symbol of exploitation. Slavery was instead a heavy obligation which the South was honorably trying to discharge. In time of war the South had risen to defend the country from invading forces. The Northeast, on the other hand, had selfishly shrunk from war in 1812. In the Hartford Convention it had conspired treasonably against the nation. Hypocritically, New England pretended friendship for the West and sympathy for the oppressed, but what had it done for its people? Look at the misery, poverty and oppression of Northern cities.[27]

Webster had known the master of this form of verbal combat, John Randolph, and was quite prepared for the simulacrum. He knew what to do. Long before, as a freshman Congressman, he had been challenged to a duel by Randolph over a trifling point of debate. He had refused to duel and had received from Randolph the next day a friendly apology.[28] The transcendent Yankee, unlike his devil-twin, was always a pacifist. The thought of bloodshed sickened him as the heartless brutality of partisan warfare had sickened Harvey Birch. He knew, furthermore, that while Hotspur raged below, his real opponent, John Calhoun, sat silently above, as the presiding officer of the Senate, wearing the mask of statesmanship. The South, he sensed, would have to be outmaneuvered by statecraft.

For two years the question of a protective tariff had vexed the halls of state. In 1828 the *South Carolina Exposition and Protest,* secretly written by Calhoun, set forth an argument for the doctrine of nullification or "state veto." The procedure was an orderly one which called for a state convention to pass on the constitutionality of a piece of legislature, and it was based on the precedent of the Virginia and Kentucky Resolutions of 1798. The doctrine was couched in legal terminology and mentioned the possibility of secession only as a last resort. It was nonetheless revolutionary since it gave to a single state the power of acting independently to nullify an Act of Congress. Calhoun had aimed this complicated legislative blunderbuss at the high tariff. He hoped he would not have to pull the trigger. In this doctrine Webster located his legitimate foe.[29]

As he stood during two January afternoons delivering his reply to Hayne, he cast his nets wide. The idea of the Union Webster saw as a garment curiously contrived of such ingredients as wool, hemp and sugar, all of which needed the protection of a high tariff. Southerners, Westerners and New Englanders contributed to its manufacture. Decked out in it, a man from Massachusetts might look very much like Uncle Sam himself. The last thing that Webster wanted was the sort of allegorical civil war which Hayne had tried to impress upon him. In his reply he was pacific and benign and nonpartisan. Pointing to his heart, he assured those present there was no anger there and no wounds. Although his opponent had aimed at him the "poison arrows" of faction, they had not sufficient force to reach him.

He began by recasting Hayne's drama:

. . . if it be supposed that, by casting the characters of the drama, assigning to each his part: to one the attack; to another the cry of onset; or, if it be thought that by a loud and empty vaunt of anticipated victory, any laurels are to be won here . . . I can tell the honorable member once and for all, that he is greatly mistaken.[30]

Through it all Webster was grandly imperturbable. He patiently pointed to the errors of fact and logic which he detected in Hayne's speech. He even corrected a reference which Hayne had made to *Macbeth*. He spoke for no special interest, no region, but for the Union. Massachusetts had, he asserted, always gone with the Union. The Hartford Convention and the Essex Junto were not matters of region but were symptomatic of dissension existing everywhere. The great Washington had always had his principal support in Massachusetts, his principal opposition in the South. The internal improvements he called for, roads and canals, were not for his good or the good of his state, but for the good of the country as a whole. *All* would profit by them. If there was an attack being launched somewhere, it was not being launched by the North or by the South or even by South Carolina. And he reminded Hayne of the citizens in his own state who found the idea of nullification abhorrent. Was Hayne to suppress this "minority" in order to defend the rights of minorities in general? The attack came from a small faction in a state whose services to the country Webster praised at length. Pickney, Rutledge, Laurens, Sumter, Marion—these were men who had fought shoulder to shoulder with men from Massachusetts. Webster then recommended judicial review rather than nullification as the final recourse in matters pertaining to the Constitution, and closed with the peroration on the Union which nearly every schoolboy for a century was to commit to memory. "Would to God," he had exclaimed toward the end, "that harmony might again return!"[31]

Harmony! On this word and the meaning he assigned to it, Webster built his political career. This word and this speech penetrated very deeply into the American's consciousness of himself in these anxious decades. Behind them, a few decades in the past, lay a period in history which for Americans symbolized harmony. Its memory was a powerful antidote for a Randolph's poisoned arrows.

Revolution was harmony! Only an American could understand the paradox. Webster understood it well and Americans understood Webster. On this occasion the divisive idea of a united South had been routed. Webster's speech was a piece of historical fiction which had captured a reading audience that would have done honor to Sir Walter Scott. In a few weeks' time one press alone distributed forty thousand copies. The speech was everywhere pirated.[32] Unlike Sir Walter, Webster was to receive his royalties. From Amos Lawrence in Boston came words of praise and, in addition, a costly silver service inscribed to the Defender of the Constitution. From every region of the country letters of praise and admiration poured in. A letter arrived from a Virginia planter, James Madison: "It crushes 'nullification,'" the Virginian wrote, "and must hasten an abandonment of secession." A British traveler commented, "From the Gulf of St. Lawrence to that of Mexico, from Cape Sable to Lake Superior, his name has become, as it were, a household word."[33]

The Yankee at Home and Abroad

In 1827, the year in which Daniel Webster entered the Senate, a Boston publishing house brought out a novel by an unknown New Hampshire widow named Sarah Josepha Hale. *Northwood* launched one of the most successful careers in the history of American literary journalism. Fifty years later Sarah Hale would finally step down from her self-created eminence as "The Lady Editor" of *Godey's Lady's Book* with one last and brief salutation to her sex. "Having reached my ninetieth year," she wrote in December, 1877, "I bid farewell to my countrywomen, with the hope that this work of half a century may be blessed to the furtherance of their happiness and usefulness in their Divinely appointed sphere."[34]

That "Divinely appointed sphere" was the American Home, a territory she had long ago pre-empted as her own. By 1860, Louis Antoine Godey, her business associate of many years, was distributing well over a million copies each year of his monthly *Lady's Book* and could number his subscribers at close to 150,000.[35] Over many American households Sarah Hale had been for years the acknowledged ruler in matters of deportment and taste. The characteristic stamp of the Lady Editor on every issue was as recognizable as her name on the masthead. A versatile talent, she had tried her hand at almost everything. She had written children's verse, including the popular rhyme "Mary Had a Little Lamb." She was the author of several cook books, some volumes on family hygiene and an encyclopedia of famous women in history. Like the name of Daniel Webster, the name of Sarah Josepha Hale was a household word.

The conjunction of these two names is not an accident. Daniel Webster and Sarah Hale, despite the difference in their spheres of activity, were alike in many ways. Sarah Buell, like Webster, had been born in the Merrimack Valley of New Hampshire, in the decade that marked the close of the Revolutionary War. Sarah's father, like Webster's, had been a captain of militia during the Revolution, and had subsequently "kept tavern." Both Sarah Buell and Webster had first known the life of a farm, then that of a provincial village; they had read voraciously and for a time taught school. Webster became a lawyer; Sarah Buell married one.[36]

Both lives were punctuated by the events which visited so many American families a hundred years ago. Webster lost a wife and three of his four children through early and unexpected death. Sarah Buell had confronted death for the first time while she was still a child, when her mother had placed Sarah's small hand on the stone-cold forehead of a dead relative. A few years later her mother and a younger sister died on the same day. Sarah Hale, who was herself a female Tithonus, early lost her husband and was survived by only one of her five children.[37]

Both lives are representative of the geographical and social mobility which characterized the period. Webster moved from Portsmouth to Boston and finally to Washington; Sarah Hale's editorial pilgrimage took her first to Boston and finally, for the last forty years of her life, to the metropolis of Philadelphia.

The lives of Sarah Hale's children underline the plight of the American family. All of them had been born in the house of

David Hale in the small town of Newport, New Hampshire. Three decades were sufficient to scatter the family over the American continent. Left a widow at thirty-four, Sarah Hale was faced with supporting and educating five small children. One was sent to relatives in New York. When she moved to Boston in 1828, she left all but one of her children in New Hampshire. David, the oldest, was later graduated from West Point and died suddenly after a short army career in Florida. Horatio was graduated with distinction from Harvard, and afterward served as an ethnologist with Charles Wilkes's expedition to the South Seas. For the rest of his life he was a successful lawyer in Chicago. William, the youngest of her sons, also attended Harvard, taught school in Virginia, read law and later became a justice of the supreme court of Texas. Frances Ann married a Philadelphia doctor and lived out her short life in that city. Josepha, like her brother William, taught school in the South, and finally settled in Philadelphia to found a successful school near her mother. It is little wonder that Sarah Hale became, like Webster, a nationalist in her outlook, or that she devoted herself before all else to sentimentalizing the close family group.[38]

Both Daniel Webster and Sarah Hale learned what it meant to rise in society and to leave the provinces behind. They found a society in flux and they capitalized on its fluidity. With all this in common, it is hardly surprising that they shared concerns and felt similar anxieties, concerns and anxieties which were characteristics of the time. Webster devoted himself to the interests of the merchant and on state occasions became his orator and poet; Sarah Hale addressed herself to the interests of the merchant's wife and provided his family with a literature and an ideology.

Mrs. Hale's stories are very little concerned with the larger contours of society; she herself was editorially nonpartisan, although she never tried to conceal her Unionist sympathies. If Webster refused to recognize a real division between North and South, Sarah Hale and *Godey's* went even further. During the Civil War and Reconstruction, *Godey's* refused to acknowledge that a war existed or had existed.[39] Such a suppression was not merely good business practice, though it was this too. It suggests the degree to which she *was* political. She accepted and developed Webster's theory of social harmony on a domestic and village scale. One of her sketches is even set in the fictional town of Harmony, New York. Sarah Hale wrote of an America harmoniously composed of the rich and the would-be rich. It was a society that believed in give and take, in compromise and reconciliation. Sarah Hale once sent a purse to the great compromiser Henry Clay and a handbag to his wife as a Yankee token of her Yankee esteem. "To speak without metaphor," she once observed, "the engrossing pursuit of Americans is wealth."[40] What American better symbolized this pursuit than the "merchant"? To those already wealthy the term denoted a kind of status; to the shopkeeper it was a flattering symbol of aspiration; even to the farmer it was a pious hope to be realized, perhaps, in the next generation.

Sarah Hale's response to the experiences of early life was, of course, in many ways different from Webster's. Daniel Webster at the end of his childhood moved into the wider expanses of a man's world and operated there for the rest of his life. In the early nineteenth century formal education was widely regarded as a man's prerogative. Webster, at a considerable hardship to his family, was sent first to an academy and finally to Dartmouth College. Sarah Buell stayed home. What she learned—and she learned a good deal—she learned secondhand from her brother Horatio and from her husband. They taught her Latin and mathematics and introduced her to "polite letters." She never forgot this early "deprivation" and all her long life she campaigned for woman's education. She was shrewd enough to recognize, however, that women, whatever their education, could not follow men everywhere. Such freedom, even should it be granted, would in her eyes have had a disastrous effect on American society, since it would have removed the woman from her pivotal place in the family, as Sarah Hale's experience with her own family must have taught her. The family, she always believed, was the principal stabilizing force of society. Fanny Wright was not for her an admirable example of the new woman. Such women, Sarah Hale concluded, threatened to debauch the institution of the family. She never expressed much sympathy with militant woman's-rights movements.[41]

The role which she evolved for the American woman was a compensatory one. In an America, she reasoned, where a man was forced to make his way and fulfill himself by the accumulation of property, the woman was left with a positive and dynamic role to play. She was destined to be the active agent of culture and moral perception. The man, by the very nature of his activities, had neither the time nor the ability to play such a role. The woman should be an example, a compensating influence to overcome the terrible and apparent dangers which existed in a society given over without reservation to the pursuit of wealth. The destiny of America, she concluded, was therefore largely in the hands of its women. Who could ask for a more challenging or ennobling task?[42]

Sarah Hale and Daniel Webster encountered each other on the common ground of the American family. To both of them, the most distressing problem of American society was the acquisitive man. How were his acquisitive inclinations, in themselves both good and necessary, to be controlled and kept within bounds? For Webster, as for William Wirt, the solution lay, as he made clear in 1826 when he eulogized Adams and Jefferson, in the worship of exemplary heroes, men who by their heroic and selfless example could enforce a standard of self-discipline on a later age. He wore alternately the mask of Puritan Father and Revolutionary Statesman. If a man could keep his eye on the constellation of the great, and in particular on the figure of Washington, he might perhaps keep his aggressions in check. There is no reason to doubt that Webster wore these masks in good faith, certainly at first. He himself was groping for the solution to a problem which in his own life assumed momentous proportions. The wildness he felt surging within he tamed, or he tried to tame, with a façade of cool reason and domestic pacifism. The transcendent Yankee was a combination of Puritan and Statesman. He was benign and he was disinterested. Webster talked a good deal about the family and the home, but finally he was a politician and a man. His principal concern was with such larger social questions as the meaning of revolution and federal Union. Sarah Hale made the home and the family her principal subject. Webster made money and delivered orations. Sarah wrote moral tales about American families and successfully edited two magazines for women.

In her long career she labored to put a better face on the Yankee by making him into a family man, something he never was or could be. If the figure of the Yankee meant anything, it meant movement—horizontal and vertical movement. Like Webster or like Melville's Captain Ahab, a Yankee might have a family but his restless spirit was always tending away from it, not toward it. For the Yankee a home and family was a point of departure, a point which defined the voyage out—or up. It was never a place of rest.

Sarah Hale seems to have sensed the dimension of her problem, even at the beginning. In her personal life she too wore a mask, the mask of *mater familias*. Although she was early a widow, never remarried, left the rearing and education of her children in good part to others and lived much of her life in boardinghouses in Boston and Philadelphia, she never abandoned the role of mother, always condemned boardinghouse life, and urged upon women and men alike the moral obligation to marry. The fashionable figure of the bachelor and the pathetic figure of the spinster woman were for her symbols of social disintegration. From the age of thirty-four, the time of David Hale's death, until her own death at ninety-one, she never once abandoned the black silk taffeta of a widow in mourning.[43]

This is not to say that Sarah Hale neglected her children or ceased to care about them. She did for them everything she could, and everything she did was in a sense for them. She was simply forced to play a double role, the role of father and mother, good provider and provider of goodness. If this involved her in inconsistencies, she could at least have argued she had never recommended the role to anyone else. She provided for her family in the only way she knew. The one successful thing she had done before the death of her husband was to compose a number of poems for local newspapers. In 1823 a number of these poems were collected and published by a local printer in a small volume entitled *The Genius of Oblivion*.[44] When her millinery shop in Newport failed to support her family, she turned wholeheartedly to literature, one of the few activities aside from schoolteaching that was open to women. Literature was to her what the law was to Webster and might have been to David Hale. It was a way out of the provinces, a way up. Beneath the soft exterior of motherhood and femininity, Sarah Hale was a shrewd and businesslike woman whose later dealings with male contributors to *Godey's* proved her more than a match for the Yankee entrepreneurs who were making their way in literature.[45] Though she may have preferred to knit rather than to whittle, she could bargain with the best of them.

She moved herself and her widow's weeds with all possible speed and with considerable address out of the provinces, into the metropolis and, in so far as she could, into the world of men. In 1826 a Boston weekly newspaper, the *Spectator and Ladies' Album*, offered a gold medal "of the value of twenty dollars . . . for the best poem" sent in. The bait was sufficient. From Newport came an envelope containing a poem entitled "Hymn to Charity" and signed "S. J. H.." It contained the lines:

> Thus selfishness, the winter of the mind
> In hate's dark bonds would human feelings bind.[46]

This rather unprepossessing piece of verse won Sarah Hale the gold medal and gave her her first encouragement as a writer, but it was really *Northwood* which turned the trick. This long, cumbersome and sketchy story caught the attention of Sarah

Hale's contemporaries and convinced a Boston clergyman that he had at last located an editor for his magazine.

The Yankee Ethos in Limbo

The very fact of the novel is a puzzle. What had made a busy and hard-pressed widow living in a small provincial town sit down in the winter of 1826 and fill page after page with the story of Sidney Romilly? Why should she have concerned herself, as she did, with the South? Her whole life of thirty-eight years had been spent in and near the small town of Newport, New Hampshire. She knew as little about the South as she did about the Antipodes. She had evidently set out to paint an agreeable picture of the small provincial world she had known since her childhood. She had wanted to show that the village of Northwood, New Hampshire, where her story was set, was, like her own Newport, a society of independent, industrious and virtuous freemen or, as she put it, a society "of contented minds and grateful hearts."[47] In Northwood a man might live by the labor of his hands in peace and plenty. To James Romilly, Sidney's father, his happy provincial home on a winter evening was a safe haven, almost womblike in its protectiveness.

Indeed, few conditions in this world of care can be imagined more enviable than that of Mr. Romilly, when of a winter evening, with every chore done, he seated himself before a "rousing fire," "monarch of all he surveyed," and listening to the roaring of the tempest without, contrasted it with the peace, plenty, and security reigning within.[48]

Such a situation seemed to provide everything a man could wish for. Why should anyone want to emerge from it? Why would Sarah Hale herself be willing to leave her own village? Why would she send Sidney Romilly forth to become a gentleman and a planter in a South she did not know?

The one thing Northwood did not provide was opportunity.

Northwood, she observed, "offered few temptations to the speculator" and its soil, unlike that of the South and the West, "promised
no indulgence to the idle."[49] If her young men and young women
were to better themselves, as she believed Americans characteristically did and should, they would have to go elsewhere to do
it. But how could they go elsewhere without being false to the
values of Northwood? Since America in her eyes was characterized by its Northwoods, how could a young man from the provinces rise and become successful without in a sense betraying
both his family and his country? How was it possible to make a
Yankee provincial into a gentleman and a Southerner? Harvey
Birch into General Washington?

The problem fascinated, almost obsessed, her. For Webster's
selfless devotion to Union, Sarah Hale substituted a selfless devotion to her family and to her sex. To young women, she
recommended the same kind of selfless devotion to family. To
young men, she recommended a more difficult combination of
benevolence and ambition, a balanced diet of give and take. For
the Yankee who had left the provinces, the solution to the
problem of emergence lay, as for Webster, in adopting a mask
of selflessness. But where could the emergent Yankee best find
an opportunity to play his selfless role? Though the answer she
gave was hedged about with all kinds of qualifications and punctuated with warnings, she nonetheless answered: "In the South."

The South which Sarah Hale created as an antipode to her
North is less a place than a moral climate: an expression of what
the North lacked and what the emergent Yankee needed. In 1829
she published her first collection of stories, or, as she preferred
to call them, "sketches." These sketches, taken together, go a
long way toward explaining why Sarah Hale felt driven to invent
a South that was different from the Northern world she was
every day evoking in this early writing. The problem which
she encountered was certainly not the one she had consciously
in mind as she set out to describe her country and her countrymen. Everything about these first inventive efforts suggests that

she wanted above all else to write "realistically," as we would say, about America. Sarah Hale's sense of realism may seem stylized and cloudy to modern readers, but she entertained the greatest scorn for writing that was derivative and European in flavor. She always insisted on a certain American verisimilitude. Her intention, she announced, was to write only about what "gives to Americans their peculiar characteristics."

To exhibit some of those traits, originated by our free institutions, in their manifold and minute effects on the minds, manners, and habits of the citizens of our republic, is the design of these Sketches.[50]

The titles which she gave to collections of these sketches are further evidence of this concern. The first of two volumes was published under the title *Sketches of American Character.* The second volume, published six years later in 1835, was entitled *Traits of American Life.* For Sarah Hale, as for Webster, the word "character" was more normative than descriptive; it was more concerned with "should" than with "is." For both of them "character" meant restraint, self-control, self-discipline.

The need for character is precisely the point of the lurid tale, "Wedding and Funeral." James Murray, the hero of the story, is the pampered son of a rich New York merchant. The story begins with a village wedding in which James Murray marries a simple country girl, Lucy Marsh. One bystander at the wedding admires the obvious good fortune of the young couple.

Few begin the world thus advantageously. They have health and beauty, wealth and reputation, and friends, and affection for each other.

Another bystander is more skeptical and cautious.

Could you add one item more to the catalogue of advantages, the earthly picture would be complete. . . . How unfortunate that the absence of that one requisite, may, perhaps, render all the others nugatory.

When the skeptic is asked to name the missing "requisite" for happiness, he replies that James Murray, while otherwise blessed, seems to be without "self-control."[51]

He is certainly right. James Murray becomes a madman and a beast. Because he had no fortune to make and no purpose in life, he had begun to tipple in college while his poorer classmates studiously prepared themselves to read law and better their stations. After his marriage he becomes a habitual drunk, spends his fortune in debauchery and finally goes berserk altogether. He riots about the house, breaks all the windows, thrashes and beats the submissive Lucy, and at last, in a moment of rage, strikes and kills his small son. Overwhelmed with sorrow, he rushes out and drowns himself, while Lucy succumbs and dies of a "broken heart." Near the end of the story Mrs. Hale has one of her characters underscore the fact that the tragedy of James Murray is peculiarly American.

When . . . men yield to temptation, to sin—suffering must follow. Indeed in our country, more than in any other on earth, deviations from morality and integrity are punished either with the loss of fame, fortune, or public confidence.[52]

Why was America so different? As this story suggests, there is more melodrama than one would suppose in Sarah Hale's *Sketches of American Character*. Every sketch was in some sense a recipe. You put together a little of this and a little of this and you get that. You put together a spoiled child, a great sum of money and a bottle of brandy, and you get violence and social chaos. You end up with "debauchery," "broken hearts" and "sorrow."

In writing about a man, you took his measure. When he went wrong, as Mrs. Hale's characters frequently did, you explained to your readers what mistakes he had made and, as a kind of *obiter dictum*, you told them how the mistakes might have been avoided. You said, "If Richard Woodcock had not bought the lottery ticket . . ." or "if Lucy Marsh had refused to marry a man who drank . . ." or "if James Murray's parents had taught him the meaning of honest labor. . . ." For every disastrous or regrettable occurrence there was a condition which would have made it avoidable.

The object of such a discussion was self-improvement and self-improvement was something in which Americans passionately believed. This is a form of speculation so foreign to our own thinking and, as we conceive of reality, so "unrealistic," that it is difficult to understand the significance that could once have been attached to it. It is difficult now to understand the amount of reality which the idea of self-improvement contained for nine-teenth-century Americans; or, put in another way, it is difficult to understand today how much reality was itself defined by change. What one fact could have loomed larger than that of change in the minds of Webster or Sarah Hale? Americans conceived of their social and institutional life as in a state of flux which, if it promised almost unlimited individual opportunity, threatened to subvert all familiar forms of order. For them, nothing was impossible. It is difficult for us to realize that their superb optimism and their terrible anxiety were functions of the same human situation.

It seems apparent that Americans in the early part of the century were quite unprepared for changes of the order of those that they experienced in their personal lives and observed in the life about them. They were also uncertain about the direction in which things were tending. Sarah Hale felt these concerns and her fantasies come very close to the imaginative center of her time. Almost instinctively she fell into the kind of moralizing for which Americans hungered; her little sketches, like the historical legends of later decades, can be thought of as parables for survival. Her writings always concerned themselves with a world gone wrong through lack of character or a world *kept* right through the exertion of character at some crucial moment.

The sketches included in these volumes were written during the years in which Webster was working out his own defensive fiction of the disinterested American. Despite the fact that her sketches appeared in ladies' magazines, she revealed an anxiety about America that was very similar to Webster's. Beneath a surface of seemingly imperturbable optimism and dogmatic certainty ran a strong undercurrent of fear and uneasiness.

Sarah Hale's argument for the preservation of an ordered society is reiterated in story after story. In a world of flux and change, only character can preserve a man—or woman—from the ruin of a James Murray or a Richard Woodcock. Nothing is therefore more important to the future of the country than the formation of a stable American character. Again and again she made the point that character is formed in the home and by the parents. It is in the home and not at schools and colleges that the habits essential to survival can be developed and reinforced. James Murray is sent to college by his merchant father, but he has not been given the values that permit him to profit from the experience. He takes to drink, and college is simply a step in his disintegration.

In the tales of merchants' sons there are few happy endings. The surest way to work out your salvation in Mrs. Hale's America was to keep your hand on the plow and stay in the provinces. In a historical tale entitled "The Silver Mine" and set in the eighteenth century in her own Newport, this point is heavily underscored. Deacon Bascom has a series of dreams in which he is visited by " a man clothed in black" who tells him he will find a silver mine under a rock near a blasted tree on nearby Sunapee Mountain. After much deliberation he yields to temptation and (like Hawthorne's Goodman Brown, whom he in some ways resembles) he leaves behind his "good wife" and threads his way through a dense wilderness to the indicated spot. Just as he is about to dig for the silver, he kneels to pray and finds the strength to leave the stone unturned and the silver unmined. Deacon Bascom is able to perform this heroic act of self-denial, he admits, only because at the crucial moment he suddenly remembered his children. Riches would ruin them. "I felt," he told his wife, "that should my children be corrupted by the riches I there sought, how terrible would be my guilt, and the accusations of my conscience!"[53]

The story has a further point that is less obvious. Sarah Hale appears to be saying that the Yankees should stay put. The wilderness through which Deacon Bascom has to make his way is described in a way that makes it appear allegorical. The wilderness is where a man goes to make his fortune; it is what separates him from his home; it is a place where a man can get lost. Like Harvey Birch, Deacon Bascom refuses wealth. As a result, "The children of that good couple were excellent men and women, and their descendents are worthy and respectable people."[54]

This curious story, which Sarah Hale referred to as an American fairy tale, is really a fairy tale *manqué*.[55] The American Cinderella *refuses* the glass slipper and lives happily ever after. Modern New Englanders, she interjects toward the end, show a falling off in character. Their one concern is riches and they leave home and sweetheart to seek their fortunes at the ends of the earth. Country society is thus deteriorating.

Alack! what a change half a century has produced. Now our gentlemen are wholly engrossed with caring for their own dear selves; marriage is slavery, and a family a bill of cost. Our fine young men, who should be the glory and strength of New England, go to find their graves in the marshes of the south, or the prairies of the west; and our fair girls go—into the cotton factories![56]

A society, to remain stable, must also remain static. The frontiers of the West and Southwest were fully as threatening and perilous to her as the metropolis. Her ruined young men die as regularly of "yellow fever" in New Orleans as of intemperance in New York City. A land of plenty was indeed a fearful place.

In her fiction the ambitious young man who leaves the provinces does so at his peril. He may not meet the melodramatic ruin of a Richard Woodcock in "The Lottery Ticket," but he is always punished in some way. With a good character and the best of intentions he may, like William Forbes in the story of that name, marry a rich and fashionable woman who makes him a stupid and uncompanionable wife; or he may, like the promising George Torrey in "The Poor Scholar," die fighting a duel in Virginia. The only kind of migration that is permissible is backward migration. A young man may be sent back to the provinces.

A return to the provinces is, in fact, one prescription for saving the character of a merchant's son. "Walter Wilson" is the story of a rich merchant's son who is left penniless at his father's death. Far from being a disaster, this circumstance alone saves him. He is bound out to a "Puritan farmer" who teaches him the self-discipline of hard manual labor. He ends by marrying the farmer's daughter, Fanny, and settling in the country. The theater-going and sophisticated Owen Ashley in "A Winter in the Country" is saved in a similar way when his father, a rich Boston merchant, goes bankrupt. Ashley is sent to find work in a small village in Vermont. At first he despairs at the thought that he is being exiled to "Bocotia." Instead of the crudeness, rusticity and ignorance that he expected, he finds in Vermont a little Eden of self-sufficient and self-instructed yeomen. In letters written to a friend in Boston, Ashley describes the cultivation and leisure of a country winter where he does not find the contrast between effeteness and poverty which characterized life in the "metropolis." The story ends with his expected marriage to the daughter of an industrious Yankee farmer.

The problem of the merchant's son could not, however, be permanently solved by a winter in the country. Owen Ashley could not be expected to stay in Vermont any more than Sarah Hale could have stayed in New Hampshire. It seems clear from the title of the story that Ashley will return to Boston with his country wife, just as certainly as Daniel Webster had taken his own country wife to the same city. The country was a place of indoctrination. Merchant's son and farmer's son alike could there be introduced to the sobering self-discipline of work. Character could there be formed to a republican model. Sooner or later many provincials like George Ticknor, Sarah Hale and

Daniel Webster would have to encounter the Great World and put their American virtue to the test. They would have to emerge from their provincial chrysalis and meet the test of the metropolis or the frontier. Sarah Hale knew very well that the American could not always leave his talent buried in the provinces like Deacon Bascom's silver.

Arthur Lloyd in "The Lloyds" had not had the "advantages" of a country childhood, but he had been provided with its moral equivalent by his rich but heroic father, another New York merchant. Arthur was never indulged or gratified in his selfish desires. He was always made to feel that a virtuous and useful life was a pleasure, not an obligation. But after all his instruction what, finally, does Sarah Hale have her faultless hero do? In a long story that is practically a novella, he does in fact very little, because there is very little he can do.

"The Lloyds" is a dull story and Arthur Lloyd, for all his careful nurture, is himself dull because nothing *can* happen to him. He already has his money. In Sarah Hale's world there is very little a rich man can do, unless he loses his money or goes to pieces and dies a suicide or an alcoholic. In her tales of rich and successful men she therefore encountered a problem she had not been forced to face in her stories of bankruptcy and moral disintegration. Everybody knew that "the wages of sin is death"; the wages of virtue, however, were another matter. Virtue inevitably brought financial success, but at a certain point in her scheme of things, financial success became a vice and the successful man became idle if he stopped earning money, and avaricious if he continued to do so. She therefore chose most often to skirt this problem and to write about poor boys who became rich, or rich boys who became poor or who came to no good. Arthur Lloyd is a stalemate. The best he can do is to practice negative virtues. By self-control he can hang on to his money, and by acts of benevolence he can maintain his unselfishness and self-control. In other words, he can live as though he were not rich and as though he were still in the competitive race.

For such a character there was one other possibility. He could tackle the problem of living as a gentleman planter in the South.

From Yankee to Southern Cavalier

It was not easy to make out in the South. Sarah Hale's fiction is strewn with the corpses of those who had tried and failed. Her Yankees who visit the South do not all die violent deaths like George Torrey, who is killed in a duel. The experience of life there has, however, a crucial effect on all of them. Either it brings out the worst or the best in them. George Torrey's mistake is to forget that the transcendent Yankee is conservative of life just as he is conservative of money. His death is wasteful and spendthrift. Like Daniel Webster, he should have refused to risk his life so senselessly and stupidly. By becoming the inseparable companion of a brilliant and extravagant young Virginian, he is made to forget for a moment his own values. The mistake costs him his life. Sidney Romilly, Sarah Hale's most important hero, does better.

Sidney Romilly, like George Torrey, promised great things. He had been named for Algernon Sidney, English republican theorist, by his hopeful father. He possessed the Websterian assets of "an expansive forehead" and "large luminous eyes" which "gave promise of uncommon genius." He early took to books. "Literature," Sarah Hale comments, "is the star and garter of a Yankee. It claims precedence and gains privileges to which wealth alone is not entitled."[57] Among the Romilly children he was the one marked for emergence. Sidney's one fault was the curious one that he learned *too easily*. He responded too readily and passively to his surroundings. Thus, while the disciplined world of Northwood made him strong, the undisciplined and leisurely moral climate which he encountered in the South made him weak and ineffective.

Some twenty years before the opening of the story, Lydia

Romilly, with whom Sidney goes to live, has married a Mr. Horace Brainard of South Carolina. Brainard exemplifies Sarah Hale's idea of the Southerner. When he visits Northwood, to see about adopting one of the Romilly children, he is carefully contrasted with James Romilly, Sidney's father. The contrast is an interesting one. The elder Romilly had made his own way; he is a devout Protestant and he believes in the virtues of work. Brainard had inherited his plantation and his wealth; he is a Roman Catholic; he lives a life of leisure. Romilly believes in the family and centers his own life there. Brainard believes in society and the Great World. Romilly has a large, happy family; the Brainards are childless. Brainard is nonetheless a sympathetic character in the novel. His errors are errors of weakness. His dissipations are those of his society and of his class. The race track, the billiard table and the theater symbolize the purposelessness of his life.

Brainard is also given many admirable traits. He is courteous and cultivated. He is a kindly and conscientious master to his slaves, and he considers them a trust, rather than an indulgence. In his other relationships he is charitable and yielding. Even his Catholicism is portrayed as a sympathetic trait when placed alongside the uninformed Protestant bigotry of his New England wife. Catholicism in this period did not yet have quite the associations it later had for middle-class Americans. It was still more associated with aristocratic George Calvert, the Carroll family and Baltimore, than with Paddy and Boston. A great many Protestant Americans, among them Harriet Beecher Stowe, felt attracted to Catholicism, if only as an antidote for an overdose of Calvinist austerity. They saw Protestantism as inclining toward Puritan fanaticism and self-righteousness, or toward the uncontrolled emotionalism of the revivals. Neither tendency could be sympathetically viewed. If Catholicism inclined toward indifference and passivity, the other face on the coin of Puritan fanaticism was Yankee hypocrisy; and emotionalism was too much associated with madness to find acceptance in an age that feared madness and the consequences of loss of control. Sarah Hale thought of Catholicism as a quiet, aristocratic religion which stood for tolerance, reason and moderation. In her personal life she, like Harriet Stowe, compromised her early Puritanism by becoming an Episcopalian "convert." Such a conversion was in the pattern of emergence in both the North and the South.

The features of Sarah Hale's fantasy-South thus become a little clearer. If Northwood stood for the Protestant ethic, the South represented a set of compensatory possibilities. It stood for *noblesse oblige*, cultivated leisure and human sympathy. One tendency of Northwood was represented by the stock Yankee villains, Deacon Jones and Ephraim Skinner, who are revealed as fanatics, misers and hypocrites. In his attitude toward money, Brainard is again set off against such Yankees. He is portrayed as free from any taint of acquisitiveness. He spends his money grandly and generously, hardly noting the cost of what he does. He is finally ruined because he honorably takes the word of a dishonorable speculator. The Southerner, despite his weakness, could be a disinterested man of honor. The greatest liability of Southern character was its tendency toward idleness and self-indulgence, the cult of pleasure. The even greater liability of Northern character was its tendency toward selfish acquisitiveness and predatory greed. It is important to note that in Sarah Hale's eyes the weakness of the Yankee was a kind of strength; the weakness of the Southern gentleman was, alas, his weakness. In her world, only the salubrious North had bad men; only the debilitating South had bad air. In other words, only the Yankee could be a villain. The Southerner was marked for a victim.

It is not the love of pleasure, the taste for amusements, that constitute the love of the world. It is the love of money, the craving desire to accumulate property, the entire devotion of the heart and soul, mind, might and strength, to the one object of increasing or preserving an estate, that bows down the lofty intellect of men, and makes their sordid souls as grovelling as the appetites of the brutes that perish. This inordinate thirst for riches is the besetting sin of Americans; situation, institutions, education, all combine to foster it.[58]

How, she asks, can you temper the acquisitiveness of the Yankee without destroying the strength which alone enables him to survive the competitive race? How could you salvage the disinterestedness and honor of the Southerner without having to accept his weakness into the bargain? Both strength and disinterestedness were requirements for a stable national character. How could they be combined?

The first attempt to superimpose the Cavalier gentleman on the Protestant Yankee almost results in Sidney's ruin. The Northwood he knew as a child was nearly all work; the Southern world into which he moved was nearly all play. He soon learned that as a young gentleman he could do exactly as he pleased. His foster parents competed for his favor; the Brainard slaves, who expected him to become their master, fawned over him and jumped at the chance to serve him. His Yankee tutor soon abandoned the hope of getting him to study. Once he found that he had no competitors, all his incentive to study and to excel left him. Why should he bother? Had he not been given Great Expectations? When Sidney was twenty his tutor was dismissed and he was introduced into Charleston society, where, it is implied, he soon cut a considerable figure. Only "those early lessons of sobriety and virtue" moderated his indulgence and prevented his becoming a rake.[59] "Sidney had never forgotten he was Yankee born, although half *raised* on a southern plantation."[60] Sidney is finally rescued from his hybrid impasse by another New Englander, who urges him to return home. At his friend's suggestion he finally returns, after seventeen years away, to visit his family in Northwood. This experience completes his re-education.

Once back in Northwood Sidney discovers at last what the Good Life really is:

Till within a few months, pleasure has been the idol of my pursuit; and I have, I believe, sought it in every place except where alone it is to be found—in a virtuous home.[61]

His education is further aided by the accidental death of his father and the death of his stepfather, who dies a bankrupt.

Sidney is left penniless and has to begin all over again. He runs the family farm, learns to work with his hands and successfully courts a virtuous Yankee girl. At this point, destiny steps in and saves Sidney for gentility. His wife-to-be becomes an heiress and Sidney mysteriously recovers Brainard's fortune. The novel ends as he once again leaves for the South to run Brainard's plantation and to become a virtuous Southern planter. This time, it is implied, Sidney has the character necessary to survive in the loose moral world of the South.

This ending is schematic and in many ways unsatisfactory, but Sarah Hale, almost inadvertently, uncovers a very serious problem in her thinking about American character. Sidney Romilly, by the end of the novel, is both an emergent Yankee and a merchant's son. He is both a young provincial on the way out and on the way up, and the rich young man whose character is saved by a reindoctrination in provincial virtue. It took two exposures to the disciplined life of Northwood to make Sidney Romilly into a gentleman who could be trusted to control himself. The first kept him from going utterly to seed during his education; the second instructed him in the responsible use of his money and his social distinction. Twice he emerged from the provinces, each time a little better able to control himself. At last, he emerged with his character formed and with the Hale stamp of approval. What was he equipped to do? The answer is simple. He had finally learned to say no. The emergent Yankee must learn to say no in order to succeed, but why must the gentleman say no? Why, in heaven's name, can he not at long last relax and enjoy himself? Why must he be continually bedeviled with tempters till the end of his days?

The Problem of American Gentility

The answer to these questions reveals the dimensions of Sarah Hale's problem. The idea of leisure was unacceptable to a great many Americans in the nineteenth century. Mr. Chapman, the Connecticut Yankee in "The Springs," a story set in Saratoga, had a go at leisure and the fashionable life of a spa and found the experience not to his liking. He believed in being useful, and leisure to him was a form of uselessness.

I don't think those gentlemen and ladies there are so happy as the persons I left at work in my factory. They do not look half as cheerful and gay. Indeed, the observations I have made, have convinced me that employment, some kind of business, is absolutely necessary to make men, or at least our citizens, happy and respectable. This trifling away of time when there is so much to be done, so many improvements necessary in our country, is inconsistent with that principle of being useful, which every republican ought to cherish.[62]

The gentleman of leisure has little place in the fiction of this period, except as a warning. When he appears at all, he is apt to appear as a rake or a villain. Arthur Lloyd's gentility is proved by his ability to detect a false aristocrat, not by his ability to be one himself. He must go on saying no. At the same time an American was expected to distinguish himself somehow and his success was measured by the distance he could put between himself and his Northwood. If he must, in fact, rise, to what could he legitimately aspire? He could not aspire to become a gentleman of leisure, because to become one would be to betray the whole meaning of his life. He would have to begin saying yes. To accept a genteel status would mean accepting Europe and denying Northwood. If an American was to become a gentleman, he would have to become an American kind of gentleman. What did this involve?

Sarah Hale's fiction contains an answer to this question. Only a kind of social distinction which was consistent with the values of the emergent Yankee was acceptable to her. Her idea of the gentleman was an extrapolation from her idea of the successful man. To become a useful gentleman it was necessary for a man to act as though he were still in the competitive race. The emergent Yankee was expected to deny himself any indulgence and to put all his energy and his time to "use." The American gentleman was supposed to place "service" before everything. What "use" was to the Yankee, "service" was to the gentleman. There was, however, an important difference between becoming successful and becoming a gentleman. It was legitimate, even necessary, for the Yankee to be ambitious, if his ambitions were proper. The American gentleman, on the other hand, could not want anything, except to be of more service, to be more selfless. In public, Webster could only aspire to join the constellation of the Great and Disinterested Statesmen whom he tried to emulate. Only in private could he want power, money and the Presidency. He could transcend his own image, but he could not wish to rise. If the emergent Yankee had to deny his desires and say no, the gentleman was not supposed to have any desires to deny. The only kind of distinction which many Americans could imagine and accept was one of moral perfection. To be better, it was necessary to be perfect. Parson Weems sensed the meaning of distinction when he inserted the cherry-tree story in his life of Washington. Washington was not simply truthful. He *could not* tell a lie.

Harvey Birch could approach Washington in his ability to say no. He proved that he had served his country disinterestedly when he refused the gold. Nonetheless, he could not *be* Washington or even Washington's friend, he could only be his "secret friend." Harvey had refused to emerge; he would forever bear the mark of a provincial. He is the transcendent Yankee pure and simple. The distinction of Washington was to be found in the contrast between what he *could* have wanted and what he did want. He was the military man who stood for peace, the empire builder who wanted no entanglements, the revolutionary who stood for harmony and the political leader who refused more political power.[63] Conversely, Webster failed to maintain his mask of disinterestedness because he could not renounce power and because he could not refuse gold. The measurement of his failure lay in the contrast between what he said he wanted and what he was revealed to have wanted. In the censorious words hurled at him in 1845 by Alabama's fire-eating William Yancey, it was Godlike Dan against hell-like Dan. Harvey Birch could hide his deerskin purse; Webster could not.

A Division of Labor

Black Dan! The chapter ends with him. Sarah Hale appears to have had him very much in mind as she wrote *Northwood*. He was the plowboy become statesman, whom Sidney Romilly envied. He was the emergent Yankee. Sarah Hale was even for a time associated with Webster during the building of the monument at Bunker Hill, that monument to national harmony. In 1852, the year of Webster's death, she paid tribute to him again. That year she had revised and reissued *Northwood*, substituting for the old subtitle, "A Tale of New England," a new one, "Life North and South: Showing the True Character of Both." Her object in bringing out a new edition was to provide an answer to Harriet Beecher Stowe's disturbing novel, *Uncle Tom's Cabin*, published the same year, and to abolitionist arguments in general. In a brief foreword to this edition she made a plea for Union and praised the statesmen who had never been betrayed into divisive tactics. She identified herself with their cause:

And from the glorious old Granite State, where the scenes of this novel begin, have come forth those great men, "Defenders of the Constitution",—who "know no North and no South",—but wherever the sacred Charter of Union stretches its cordon of brotherhood, and the Eagle and the Stars keep guard, is their country. In the same spirit our book goes forth.[64]

The Union, in other words, was a kind of family. She went on to emphasize the point that a war between North and South would be a war between brothers. "The great error of those who would sever the Union rather than see a slave within its borders, is, that they forget the *master* is their brother, as well as the *servant*." She had made this point, she said, in 1827, and she had found it necessary to revise very little of what she had then said. Sidney Romilly, a Yankee, had become a Southerner and a gentleman. "The few additions made to the original work are only to show more plainly how the principles advocated may be effectually carried out."[65]

In 1826 Sarah Hale was living the isolated life of a provincial widow. She was poor and the race was ahead of her. Twenty-five years later she had achieved fame, success, influence—call it what you will. She had emerged, and she was living in Philadelphia, an editor, *the* editor really, of *Godey's*. *Godey's*, furthermore, had reached the peak of its influence. Thereafter it met increasing competition from such new publications as *Harper's Magazine*, founded in 1850, and the *Atlantic*, founded in 1857. Sarah Hale was sixty-four and, vigorous as she was, even she must have known that her life lay behind her. She would have looked back on her struggles and those of her hero with a certain detachment which would not have been possible twenty-five years before. Her knowledge of American life had, of course, increased immensely over the years, and America itself had changed, changed tremendously. The South, which was virtually unknown to her before, was now a part of her everyday experience as an editor of a national magazine with many Southern subscribers and contributors. She knew about it as a mother as well. Three of her children had made their lives, or part of their lives, in the South. The surprising thing, really, is not that she made changes in *Northwood*, but rather that she did not make more. The race, it appears, looked much the same from either end.

The first edition of *Northwood* had said little or nothing about Sidney's plans. The last chapter had ended with his departure for the South. The new chapter is much more specific. Sidney has adopted the view that slavery is sanctioned by the Bible. For the Negro slaves, slavery had been, in fact, a great opportunity. The Negro had become a Christian and he had been introduced to civilization in the most advanced nation the world had ever known. In America, however, the Saxon is destined always to be superior. The future of the Negro, therefore, lay in Africa. There he might carry Christianity and civilization to his less fortunate "countrymen." Sidney had thus been made a mouthpiece for the arguments of the American Colonization Society, an organization founded in 1817 with the purpose of sending Negroes back to Africa. Although its program was unacceptable to either abolitionist or fire-eater, and its activities limited, it had a considerable appeal in the border states and listed among its members the leading spokesmen of the Whig party, Henry Clay and Daniel Webster. Sidney had worked out a plan for permitting his slaves, Yankeelike, to earn their own emancipation.

The principal danger of slavery, Sarah Hale contended, was not its effect on the slave but its effect on the master. Planters tended to forget that in the absence of work, they must fill up their time with duties, that they must live a life of service. All too frequently, a young Yankee tutor wrote to Sidney, young Southerners returned from college "where they often give promise of great talent, to smoke cigars in a veranda, or lie in the shade reading *cheap* novels!"[66] The English language, he wrote, was being bastardized by a promiscuous association with Negroes, and lovely Southern women spoke in a "niggerish" way. There is a strong hint in this last chapter that more than language was being bastardized.

Thus the system of slavery increases the temptations to sin, and only the most resolute courage in duty and humble reliance on Divine aid can struggle on successfully against the snares of evil around the slaveholder.[67]

Despite all these dangers and temptations, however, Sidney and his wife were completely happy in the South and fully up to its demands and its challenge. "Sidney and Annie Romilly are *at home!*" she wrote. "To them the word is full of meaning."[68] Surrounded by their own children and the numerous slave "children," they enjoy the satisfactions of an extended family. In such a family, the woman supplied the moral force while the man was kept busy with material concerns and with politics. Only the woman, she felt, could be really "disinterested," because only the woman was completely unconcerned with making money—and untempted by sensuality. In the North she must protect against overacquisitiveness, greed. In the South she must protect her family from falling prey to self-indulgence and idle pleasure. Southern men and Northern men must meanwhile work out a compromise which would hold the Union together, and combine the best features of both regions. " 'Constitutions' and 'compromises' are the appropriate work of men; women are the conservators of moral power," she concluded. Surely she must have had Webster in mind as she went on to explain. Appropriately, she took her supporting text from John Bunyan's *The Pilgrim's Progress:*

His hero Christian, with all the man's power, knowledge, and force of will, could hardly hold on his way to the "Celestial City". What doubts beset him! What dangers and delusions! He went *alone,* and only one soul joined him on the long pilgrimage. But when the *woman,* Christiana went, *she took the children with her.* She drew nearly all she met to join her, and angels led them on through pleasant ways to heaven and eternal life.[69]

Daniel Webster and Sarah Hale as Christian and Christiana went their separate ways. It is unknown if they ever met face to face. Still, there was a kind of marriage of purpose, and for a number of years they presided as master and mistress over the house of Whiggery. Between the two of them they also licked the platter clean

PART TWO

THE SUSTAINING
ILLUSION

CHAPTER IV

Holding the Wolf by the Ears: The Plantation Setting and the Social Order

The greatness of the past, the time when Virginia had been the mighty power of the New World, loomed ever above him [the Southern gentleman]. It increased his natural conservatism. He saw the change that was steadily creeping on. The conditions that had given his class their power and prestige had altered. The fields were worked down, and agriculture that had made his class rich no longer paid. The cloud was already gathering in the horizon; the shadow already was stretching towards him. He could foresee the danger that threatened Virginia. A peril ever sat beside his door. He was "holding the wolf by the ears."

THOMAS NELSON PAGE[1]

What is the reason, when we get down south, here, everything seems to be going to destruction, so? I noticed it all the way down through Virginia. It seems as if everything had stopped growing, and was going backwards.

HARRIET BEECHER STOWE, *Dred*[2]

By the eighteen thirties the soil had been prepared in both the North and the South for the growth of what can only be described as a plantation legend, a set of popular beliefs about the Southern planter, the plantation family and what was assumed to be the aristocratic social system which existed in the South. Southerners had become obsessed by feelings of social decline, by a conviction that the civic values and ideals of the Revolutionary generation had been eroded away by a half century of democratic change and territorial expansion. They grasped for symbols of stability and order to stem their feelings of drift and uncertainty and to quiet their uneasiness about the inequities within Southern society. Soon they would be forced to answer directly charges concerning Negro slavery leveled at them from the North. The North itself, meanwhile, had been suffering from growing pains of the most acute kind. A fear that America had become the scene of a wild scramble for riches and material comforts was widely felt. Everywhere one finds evidence of deep concern lest the last vestiges of Revolutionary idealism and social coherence disappear. There was a great hankering for intellectual distinction, genteel taste, private and public decorum. It is scarcely surprising, in view of feelings of this kind, that the North itself turned admiringly toward the South despite grave and growing reservations about slavery. Caught between the predatory Yankee and the genteel Southern slaveholder, Northerners were quick to indicate their preference for the latter.

Everywhere in America, at the same time, a set of well-defined fears and misgivings began to focus on the institution of the family. Fifty years had been sufficient to break up the kinship groups which remained along the Atlantic seaboard at the close of the Revolution and disperse them across the continent. Men and women died hundreds—and sometimes thousands—of miles from the place of their birth. Traditional modes of authority which had persisted within families during the colonial period had to be abandoned through the sheer impossibility of family councils and the difficulty of exercising patriarchal power on a shifting social scene. The nineteenth century was thus left to reckon with the dismembered family unit which it chose to call the Home and to accommodate itself to the changing roles of those within the Home—men, women and children. The reduction of men from heads of family to breadwinners, the new moral authority assumed by American women, and the sentimental obsession with childhood innocence and wisdom all required an airing in popular literature, and for this purpose the plantation novel of the thirties, forties and fifties proved an effective outlet, especially in the South, where the fear of social dissolution was most intense.

In the rash of plantation literature produced in the South during these years women were given the same kind of new role they assumed in Northern writing which examined the Yankee ethos. If the men were necessarily acquisitive, Northerners like Sarah Hale had reasoned, perhaps it was the responsibility of women to act as their intellectual and ethical tutors and to provide society with necessary moral restraints. The necessity in the South of accounting for the decline of the Tidewater led Southerners to a growing distrust of the acquisitive value system which they associated with progress and the North. It also induced them to undertake a closer scrutiny of the Cavalier ethos than that which had been taking place in the North. If the planter was to appear aloof from money-making and the plantation was to be represented as something other than a setting for human and economic exploitation, what positive, alternative values could the Southern gentleman be given?

The problem was complicated by the fact that Southerners tended to associate male effectiveness not only with horsemanship and other soldierly and outdoor qualities but also, as Northerners did, with financial success. Again like Northerners, they also tended to associate such qualities as moral consciousness, sentimentality, introspection and benevolence with femininity. It became a question of how it was possible to endow the plantation with some of these attributes without robbing the Southern gentleman of his manhood. The Southern answer to this question lay in the cult of chivalry—in having the Cavalier kneel down before the altar of femininity and familial benevolence. This was not an entirely comfortable compromise, however, and a very clear limit had to be imposed on the scope of the woman's new moral authority. She was given the Home on the understanding that her benevolence was to stop at the bounds of the family. Women were projected into the center of the plantation legend and the plantation became a kind of matriarchy. Nonetheless, behind the plantation portico there can frequently be heard, faintly but distinctly, the still small voice of an awakening Southern consciousness that wrong has been and is being done behind the complacent façade of the planter's social code.

The Plantation Legend and Southern Introspection

The fictional Southern plantation which Ellen Glasgow, William Faulkner and other twentieth-century writers inherited was principally the creation of two active periods of literary and social ferment. The first and most interesting of these lasted from about 1832 until the mid-fifties, when the literary energies of both North and South were drawn off into purely polemical writing. The second period lasted from about 1880 to the end of the century. The image of Southern society which emerged from this first and far less publicized period of preoccupation with plantation life was, by and large, complex and fluid, especially when contrasted with the saccharine and sentimental stereotype which proved so popular in the eighties and nineties.[3] The interest of this earlier fiction, however, springs mainly from its qualities of complexity and suggestiveness, since as literature these first efforts are for the most part inept performances rarely distinguished by imaginative force or creative originality. If the later writing was often slick and predictable, the prewar efforts were amateurish at best and often the work of complete novices. The first novel to employ the plantation setting in any important way was *The Valley of Shenandoah* (1824), the work of George Tucker, a Bermuda-born Virginia Congressman and constitutional lawyer who had never before written fiction. Real literary interest in the plantation, however, did not come until the early thirties, when a number of books of a similar sort appeared in quick succession. In 1832 a young Baltimore lawyer, John Pendleton Kennedy, opened his literary career with a book entitled *Swallow Barn* which described life on a Tidewater plantation. The same year, James Kirke Paulding, a New Yorker of Dutch extraction—and a prolific writer—devoted the first part of his *Westward Ho!* to the household of an improvident Virginia gentleman. In 1834 William Alexander Caruthers, a young and ambitious Scotch-Irishman from the Shenandoah Valley, published his first two novels, one of them historical, and both of them concerned with the Tidewater gentry. *The Kentuckian in New York* and *The Cavaliers of Virginia* appeared within months of each other under the imprint of Harper & Brothers. Caruthers' third novel, *The Knights of the Horseshoe*, although written soon afterward, did not appear as a book until 1841. In 1836 Nathaniel Beverley Tucker, a son of St. George Tucker and a half brother of John Randolph, published two novels, *The Partisan Leader* and *George Balcombe*, both of which concern the Virginia Cavalier and touch on plantation life. *George Balcombe*, which is set in Missouri, also interestingly reflects the effect of Tucker's eighteen years' residence on the Southern frontier.

Meanwhile, the *Southern Literary Messenger*, founded in 1834, had begun to provide an outlet for fiction of a briefer kind about the Old South, and novelists outside Virginia, like William Gilmore Simms of South Carolina, were beginning to focus on the social life of the plantation elsewhere. After the eighteen thirties there was a lull of some years in literary planting and there was nothing quite like this first intense interest in Southern life until the eighteen fifties when *Uncle Tom's Cabin* was followed not only by a rash of "answers" but also by a great mass of nostalgic writing about the South which was seemingly unrelated to the slavery issue. It was during this period, for example, that Simms finished his fictional history of the American Revolution in South Carolina and John Esten Cooke, taking his cue from Simms, published the first of his many historical romances about social life in the Old Dominion (the name by which the pre-Revolutionary "Colony and Dominion of Virginia" came to be known). By 1860, certainly, enough had been said about the culture of the gentleman planter to suggest the kind of concerns which had precipitated much of this discussion and provoked so many Southerners, at least briefly, to undertake literary ventures.

Previous attempts to deal with the sudden appearance of this interest in the plantation have focused almost entirely on the propaganda value which this literature was supposed to have had in justifying the "slavocracy." According to this argument Southern Whigs became fearful after 1832 that the abolitionist attacks upon the South would lead to the defection of Northern conservatives from the Whig alliance. In response to this threat they undertook to retouch the image of plantation society with the explicit object of "keeping the moneyed classes of the North persuaded of the virtues of the slavocracy."[4] One trouble with this kind of analysis is that it ascribes to all of these writers a singleness of purpose and a kind of political partisanship which most of them did not possess. But even assuming that this writing was undertaken "to express the ideal ends of the slave system," as Henry Nash Smith has put it,[5] the novels which were produced fall far short of such an objective. Anyone expecting to find in these novels anything resembling a consistent celebration of the plantation economy, slavery or the Tidewater aristocrat is in for a surprise.

After the Civil War had removed most things at issue, such as slavery and secession, the literary plantation did become more of an idyllic sanctuary, a kind of sunny Shangri-la, into which the cares of the world rarely intruded,[6] but in this earlier period there is a marked tendency to view the Tidewater planter critically or satirically, and to see his world as tragically flawed, or at least seriously threatened by disruptive forces in its very midst. Disruption, in fact, is a key to much of this writing, since Indian wars, rebellions, the Revolution, economic upheaval and bankruptcy are its stock in trade. The most prominent feature of these novels is not their advocacy of the Southern position on such sectional issues as slavery and secession, but rather their introspection—their preoccupation with intramural problems and their concern with issues which divided the South and about which individual Southerners were themselves undecided. While it is not possible to discount altogether more conventional literary ambitions, which in the case of Kennedy, Caruthers and especially Simms seem to have run quite high, it is probable that a good many of those who wrote their first novels under the stimulus of these years did so as a means of resolving problems and working through anxieties which could not be handled in any other way. Certainly the Old South revealed in these novels seems to belong less to a literature of affirmation or advocacy than to a literature of reconciliation and self-admonition. In fact, much of the usefulness of such writing would disappear if it were simply a recasting of polemical postures into story form. Fiction, even bad or indifferent fiction, often taps levels of the imagination which are not reached in conceptual writing and turns up reservations and contradictions which do not appear in polemics.

From Hotspur to Hamlet

A certain tension existed from the outset between the ideal of the Southern gentleman and the capacities he exhibited in fiction. In 1860 a young Alabama lawyer named Daniel Hundley published—in response to "exaggerated romances of the Uncle Tom school"—an interesting and complex analysis of Southern society in which he included a sketch of the Southern gentleman which sums up much of the prewar speculation about him.[7] Hundley, whose family was Virginian, had studied at Harvard and the University of Virginia. He had also traveled widely in the North and lived for a time in Chicago.[8] He was therefore an unusually sophisticated and experienced observer. He painted a far from idyllic picture of the South. His brilliant and satirical chapters on "Cotton Snobs," "The Southern Bully" and "The Southern Yankee" contain many illuminating insights into the structure of antebellum society and convey his awareness of the South's problems. Nonetheless, his depiction of the Southern gentleman is pure myth.

The gentleman was, to begin with, free of any taint of new wealth or old European corruption. Hundley was careful to distinguish him not only from his parvenu imitators in the South— "the new-rich swells"—but also from the International Gentleman—the Chesterfield and the Beau Brummell.[9] His real Southern gentleman was, however, invariably a man of aristocratic lineage. In Virginia he was apt to be a descendant of English Cavaliers, in Maryland he was most likely to be an Irish Catholic and related to the Proprietor, Lord Baltimore, while in South Carolina he was generally of French Huguenot ancestry. In the Southwest, on the other hand, his forebears had been "Spanish Dons and French Catholics." The gentleman was tall, slender and generally characterized by "faultless physical development." Life in the open air and the Southern passion for field sports had conditioned him to combine "firmness" with "flexibility" and had made him a more resilient and more balanced individual than his excitable and hare-brained Northern counterpart. Nonetheless, he was highly educated, frequently at the University of Virginia or at some comparable institution, after which he was apt to have made the Grand Tour of Europe. He possessed a natural dignity which was partly the result of exercising from childhood the habit of command and partly a trait inherited from "those mailed ancestors who followed Godfrey and bold Coeur de Lion to the rescue of the Holy Sepulchre."[10] He governed his plantation with a patriarchal authority which was based on natural traditions of family rule rather than on any artificial kind of coercion. Planting, politics and military service rather than the professions were his preferred occupations. In every way, Hundley seemed to indicate, the Southern gentleman was characterized by virility and by a mastery of his environment.

The most striking characteristic of the Southern gentleman in fiction, on the other hand, is his remoteness from this ideal. Certain of these qualities may be claimed for him, but his place in these stories and novels is not the one which Hundley and others who theorized about the gentleman would have assigned him. He is not the master of his own house, to say nothing of his environment, and he is frequently patronized by the novelist himself. Often he has died before the story opens and exists only as a memory.

In *The Valley of Shenandoah*, for example, Colonel Grayson is dead and the story begins as his family is struggling out of the indebtedness which he has settled upon it. They have placed their overseer in charge of their Tidewater plantation and moved west to the valley in order to reduce their expenses and escape from the crushing burden of the colonel's reputation for hospitality. Even this drastic step does not solve the problems which the family has inherited and Tucker is finally forced to concede that his theme is the "ruin of a once prosperous and respected family."[11] The planter's son in this fiction, no less than his father, is in full flight from solvency. If he is not spending the family fortune or gambling it away, he is apt to be drinking himself to death or destroying himself with more dispatch in duels and brawls. "Our young Virginians," one character comments, "live as if they could never get rid of their constitutions or estates soon enough; and yet many of them contrive to wear out both before they are thirty."[12]

If the planter is not a spendthrift, a gambler or a dueler (a role, incidentally, frowned upon by all of these novelists), he is often the dupe of his overseer or the victim of a confidence scheme. In

Beverly Tucker's *George Balcombe* the narrator's father, Colonel Craigenet, had supplied the Revolutionary armies without demanding compensation, had been cheated out of an English fortune through carelessness or indifference (it is difficult to tell which) and had fallen so heavily in debt that at his death his plantation had been seized to help meet his financial obligations. In Paulding's *Westward Ho!* Colonel Cuthbert Dangerfield, the Tidewater hero, is a very model of financial irresponsibility. His lavish scale of entertainment, his headlong fashion of laying huge bets on his horses and his entire neglect of the business side of planting (he keeps no books) eventually force him to sell out to his Scotch merchant and move to Kentucky. If these writers have anything to say about the place of the Cavalier gentleman in the nineteenth-century South, it is to call his usefulness into question. His characteristic improvidence, his almost childish impetuousness and irresponsibility, his lack of enterprise and his failure to move with the times—in sum, his inflexibility and inadaptability—spell his doom.

Effective characters, on the other hand, are apt to be "orphans," like Caruthers' Nathaniel Bacon, and Tucker's George Balcombe, or men of mixed, unknown or unspecified ancestry, or even yeomen of Scotch-Irish or German ancestry—from the South's "new" immigration—like Kennedy's Galbraith Robinson or Beverley Tucker's Christian Witt and John Keizer, or George Tucker's Ariosto-reading, Scotch-Irish mountaineer, M'Culoch. There is really no mistaking the implication embedded in all of these novels that the aristocratic South is in for a bad time.

The plantation itself tells much the same story. Perhaps more than anything else, the planter's house and grounds are used to symbolize the decline of the Tidewater aristocracy. Scarcely a single novel omits the opportunity of depicting a ruined plantation house and the desolation which surrounds it. The terms of such descriptions, in fact, soon become so fixed that their recitation becomes a kind of ritual. There is the mansion itself which is nearing a state of decay, its doors rotting on the sills, its steps eroded by frost, the portico littered with debris and, inside, the paper hanging loose from the walls, the wainscotting warped or shrunk, the cornices chipped, the mantel cracked and the carpets in shreds.[13] When the scene of action in these novels is located in the past, it is always in a time of trouble—during the American Revolution, or Bacon's Rebellion or an Indian war—and desolation is always implied or threatened. It would be difficult, for example, to distinguish between most nineteenth-century plantation ruins and the desolate plantation home to which in 1783 Captain Porgy returns in Simms's *Woodcraft*. It is significant that not a single plantation novel was set in the bountiful heyday of plantation prosperity of the mid-eighteenth century.

In searching out an explanation for this persistent theme of economic decline in plantation fiction it is important to recall that these novels were almost entirely the work of writers who had been brought up not in the Southwest but in the seaboard South, and especially in Virginia. To a very considerable extent their works reflect the results of the prolonged rural depression which struck the eastern counties soon after 1800 and continued to wear away at their prosperity for close to thirty years. This depression, which was especially acute at the close of the war of 1812, dealt the Tidewater a blow from which it never fully recovered and precipitated a major exodus of Virginians to the West. By 1830, it has been estimated, close to a third of those born in Virginia and Maryland around the turn of the century had crossed the Alleghenies, among them the future novelist Beverley Tucker, who found himself unable to earn a living in Virginia.[14] The decline of plantation prosperity in the Carolinas came somewhat later, after the opening up of the Southwest—and with it a kindred nostalgic literature of economic decline. The need to understand this phenomenon, the causes of which were obscure at the time, probably explains in part the sudden appearance of literature about the Tidewater planter as well as the ambivalent attitude which it expressed toward him. For if there was a kind of sadness associated with the passing of an old and more ample and decorous style of life, there was also a need to accept, or at least understand, the social style which seemed to be replacing it —and the forces which had brought this change about. Partly, too, these novels seem to reflect a growing awareness of the east-west cleavage which was developing within the seaboard states, and again, especially in Virginia. This cleavage first became apparent during the constitutional convention held in 1829, but many Virginians like John Randolph had been long aware of the impending disunity. Whatever one felt about the issues which were raised, no one could mistake the threat which "King Numbers" in the west posed for the minority of aristocratic, slave-holding planters east of the Valley who held some 400,000 of the state's 447,000 slaves and ruled the state through their domination of the legislature (by virtue of the three-fifths rule which gave slaveholders representation for three-fifths of their slaves) and their control of the powerful county courts. The serious western attack on slavery two years later was anticipated by discussions which provoked Randolph to refer ominously to the French Revolution and the destruction of all property rights.[15]

By 1830 Virginians themselves had clearly raised the issue as to whether the yeoman west or the aristocratic east were best fitted to retrieve the fortunes of the state. The argument, as men like Randolph conceived of it, ran a little like the plot of a plantation novel. Virginia had once been a wealthy and influential state; she had once possessed large expanses of land and a harmoniously ordered society. Now her wealth was gone, her influence was on the wane and she had long since squandered away her title to her western lands without any thought to her own future. Who should bear the responsibility? Randolph, during the Congressional debate on the tariff in 1824, sardonically laid the blame on the Improvident Gentleman, who had shown himself incompetent to conduct the affairs of his own household.

Virginia . . . must now begin to open her eyes to the fatal policy which she has pursued for the last forty years. I have not a doubt, that they who were the agents for transferring her vast, and boundless, and fertile country to the United States, with an express stipulation, in effect, that not an acre of it should ever inure to the benefit of any man from Virginia, were as respectable, and kind hearted, and hospitable, and polished, and guileless Virginia gentlemen, as ever were cheated out of their estates by their overseers; men who, so long as they could command the means, by sale of their last acre, or last negro, would have a good dinner, and give a hearty welcome to whomsoever chose to drop in, to eat, friend or stranger, bidden or unbidden.[16]

At the end of the century Thomas Nelson Page, looking back on the antebellum period, noted that there had been three distinct generations of Southern gentlemen before the Civil War. Of these, the Revolutionary gentleman, he felt, had been the most active and enterprising since "he had been a performer in the greatest work of modern times, with the scaffold over him if he failed." His son, less active and more introspective, "had faced the weighty problems of the new government, with many unsolved questions ever to answer." His grandson, who belonged to still another generation of Southerners, had been left to brood over the declining fortunes of the South. It was he who anxiously held "the wolf by the ears."[17]

Few Virginians exhibited better than Randolph so many of the qualities Page ascribed to his legendary third-generation Southern gentlemen. The Randolph family had figured importantly in every phase of Virginia life from the time that William Randolph acquired Turkey Island on the James in 1684. For a period of almost thirty years after 1800, John Randolph had paraded his eccentricities before the nation as a Virginia Congressman. "Booted and spurred, he swaggered about the House, whip in hand," exhibiting opinions that were no more conventional—or predictable—than his dress or his manners.[18] He was the opponent of all compromise, all temporizing, and he never hesitated to strike out insultingly at any detected sham or pretense. Henry Adams, who did not like him, later referred to him as a "Virginian Saint Michael, almost terrible in his contempt for whatever seemed to him base or untrue."[19] He was almost always an opponent of national measures, and in this respect was more Jeffersonian than Jefferson himself. His strict adherence to the doctrine of state sovereignty finally carried him out of the Republican party and into an eccentric political posture of his own. "Asking one of the states to surrender part of her sovereignty," he once observed, "is like asking a lady to surrender part of her chastity."[20] Throughout his political career he was more or less always in opposition. He knew how to do one thing, and he did it superbly. He knew how to resist.

In his personal life he was no less idiosyncratic. The heavy drinking of his early years, his addiction to horse racing and to the code duello paralleled his devotion to Virginia in political matters. Opposition to one of his measures in Congress might lead to a challenge, as it had for Webster. Throughout much of his life he was in ill health and, in his last years especially, given to fits of madness. He never matured physically, looked like a boy and spoke in a rich soprano voice. He died, probably of tuberculosis, in 1833, after an illness of several years in which he took to opium, drank to excess and treated all about him, including his slaves, harshly and brutally. An autopsy performed after his death determined that he had in fact been sterile.[21] Although he was in almost every respect an unrepresentative Virginian and Southerner, Randolph set the pattern for the doomed Southerner in the same way that Franklin had earlier set the pattern for the emergent Yankee. Everything about him—his rakish youth, his fierce Virginia patriotism, his touchy pride, his arrogant aristocratic manner, his high sense of integrity, his rapierlike wit, his consumptive appearance, his hypochondria, his final madness and even his impotence—fitted him for the role. More than almost anyone else he possessed a tortured consciousness of Virginia's tragic decline. To Virginia he had given the full measure of devotion, and yet, finally, he had succeeded in doing very little except place a finger in the crumbling dike of state particularism and shout his literate and incisive imprecations at the tides of nationalism which at last overwhelmed and destroyed him. It is little wonder that Virginians did not easily forget him, and it is certain that Page had him first in mind as he attempted to catch the qualities of the Virginia gentleman during these difficult years.

Any typology of the Southern gentlemen who stalk through these novels would include at least two types who owe something to Randolph, whose death in 1833 closely coincided with this first outburst of fiction about the plantation. There were a number of types, generally minor characters, of a quite different sort, like the genial squire, the proud old Tory and the dilettante-dandy (usually, in Virginia fiction, a South Carolinan), but any selective list of planter-heroes would give priority to the Southern Hothead and the Southern Hamlet. George Bagby was probably thinking of Randolph when he defined the Hothead or Fire-eater as "a red Indian imprisoned in the fragile body of a consumptive old Roman."[22] (Randolph had always boasted of his kinship to Pocahontas.) The Hothead, who combined in his person all the touchy pride and aggressiveness of Randolph, owed something to Patrick Henry as well, since Henry, in the popular image of him created by Wirt, was the first Virginian to be known as an instrument of pure insurgency. When Beverley Tucker came to write *The Partisan Leader*, which concerns an imagined war between Virginia and the North (against the "Yorkers and Yankees"), he gave many of his half brother's traits to his partisan commander Bernard Trevor. In 1854 a similar figure appears, anachronistically, with Patrick Henry in a description of the Stamp Act Crisis—a sort of great rehearsal for 1860—at the end of John Esten Cooke's *The Virginia Comedians*.[23] This personage came to stand for a narrower and narrower range of Southern possibilities which certain of these novelists anxiously explored. Along with the Patrick Henry of the Virginia ratifying convention, he became a hero of states' rights. He came to symbolize honorable failure and the lost cause. As the sectional crisis intensified, he became more and more strident until finally, in 1860, in Edmund Ruffin's *Anticipations of the Future*, the novel itself is narrated from this point of view. Ruffin took as the epigraph of his novel Henry's provocative line: "If this be treason, make the most of it." But when all of these novelists were finished with the Randolph-Henry Hothead the figures of Henry and Randolph had lost their historical identity. There was still enough of Randolph's real complexity of attitude left to suggest the outlines of a kind of character who had more expressive possibilities for the novel—and for the South—than these rebels.

The most interesting kind of Southern gentleman to make his appearance in this early fiction is the Southern Hamlet, a man who, like Horace Brainard in *Northwood*, is introspective, given to brooding—one in whom the springs of action have become somehow impaired. The introverted gentleman has a long history in Southern fiction which runs the gamut from Poe's neurasthenic Roderick Usher to Faulkner's Quentin Compson III and includes along the way contributions by Simms, Harriet Beecher Stowe and practically all the talents large and small that have examined Southern life. At their worst, these figures were simply the personification of Southern lassitude. The best of them, however, are made to bear the full weight of remembered greatness and suffering, just as they are made to bear the burden of the South's injustices and inhumanities, both inflicted and received. They are the consciousness and the conscience of the South and they are paralyzed by their knowledge. This was the type of Southerner whom Harriet Stowe selected to illustrate her own theories about the nobility and the weaknesses of Southern character. Augustine St. Clare in *Uncle Tom's Cabin* is such a figure. Indolent, conscience-striken and emasculated, he nevertheless becomes the prophet of world revolution—"a mustering among the masses, the world over"—and foresees a cataclysm which will topple the unjust. St. Clare had once contemplated a bold course of action, but tortured by uncertainty and self-doubt, he had permitted his resolution to slacken. "There was a time," he tells his cousin from Vermont, "when I had plans and hopes of doing something in this world, more than to float and drift. I had vague, indistinct yearnings to be a sort of emancipator,—to free my native land from this spot and stain. All young men have had such fever-fits,

I suppose, some time,—but then—"[24] In Mrs. Stowe's *Dred*, published in 1856, aristocratic Edward Clayton is a classical Southern Hamlet. He was:

tall, slender, with a sort of loose-jointedness and carelessness of dress, which might have produced an impression of clownishness, had it not been relieved by a refined and intellectual expression on the head and face. The upper part of the face gave the impression of thoughtfulness and strength, with a shadowing of melancholy earnestness; and there was about the eye . . . that occasional gleam of troubled wildness which betrays the hypochondriac temperament. [25]

About all of these figures there is an obvious lack of vitality and masculinity, the very qualities which the legend most insists upon. Mrs. Stowe emphasized these feminine characteristics of the Southern gentleman just as she embodied in Legree and some of her Yankee slave traders most of the distasteful male traits she could bring herself to describe. Edward Clayton's mouth is described as "even feminine in the delicacy and beauty of its lines," and his nature, she noted, was "veined and crossed with that of the mother."[26] It seems evident from the emphasis which she places on such details that in her own thinking, if you carried the potentialities of each section to the limit, the South became pure sensibility while the North became the naked impulse to wealth.

It was not simply Mrs. Stowe who reached such conclusions about the diminished vitality of Southern character. Now and then a perceptive Southerner even noted that the traits of the Hothead and the Hamlet were expressions of the same fundamental failure of character. On June 5, 1862, Mary Boykin Chesnut, the wife of a Confederate official and former United States Senator from South Carolina, noted in her diary some of her own reflections on the Southern gentleman. The war, she felt, had already disproved the old shibboleths about the Yankee's cowardice, and events were beginning to suggest some of the shortcomings of the Cavalier. "Our planters," she wrote, "are nice fellows, but slow to move; impulsive but hard to keep moving. They are wonderful for a spurt, but that lets out all their strength, and then they like to rest." The Southerner's indolence and inability to act, furthermore, lay deeper in his nature than the weather.

> This race have brains enough, but they are not active minded. Those old revolutionary characters—Middletons, Lowndeses, Rutledges, Marions, Sumters—they came direct from active-minded forefathers, or they would not have been here. But two or three generations of gentlemen planters and how changed the blood became![27]

This tendency to explain what was probably the unavoidable decline of the seaboard economy and defeat of the South as a failure of blood and a failure of nerve persisted long after the war. Margaret Mitchell's genteel Ashley Wilkes, for example, in *Gone With the Wind* "was born of a line of men who used their leisure for thinking, not doing, for spinning brightly colored dreams that had in them no touch of reality."[28]

The Plantation Becomes a Matriarchy

The real focus of fictional plantation life was not the planter but his wife, whose benevolent rule extended over the entire household, white and black. Alongside the Southern matriarch, the gentleman planter becomes a shadowy figure, hovering in the background or, as we have seen, he disappears altogether and leaves the woman to preside over the family unobstructed. Again it is Hundley who sums up the legend:

> In this her proper sphere woman wields a power, compared to which the lever of Archimedes was nothing more than a flexible blade of grass. She it is who rules the destinies of the world, not man. The raging tornado treads with the tramp of an army along the mountain's sides, uprooting loftiest cedars in its fury, but there its power ends; while the silent night dews, stealing without noise or bluster into the heart of the solidest rock, rend the very mountain itself asunder. So man, although he shall march with banners flying and to the music

of fife and drum to the world's end, will always find that there is a power behind the throne greater than the throne itself.[29]

Thomas Nelson Page, recalling the role of the antebellum plantation mistress, draws much the same picture. She was "the most important personage about the home, the presence which pervaded the mansion, the centre of all that life, the queen of that realm." The master, Page goes on to say, simply carried out her directions and yielded her authority in everything "not because he was afraid, but because he recognized her superiority." Though often delicate, nervous and even an invalid, her force of character was able unobtrusively to rule "as unseen yet as unmistakably as the power of gravity controls the particles that constitute the earth." "She was mistress, manager, doctor, nurse, counsellor, seamstress, teacher, housekeeper, slave, all at once."[30]

The plantation mistresses of these early novels conform, on the surface, to this ideal of the planter's wife. They are not only solidly committed to the plantation system, they are the heart and soul of it. While aristocratic life has destroyed the planter's initiative and made him passive and indolent, the demanding routines and unending responsibilities of the plantation household have made the woman stronger and increased her status and dignity. The planters of his own day, George Tucker felt, showed a falling off from former times. The women, however, had improved themselves. "They have gained, generally speaking in mental improvement, without losing in delicacy or purity."[31] Mrs. Grayson in *The Valley of Shenandoah*, after the colonel's death, has taken over the management of his estates and runs them more efficiently than her husband had. At the neighboring plantation, "The Elms," Major Fawkner has fallen under the domination of his wife. In *Swallow Barn* the same situation prevails: "Whilst Frank Meriwether amuses himself with his quiddities, and floats through life upon the current of his humor, his dame, my excellent cousin Lucretia, takes charge of the household affairs, as one who has a reputation to stake upon her administration." She only pretends to yield to her husband when differences arise, "since she is confessedly and without appeal, the paramount power."[32] Mrs. Dangerfield in *Westward Ho!* gently but firmly rules her impetuous and headstrong husband and Ann Clayton, after her marriage in *Dred*, is described as an Amazon queen:

Ann Clayton, in a fresh white morning-wrapper, with her pure, healthy complexion, fine teeth, and frank, beaming smile, looked like a queenly damask rose. A queen she really was on her own plantation, reigning by the strongest of all powers, that of love.[33]

Even the young belles, whether timid or flirtatious, possess like Lucy and Victorine in *Swallow Barn* the incipient strength of their mothers.[34] One of John Esten Cooke's heroines, for example, who is "just on the threshold of womanhood," at once communicates the qualities which will distinguish her as a mature woman.

But a single glance at the young face showed that her nature was not weak—on the contrary, that her character was strong and resolute. She was, indeed, all woman in her organization—both timid and firm, both pliable and unbending. Under the shy manner you could see this force of character, and felt that if the moment came this girl would be capable of opposing her will with unfaltering **nerve** to any obstacle in her path.[35]

The pattern of Southern chivalry, as it developed in these decades, thus becomes a little clearer. If we are to believe the novelists, the plantation house was populated by generous-hearted but improvident or indolent men and single-minded and domineering women and their incipiently Amazonish daughters.

It is interesting to note, furthermore, that the characteristics of the planter and his wife in this fiction remain much the same whether the author is a Northerner or a Southerner, a man or a woman. Sarah Hale imagining a Southern plantation from her perch in New Hampshire and Harriet Stowe working from Brunswick, Maine, on very slender personal experience see the plantation family in much the same light as seasoned Southern observers such as Kennedy and George Tucker. This was not the South's image concocted to propagandize the North, nor was it the woman's or the man's: it was the nineteenth century's. Thackeray's plantation was scarcely different.[36] Of all these writers, only Beverley Tucker spoke from the point of view of the professional Southerner and Tidewater aristocrat, and even he wrote with eighteen years in Missouri fresh in his mind. All of the others came to their subject with something of the perspective of an outsider. George Tucker, though long a resident of the Tidewater, had come from Bermuda at the age of twelve to live with his distant relative, St. George Tucker, in Williamsburg, and it is interesting to note that the novel is set in the Virginia of 1790 which he first came to know. Paulding was a New Yorker, Kennedy a Baltimorean familiar principally with the valley. John Esten Cooke, too, had been reared in the western part of the state. It is therefore necessary to look beyond any narrow aristocratic partisanship for the explanation of many of the features of these novels.

The Origins of Southern Chivalry

Among the concerns of national scope which play over these novels few figure more importantly than the changing position of women. In attempting to understand what lies behind some of this fantasy it is therefore helpful to recall that the first appearance of plantation fiction coincided not only with the appearance of militant abolition in the North but also, and I think just as significantly, with the first stirrings of the movement for woman's rights, which occurred at about this time and appealed to—as well as alarmed—many of the same people. The popular New England novelist Lydia Maria Child published her influential tract, *An Appeal in Favor of That Class of Americans Called Africans* in 1833, just a year after her comprehensive *History of the Condition of Women*, which appeared in the same year as *Swallow Barn* and *Westward Ho!* The expatriate Grimké sisters were publishing pamphlets concerned alike with slavery and the status of women throughout this decade. Angelina's *Appeal to the Christian Woman of the South* was published in 1836, and Sarah Grimké's *Letters on the Equality of the Sexes and the Condition of Woman* appeared in 1838.

Such agitation as there was, however, took place almost entirely in the North, where women had seen themselves bypassed by egalitarian reforms which extended the suffrage and liberalized the legal restrictions placed upon other groups. Nowhere in the eighteen thirties could women vote, or if married, own property in their own names. Divorce was almost impossible. Higher education was rarely available and all of the professions, including the ministry, and most jobs were still closed to them. Married women lived in a kind of legal bondage to their husbands. Women soon learned bitterly that even certain of the reform movements—even, ironically, parts of the antislavery movement—did not welcome them. It was this knowledge, more than anything else, that precipitated the convention held in Seneca Falls, New York, in 1848 —a year of revolution, some of the women noted—and the Declaration of Sentiments in the spirit of '76 protesting the tyranny of man which the convention issued. The movement for woman's rights which grew out of this and other conventions made only modest progress before the Civil War, but the activities of rebellious groups of women were widely commented upon and caused considerable uneasiness, especially in the South.[37]

The authors of these plantation novels, whatever their differences on the slavery question, were unanimous in their condemnation of "the new woman" as she was represented by Fanny Wright, Mrs. Bloomer and protosuffragettes like Elizabeth Cady Stanton. Though the threat was then no bigger than a woman's hand, all of them, like Sarah Hale, saw in militant feminism a force which could ultimately destroy the home and family. Sarah Hale and Harriet Stowe each in her own way championed the position of women and by her own example enlarged the sphere in which they were permitted to move, but in this endeavor, as in her crusade to free the slaves, Harriet Stowe eschewed the extremists and sought, to use her own word, for an "intermediate" way. As her biographer observed of her, "she was never one to ally herself uncompromisingly even in private communications with causes that were unpopular or dubious."[38] Quite the contrary, in fact. Her distaste for the female Left grew to such a pitch that in 1871 she wreaked her vengeance on the suffragettes (and emancipated women in general) in her wickedly satirical *My Wife and I*, in which Mrs. Stanton appears as the virago Stella Cerulian. About the others, there was never really any question. Kennedy in *Swallow Barn* holds forth on the advantages of educating young women in the home and guarding them throughout their lives from the rivalries and impurities of the world.[39] Paulding was fanatical on this subject, as was Beverley Tucker. All of them seemed willing to offer the American woman the dominion of the home, provided she would stay there; and with varying emphasis and pitch of feeling they sought to make the home a fortress worth keeping and a charge worthy of her dignity. In this they allied themselves with the authors of the so-called "domestic novel"—the sentimental novel of the home and family—which rapidly gained ascendency over all other forms of fiction by mid-century, as Helen Papashvily has shown.[40]

It is difficult to know with much exactitude how feeling ran among Southern women in this period and what, in particular, stirred up the anxiety and stimulated the interest which was focused on them. Nonetheless, it is impossible to read widely in the literature of the South without gaining the impression that Southern women in a certain sense were being bought off, offered half the loaf in the hope they would not demand more. One or two incidents, such as the defection of the aristocratic Grimké sisters of Charleston to abolition and militant feminism, were widely commented upon, but the strait jacket of rigid convention in which Southern women lived, and men knew they lived, probably composed the principal threat. Stripped to its barest essentials the deference shown to them in the form of

Southern chivalry was the deference ordinarily shown to an honored but distrusted servant. "'Man almost always addresses himself to the weakness of woman," commented Sarah Grimké in 1838:

By flattery, by an appeal to her passions, he seeks access to her heart; and when he has gained her affections, he uses her as the instrument of his pleasure—the minister of his temporal comfort. He furnishes himself with a housekeeper, whose chief business is in the kitchen, or the nursery. And whilst he goes abroad and enjoys the means of improvement afforded by collision of intellect with cultivated minds, his wife is condemned to draw nearly all her instruction from books . . . whilst engaged in those domestic duties, which are necessary for the comfort of her lord and master.[41]

Wilbur J. Cash is probably correct in attributing some of this deference to the guilt which widespread miscegenation caused among Southern white men,[42] but it is hard to believe that the grievances of plantation women or the malaise of their husbands began or ended with the simple fact of miscegenation. One example may suggest the complexity of women's feelings in the South. Mrs. Chesnut is far from a typical Southern woman (in the North, one feels, she would have become the novelist she dreamt of being), but in her literate and sensitive diary she managed to note down much more than the gossip of the Confederacy, although she did this extraordinarily well. Having grievances of her own, she was particularly attuned to the dissatisfactions of Southern women, and through the conversations which she recounts with other women, she succeeded in communicating a state of feeling which, if it were widespread, would explain some of the defensiveness of Southern writers. For her and for her friends every day seemed to hold its small trials and humiliations—the constant necessity of asking her husband for pin money (it was not thought proper for women to handle money), the patronizing attitude of a male friend, the insubordination of a servant—but the stories they exchanged range far beyond these petty annoyances and focus on the plight of women forced to live, as she once put it, in the middle of squalid Negro villages. She tells the story of a neighbor murdered by her slaves while staying alone on her plantation. "Fancy how we feel," she confided in her diary. "I am sure I will never sleep again without this nightmare of horror haunting me." Someone in a gathering of women tells the story of a planter who had not gone to bed sober in thirty years and the women speculate whether they would have endured it—"to think," someone comments, "that for no crime a person may be condemned to live with one [a drunk] thirty years." She visits her sister only to find her pale, nervously shattered, her hair suddenly turned gray after an epidemic has swept her household and taken the lives of two of her children.

Most revealing of all are the entries which portray the shameful duplicity and self-deception with which women lived with miscegenation. There was the man, for example, whose mulatto children were kept in full view and provided for in his will. "His wife and daughters, in their purity and innocence, are supposed never to dream of what is as plain before their eyes as the sunlight." Mrs. Chesnut bristles on another occasion, recalling a flagrant instance, at the revolting thought of being tyrannized and righteously railed at by a man who has only just returned from "the quarter." "You see," she noted, "Mrs. Stowe did not hit the sorest spot. She makes Legree a bachelor." On the subject of slavery she minces no words. "I hate slavery," but so too did she despise and distrust the slaves, especially the women with their open sensuality and slatternly, provocative manner. When an old and trusted overseer visits them and states his own conviction that slavery is wrong—"Slavery is a thing too unjust, too unfair to last"—she tacitly agrees as she had agreed earlier to his statement that most planters' wives were "abolitionists in their hearts, and hot ones, too." Her entry closes with an edgy confession of futility. "Our votes are not counted. We are women, alas!"[43]

A certain amount of writing originating in the South appears to have been addressed to the Mary Chesnuts—and to their husbands. In 1835, the year before the appearance of Tucker's two novels, Thomas R. Dew, proslavery theorist and Tucker's colleague at William and Mary, wrote three long and scholarly articles for the recently founded *Southern Literary Messenger* under the general title, "On the Characteristic Differences between the Sexes, and on the Position and Influence of Woman in Society."[44] What emerged from Dew's discussion was a careful formulation of what might be described as the stand-pat position on the status of women, a view which was characteristically—but not at all exclusively—Southern. Dew began by assuming certain physiological differences between men and women. Man was physically stronger, for example, and was therefore destined to be the aggressor in the business of life; the woman's physique was to a great extent determined by her childbearing role: she was weaker, more passive and, in her psychology, more internally oriented. "Her inferior strength and sedentary habits confine her within the domestic circle; she is kept aloof from the bustle and storm of active life."[45] Because the woman was weaker and because she required the protection of the stronger male for herself and for her young, she was early driven to find other means than force for exercising her will, and she soon discovered that the greatest power on earth was not the muscularity of the man but her own powers of allurement—in short, her sex appeal: "Grace, modesty and loveliness are the charms which constitute her power. By these, she creates the magic spell that subdues to her will the more mighty physical powers by which she is surrounded." So great is her power, he concluded, it is almost Godlike: "it subdues without an effort, and almost creates by mere volition."[46]

The experience of motherhood, Dew continued, is the fundamental drive in the psychology of all women and makes them less self-centered, more outgoing and sympathetic than the man, whose roles as guardian of the home and provider force him to do battle with the world. The essence of womanhood, on the other hand, was love, while the essence of manhood was predation. "Man is necessarily an active, restless, energetic, impatient being.

[170]

This character is generated by the functions which he has to discharge in this world."[47] Both historical and physiological experience have inured the woman to suffering and, even, to brutality, and schooled her in resignation and in the arts of concealment. Both in the act of childbearing and in her traditional role as trophy of war she has always been subjected to forces beyond her control. While Ulysses fought and wandered, Penelope, through the use of artifice, held a houseful of suitors at bay.

In many ways—in all *possible* ways, Dew felt—the situation of the American woman represented an improvement over the past. She was no longer a warrior's pawn, like Briseis in the *Iliad*; she was spared from the degradations of the seraglio, and she was rapidly freeing herself from the arranged marriage and establishing her right to choose her own partner in matrimony. In almost every way she had become the social equal of man. She could scarcely ask for more. Legal rights, property rights and the "right" to participate more extensively in the affairs of the world would only encourage her to violate her own nature. As soon as women begin to make overt demands and exact satisfactions for grievances, Dew continued, they lose the fateful charm to which they owe their power and are thrown back upon their inferior physical strength—and all for a few pages of foolscap. Woman's nature dictated the opposite course from that of rebellion and counseled her to suppress her dissatisfactions and win alleviations by means of her sympathetic powers rather than through stridency.

In no event, Dew felt, could the woman ever hope to win equality with the man in all respects. She could not, for example, ever hope to be the sexual equal of man and she would therefore always have to wrestle patiently and quietly with her passions and her frustrations:

She cannot give utterance to her passions and emotions like man. She is not to seek, but to be sought. She is not to woo, but to be wooed. She is thus frequently required to suppress the most violent feelings; to put a curb on her most ardent desires, and at the same time to wear that face of contentment and ease which may impose upon an inquisitive and scrutinizing world.[48]

Since her moral perceptions provided the stabilizing basis of family life, furthermore, a set of rules more rigid than that of the man necessarily governed her conduct. In certain other respects as well she was limited, if not by aptitude at least by experience and training, in what she could legitimately expect from any society. Women had never exhibited a capacity for intellectual attainment of a high order. Metaphysics, abstract thought, scientific experimentation were beyond her present abilities and probably would continue to be. Even the arts were properly the province of men, though one or two exceptions suggested women might occasionally aspire to perfection at least in one of the performing arts. In literature, especially, the sensitivity, perceptiveness and moral insight of women might be expected to find an outlet, particularly in such a form as letter writing, where the relationship expressed was intimate and the formative sense was not overly taxed. Since their sphere of interest was limited to the family circle and since they were by nature passive and yielding, women could scarcely have been less fitted for politics or war. The fable of the Amazons was just a fable, Dew concluded reassuringly. No evidence had ever been produced to show that women had successfully done battle with men, or ruled over them. On the contrary, any close look at the Bible made it clear that God had seen fit to place woman in subjection to man and to develop the family around the harmonious interdependence of men and women. Any effort to alter this fundamental arrangement of nature, he sternly warned, would bring with it dire and unforeseeable consequences.

Women and Negroes: One and Inseparable

These articles in the *Messenger*, their tone, rhetorical pitch and the would-be "new Southern woman" to whom they are so obviously directed, provide better evidence than anything else that the woman question was being widely discussed and that many Southerners were convinced that the Southern home was threatened. Anyone remaining skeptical would find supporting evidence in plantation fiction generally and especially in Beverley Tucker's *George Balcombe*, published in 1836. A casual glance at Tucker's novel is sufficient to establish his indebtedness to Dew and the similarity of his aims. (He also drew from Dew's authoritative defense of slavery, which appeared in 1832.) Unfortunately for him, Dew's ideas were easier to restate than to dramatize and Tucker, who was a literary novice, could do little more than permit his titular hero to preach the gospel according to Dew in scene after scene. In general this novel, interesting as it is, exhibits all the worst traits of the college professor turned novelist. Mrs. George Balcombe, for example, is described as the model wife: she is lovely and dependent and she displays her domestic prowess by the ingenuity with which she has brought to a double log cabin in Missouri most of the comforts and elegancies of a plantation house in Virginia. Otherwise, she is suffered to remain discreetly in the background, fulfilling the role which Dew assigned to her and listening to her husband talk. George Balcombe, an orphaned Virginian who shows himself in Virginia matters more pious than the Pope, is the principal mouthpiece for Tucker's theory of the organic state and the social hierarchy. The irony of allowing this curious brand of neo-medievalism to be beamed at America from the lawless and fluid Missouri border revealed in the novel does not seem to have occurred to Tucker, whose social system Balcombe proceeds to unfold. Within the gradations of society provided for by a beneficent deity, every group is assigned a place. At the top is the Cavalier gentleman of English ancestry and unmixed blood and below him are ranked other groups whose subservience to the gentleman is constantly asserted: German and Scotch-Irish "peasantry," women and Negroes. Balcombe, whose claims to the first rank are somewhat doubtful, expresses considerable satisfaction in the order of nature. "For my part," he tells the narrator:

I am well pleased with the established order of the universe. I see gradations in everything. I see subordination everywhere. And when I find the subordinate content with his actual conditions, and recognising his place in the scale of being as that to which he properly belongs, I am content to leave him there.[49]

Tucker's extreme position on the status of women parallels his position on slavery and by its very extremity lays bare the kind of thinking which underlay the sentimental image of the plantation. For him, too, the threat of insubordination was evidently very great but, unlike the others, he approached the problem conceptually—far more bluntly, in fact, than Dew—and the result is most revealing. When the narrator speaks of educating women, Balcombe abruptly retorts, "No, William. Let women and negroes alone, and instead of quacking with them, physic your own diseases. Leave them in their humility, their grateful affection, their self-renouncing loyalty, their subordination of the heart, and let it be your study to become worthy to be the objects of these sentiments."[50] The affectional world which the woman inhabited made her, Tucker felt, immune to intellectual and social questions. This "indisposition" of the woman, furthermore, was something to be "cherished," since any effort to change her in some artificial way would create a threat to the supremacy of the man. If anyone should try to make "her something that God did not make her, nor mean that she should be, she will struggle for supremacy, and contend for distinction with her husband."[51]

The flawless and harmonious social order which men like Dew and Tucker proposed as a God-given mandate scarcely concealed the anxiety which lay behind it. Their insistence upon a fixed hierarchy, upon the subjection of woman, slave and yeoman to the Cavalier, was an obvious result of their alarm at the spectacle of a society adjusting itself according to the natural capacities of its individual members. An open society such as that which they saw developing seemed to promise a change of status to everyone, at least eventually, and already diabolically persuasive spokesmen in the North had begun to argue for the equality of both women and Negroes. The particular challenge posed them by women was partly the result of their inability to believe in the effectiveness of the gentleman planter. This doubt itself was a result of their association of the planter with the decline of the plantation economy in the East. They too, without quite recognizing it, had been seduced into identifying effectiveness with the ability to make money and, deprived of this, their Cavalier heroes are at a loss to explain themselves. In addition to this they were forced to reckon with the place which women had been assigned in the plantation legend. The same impulse which had induced the novelists to flatter the woman by placing her in charge of the household and making her the moral custodian of the family also attributed to her a moral sensibility that was keener than the man's. This concession to the woman, however, had been made at a time when the moral preoccupations of the society were assumed to be of secondary importance. As slavery more and more developed into a moral rather than a social or an economic problem, however, and it became clear that the ultimate outcome of the debate over its preservation would be decided on moral grounds, certain Southerners began regretting the moral autonomy which they had assigned to women. The old division of labor between men as providers and women as moral preceptors began to be seriously questioned, especially when it became apparent that women were in fact aligning themselves in number with the forces that were attempting to disrupt the social system in the South. Unfortunately, Tucker's solution, which was to lump the woman with the slave, only further emphasized the ridiculous predicament which the Southerner had created for himself. Far from suggesting the need for reclassifying the woman, he only, by association, succeeded in emphasizing the humanity of the slave and calling attention to the need for emancipating them both. But, apart from the importance given to it by a few individuals like Dew and Tucker, this was a problem which did not assume serious proportions until the fifties. For the time being it was the Cavalier and not his lady who was to be the principal subject of investigation.

CHAPTER V

A Squire of Change Alley: The Plantation Legend and the Aristocratic Impulse

Some years previous to this period Mr. Petigru had engaged in the ordinary and legitimate proceeding of investing his professional profits in a plantation and negroes. It was the approved Carolina custom in closing every kind of career. No matter how one might begin, as lawyer, physician, clergyman, mechanic, or merchant, he ended, if prosperous, as proprietor of a rice or cotton plantation. It was the condition that came nearest to the shadow of the colonial aristocracy which yet remained.

WILLIAM J. GRAYSON, *James Louis Petigru*[1]

THE PLANTATION NOVEL of the eighteen thirties provided more than a sentimental portrayal of country life and an idealization of the colonial and Revolutionary past. At the hands of the more talented and inventive practitioners like John Pendleton Kennedy it ranged far beyond the elegiac and the sentimental and probed the significance of the South's mixed cultural heritage—the old English stock and the "new" immigration. The literary techniques for this undertaking were derivative—and often not very thoroughly learned—but the problem was American and, in fact, Southern. From English portrayals of squire and manor house Southerners learned to edge their characterizations of the planter with irony. From Scott's form of the historical romance they learned to deal in cultural contrasts between aristocrat and plebeian, gentleman and commoner, Highlander and Lowlander. In the plantation novel, however, the commoner and the genteel half-breed rather than the gentleman began to receive the most creative emphasis. The gentleman planter for writers like Kennedy —himself half Scotch-Irish—became less a cultural ideal than a touchstone against which the emerging stock could measure its historical credentials, its vitality and its promise. The result of this fictive introspection was a virtual revolution within the social world of the novel, a near overturning of the social order on the legendary plantation and the emergence of the Scotch-Irish yeoman as a chivalric hero second to none. This revolution accomplished, aspiring men like Kennedy turned their attention to other and more serious matters. For them a literary career was simply one brief phase of a life devoted to business and public affairs. It had scarcely begun before it was over. *Sic transit gloria litterarum.*

The Literary Origin of the Plantation Legend

In the month of May, 1832, William Wirt turned from his cares as a Presidential candidate and his concern with the "national good" long enough to read a small book which had been published by Carey and Lea of Philadelphia the month before. The book had been dedicated to him. On May 23 he wrote to his friend Dabney Carr in Virginia: "Pray have you seen a new work called 'Swallow Barn' which is dedicated to *me*. It is said to be by John P. Kennedy, a right merry young lawyer of this place." Wirt left no doubt that, despite the dedication, he found very little in Kennedy's book which he liked. "It is a *sort* of a novel," he commented, "of which the scene is laid in Virginia—but it is a *non descript* sort of a novel—very little incident—& a great deal of what is called sketches of characters—It is said to be much puffed in Philadᵃ. . . ." The book, he found, reminded him in an unpleasant way of Paulding's early writing. Wirt sounded, in fact, a little like Thomas Jefferson discussing the writing of William Wirt. "But it is too much like Paulding's conceited style for my taste—too much verb[i]age & too little matter—a light, trifling, fantastic style—flippant & smart enough—but no deep . . . solemnising." Wirt, it appears, had not liked *Swallow Barn* at all. It was showy, shallow and pretentious. He was also somewhat embarrassed by the dedication and urged Carr to be discreet. "This is *entre nous*—for as I am complimented by the dedication, it wd. seem ungrateful in me to decry the work—but to you I say whatever comes uppermost."²

The full title of Kennedy's book was *Swallow Barn, or A Sojourn in the Old Dominion*. After the convention of the time, Kennedy had employed a *nom de plume*, "Mark Littleton, Esq." Although the dedication was very complimentary and mentioned Wirt's lasting literary achievement and "the purity and worth" of his character, it suggested at least one strong reason why Wirt may have been displeased. The book which Kennedy singled out for praise was not Wirt's *Patrick Henry*, over which he had labored for years, or the group of essays he had written a few years earlier for *The Old Bachelor*. Kennedy referred only to Wirt's earliest and most casual book, *The Letters of the British Spy*, written almost thirty years before. "Some years gone by, you carelessly sat down and wrote a little book, which has, doubtless, surprised yourself by the rapidity with which it has risen to be a classic in our country." The *British Spy* was the model which he had adopted, Kennedy said, though he modestly added that he was without "the wings that have borne your name to an enviable eminence."³

Wirt had long ago forsaken social satire for social elegy, or "deep solemnising," as he called it, and he must have found Kennedy's preface as little to his taste as the dedication. Kennedy stressed his intention to poke a little fun at country life in the Old Dominion rather than to sentimentalize it:

If my book be too much in the mirthful mood, it is because the ordinary actions of men, in their household intercourse, have naturally a humorous or comic character. . . . The undercurrents of country-life are grotesque, peculiar and amusing, and it only requires an attentive observer to make an agreeable book by describing them.[4]

Kennedy's Old Dominion, like Paulding's Southlands and Wirt's Old Virginia, began as a jest. He was finally no better able than others to sustain the jest, and soon himself forgot how to take his own jokes, but in his first book the "mirthful mood," as he called it, prevailed.

The immediate popularity and lasting success of *Swallow Barn* —Kennedy once referred to it as a "prosperous" undertaking[5]— requires some explanation. On the surface, it appeared to offer little novelty. Kennedy's literary debts were obvious at the time and even now hardly require listing.[6] Wirt, offhand, would seem to have been the least of his creditors. The book suggests his familiarity with a long tradition in English letters which had been concerned with the whimsical portrayal of country life, with special emphasis on the character of the country squire. The literary ancestry of Kennedy's Virginia planter, Frank Meriwether, goes back, at least, to Joseph Addison's Sir Roger de Coverley and includes such figures as Fielding's admirable pair of country gentlemen, Mr. Allworthy and Squire Western from *Tom Jones*, as well as some of Jane Austen's parochial lords of manor. His most obvious literary debt, however, was to a friend and fellow American, Washington Irving. Ten years before, in 1822, Irving had published a volume of connected sketches entitled *Bracebridge Hall*. In *Bracebridge Hall* Irving had portrayed the life which circulated in and about an old manor house in Yorkshire. The amiable and eccentric Frank Meriwether owes much to Irving's amiable and eccentric Squire Bracebridge. Kennedy was also indebted to Irving for the form of his book. As Wirt had noted, *Swallow Barn* like *Bracebridge Hall* was somewhere between a sketchbook and a novel. Like *Bracebridge Hall*, too, it focuses on the life within a single household. What the manor was to Irving, the plantation became for Kennedy. It was Kennedy's contribution to see—and to stress—the similarity.

One important aspect of the legend which developed about the figure of the planter was his similarity to the English squire. The most common source for the American idea of the squire was, of course, English literature. Throughout the century Americans looked upon the country gentleman and his way of life—in fact and in fiction—with an affectionate regard which they did not extend very often to other aspects of European society. If they regarded the metropolis with suspicion and concealed envy, they opened their hearts to the squire. In so far as they could, they tried to make his style of life their own. Among the European experiences which met with George Ticknor's unqualified acceptance were the two or three occasions when he encountered English country society. In January of 1819 he visited successively two countryseats, one belonging to the Marquess of Salisbury and the other to the Duke of Bedford. What particularly appealed to Ticknor was the parochialism of country society, its openness and its air of rusticity. "I liked this sort of hospitality," he commented, "which is made to embrace a whole county." He was delighted with the excitement of a hunting party leaving or arriving, with the merriment and wholesome good humor of country sport. "It was certainly," he concluded, "as splendid a specimen as I could have hoped to see, of what is to be considered peculiary English in the life of a British nobleman of the first class at his country-seat. I enjoyed it highly."[7] Other Americans enjoyed it too—or at least enjoyed reading about it—as Irving had guessed they would. John Pendleton Kennedy, more than anyone else, succeeded in transporting the squire to America.

Mark Littleton, Kennedy's narrator, is a familiar literary type.

Like Irving's Geoffrey Crayon he is a Citizen of the World, an inveterate traveler and carefree bachelor. He provides an outside, uncommitted point of view. Like the narrator of Paulding's *Letters from the South*, Littleton is a New Yorker. His observations on Virginia life are addressed to a fellow townsman, Zachary Huddlestone of Preston Ridge, New York. Earlier literary descriptions of the Old Dominion, like those of Paulding and Wirt, had rambled discursively over the countryside. Kennedy gained focus by concentrating his attention on the life of a single plantation. Littleton's reflections, which he shares with Huddlestone, are confined to the activities in and around "Swallow Barn," a tobacco plantation on the lower James River, where he goes to spend the summer of 1829 with his Virginia cousins. At "Swallow Barn" live Frank Meriwether, known as "Master Frank," his wife Lucretia, who is Littleton's cousin, and Ned Hazard, another cousin who is about Littleton's age and who becomes his companion for the summer. Together the two young men share the experiences of a plantation summer.

The other members of the little community at "Swallow Barn" are introduced one by one. In addition to Frank and Lucretia Meriwether, who are master and mistress of the plantation, there are two adolescent daughters, Lucy (a blonde) and Victorine (a brunette), Prudence Meriwether, Frank's maiden sister, the Reverend Mr. Chub, a vascular country parson, and Scipio, a free Negro servant whose memory stretches back to the "palmy days" before the Revolution. At an adjacent plantation, "The Brakes," live an old Loyalist planter, Isaac Tracy, his son Ralph and his two daughters, Catherine and Bel. Old Mr. Tracy has the charming formal manners and quaint, fixed views of the old regime; his son Ralph is a typical Southern sportsman, and Bel Tracy is a typical romantic heroine who persists in trying to force the chivalric image on the life about her. Still other characters arrive from time to time to crowd the scene and vary the comic fare.

From Jest to Sentiment

A whimsical analogy between life on a tobacco plantation and life in a medieval manor house is sustained throughout the book. The plantation house is referred to as "an aristocratical edifice"; Frank Meriwether is described as a comical lord of manor in a chapter entitled "A Country Gentleman" and references to feudalism and chivalry turn up in almost every chapter. Chapters entitled "Traces of the Feudal System," "Knight Errantry," "A Joust at Utterance" and "The Last Minstrel" hammer home the suggested parallel. While the tone of Kennedy's narrative is generally light and playful, the attitude which he wished to have his readers feel toward the chivalric pretensions of life at "Swallow Barn" is not always clear. In most instances, however, he treats the fanciful claims of his characters with gentle, smiling satire. Frank Meriwether's efforts to play the squire, it is implied, make him a genial host, a pompous justice of the peace, a garrulous and dominating conversationalist and a political bigot. His provincial isolation and parochial narrowness lead him to translate *droit du seigneur* as the *correctness* of the lord. Littleton's cousin, Ned Hazard, had gone off "a knight errant" to Peru a few years before to fight for the patriots. "However," Kennedy comments, "he came home the most disquixotted cavalier that ever hung up his shield at the end of a scurvy crusade."⁸ Bel Tracy of "The Brakes," whom Ned Hazard courts throughout the story, is given outlandishly romantic notions. "She reads descriptions of ladies of chivalry, and takes the field in imitation of them," Ned Hazard observes. "Her head is full of these fancies, and she almost persuades herself that this is the fourteenth century." She dabbles in falconry, using an uncooperative hawk as her falcon and a bewildered Negro boy as her falconer. She also attempts to train an eccentric Hessian veteran of the Revolution to act as her minstrel. Most of all, Ned Hazard believes, she wants "a gallant cavalier to break a lance for her."⁹

In most episodes of the book Kennedy plays with the comic inappropriateness of the chivalric image. When Bel's falcon, "Fairborne" the hawk, escapes and is recaptured, he is described as "a tawdry image of a coxcomb. His straps and bells hanging about his legs had the appearance of shabby finery; and his whole aspect was that of a forlorn, silly, and wayward minion, wearing the badge of slavery instead of that of the wild and gallant freebooter of the air so conspicuously expressed in the character of his tribe."[10] "I live in my lady's grace" is inscribed on a silver ring on Fairborne's leg. The chapter entitled "A Joust at Utterance" describes a fist fight between Ned Hazard and a local bully at a crossroads store. Many absurdities of Southern character (including the absurdity of Southern names) are lumped together in the figure of Singleton Oglethorpe Swansdown, Ned's competitor for Bel Tracy's hand. Swansdown is a man of many accomplishments. He is heir to a large plantation in one of the eastern counties; he has traveled about the country, pretends to know everything and everyone, dresses fashionably, has run for Congress and has written a long poem, "The Romaunt of Drysdale," in the manner of Sir Walter Scott. He is the personification of the Southern literary dilettante. Old Mr. Tracy's stubbornness in pursuing a boundary dispute with his neighbors is also treated satirically. "The lord of a freehold coming by descent through two or three generations, and especially if he be the tenant in tail, is as tenacious as a German Prince of every inch of his dominions. There is a seigniorial pride attached to his position . . . it manifests a contemptuous defiance of the feudal dignity."[11]

On the other hand, Kennedy's satire is not always sustained. At certain points the whimsy gives way to nostalgic sentiment, especially when he is discussing Virginia's past rather than her present. John Smith, for example, "was moulded in the richest fashion of ancient chivalry." If he had been of noble birth, Kennedy observes, "he would have been as distinguished in history as Bayard, Gaston de Foix, Sir Walter Manny, or any other of the mirrors of knighthood whose exploits have found a historian."[12]

The chapter entitled "Traces of the Feudal System," which contains a satiric portrait of Frank Meriwether as a lord of manor, also contains a perfectly straight account of the aristocratic ancestry of the Virginia planter. The aristocratic manners of the Virginian could be explained, Kennedy felt, by the position which Virginia had once held within the British Empire, and by the circumstances surrounding her settlement. She had been a favored colony, her population "consisted of gentlemen of good name and condition, who brought within her confines a solid fund of respectability and wealth"; her territory had once been more extensive than that of any other colony. The Virginian nevertheless soon outgrew his English ancestors. In Virginia the traditional spirit of English liberty had grown and expanded, making the Southern planter a more wholesome kind of aristocrat than his English equivalent, the country squire:

This race of men grew vigorous in her genial atmosphere; her cloudless skies quickened and enlivened their tempers, and, in two centuries, gradually matured the sober and thinking Englishman into that spirited, imaginative being who now inhabits the lowlands of this state.[13]

The flights of sentimentality and of nostalgia which punctuate *Swallow Barn* are not so much lapses as they might appear. It was Kennedy's method in his first book to mix comedy and sentiment in almost equal parts, as he himself noted in a later preface. He was very gingerly in asserting the chivalric parallel. "Our old friend Polonius," he wrote in 1851, "had nearly hit it in his rigmarole of 'pastoral-comical, tragical-comical-historical-pastoral.' "[14] His literary method involved him in a form of emotional Indian giving. He presented his readers with a flattering image of "feudal" Virginia and then withdrew it smilingly. He catered to the prevailing popularity of the chivalric romance and to the sentimental attachment that Americans had come to feel for the Middle Ages; he indulged them in their desire to see continuity between their own social world and the social world of Europe.

On the other hand, he carefully protected their sensitivity to invidious comparisons by assuring them that Virginia was, after all, superior.

The fact that Kennedy was the kind of literary eclectic which this description suggests probably explains, at least in part, the popularity of *Swallow Barn*. Nineteenth-century readers would have found many parallels between it and English books which they knew and admired. The fact that the novel was derivative would not have decreased their enjoyment. When American critics asserted that they wanted a literature different from that of England, most of them only half meant what they said. They did not want a literature which was totally new. American readers as a whole continued through the century to prefer European and English books to native writing. When they did read books by Americans, their own cultural insecurity led them to prefer those American books which bore some obvious similarity to the literature they were familiar with. Popular American writers, men like Cooper, Irving and Simms, owed much of their rather modest popularity to the successful adaptation of European literary conventions to the American scene. In *Swallow Barn* there was just enough which was familiar to make the book reassuringly literary, and there was just enough which was local and novel to make it American. This was not, however, the extent of its attractions.

The continued popularity of *Swallow Barn* owes something to a growing need—a need which was strongly felt in America as elsewhere—to sentimentalize country life. The uncertainty which Americans began to feel in the first half of the century about the general drift of their civilization led them to attach great significance to their pastoral setting. Americans like Webster, Sarah Hale and William Wirt who left the provinces to live in coastal cities were inclined to look upon provincial life as stable and untouched by progress. From the perspective of Baltimore, New York or Philadelphia, a Virginia plantation came to seem like a haven from the new and disruptive changes which they saw taking place around them. It was obvious from the beginning that *Swallow Barn* was a city man's somewhat patronizing argument for the parochialism of the country. At one point Mark Littleton exclaims, "You will never know your friend so well, nor enjoy him so heartily in the city as you may in one of those large, bountiful mansions, whose horizon is filled with green fields and woodland slopes and broad blue heavens. . . . There is a fascination in the quiet, irresponsible, and reckless nature of these country pursuits, that is apt to seize upon the imagination of a man who has felt the perplexities of business."[15]

As the years passed Kennedy himself became much more sentimental and less satirical about the kind of life he had described in *Swallow Barn*. In a revised edition, published in 1851, he softened the satire at many points,[16] and wrote a new preface in which he expressed his altered sentiments about the book he had written twenty years before. In his first literary effort, he noted, he had paid tribute to the "homebred customs, which are said to strengthen local attachments and expand them into a love of country." Since 1832, he felt, much of the old "raciness" had disappeared from manners in the Old Dominion. "Time and what is called 'the progress,' have made many innovations there, as they have done every where else." Gone or disappearing was the "mellow, bland, and sunny luxuriance of her old-time society— its good fellowship, its hearty and constitutional *companionableness*, the thriftless gayety of the people, their dogged but amiable invincibility of opinion, and that overflowing hospitality which knew no ebb."[17] In particular, he regretted the passing of the "insulated cast of manners" which had once characterized life in the American provinces. He felt that he detected a pale uniformity creeping into American life, a uniformity which was partly the result of modern technology and partly the result of aping European fashions. "What belonged to us as characteristically American, seems already to be dissolving into a mixture which affects us unpleasantly as a tame and cosmopolitan substitute for the old warmth and salient vivacity of our ancestors." What was missing, he concluded, was "something which belongs to us and to no one else."[18]

The sketches contained in *Swallow Barn* had, therefore, in the course of twenty years become historical. "They have already begun to assume the tints of a relic of the past, and may, in another generation, become archaeological, and sink into the chapter of antiquities."[19] Virginia in 1829 became for Kennedy what Virginia in 1765 had been for Wirt: a Good Society. The preservation of the values of such a society became for Kennedy as for Wirt a serious preoccupation. The temporal location of the Old South varied a good deal from elegist to elegist through the century, but no chronicler of the Old South, no matter how critical or mirthful he may have felt at the beginning, looked upon his subject as a joking matter for very long.

The Mythmaking Ethos

What, one wonders, had induced "Mark Littleton, Esq." to express such concern for the passing quaintness and distinctiveness of manners in the Old Dominion? Kennedy had no significant personal or ancestral ties to the Virginia Tidewater. He was hardly more of a Virginian than Paulding or Wirt. His father, John Kennedy, had immigrated to America from northern Ireland in the last quarter of the eighteenth century and established his residence in Maryland. His mother had been Nancy Pendleton of Martinsburg, in western Virginia; she was a member of a Virginia family of some distinction which had produced several prominent Revolutionary lawyers, among them Edmund Pendleton.[20] Until his bankruptcy in 1809, when John Kennedy had retired from active business, he had been a merchant in Baltimore. When Kennedy was fourteen, his family left Baltimore and moved to a farm in Jefferson County near Charles Town in what is now West Virginia. During the final years of John Kennedy's life, the family lived at the Pendleton plantation, "The Bower," near Martinsburg, also in Berkeley County. Kennedy himself remained behind in Baltimore to attend college, read law and finally, in 1816, to begin the practice of law. His knowledge of

Virginia was therefore gained from summer excursions when he set out on horseback like Mark Littleton, Esq., to visit his Virginia cousins, the Pendletons at "The Bower." When he came to make a book of these experiences, Kennedy moved "The Bower" to the Tidewater and changed the name of the plantation to "Swallow Barn." Otherwise he made few alterations. The Virginia which Kennedy knew was the western part, the Shenandoah Valley and the mountains. Many of the details from *Swallow Barn*—the hipped roof of the plantation house, the nearby German settlers— suggest its original valley location.

In Sarah Hale's scheme of things Kennedy was thus a merchant's son. There is little doubt that his life was considerably influenced by his father's business failure, which had forced the removal of the family from Baltimore to the country. Like Owen Ashley and other Hale heroes, Kennedy became the man whose life was "redeemed" by an exposure to vigorous and healthful provincial life. Kennedy's interest in Virginia had from the beginning a decidedly literary cast. He was inclined to patronize the Pendletons in the same way that Mark Littleton had patronized the Meriwethers, the Hazards and the Tracys. "The Bower" was for him a version of the pastoral; he went to Virginia, he said, to seek out the picturesque. He never felt entirely at home outside the city. As a young boy he had learned to ride on the family farm by taking "swearing work horses to water after a hard day's plowing."[21] He was always a little insecure when cast in the role of a Cavalier. During the summer excursions to "The Bower," he tried to enter into the sports of the Pendletons. He resolutely fished, hunted and rode horseback with his Virginia cousins, but his greatest delight was in the landscape. "But still I confess," he wrote in his autobiography, "that all these occupations were subordinate to the interest I took in the scenery, and the country life with which these amusements were connected. I was ever in the pursuit of the picturesque, and found more enjoyment in sketching a party of gunners or fishermen than in aiding them to take their prey."[22]

Kennedy's real interests and aspirations, however, centered in the city of Baltimore, where he made his life. Although he attended an academy and took a degree, at the age of eighteen, from an institution known as Baltimore College, his education was largely his own doing. Like emergent Yankees he was forced to make his own way in the world. He later described the program of study which he undertook in the small attic room where he lived in Baltimore. He gave himself a strenuous course in "how to become a gentleman before dawn."

I studied Greek a whole winter by rising before daylight; I read Locke, Hume, Robertson—all the essayists and poets, and many of the metaphysicians; studied Burke, Taylor, Barrow, worked at chemistry, geometry, and the higher mathematics, although I never loved them; made copious notes on all the subjects which came within my study; sketched, painted (very badly), read French, Spanish, and began German; copied large portions of Pope's translations from Homer, and wrote critical notes upon them as I went along; in short, I thoroughly overworked myself through a number of years in these pursuits, gaining much less advantage by the labor than, I am confident, I could have secured with better guidance in half the time.[23]

From this period of self-culture he emerged to become one of the city's first citizens. His name was as closely associated with Baltimore and with Maryland as that of any man of the period. He served his city, state and nation as a practicing attorney, a railroad promoter, a representative and speaker in the state legislature, a Congressman, and as an officer of several municipal and state institutions. He was twice appointed provost of the University of Maryland, and he was a founder and the first president of the Peabody Institute. His brother Anthony was a United States Senator from Maryland. Kennedy himself was offered, and refused, the nomination as governor of the state.

There was very little indeed about his social views and political activities which bore the stamp of John Randolph's form of Virginia particularism. The "right merry young lawyer" at whom Wirt had aimed rather sharp criticism was in Wirt's eyes

otherwise unexceptionable. He himself recommended him for
political preferment.[24] Kennedy never, even momentarily, deviated
from sentiments which were from the beginning Unionist and
nationalist. During the Civil War he gave his allegiance to the
Union. In 1860 he supported Everett and Bell; in 1864 he was for
Lincoln. In 1868 he enthusiastically supported General Grant and
advocated a policy of forgiveness toward the South.[25] He was associated with the Whig party throughout its existence and served
three terms as a Whig in Congress. He wrote a number of widely
circulated pamphlets and small books in behalf of his party, including a heavy-handed satire of Jacksonian Democracy, *Quod
libet*, and an attack on Tyler for his apostasy, *A Defense of the
Whigs*. On one occasion his literary labors brought him the personal thanks of Henry Clay.[26] After 1830 he became a friend of
Clay's and a forceful spokesman for his American Plan. Throughout his political career Kennedy was known as a warm supporter
of internal improvements, the protective tariff and other measures
favorable to commercial and manufacturing interests. Daniel
Webster was sufficiently impressed with his abilities to request his
services in 1840 as Assistant to the Secretary of State. Twelve
years later, in 1852, President Millard Fillmore appointed him to
his cabinet as Secretary of the Navy.

Kennedy may have courted in fancy some distant Virginia
cousin who resembled his heroine, Bel Tracy, but his heart remained loyal to the city of Baltimore. There is little question
that he thought of marriage as a means of social advancement.
In both of his two marriages he allied himself, like Wirt before
him, with the so-called merchant-class. Soon after he began to
practice law, Kennedy began to frequent the house of William
Pinkney, who was Baltimore's leading lawyer, and he was engaged
for a time to one of Pinkney's daughters. After this engagement
was broken off, he married Mary Tennant, the daughter of a
prominent Baltimore merchant, who died in childbirth within a
year. Five years later, in 1829, he married Elizabeth Gray, the
daughter of an enterprising Irish textile manufacturer named

Edward Gray who owned a large mill on the Patapsco River near Baltimore. After the death of his father-in-law in 1856, Kennedy directed the Gray estate and assumed the management of the mill.[27]

Kennedy did not have to improvise step by step the movements of his life. There were models for him to follow and he was well aware of them. Other men had come out of the provinces and edged their way up through the practice of law and through happy alliances by marriage. It would be wrong, of course, to imply that Kennedy or any of the others whose lives fell within the pattern of the emergent Yankee proceeded by deliberate calculation. They did, in fact, what came naturally. They aimed high, worked hard and married cautiously and well. To a young man convinced of his ability it would have seemed ridiculous to do anything else. Few things could have been more obvious to Kennedy than the fluidity and mobility of the social world about him. His father had become a bankrupt. His father-in-law, Edward Gray, on the other hand, had walked onto the pier in Philadelphia one day in the seventeen nineties, penniless and still in Irish homespun. In thirty years he had worked his way to the top of the mercantile and manufacturing world of Baltimore, despite several almost disastrous economic misadventures.[28]

The exploration of the past presented Kennedy with problems which were as much personal as they were social or political. Men of such different origins as Paulding, Wirt and Kennedy himself found it necessary as they assumed places of importance in American life to dispose of their own cultural heritage in some fashion. They were inclined to identify themselves with Americans of English ancestry. As Kennedy once candidly observed, "There is not a man in the world who cannot make out a pedigree."[29] Sarah Hale was inclined to forget that her maiden name was Sarah Buell, there was always some confusion about the national origin of Hugh Swinton Legaré and Paulding's son went so far as to deny the family's Dutch ancestry. William Wirt in 1833 seemed quite unaware of his ancestral connections with the

Württemberg Germans, whom he alternately patronized as "simple-hearted" and scorned as "cattle." This was not a form of deceit, nor was it peculiar to these men. Every American was forced to refashion his cultural heritage to some extent. Kennedy was hardly different in this respect from his contemporaries. In his speeches and addresses he talked of Saxon ancestry, discoursed on the manners of the Old Dominion and reminisced about Cavalier Maryland as though the Kennedys had settled Jamestown or arrived with the first party in St. Mary's. Nevertheless, when Kennedy's Scotch-Irish consciousness was not altogether muted, and when he wrote from the deeper levels of his imagination, the complexity of his cultural heritage found forceful expression.

The Cult of Chivalry and the New Immigration

The two cultural strains which commingled in Kennedy's consciousness—"Cavalier" Pendleton and mysterious Scot, the old immigration and the new—work dialectically in his most important historical fiction, the novel *Horse-Shoe Robinson*. What emerges from this dialectic is an expression of national consciousness which had a very wide appeal among Kennedy's contemporaries. While at work on *Horse-Shoe Robinson*, he was living in William Wirt's house in Mount Vernon Place. He occupied his days as a railroad promoter, doing now and then a little legal work, and spent his evenings writing historical romance.[30] He was dividing his energies as before between the past and the future. The book appeared in the early summer of 1835 with the full title *Horse Shoe Robinson, a Tale of the Tory Ascendency. By the Author of 'Swallow Barn.'* It was dedicated to Kennedy's friend and fellow author, Washington Irving, himself a kind of mysterious Scot.[31] In a brief note to the reader Kennedy observed that the search for traditions in the American Revolution had begun "in good earnest." Fifty years had passed, he noted, since the events he was about to describe had occurred, "that being deemed the fair poetical limit which converts tradition into truth, and takes away all right of contradiction from a surviving actor in the scene."[32]

The historical circumstances into which Kennedy projects his leading character serve as little more than a backdrop. The events of the story take place in Virginia and the Carolinas during the dark months of 1780 when the British are besieging Charleston and the Tories appear to have the upper hand throughout the South. The novel begins in July of that year, when Brevet Major Arthur Butler of the Continental army secretly visits his wife, Mildred Lindsay, near her Loyalist father's home in western Virginia. Butler is on his way south on a secret mission to help raise the siege of Charleston and turn the tide of battle against the British. The novel ends with the Patriot victory at King's Mountain in the fall of the same year.

In the course of the story Butler journeys south, is captured in South Carolina, escapes, is recaptured and almost executed, and is finally freed at the concluding battle at King's Mountain. Throughout these adventures Butler is accompanied and served adroitly by a famous soldier, Sergeant Galbraith "Horse-Shoe" Robinson. The emphasis of the narrative falls on the characters of the two Whig soldiers, one of them a South Carolina gentleman planter, the other a yeoman-blacksmith from the Virginia mountains. It is the latter, of course, who finally provides the principal interest of the story and gives the novel its name. Major Arthur Butler is useful to Kennedy chiefly as a foil for exhibiting the resourcefulness, soldierly virtuosity and high moral qualities of Butler's "squire," Horse-Shoe Robinson.

Poe, who reviewed the novel for the *Southern Literary Messenger*,[33] was quick to appreciate the boldness of Kennedy's innovation. By all standards of polite fiction, Poe noted, Butler, not Horse-Shoe, would have been made the central figure, the hero, of the novel. Butler is regarded throughout the story as Horse-Shoe's social superior and Butler, of course, "gets" the heroine at the end of the book. "But Mr. K.," Poe remarked with approval, "has ventured, at his own peril, to set at defiance the common ideas of propriety in this important matter."[34] Poe had forgotten, or chose not to mention, Cooper's quite similar innovation in *The Spy*. In any case, Horse-Shoe Robinson, like Cooper's hero, makes the novel his own, and, despite his Southern origin, emerges as a transcendent Yankee in many ways similar to Harvey Birch. Major Butler, furthermore, shares many qualities with young Henry Wharton, the official hero of Cooper's *The Spy*.

At first glance Horse-Shoe Robinson seems in most respects Butler's opposite. He is a yeoman. He is rough and good humored in his manner, and he speaks a curious dialect—saying "mought" for "might," "sarvices" for "services" and "incarnivorous" for "carnivorous." In the matter of wearing a disguise, he is as resourceful a chameleon as Harvey Birch. At various points he plays a buffoon, a genial Tory irregular, and the part of the formidable and diabolical Jack O'Lantern, a mysterious and almost superhuman night raider. Even Butler is occasionally unable to detect his disguise. The Tories describe him as a man "as big as a horse" and associate him with the devil. Horse-Shoe himself exclaims at one point: "My name is Brimstone, I am first cousin to Belzebub."[35] As his name suggests, he is closely associated with fire. He compares himself to a malleable piece of iron. When he expresses his ideals to a fellow patriot, he apologizes for his appearance by observing:

You mought hardly expect to find much thought of such things left in a rough fellow like me, that's been hammered in these here wars like an old piece of iron that's been one while a plough coulter, and after that a gun-barrel, and finally that's been run up with others into a piece of ordnance—not to say that it moughtn't have been a horse shoe in some part of its life, ha! ha! ha! There's not likely to be much conscience or religion left after all that hammering.[36]

He is, of course, understating his moral qualities, which are stressed all along. Like Harvey Birch, he only seems to be without conscience and religion, and Kennedy does not mean to have the reader take him at his word.

Horse-Shoe and Harvey Birch are not, however, in every way similar. One important difference between them underlines the fact that *The Spy* is a Northern book and *Horse-Shoe Robinson* is a Southern book. Despite his attention to Captain Jack Lawton and the Virginia dragoons, Cooper was not fundamentally interested in exploring the soldierly qualities of his characters in *The Spy*; he showed very little interest in the military aspects of the Revolution. Harvey Birch had been sickened by the cruelty and bloodshed of partisan warfare. The quality which he is revealed to have and which he is implied to share with General Washington is the quality of disinterestedness. He is above acquisitiveness. Like the Honorable Daniel Webster he is cool and peaceable. He is a gentleman of honor, not a chivalrous knight. The concept of chivalry, however, finds a very prominent place in *Horse-Shoe Robinson*. In his second book, Kennedy was not always jesting when he referred to knights and ladies and the gentlemanly code of honor. He teased young Henry Lindsay for his chivalric pretensions (Henry compares himself to Coriolanus) just as he had teased Bel Tracy in *Swallow Barn*; but he clearly, in all earnestness, thought of Arthur Butler as a knight-errant and of Horse-Shoe as his squire.

The soldierly qualities of Horse-Shoe are apparent from the first. He is given the military title of "sergeant." He is a mounted soldier, not a peddler on foot. He uses his saber as cleverly as he uses his tongue. Horse-Shoe is also capable of taking vengeance when he has the Tory irregulars at bay:

"Cut them down," cried Horse-Shoe, "without marcy! remember the Waxhaws!" And he accompanied his exhortation with the most vehement and decisive action, striking down, with a huge sabre, all who opposed his way.[37]

When one of the irregulars pleads with Horse-Shoe for mercy he gets an un-Birchlike reply:

"You get no quarter from me, you cursed blood-lapper!" exclaimed Horse-Shoe, excited to a rage that seldom visited his breast; "think of Grindall's Ford!" and at the same instant he struck a heavy downward blow, with such sheer descent, that it clove the skull of the perfidious freebooter clean through to the spine.[38]

The rough and merciless soldier is, however, simply Horse-Shoe's surface character. He, like Harvey, transcends his appearance. Harvey becomes a disinterested gentleman like General Washington; Horse-Shoe a knight-errant like Arthur Butler. When Horse-Shoe sets off for "Dove Cote" to bring the news of Butler's capture, Kennedy comments that "he rode forth with as stout a heart as ever went with knight of chivalry to the field of romantic renown."[39] If Horse-Shoe can more than hold his own with the wild and ruthless back-country Tories of the South—one of them skins a wolf alive—he can also hold his own with Arthur Butler. He conducts Mildred, young Lindsay's sister, from Virginia into South Carolina *"sans peur et sans reproche."* Horse-Shoe is the Southern Yeoman become Chevalier Bayard; he is the wild Scot become gentleman warrior. Horse-Shoe Robinson is to the South what Harvey Birch was to the North: a defensive fiction. Harvey was a triumph over predatory greed. Horse-Shoe was a triumph over back-country brutality. Each in his own way held American wildness at bay. Horse-Shoe's superiority to Butler lay in the fact that he belonged to the American present and future, while Butler took his gentlemanly social values from the European chivalric past. Horse-Shoe was a Scotch-Irishman's symbol of hope; Arthur Butler was a part-Englishman's idea of a conventional gentleman. Horse-Shoe accommodated to the American present those qualities which Kennedy admired in his Pendleton ancestors; he promised to carry these qualities into the future. He was a mounted knight with his feet on native ground, a Cavalier who could shoe, as well as ride, a horse.

Horse-Shoe, like Cooper's Harvey Birch, was of obscure origin and uncertain social status. Like Harvey Birch, he was a kind of transcendent Yankee: he pursued the object of his quest as though that object were money. He was a hard-boiled idealist; he knew how to disguise his high purpose beneath a convincing veneer of craft and guile. He could handle himself in the present in a way the Cavalier could not. When difficulties arose, he knew what to do to get himself and his gentleman companion out of a scrape. Gentleman Cavalier and Transcendent Yankee, aristocrat and yeoman, were, in fact, virtual twins. Either was incomplete without the other. Together they made the world of American fiction go round. Placed together in the past, they over and over again performed a ritual of national survival. The pathfinder, the transcendent Yankee, taught his genteel companion the art of overcoming both savagery and civilization, both wilderness and Europe. He was equally clever at reading natural signs in the forest and fathoming the sophisticated strategies of a European enemy. He was always in some sense a "spy." Although the gentleman Cavalier was always placed above him in the social world of American fiction, works of fiction in which he found a place were always primarily about *him*. He stood for what the American gentleman needed, what he lacked. In the drama of national character, he was a natural force, an indigenous residue of strength.

John Pendleton Kennedy might jest about his Kennedy forebears, call them cattle thieves and barn burners, but he created in the character of Galbraith "Horse-Shoe" Robinson a mysterious Scot who could rob, steal, fight and burn, and still be a kind of Cavalier. At the end of the novel Horse-Shoe even displays a democratic version of the Southern gentleman's characteristic habit of command. He steps in to prevent a group of Patriot irregulars from lynching a fierce and treacherous Tory back countryman whom they have captured. " 'Friends,' said Horse-Shoe calmly to the multitude, 'there is better game to hunt than this mountain-cat. Let me have my way.' " He carries the day. " 'None has a better right than Horse-Shoe Robinson,' said a speaker for the group, 'to say what ought to be done.' "[40] Even his name contained suggestions of English (Robinson) and Scottish

(Galbraith) origin. In the words of a contemporary critic, he was "One of nature's true noblemen, a self-devoted champion of freedom, full of resources in perilous times and with as much prudent foresight and practical wisdom as native courage and benign sympathy." Although "he yet made a sad havoc with the King's English, could not sign his name" and was "destitute of all clerkly arts," he "had the soul of a true cavalier."[41] Kennedy could hardly have been aware of the source of his pride in Galbraith Robinson. Edgar Allan Poe and William Gilmore Simms, both, like Kennedy, of Scotch-Irish and English ancestry, responded sympathetically, but neither, try as he would, was able to put his finger on exactly what attracted him to the character of Horse-Shoe.[42] Horse-Shoe was finally a convincing embodiment of male effectiveness as well as an expressive amalgam of the mixed cultural ingredients which Kennedy and many of his contemporaries contained unreconciled within their own consciousness, a mixture of hope and memory, but also a mixture of shame and pride.

Literature and Aspiration

The first issue of the *Southern Literary Messenger*, which appeared in August of 1834, was prefaced by testimonials from six "prominent Americans," who wished the new literary venture Godspeed: Kennedy, Irving, Paulding, Cooper, John Quincy Adams and a man now forgotten, Peter A. Browne,[43] all welcomed the prospect of a purely literary magazine in the South. Three years after he had begun to write, Kennedy thus became a spokesman for the profession of letters. On the basis of *Swallow Barn* alone, he had reached a kind of literary eminence. The publication of *Horse-Shoe Robinson* a year later brought him something close to critical acclaim, although his financial rewards were indeed modest.[44] After 1835 he devoted his energies increasingly to politics, pamphleteering and various civic undertakings. He became a publicist for the Whig party, a memorialist, a lecturer and a man of letters of a sort, but—except for his last and unsuccessful historical romance—he was never afterward primarily a writer. Whatever it was that took him off to his study night after night to compose works of fiction left him on the threshold of public life. Whatever he had wanted from the career of literature he had apparently got—or despaired of getting. After the publication of his last novel in 1838, he lived for another thirty-two years without writing another book which was not in some sense topical. His literary apprenticeship was hardly at an end before he abandoned literature altogether.

For Kennedy, as for so many Southerners who seem for a time to have pursued a literary career, literature was not an end in itself. His own activity as a creative writer, like that of the others, was very brief—in his case a bare seven years. For these men authorship marked the final stage in a long and difficult course of self-cultivation and signified to them and to their contemporaries that they had attained gentility, that they had in some sense "arrived"; but it was more than this. Most immediately, of course, writing brought them to public attention and earned them a place of respect in the community, but their writing, at its best, provided them with a means of dealing with the problem of their American identity and with an opportunity to lay the complex ghost of their cultural heritage. Even at its worst, their writing expressed their need to discover an alternate set of values which would provide them with some perspective toward their own times, toward the Puritan-Yankee-utilitarian present, the syndrome of values which they referred to as "the Progress."

The strategy of procedure was to admire what you were not. Protestant John Kennedy sentimentalized Catholicism, parvenu John Kennedy idolized the established Baltimore. Finally, of course, aristocratic and Catholic Old Maryland, the subject of Kennedy's last—and least successful—novel, *Rob of the Bowl*, was hardly more believable than the aristocratic and Catholic South Carolina which Sarah Hale had created for Horace Brainard and Sidney Romilly. The difficulty with such a fiction was not that one soon ran short of imaginative materials in which to embody it; the story of the antipode South could be told over and over—and it was. The deficiency was in the imaginative terms through which it was expressed. The scene of action could shift from century to century, from rebellion to rebellion, from Virginia to South Carolina, without escaping from the inevitable repetition imposed on the past by such a limited point of view. The difficulty lay in the growing inclination to see in the past what could not be found in the present: because polite manners seemed threatened, one saw them as flourishing in the past; because Protestantism dominated the present and seemed fanatic and narrow, one regarded the past as Catholic and Catholicism as tolerant and reasonable; because a driving ambition to succeed seemed to possess contemporary Americans, one imagined a past in which men were motivated by purity of heart and chivalric honor. Writers came to believe in their own fictions. Old South and new South, chivalric South and Yankee South, became confused and indistinct. Kennedy moved from Baltimore to the Gray estate on the Patapsco in 1856 to live as a country gentleman. He was himself shocked and outraged to learn of the unchivalric atrocities committed by Confederate soldiers during the Civil War.[45]

Protestant, acquisitive America never made satisfactory contact with a Catholic, chivalric past, but the effort to establish such contact, the search for materials, the groping for adequate terms nevertheless went on. Kennedy himself never tried again. In the last paragraph of *Rob of the Bowl* he spoke hopefully of sometime looking "again into the little city"[46] of St. Mary's, but he died in 1870 with his sequel unwritten and his aspirations of many years before no doubt forgotten.

CHAPTER VI

The Promised Land

Shall it be said in after-times that the descendants of the
noble Cavaliers and gentlemen, who conquered and re-
claimed this country, had become so degenerate as to
suffer this great inheritance to pass from us? Oh, never
let it be said! Gird on your armor, Virginians, and follow
me at least to the mountain's brow! Take one glance over
those hitherto impregnable barriers, the great Appalachee,
and I will show you a finer country than that promised
land which Moses beheld, but never reached. . . . Shake off
the lethargy which oppresses you, and go with me to this
great, this boundless country—this future seat of empires.

WILLIAM A. CARUTHERS, *The Knights of
The Horseshoe*[1]

THOSE NOVELS WHICH give expression to the racial theories of the
Old South, the reiterated appeals to an English ancestry (even
by those without one) and the Cavalier ethos of war and honor
best embody the aspirations and the sense of destiny of Southern
society as a whole. These themes originate in thinking of a kind
similar to Kennedy's and among men vexed by many of the same
problems which concerned the other plantation novelists. Pre-
eminent among these problems was the failure of the seaboard
South, and especially Virginia, to hold its own in power and pres-

tige as the century advanced. Many Southerners like Kennedy, however, tended to abandon the Cavalier ideal and sought the explanation for decline in the waning vitality of the old English stock as symbolized by the planter-aristocrat. For them the future of the South lay in its yeomanry, in which they themselves as successful exemplars of the new immigration came passionately to believe. For them, too, the decline of the Cavalier became curiously associated with their own personal success and their own arrival at a new kind of republican gentility and democratic nationalism. For still others, however, the decline of the eastern South became identified with personal failure and frustration, as it had for the Southern Mugwumps. As a result, their own rationalization of what they saw occurring pursued a different line, and they sought to solve their historical predicament, finally almost in defiance of reality, by propounding a magnificent dream of expansive vitality and racial purity in which Cavalier ideals were to be carried west into a beckoning future of empire and domination. Like contemporary revivalists they exhorted the backsliding South to return to the altars of ancestral and racial piety.

No explanation for the decline of the seaboard South had greater and more sustained appeal than the idea of a dynamic, expanding South, racially and culturally homogeneous, spreading across the mountains and out toward the fertile Mississippi delta and extending itself on into Mexico and even down into the tropics. Expansionism, to be sure, was an obsession which gripped the imagination of Americans in general and found its advocates in the North, some of its most articulate advocates, in fact; but nowhere were Americans so willing to fight, live and die for the idea as in the Southern states. Southerners filled the rolls and commanded the armies which fought the Mexican War, and Southerners appeared to be willing to undertake a filibustering expedition at the drop of a hat.[2]

The concern with a dynamic, expanding South no doubt owed some of its appeal to the hope of extending the institution of slavery and bolstering the proslavery forces in Congress, but its

appeal was finally more generalized than this and found many supporters among Southerners whose interest in extending slavery
was at the time marginal at most. Much of the appeal lay in the
general conception of a separate and preferable Southern destiny,
a destiny not in pursuit of the main chance, as in the North, but
rather in pursuit of some elusive ideal, always couched in para-
doxical language. "A warrior race," asserted the *Southern Quarterly Review*,

will found an empire, illustrious in arms, as renowned in arts, and
show the Cavalier blood to be still worthy of its Norman origin. Its
empire will be peace; but the sword will share the supremacy of
the spade, the rudder and distaff, and make the camp contribute no
less to the national glory than the forum and the senate.[3]

Other spokesmen called for a great democratic monarchy, a
republican empire—some form of transcendent and beneficent
conquest, like the pursuit of the Holy Grail. It was an undertaking fit for a knight.

A Scotch-Irishman Takes Stock

In March of 1846 the Virginia novelist, William Alexander
Caruthers, wrote from Savannah, where he was then living, to a
friend in Virginia who had established a certain reputation as a
historian and antiquary. Caruthers' literary production had virtually come to a halt five years before with the magazine publication
of his last important novel, *The Knights of the Horseshoe*. He had
meanwhile toyed with one or two further ideas which had come
to nothing, and he now felt hard put to it. He was committed, he
said, to writing two tales before the end of the summer, and he
found himself without the resources for doing so. "Will you, my
dear sir," he wrote, "furnish me with some old tradition upon
which I can weave a story, and the localities if necessary. I know
your head is full of them." As an afterthought he added: "I am

sadly in want of the old anterevolutionary names of Virginia. I wish you would give me a dozen or two aristocratic, as well as plebian [sic], but especially the latter." The friend, Charles Campbell, obligingly responded with a long list of names and the suggestion that Caruthers spin a romance about the colorful life of Edward Teach, known as "Blackbeard the Pirate," whose career had been terminated by Governor Spotswood in 1718. Caruthers answered Campbell, thanking him for the names but expressing doubts about the idea. "I have no turn whatever for the Jack Shepherd[4] school of novels. I want the family and fireside traditions of the Old Dominion."[5]

Caruthers, already ill with tuberculosis, did not live to weave another story around an old Virginia tradition. He died at the end of the summer at Marietta in the mountains of Georgia, at forty-four. His long silence and the thematic repetitiousness of his writing make it seem likely, however, that he had said his say and that his imagination had spun itself out in the novels and assorted sketches and essays which he left behind him.[6] Much of what Caruthers had to say bears a certain easily recognized resemblance to the writings of other Virginians of the period. Like Kennedy and like Wirt earlier, he had begun with a contemporary study of Southern manners and then plunged himself into Virginia's colonial past.

Almost nothing in Caruthers' background at first glance seemed to destine him to become a "Chronicler of the Cavaliers," as his biographer has called him. Born in a part of the Shenandoah Valley which was "as completely Scotch-Irish as though it were located in Ulster,"[7] reared in a merchant's family in Lexington, trained as a physician in Philadelphia and long a resident of New York City, he could scarcely have had less contact with the cultural heritage he examined in his novels. The Blue Ridge at Lexington formed an almost impassable barrier which restricted communication with the counties of the Piedmont and Tidewater, and Lexington had been content to do its business up and down the prosperous valley floor along the route which the

Carutherses had taken after their arrival in Philadelphia early in the preceding century. They were part of the wave of Scotch-Irish immigration which had brought the Calhouns, Petigrus (then spelled Pettygrew) and Simmses to South Carolina and the Kennedys to Maryland. His mother's family, the Alexanders, who had come to America at the same time, had been closely identified with the Presbyterian Church and an uncle, Archibald Alexander, had been the first professor of theology at the College of New Jersey, for many years the intellectual center of Scotch-Irish America.[8]

Yet his imagination leapt the mountain barrier and roamed the older parts of Virginia, even if he personally did not. A hankering for the gentleman's culture seized him as a young man, and his adoption of what he took to be a gentleman's style of life was the cause of his financial ruin. In 1823 he married the daughter of a wealthy sea-island cotton planter and added her dowry of seventy-nine Negro slaves to his already sizable fortune. He then settled down in Lexington, ostensibly to practice medicine, although at no time, either there or in New York or afterward in Savannah, did he practice with much success. Meanwhile, he bought a house to which he soon added "a three-story Piassa with white Pillars" and other appurtenances of a Tidewater mansion and commenced to offer entertainment on a grand scale. In six years he managed somehow to run through his own fortune and that of his wife and encumber himself with debts he was never able to pay. Paulding's Cuthbert Dangerfield could not have spent his patrimony with more abandon. Finally, in 1829, he took an oath of insolvency and moved himself and his family to New York City.[9]

Caruthers, for all his pretensions to Cavalier gentility, never succeeded in fully shaking his Scotch-Irish heritage, although his estimate of Cavalier culture rose as his worldly prospects diminished. In his own mind there appears to have been a close association between gentility and failure. His financial ineptitude was legendary among members of his family. As his own profes-

sional failure grew more apparent, he was early compelled to resort to the improvisations of the shabby genteel. At the same time
he came to condemn in himself the Cavalier qualities which he felt
had unfitted him for American life. He created for himself out
of his Scotch-Presbyterian background a counterimage of a
different kind of American whom he identified historically with
New England, Puritanism, male effectiveness and heroic self-
control.

These two character types are played off one against the other
throughout much of his fiction. Neither was altogether a model
to him and, for a time at least, he sought to combine in his
heroes the best qualities of both. The central figures in his fiction
are none of them content to settle back into the static world of
the plantation legend. Each of them is some kind of rebel against
his society and his time, and each is endowed with a prophetic
compulsion which drives him to seek some elusive ideal of national greatness. Each, like Wirt's Patrick Henry, disguises his
personal ambition behind a façade of providential necessity. His
Daniel Boone, his Nathaniel Bacon and his Alexander Spotswood
are all cast as visionaries whose concern is with the democratic
future of the country rather than with the aristocratic past.
Caruthers injected only enough nostalgia into the narrative of
events to suggest his personal regret for the passing of the more
spacious and decorous social world which he imagined as having
once existed on the other side of the Blue Ridge.

The move to New York, which was made in the winter of
1829, was intended to be a fresh start, but by 1832 he was again
in financial straits: his rent was unpaid, and he was under pressure
from both New York and Lexington creditors. At about this time
Caruthers commenced the activities which were to bring him a
kind of prominence during his life. He began to make himself
into a man of letters. This was not entirely a new departure.
While he lived in Lexington he had made regular use of the books
owned by the Washington Literary Society and the Franklin
Society, to both of which he belonged. To judge from the record

of his withdrawals, he spent much of his time in Lexington reading the standard English authors, although he exhibited a strong preference for Scott, Byron and, in an English translation, Cervantes. Among the books which he withdrew during his final months was Cooper's *The Spy,* which he apparently raced through in three days.[10]

Whigs and Harmony

Sometime in 1834 *The Kentuckian in New York, or The Adventures of Three Southerns* "by a Virginian" was issued by Harper. Even among literary nationalists the novel was not acclaimed. *The Kentuckian* is nonetheless an interesting failure. In his effort to win a place for himself in the chaotic world of early American letters, Caruthers had taken no chances and included a little of everything. To the melodramatic plot of a beautiful young woman mysteriously pursued, he added accounts of American manners, North, South and West. The novel, which borrowed extensively from a popular play by Paulding,[11] tells of a trip to New York City by two young South Carolinians and contains their letters to a friend in Virginia. The rest of the book is devoted to the Virginian's description of a journey to South Carolina.

In the course of their journey the two South Carolinians, Victor Chevillere and Augustus Lamar, fall in with "an American Yeoman of the West," a Kentucky drover named Montgomery Damon, whose comic naïveté and colorful high jinks provide some of the story's better moments. With his two-story hat, homemade clothes and bandanna, and his vernacular commentary on city life, Damon exhibits the full range of Western eccentricity. His prominence is not, however, what the title might suggest. Most of the novel is given over to Chevillere's reflections on life in a Northern city and to the Virginian's reflections on the lower South.

Victor Chevillere is a Whig archetype. While Caruthers lived in Lexington he had nominally allied himself with "that large and intellectual party" which later "assumed the appellation of Whig." When he moved to Savannah some years later he was actively engaged in politics and twice held local office as a Whig.[12] In the novel Chevillere is a mouthpiece for Caruthers' Whiggish social views. He speaks for nationalism, harmony between the sections and personal moderation and self-control. When Lamar criticizes some riotous young men and calls them Yankees, Chevillere scolds him for his sectionalism. "The mutual jealousy of the North and South," he continues, "is a decided evidence of littleness in both regions, and ample cause for shame to the educated gentlemen of all parties of this happy country."[13] When the Virginian, whose name incidentally is Randolph, writes to Chevillere that he "hates Yankees," Chevillere replies by reminding him that the term Yankee is relative and that in Paris or London he too would be called a Yankee. Cities, commerce and competition make the Yankee what he is, he remarks. Southerners, furthermore, can learn something from the Yankee, just as they can learn something from the industrious and prosperous yeoman of their own back country.

At this point Caruthers, characteristically, thought of the American character in mediating terms. No region, he felt, contained the perfect American. North, South and West, Roundhead, Cavalier and Kentuckian, all have something to contribute to a stable American character. The weakness of Northern civilization, he felt, was to be found in its mercenary values, its impersonality and the moral degeneration of its cities.[14] The weakness of Southern society was the financial ineptitude, indolence and self-indulgence of the traditional gentleman planter. Both societies, finally, had much to learn from the self-sufficient and vigorous Western yeoman, who in turn could do with a little civilizing from the East.

Nonetheless, Chevillere, not Damon, is Caruthers' recipe for a stable American character. Damon's provincialism, his vernacular speech and his "ludicrous fancies" destine him to the social status of a menial and to the dramatic role of a clown. Lamar, with his taste for brandy, cigars and dueling, is the typical Southern hothead; Chevillere and Randolph come to represent, respectively, the Thoughtful South Carolinian and the Thoughtful Virginian. Chevillere's greatest virtue is his self-control. He neither drinks nor smokes. He strongly opposes the custom of dueling, as did Caruthers himself. Meanwhile, from South Carolina, Randolph was writing that there was no yeomanry, that slaves were harshly treated and that "the seeds of decay are sown" all about.[15]

The image of life in the Old South provided by Caruthers in his first novel is not very surprising. Mostly he wished to convey the lack of vitality in the South. Randolph finds the Tidewater counties of his own state worn-out and their occupants decadent and living on memory. The vigorous stock of the Southern states, he concludes, has already pulled up stakes and headed west toward the country of Montgomery Damon. What Caruthers had seen in his excursions through Virginia and down the Southern seaboard to Savannah was precisely what innumerable observant Southerners had noted before the century had progressed very far: evidence of social decline. In his first novel he had formulated a means of expressing what comes very close to being *the* Southern problem of these years, and virtually all of his subsequent writing was directed to explaining the problem and examining some of its terms in historical perspective.

Yankee and Cavalier

Caruthers' next literary venture, which followed *The Kentuckian* by a matter of months, took him into the very center of the historical legend, to the myth of the colonial origins of the American people and to an investigation of the key terms, Cavalier and Roundhead. Sometime late in 1834 Harper issued *The Cavaliers of Virginia, or The Recluse of Jamestown. An Historical*

Romance of the Old Dominion as part of its "Library of Select Novels." *The Cavaliers* is set in Virginia in the third quarter of the seventeenth century. Its action is concentrated in 1676, the year of Bacon's Rebellion, and its plot is concerned with the efforts of Nathaniel Bacon, the novel's hero, to protect the Virginia frontier from the attacks of hostile Indian tribes. Because of the vacillating policies and ultimate reluctance of the colonial governor, Sir William Berkeley, to take decisive action, Bacon is forced to act independently, and his hastily assembled "People's Army" eventually wins a definitive victory over the Indians near the future site of Richmond. Bacon then returns to defeat the forces of the irate governor and, finally, to burn Jamestown. The military skirmishes with which the novel abounds are interwoven with another plot which concerns the personal efforts of Bacon, whom Caruthers makes an orphan, to establish his identity and to win the Fairfax family's consent to marry their daughter Virginia, the novel's heroine.

As historical sources Caruthers used John Daly Burk's *History of Virginia* and several other books, the facts of which he greatly elaborated.[16] An occasional footnote which reads "Historical" or "see Burk" suggests a certain concern with authenticity, but Caruthers freely admitted that he "had intentionally transposed the historical order of events" and made other changes demanded by the conventions of the romance.[17] He had, for example, made Bacon single and eligible when he was in fact married, and he had ended the novel with the intimation that Bacon and Virginia would "live happily ever after" when Bacon actually died within the year. He also introduced a mysterious Recluse, who is later revealed to be General Edward Whalley, one of the three regicide judges of Charles I. The Recluse, who is of giant size and almost superhuman capacities, plays a central part in the story, as the subtitle suggests. He rescues Bacon from a number of scrapes and in the battle scenes performs as a Roundhead superman. He represents one of the social poles in the novel. At the other extreme is Governor Berkeley, who is portrayed by Caruthers as a typical Cavalier gentleman.

Bacon is seen in relation to these two men and the values which they represent. The Recluse is a solitary figure, like Harvey Birch, who lives in almost monastic seclusion in a hidden cavern outside of Jamestown. His movements are as mysterious, his appearances and disappearances as sudden, as those of Harvey. In other ways, too, the Recluse is the very image of the transcendent Yankee. He is characterized by his almost priestlike detachment and disinterestedness. (Both Bacon and Virginia Fairfax call him "Father" when they converse with him.) He is also distinguished by an extraordinary combination of self-control and zeal. "The expression of his countenance," Caruthers remarks, "was decidedly intellectual; and about the lower part of his face there were some indications of a disposition to sensuality, but tempered and controlled in no ordinary degree by some other fierce and controlling passion."[18] Berkeley, by contrast, is always seen in the midst of his courtly retinue, never alone. He is the leader of the Cavalier party, whom Caruthers describes as "the first founders of the aristocracy which prevails in Virginia to this day . . . the immediate ancestors of that generous, fox-hunting, wine-drinking, duelling and reckless race of men, which gives so distinct a character to Virginians wherever they may be found."[19] Berkeley stands for unswerving loyalty to the King, for a hierarchical society and the arranged marriage—in other words, for European social rigidity and courtly decadence.

Caruthers rigged the historical stage on which he placed his characters so as to make the Old Dominion, like Cooper's Westchester in *The Spy*, a neutral ground over which the component forces of national character might skirmish to some issue. Virginia becomes America in microcosm. Just as Cooper had imported a troop of Virginia dragoons and other Southern characters to round out his *dramatis personae*, Caruthers, on slender evidence, undertook to settle Virginia with enough Roundheads, Cromwellian veterans and the like to create serious cleavage in the colony, which was, he reported, "alternately subjected to the sway of the Roundheads and Royalists."[20] There is no historical basis whatsoever for bringing General Whalley to Virginia from

New England, where he is thought to have remained in hiding until his death about 1675. Caruthers, who read Whalley's story in a book by a president of Yale, apparently felt the need to introduce a figure of romance from out of Yankee folklore.[21]

The extremes of both Roundhead and Cavalier character are constantly criticized and satirized. The Cavalier courtiers, Frank Beverley and Philip Ludwell, are scheming, cowardly and dissolute "after the corrupt fashions of the parent court and country." The Cromwellian veterans who compose the insurgent forces of the Roundhead party are portrayed as self-righteous, contentious and socially irresponsible, "the most desperate, reckless and restless of the republicans who . . . had fled to Jamestown after the restoration."[22] Ananias Proudfit, the spokesman of the rebels, is broadly satirized when he attempts to speak for the Roundhead cause in a pastiche of Biblical jargon:

"Here am I," said a short black-visaged thick-set man. "Here am I, Ananias Proudfit, whom the Lord hath commissioned this night to take away the wicked from the land, and to root out the Amalekite, and the Jebusite, and the Perizzite, and the Hittite, and the Girgashite and the Amorite. And are not this council and this wicked Governor justly comparable to the five kings who took shelter in the cave of the Makkedah. . . ."

Proudfit is effectively silenced by the Recluse, who thunders, "Peace, brawler, peace, and cease to pervert the word of God to thy murderous and unholy purposes."[23] The Recluse is not made the leader of the "Crop-ears" or "Rumpers," as the rebels are called, although he holds some curious power over them. Having once himself acted out of self-righteousness, he is portrayed as a repentant revolutionary who now wishes above all to establish social harmony in the colony. Caruthers refers to him as an "umpire," and his timely arrival and awesome strength put the rebels to flight and terminate the Cromwellian rebellion, which takes up roughly the first half of the novel.

The plot of the novel is concerned with establishing Bacon's social position in the colony and with solving the riddle of his parentage. While he is attached as a sort of stepchild to the family of Gideon Fairfax, who is a Cavalier and a supporter of Berkeley, the rumor persists that his parents were active in the Commonwealth cause and that he himself has Roundhead leanings. He finally demonstrates, however, that while belonging to neither, he possesses the best traits of both parties: the aristocratic grace and sense of honor of the Cavalier, and the self-discipline and zeal of the Puritan, which he owes to the tutoring of the Recluse, who for a time mistakes him for his lost son. At the end of the novel he is revealed to be half Cavalier and half Roundhead, the son of an officer in the Commonwealth army and an English lady. He is given the best of both worlds and is the mediator between them.

Only Bacon, in fact, has the vision to see the real significance of his fight with Berkeley. To Caruthers, too, Bacon's Rebellion was the opening skirmish of the American Revolution; 1676 became a rehearsal for the events of 1776. "Here," he observes, "was sown the first germ of the American revolution. . . . Exactly one hundred years before the American revolution, there was a Virginia revolution based upon precisely similar principles. The struggle commenced between the representatives of the people and the representatives of the king." At the same time Caruthers carefully preserves Bacon from any imputation of personal ambition. Bacon sees his victory over the governor's forces less as a personal triumph than as a triumph of American destiny. "I have been but an humble instrument," he tells Berkeley, "in the hands of the Great Mover of these mighty currents."[24] Since he is half Cavalier as well as half Roundhead, his personal zeal for the future is qualified by a profound sense of loss. He is conscious that he must murder to create. Both the defeat of the Chickahominys at Orapacs and the burning of Jamestown produce in him full-blown expressions of nostalgia. Destiny alone, he feels, justifies him in what he is forced to do. Providence has decreed that the Indian must yield to the white man so that America's lands may serve their predestined purpose. Everything—English colonial policy and the improvident savage—must give way before the dynamic tide of European settlement. "Cast your eyes over this vast and fertile country," Bacon tells an Indian princess,

and you will begin to see the necessity which is driving your red brethren to the far west. . . . You will see the great comprehension and sublime spectacle of God's political economy![25]

There is nothing in Caruthers' conception of "God's political economy" which suggests that he had consciously in mind a separate and distinct Southern destiny. Quite the contrary, in fact. Bacon is portrayed as a European hybrid who takes root and flourishes in American soil, and Caruthers' Virginia with its Cavalier-Roundhead dialectic closely approximates the whole of the American colonies in the seventeenth century as Caruthers' contemporaries thought of them. The belief that America had a westward-marching destiny which was manifest and part of the design of things was, of course, a belief subsequently held by Americans in nearly all regions of the country and expansionism soon became the policy of the Democratic party.[26]

Two things, however, are significant and novel in Caruthers' scheme of things: the determining role assigned to the Cavalier strain of American nationality and the application of Providential necessity to a contemporary Southern problem, Indian removal in the Southwest. The year 1835 marked the conclusion of a long and well-publicized struggle between the Cherokee tribes and the state of Georgia, which ended in defeat and capitulation for the Indians. In that year the Cherokee signed a treaty ceding their lands east of the Mississippi for a large and supposedly barren tract of land in what is now Oklahoma. The arguments which were developed in this struggle, arguments concerning the destined use of American soil and the superiority of white civilization, provided a theoretical basis for expansionists throughout the century. It was an easy "logical" step from the Cherokee to the Mexican.[27] It was also an easy step from the Cavalier-Roundhead expansionist to the Cavalier conquistador, and from the fictional

Knights of the Golden Horseshoe to the real-life filibustering Knights of the Golden Circle.[28]

From Whig Harmony to Cavalier Insurgency

Whatever destiny was sweeping America westward into an ever more prosperous future seemed to have bypassed Dr. William A. Caruthers and left him resourceless in New York City. In 1835 he was on the move again, first back to Lexington for about two years and finally, in 1837, to Savannah, where he remained unprospering until a few months before his death. The fantasies he conceived stand in curious apposition to the events of his own life. Every effort to make the grade was for him punctuated by defeat of some sort. In the communities in which he lived his position economically and socially was never much more than marginal. Even in Savannah, which was a boom town during the years he knew it, he found a medical practice difficult to acquire and was reduced to taking over the patients of doctors temporarily absent from town. He finally took to selling everything from real estate and horse carriages to newspaper subscriptions. He won for himself a certain respectability as a literary man and gentleman of polite learning, but his economic situation must have made it very difficult for him at times even to maintain appearances—in a world, furthermore, where appearances terribly mattered. He nonetheless did what he could. He was active in the Georgia Historical Society, served twice as a Whig alderman in Savannah and even, it appears, changed his religion. The register of St. John's Episcopal Church in Savannah, the church of the social elite, contains the following notation under Caruthers' name: "New Communicant—Convert from Presbyterianism, 11th Sunday after Trinity, August 7, 1842."[29]

Caruthers' next—and last—sortie into Virginia's past, the work of his first years in Savannah, was a novel set in the second decade of the eighteenth century to which he gave the title *The*

Knights of the Horseshoe; A Traditionary Tale of the Cocked Hat Gentry in the Old Dominion. The *Knights,* which was published serially in *The Magnolia* in 1841, has as its central episode an event in the career of Governor Alexander Spotswood, an expedition which he took into the valley of Virginia in 1716. In its form and its themes, it is very similar to *The Cavaliers.* Again Caruthers took an actual historical event and dressed it up in the trappings of romance, magnified its importance and slanted its significance toward the present. Spotswood, like Bacon, is portrayed as an intelligent and resourceful modern man, very much alert to the future needs of Virginia and America. He is, in fact, a militant and articulate advocate of Manifest Destiny, and his "tramontane expedition" into the territory of hostile savages is described as a kind of filibustering venture, which leads to the creation of a knightly organization, "The Tramontane Order." This Order, which adopts a golden horseshoe as its emblem, is devoted to westward expansion. Spotswood, again like Bacon, has to face the opposition of the ruling clique within the gentry, those whose aristocratic but obsolete values attach them to England and to the past.

In other respects *The Knights* is somewhat different from its predecessor, at least in its emphasis. The gentry are treated in far greater sociological detail, and the novel's hero is not Spotswood but a young man, Henry Hall, who arrives in the colony in disguise and is forced to make his way among "the chivalry" by his wits and his promising appearance. He is later revealed to be the aristocratic Francis Lee, who had gone off to Scotland some years before to fight for the Pretender.

Roughly the first half of the narrative, which is bedeviled by a plot of extraordinary complexity, is devoted to establishing the character of Hall, who becomes the tutor at Spotswood's plantation near Yorktown. Hall is tested, scrutinized and discussed by most of the characters in the novel, male and female. The women, and Spotswood, are disposed to call him a gentleman. He shows himself adept at the genteel accomplishments: he is expert with the small sword, has read widely in military history, mathematics and in the classics, and he exhibits manners which are described as "faultless." Nevertheless, most of the gentry or the Cavaliers, as they are variously called, persist in thinking him an impostor. "Squire" Carter is able to dispose of most of Hall's acquirements— his swordsmanship ("any French dancing-master may and often does possess such tricks"), his knowledge of military history ("learnt no doubt, while acting as drummer or fifer to some marching regiment"). Only Hall's literary erudition gives him trouble. Spotswood himself singles out Hall's polite learning as the most certain evidence of his gentility. "If Hall is a hypocrite and impostor," he tells Carter,

> he is one of the most accomplished swindlers that ever I have met with. It is a rare thing in my experience of human nature . . . to see a man descending in villainy, and elevating himself at the same time in all the elegant courtesies of life. Neither is it common to see men of that stamp cultivating their minds highly.[30]

Caruthers' idea of self-improvement, self-cultivation, as it is expressed here, is of course a nineteenth-century idea which applied most particularly to young men like Caruthers who were attempting to "elevate" themselves out of the middle class and to find their way to a status which they thought of as aristocratic. The central problem in Caruthers' fiction and in his life—was posed by vertical mobility: how to become a gentleman without losing American identity, without carrying along the excess baggage of the Cavalier. To arrive at his "solution," Caruthers investigated the past and selected those traits which promised a stable American character and rejected those which smacked of antiquated and degenerate ways. The American gentleman, whatever he may have been in fact, was in fiction an eclectic figure, an anthology of historical virtues. He must possess qualities of the Cavalier, the Roundhead and the frontiersman: the Cavalier's gracious manners and disinterestedness, the Roundhead's sense of direction, self-control and zeal for work, and the frontiersman's self-sufficiency, his ability to survive in an environment far removed from civilization. He must not drink or duel.[31] Most important of all, the American gentleman must possess vision, the apocalyptic gifts of a seer. He must not only ride with destiny but, like Bacon and Spotswood, anticipate its course.

During his years in New York Caruthers had taken on the assignment of preparing a brief sketch of Daniel Boone for *The National Portrait Gallery of Distinguished Americans,* an anthology-encyclopedia of famous American lives which was issued in four volumes during the eighteen thirties. Most of what Caruthers had to say about him was taken from John Filson's *Discovery, Settlement and Present State of Kentucke,* which had appeared in 1784. Beginning with the tribute to him which appeared in Byron's *Don Juan,* Caruthers portrayed Boone as a solitary, fearless and self-sufficient man, "preëminently the architect of his own character and fortunes." In the Caruthers sketch, as in Filson, he is preoccupied with fleeing from the onrushing tide of civilization, and the sketch ends with his setting off for Missouri exclaiming: "Too crowded! too crowded! I want more elbow room." In Caruthers' eyes he became the very image of the visionary man. From the mountains looking off into Kentucky, he becomes a kind of Hebraic prophet peering far into the future. "Here, from the top of an eminence," Caruthers comments, "Boone, like Moses of old, beheld the land of promise, here the broad bottoms—skirting the since far-famed Kentucky, first greeted his longing eyes." In the course of his narrative Caruthers made one observation, however, which he later chose to alter, at least in emphasis. Beside the figure of Boone, he felt, the "golden honors" of Spotswood's knights "would have dwindled into insignificance."[32]

When Caruthers came to write *The Knights* he included a Boonelike figure in the hunter and scout, Joe "Red" Jarvis, who acts as a forest tutor to Spotswood and Frank Lee during the expedition. When the unshod horses of the Knights suffer from the rocky mountain terrain, Jarvis teaches the governor how to shoe a horse. He also instructs Lee in subtle arts of woodsmanship, the stalking of wild game and the accurate reading of Indian tracks. He finds the impractical behavior and dress of "the gold-laced gentry" both ludicrous and trying, particularly when the expedition engages in a pitched battle with hostile Indians. Only Spotswood and Lee succeed in winning his respect. Spotswood, he comments, "is a tip-top old feller in the field. He don't know nothing about fightin' Ingins yit, but I'll tell you, he'll catch it mighty quick." The old governor, he writes to a friend, drinks gunpowder in his bitters each morning, "and as for running away . . . it ain't in his dictionary." Frank Lee receives praise, and for much the same reasons: "when they made a gintleman of him they spiled one of the best scouts in all these parts."[33]

Frank Lee's willingness to shed his gold lace and adapt to forest life is just as important to Caruthers as his ability to pass among gentlemen and to outdo them in the more sober virtues—and for a very good reason. If the liability of the Cavalier was his tendency to self-indulgence and his historical shortsightedness, the failing of the frontiersman was his pronounced hostility to society of any kind. In his sketch Caruthers had given Boone a Catholic-Maryland ancestry and made him a gentleman. Joe "Red" Jarvis is a typical comic frontiersman in the tradition of Ambrose Bushfield and Caruthers' own Montgomery Damon. He is hardly an exemplary social type, although Caruthers had tried half-heartedly to make Damon more than the butt of a gentleman's jokes. Jarvis is consistently treated as a menial, speaks dialect and has little truck with civilized ways. At the end of the novel he lights out for the Territory like Huck Finn. The governor's vision of an empire in the West leaves him cold. "I'm a hunter by trade," he exclaims, "and settlements have been crowding on me for some time, and this here mountain scheme of the governor's . . . is going to make things a heap worse with me."[34]

Out of the grab bag of historical types Caruthers had thus gathered together the traits of character which he felt best met the requirements of his own time. He had begun by assuming that

Roundhead, Westerner and Cavalier all had something like equal contributions to make, but he had discovered as he progressed that his mixture was thinning down. He had abandoned as types both the frontiersman and the Roundhead, and confined his attention in his last novel to the Virginia gentleman, the Cavalier. Both Spotswood and Lee are of unmixed blood, and they, virtually alone, carry the day for expansionism and empire. It is Spotswood who summons the gentry to gird on their armor, march across the mountain barrier into the West and redeem the name of the English Cavalier.

Caruthers himself was electrified by the idea of empire as he was by few others. Constantly he reminds his readers in his own voice and through his characters of "the grandest enterprises yet in the womb of time and destiny." Spotswood, he felt, had made a beginning, but the most exalted of all enterprises lay ahead, shrouded in time. "Grand and enthusiastic as were the conceptions of Sir Alexander Spotswood," he comments,

they had little idea that they were then about to commence a march which would be renewed from generation to generation, until in the course of little more than a single century it would transcend the Rio del Norte, and which, perhaps, in half that time may traverse the utmost boundaries of Mexico.

Beyond the mountains, in Texas, Mexico and far beyond, endless opportunity awaited the race, not simply the opportunity to acquire new territory, wealth and power but the opportunity of working for the social and spiritual salvation of inferior peoples, "of advancing the cause of civilization, and of carrying the Cross of our blessed Redeemer into unknown heathen lands."[35] Here was a crusade fit for a nineteenth-century knight.

Everything about the Cavalier seemed to equip him, and him alone, for such an undertaking: he was warrior, Christian, administrator and civilizer rolled into one. His historical failings were notable, to be sure, but by 1830 the Cavalier had been seasoned, it was felt, by two centuries of American experience and many a

Jarvis had shared with him his knowledge of the forest and the Indian. The time for action seemed ripe, indeed somewhat overdue. The century had provided little to challenge his imagination and engage his energies until the great push into the Southwest which took place in the eighteen thirties. A crusade was needed, Caruthers felt, to call forth the Southerner from personal lethargy and social inertia.

William Alexander Caruthers had spoken, but his voice trailed off in a series of fanciful proposals which he appears to have had neither the energy nor the capacity to complete. It is indicative of this new-found Southern loyalty that he had made the mistake of giving his last novel to a publisher in the South who was without the facilities for publicizing it. It did not sell. His dreams of eminence seem to have evaporated during his Georgia years, and disease did the rest. Here and there in his writings are passages punctuating his rhapsodic optimism, which suggest his consciousness of the illusion which he had been sustaining through miscalculation, hardship, failure and frustration. "The experience of our race," he commented in *The Knights*, "seems to be everywhere the same. Not only was it cursed and condemned to earn its bread by the sweat of the brow, but the sentence extends much farther. . . . We are just allowed to peep into the Garden of Eden, and then banished forever amid the dark by-ways and crowded thoroughfares of a busy life."[36] His gloomiest observation about the futility of existence, however, was made in 1845, the year before his death, on the theme of "all the world's a stage." "In real life," he commented, "the actors lead off in broad farce, and as invariably end in dire tragedy. Oh! if this life is indeed but a frolic for the amusement of the Gods, it is a bitter jest at which angels might weep."[37]

Caruthers' last published work was a novella entitled *Love and Consumption*, which appeared serially in the *Magnolia* in the summer of 1842. It was a fantasy which came close to home. The story, which is set in the valley of Virginia, tells of an impetuous and gifted young Southerner who deserts his childhood sweetheart to marry a rich and socially prominent Tidewater belle. Before his marriage he had shown promise as a lawyer and an orator. Afterward, he abandons his profession and submits to the tyranny of his wife, who rules him by threatening fits of hysteria. "He is but the wreck," a friend comments, "of the most promising man I have ever known." Weakened by "those delicate domestic troubles, which are making such sad ravages upon this miserable frame," he goes into consumption and at the end of the story dies repentant at one of the Virginia springs.[38] Four years later Caruthers, his feelings unrecorded, died of tuberculosis at a spa in the mountains of Georgia. Neither his own grave nor that of his wife has ever been located.

CHAPTER VII

A Northern Man of Southern Principles

When the morning was up, they had him to the top of
the house and bid him look south. So he did, and behold,
at a great distance he saw a most pleasant mountainous
country, beautified with woods, fountains, very delectable
to behold.

JOHN BUNYAN, *The Pilgrim's Progress*[1]

THE ATTACHMENT WHICH Southerners like Caruthers came to
feel for the Cavalier was more than a matter of idiosyncrasy or
simple regional loyalty. Men of widely different experience and
temperament enlisted in the Cavalier cause, and some of the most
ardent crusaders were not even Southerners. James Kirke Paulding
is a case in point. A New York Democrat of Dutch extraction,
Paulding began with a view of the South scarcely distinguishable
from that of most of his Northern contemporaries, yet before
his death in 1860 he had assumed a set of attitudes which allied
him to the Southern extremists who worked to advance the
cause of secession. History provides few examples which depict
with greater clarity the force with which the Yankee-Cavalier
dialectic operated in American cultural speculations.

From Provincial to Citizen of the World

In the months preceding the election of Abraham Lincoln, the steam-power presses of Evans and Cogswell, Charleston printers, were kept busy turning out pamphlets for the 1860 Association. There was no mistaking the objective of this organization. Each pamphlet was designed to nudge its readers into favoring secession. Tract No. 2 was inflammatory like the others. At the bottom of the title page in bold print the reader found the instruction: READ AND SEND TO YOUR NEIGHBOR.

Among its offerings Tract No. 2 contained a letter, not by a Carolinian nor, for that matter, by a Southerner. "The following letter," commented the nameless editor, "is worthy of attention, not only for the sound views it contains, but also on account of the latitude from which it comes."[2] The letter was dated from Hyde Park, New York, September 6, 1851. It was signed by a former Secretary of the Navy, James Kirke Paulding. Paulding, the letter made clear, had been invited some nine years before to address a convocation at Charleston following the Compromise of 1850. He had been unable to make the journey because of ill health, but he had been willing to go on record as supporting the South in its efforts to win redress before the nation. The compromise, Paulding felt, represented "a most unjustifiable attack on the rights, interests, safety, and happiness of one-half the States composing it [the Union], accompanied by insult and obloquy." The right of a state to secede, Paulding concluded, could not be questioned. The honor of the South demanded that Southerners stand up and be counted; it required that they not retire cowering from the field of action.[3]

Paulding died quietly on his Hyde Park farm in April, 1860, an old man of eighty-two. In all probability he was unaware that his incendiary letter written years before was circulating from household to household in a city he had never visited. He died, one may judge, unaware of the consequences of the movement which his letter did something, however slight, to further. How had this descendant of Joost Pauldinck come to identify himself so combatively with the most extreme Southern point of view? In doing so he departed radically from the position taken by other New York Democrats who were his friends and associates. His feelings about secession were more extreme than those of many Southerners. What, after all, was the South to him?

Nothing at first glance seems less likely than the conversion of a New York provincial from the Hudson Highlands into a kind of Southern fire-eater. The history of the Old South, however, is full of surprises. Paulding is certainly one of them. He never owned a slave nor planted an acre of cotton. While he did not, like Sarah Hale, have to spin his South out of the whole cloth, his concrete knowledge of Southern life was gained from two brief summer trips. During much of his active life he served as an appointed government official in New York City and Washington. The last fifteen years of his life he lived in retirement on his Duchess County farm. If there is a convincing explanation for the drift of Paulding's feelings about Southern life, it is not to be found in anything so obvious and clear-cut as sectional or party interest. In his books about the South and about Southerners Paulding often criticized and satirized the gentleman planter, sometimes very astutely. He never became an unqualified apologist for slavery or the plantation economy. In the last analysis, he seems to have been less attracted to the South than repelled by the North. For him as for Sarah Hale, the South was an antipode to life in the North, a possible alternative. If he was better instructed than she, his sense of alienation was even greater. She, like Daniel Webster, tried to remain neutral. For an editor of a national magazine or for a spokesman of a national party, neutrality paid off. American life for a while brought very indifferent returns to James Kirke Paulding.

Paulding's family had fled from their Tarrytown home during the Revolution and lived for a few years in the small village of Great Nine Partners slightly to the North. There Paulding was born in 1778 in a house so small that the modest Tarrytown house to which the family returned a few years later seemed to the boy like "a church without a steeple." Many years later, when he had lived for a time in New York City, he returned to find that the same house "had dwindled into a very insignificant building."⁴ For the provincial there were no absolutes. Everything was defined by change. Paulding's provincial isolation was further increased by the cultural autonomy of the Dutch community at Tarrytown. Dutch was spoken at home by his grandparents and Dutch was the language used in the village church which the family attended. Paulding lived for almost a quarter of his long life without ever venturing out of this closed world. Life had almost a European pattern. With only slight exaggeration he reported that he lived "to the age of eighteen or nineteen, without ever going five miles from home."⁵ When Paulding sailed down the Hudson River to New York City in 1796, he, like Sarah Hale in 1827, knew only the life of an American village.

His experience of this limited world left indelible tracings on his mind and temperament. His country childhood was not a happy experience. Paulding's Tarrytown was very different from Sarah Hale's Northwood. Tarrytown for him was half tragedy and half fairy tale. The decade of the seventeen eighties was a period of grinding poverty for his family. His father had come to Tarrytown about 1767 and set himself up keeping store. For a time he seems to have enjoyed moderate success. He had even been a commissary for the Revolution army. For this service he was apparently never compensated. The unsettled and inflationary economy of the postwar years brought about his ruin. In Sarah Hale's scheme of things he was the merchant who went down.

William Paulding went bankrupt in 1785 and was taken off to jail as a debtor. It fell upon Paulding, then a boy of seven, to ride a borrowed horse to the jail at White Plains, six miles away, every Saturday to bring food and clothing to his despondent father. Many years later he had not shaken the memory of this ride. "It was a melancholy journey," he later recalled, "and I cannot think on it, even at this distant period, without painful emotions."⁶ Although the jail burned down a few months later and William Paulding walked away scot-free, he never again recovered his initiative. For the remainder of his ninety years he seems to have withdrawn into a world of his own, a world nourished by the books he read and memories of his own years at sea. Story and memory, fantasy and fact, became to him indistinct and confused. Paulding remembered that his father would gather his children about him and "tell them stories of his own adventures, or those of Sindbad the sailor, or some other hero of The Arabian Nights."⁷ He also remembered that his father always carried about him a pocketbook stuffed with worthless Continental currency, a symbol of his ruin.

Paulding, like so many American writers, was brought up almost entirely by his mother. From the time of his father's imprisonment his mother, Catherine Ogden Paulding, was the *de facto* head of the household. She somehow kept her family together, earned what little she could by taking in sewing and saw to it that her sons received a little education. "All that I have ever been," Paulding later recalled, "I owe to her." It was she who arranged for Paulding to live with an uncle for a brief period and attend a nearby school. But for all of Catherine Paulding's energy and good will, the years of Paulding's youth were hard years. The Pauldings, to use his own words, "were not only poor, but steeped in poverty." They were painful years for him to remember. "I never look back on that period of life . . . without a feeling of dreary sadness. From the experience of my early life I never wish to be young again."⁸

He was surrounded by human derelicts, men broken or deranged by the Revolutionary upheaval. His grandfather Ogden, who had suffered a head injury during the war, provided a spectacle which Paulding found hard to forget. He remembered him "walking along the beach at Tarrytown, picking up sticks, and talking to himself about the reign of Queen Anne." He was an unsentimental version of Irving's Rip Van Winkle. While Paulding lived with his uncle on the Saw Mill River, his fellow boarders were an impoverished Revolutionary soldier and his small daughter, who was a mute. When a neighbor committed suicide Paulding began to fear that he was losing his mind. The terrible loneliness, the long winter trek to school and the terrifying agitation caused by a religious revival combined to send him back to his mother.[9]

These years were not unrelieved by pleasures of a sort. To judge from Paulding's experience, the curse of American village life was not hard work but the long periods of unrelieved and enforced idleness. Families were large and there was no problem finding hands to do the work. The problem was finding work to do, especially during the winter months. Paulding liked to fish and hunt; he also came to enjoy the vacant dreaming, the castle building, which accompanied these activities. He read when he could find books, or he sat by the fire at night listening to his father or some neighbor ramble on about the war; but mostly he appears to have mused. He became convinced that "the present was a blank and the future almost a void." He felt cut off and isolated from the sources of life. "I lived," he once recalled, "pretty much in a world of my own creating."[10]

In his fancy he gradually began to explore the larger world which he knew lay somewhere beyond the limits of Tarrytown. While he was living with his uncle he came across a copy of Oliver Goldsmith's *The Citizen of the World*, purportedly the letters of a Chinese visitor to eighteenth-century London. "I read it I believe twenty times at least, and if I have any taste or style, I owe them to that charming work of the most delightful of all English writers."[11] This book seems to have provided his hungry imagination with its first glimpse of metropolitan life; it also provided him with the loose literary form which he used several times: the fictional book of letters.

In 1796 Paulding experienced the first great change of his life. "At length the time came for emerging into that world I had hitherto only contemplated through the medium of fancy." Sometime in that year a very green provincial sailed down the Hudson River from Tarrytown and disembarked in the metropolis of New York City. The humiliation and discomfort which were to characterize these first years in the Great World began before he was properly on land. "I well remember," he later recalled, "the first shock given to my sensitiveness was being laughed at by the rabble about the wharf."[12]

It seemed to help very little that Paulding, the eighth of nine children, had the way prepared for him. The Paulding outward migration had begun several years before when a sister had married Washington Irving's brother William, a merchant and a politician. Paulding's own brother William, later mayor of the city, had also been living in New York for some time. It was he who secured Paulding a job with the United States Loan Office, and it was with him that Paulding lived during this first bewildering exposure to city life. Through his brother and his brother-in-law, Paulding began to meet young men who, though more sophisticated than he, nonetheless shared his literary inclinations. He already knew Washington and William Irving. He soon met a number of other literary dilettantes who became his friends and associates for the rest of his life—doctors, lawyers, politicians and merchants. One of them, Gouverneur Kemble, a few years later became his brother-in-law.[13]

Sarah Hale and Webster discovered their vocations in the provinces. When Sarah Hale moved to Boston she had published stories and poems and had a successful novel to her credit. She was almost forty and her self-education was nearly completed. She moved toward opportunity and success. When Webster moved to Boston in 1816 he had practiced law successfully in a provincial capital and had already served a term in Congress. He had gathered a full head of steam. When Paulding drifted into New York City from up the river, he was a raw bumpkin, as he himself put it, and had very little notion of what he wanted to do. His self-education had hardly begun and he had very little to recommend him to the world but his sensitivity and his receptiveness. He knew that behind him lay poverty and defeat, a broken father and an exhausted mother. He was very little prepared for the painful experience of his metropolitan initiation. The young men with whom he spent his free hours were themselves provincials, but they had already assumed a high gloss of sophistication. There is no crueler taskmaster then the provincial who "arrived" yesterday. Paulding assumed his protective coloration in the midst of humiliations which he never forgot:

Thus I fell, as it were, among the Philistines; for the circle in which I moved—though I can scarcely say had a being—was composed of young men, many of whom have since made no inconsiderable figure in the world. I was excessively thin-skinned—I may say, perfectly raw—and nothing was so painful to me as ridicule. They broke me in by quizzing me most unmercifully; but, though the perspiration of almost agony sprung from the very hair of my head, I bore it like a martyr, for I was too proud to show how I suffered.[14]

A few years of such hazing were sufficient to clothe the green provincial with the garments of a bantling literary playboy, cut to the model of his friend Washington Irving. If the fit was inexact, the illusion was sustained through life and the painful ridicule finally ended. A bumpkin, a subject of satire, became a satirist. This was to be his surest defense. It was hard to smile at a provincial who was smiling back. Paulding joined his friends in the frolics at Cockloft Hall, the fictional name for the Kemble house on the Passaic in New Jersey, and he became one of the "Nine Worthies" or the "Lads of Kilkenny," two different names which the group took. His feelings about this association were always somewhat mixed, however much he tried to be grateful for the experience in later life. "Though I look back on it with something like horror," he once recalled, "I have always considered the lessons worth the purchase. It was the best school in which I ever studied."[15]

Paulding's career as a satirist began in January, 1807, with the appearance of the first number of the *Salmagundi*.[16] These miscellaneous satirical sketches, published at intervals, were obviously based on the form of the eighteenth-century English newspaper essay. Although others contributed, the sketches which appeared were principally the work of Paulding and Irving. Everything about them now seems jejune and affectedly self-conscious. Indeed, Paulding in the preface to a later edition refers to their "evident juvenility" and Irving was inclined to disown them altogether. The provincial who chose for himself a literary career was almost forced to fake a bit in order to attract attention to himself. Cooper's first novel was, after all, something of an imposture; Melville first gained attention as "the man who had lived among Cannibals" and Poe was a master of the literary hoax. Posturing and imposture verged one upon the other. Certainly, the roles assumed by the youthful essayists in the *Salmagundi* papers express the uncertain and mannered pose of newly assumed sophistication. In order to be a Citizen of the World, it was necessary now and then to don a mandarin robe or play with a name from *The Arabian Nights*. In Paulding provincialism and cultural alienation were compounded. He came to think of English culture and manners as an invading force, like the Redcoats of '76, which was violating America's natural and admirable integrity in much the same way that the British had once invaded Tarrytown.

While Washington Irving sought out the quaint, the curious and the remote in Old England and published his findings in *The Sketch Book* and *Bracebridge Hall*, Paulding, after the completion of the *Salmagundi*, published a series of books which expressed his growing bitterness toward England and his progressive alienation from English culture. The first of these books, published in 1812, was *The Diverting History of John Bull and Brother Jonathan*, an allegorical burlesque in which Squire Bull plays the role of England and Brother Jonathan the United States. *The United States and England*, published in 1815, is a pamphlet directed primarily at the severity of criticism of America appearing in the English and Scottish reviews. Two more books, published almost a decade later, advance the same arguments with increased acidity.

In 1822 Paulding published *A Sketch of Old England*, purportedly the travel letters written by a Yankee in London to his brother in America. Brother Jonathan was answering Squire Bull in kind. Three years later Paulding published *John Bull in America; or The New Munchausen*, a bitterly satirical parody of English travel books about America. In all of this writing Paulding resorted to the old strategy of employing ridicule as a defense against ridicule. English ridicule of provincial American culture was intolerable to a man whose situation within his own culture was as defensive and insecure as Paulding's. In his eyes the only thing more ridiculous than a fashionable Englishman was an American who tried to imitate him. For Paulding, as for Sarah Hale, the real America was not found in New York but in the village and on the farm. America was Tarrytown without its suffering and without its pain. By this time, however, Paulding was repeating himself and the literary battle with England had begun to lose its interest and vitality. Paulding never forgot or forgave the Old Enemy, but at this point he had already turned his attention to concerns which were more exclusively domestic.

A Southern Exposure

Paulding had by 1825 established himself as a literary patriot. The kind of partisan patriotism which he expressed in *The United States and England*, written almost ten years before, had paid him a good return. This book, soon after its publication, came to the attention of President James Madison and resulted in Paulding's appointment in April of 1815 as secretary to the newly created Board of Naval Commissioners. He left New York and moved to Washington in the same year. For a period of twenty-five years, from 1815 until 1840, Paulding was to serve as an appointed official in Republican and Democratic administrations. When he resigned his first job with the Navy in 1823 and moved back to New York, he was appointed Navy Agent for New York, a sinecure which he held until 1838, when Van Buren, having first offered the position to Irving, made Paulding his Secretary of the Navy. When Paulding retired from the cabinet in March, 1841, he had served in appointive offices for close to forty-three of his sixty-two years. This experience, probably unique among American writers, profoundly conditioned his social views.[17]

Paulding's remoteness from practical politics only intensified his isolation from other aspects of American life which played a prominent part in conditioning the lives of his contemporaries. It paralleled his isolation from Europe. Unlike his friend Martin Van Buren, for example, Paulding never attended a party caucus or ran for either state or federal office. Among the writers who concerned themselves with the South, Paulding is the exception that proves the rule. He was neither lawyer nor judge. He was never even an attorney general! If he was never, like Webster, a Congressman or a Senator, he was never, like William Wirt or Hugh Legaré, concerned with legal statesmanship. He was not even in any strict sense a professional man; neither was he a merchant. If Washington Irving and George Ticknor began as lawyers and soon abandoned the practice of law, they nonetheless made their own way in a sense that Paulding did not. At first glance, Paulding's life hardly conforms to the pattern of the emergent Yankee. Although he was surrounded by successful businessmen and successful politicians, he himself never won an election nor met a business payroll.

The success which he enjoyed was largely owing to the good offices of others. His Democratic friends and in-laws secured for him the important appointments which he held. There is no evidence that he himself ever solicited an office. When he went to Washington in 1815, he made it clear that he went in the hope of escaping the competitive race, not with the expectation of entering it. He did not seek advancement, he sought leisure and respectability. He wrote to Irving in the same year that his new situation provided him with "leisure, respect, and independence. . . . All my life I have been fettered by poverty, and my vivacity checked by the hopelessness of the future."[18] After the death in 1823 of his father-in-law, wealthy Peter Kemble, Paulding, through his wife, came into a considerable inheritance. On this occasion, he wrote to Irving with characteristic detachment that "if living in a great house constitutes a great man after the fashion of New York, a great man I am, at your service." He seemed more ambitious for his brother than for himself. "My brother William is already Brigadier-General and Mayor of the City, and these are sufficient glories for one family. Still I can't help hoping with you that we shall yet hang our hats on the next peg before we die."[19] When success did come, it came as a gift of the gods, unasked for and unsolicited. Paulding's first brush with liberal capitalism through his father cured him for life. He never forgot that the antipode to entrepreneurial success was to be found in his boyhood memories of the jail at White Plains. It was hardly worth trying. It was better to be a successful failure than to be a fallible success. It was better to go South.

Paulding saw the South below Washington for the first time in 1816. In May of that year he was sent to Annapolis on business for the navy. The following July he set out from Annapolis with the navy commissioners on a survey of Chesapeake Bay which took him as far as Norfolk, Virginia. Because of ill health he left the government party in Norfolk and traveled alone through Virginia for the balance of the summer. He returned to Washington only late in the fall. The itinerary which he followed took him to Yorktown and Williamsburg, west through the Tidewater, across the Blue Ridge and along the Shenandoah Valley north to the mountains. On the way he "did" the Virginia springs after the manner of the time, "taking the waters" at the various fashionable spas along the route.[20] It was customary to move from spa to spa rather than to stay very long at any one place. One's health depended on it—and so did one's friends.[21] Paulding followed the custom. He appears to have visited "the Warm," "the White,"

Sweet Sulphur Springs and finally Berkeley Springs before he emerged, apparently cured, at Harpers Ferry and set off for Washington. In the course of his leisurely traveling he had seen something of the Virginia Tidewater, the Piedmont, the Great Valley and the mountains. Among other things, he had discovered that Virginia, peddlers' legends to the contrary, was not all of a piece. The same year he set about correcting the record.

Paulding set down his impressions of this summer excursion in a long, rambling book which he published the following year. The *Letters from the South* appeared in two volumes in 1817. The so-called "letters" were in fact random essays loosely held together by the fiction that they were written by a Northern traveler to a friend living in a large Northern city. While the essays which Paulding wrote are here and there critical and satirical, they leave little doubt that on the whole he liked very much what he saw. Frank Oliver, the city friend to whom the letters are addressed, is constantly reminded that in the South he may find salubrious country life, leisure and independence— the very qualities which Paulding himself desired. The displeasing aspects of Southern life were not in Paulding's eyes character- istically Southern; they were faults which characterized the nation as a whole. The South, which to Paulding meant Virginia, was America in microcosm. Southerners, he discovered, were very much like everybody else—only better.

Before his summer journey through Virginia, Paulding had con- ceived of Southern life in much the same terms as Americans in other parts of the North. The representative Southerner was the planter and the planter was variously described as belligerent, spontaneous, fantastical, romantic and chivalrous. In *John Bull and Brother Jonathan*, the allegorical Southlanders are a sum- mation of an existing stereotype of the Southerner. Probably the prevailing view of the Southerner held in this period by a great many Northern writers was that of the provincial barbarian. Cooper's Jack Lawton was of the type. Emerson, at the time of his graduation from Harvard in 1821, wrote to a friend in Baltimore: "You know our idea of an accomplished Southerner; to wit, as ignorant as a bear, as irascible and nettled as any porcupine, as polite as a troubadour, and a very John Randolph in character and address." Emerson had spent the winter of 1826-27 traveling in the vicinity of Charleston, yet his conception of the South had hardly altered by 1837 when he again, and more earnestly, blasted the Southerner. The Southerner who came as a student to Cambridge was "a mere parader," "a mere bladder of conceit." It must have been difficult for a defensive Southern provincial to attend Harvard College before the Civil War, and it is hardly surprising that tempers now and then flashed. Emerson's description of Southerners in Cambridge makes them sound very much, in fact, like American provincials in Europe. "Each snippersnapper of them all," he complained, "undertakes to speak for the entire Southern States."22

The single characteristic of the Southerner which Emerson and other Northerners found most troubling can be summed up by the word "wildness." In 1837 Emerson wrote in his journal a neat formulation of his feelings about the North and the South. "The Southerner," he observed, "asks concerning any man, 'How does he fight?' The Northerner asks, 'What can he do?' "23 The Southerner, he conceded grudgingly, is "more civilized than the Seminoles . . . a little more."24 The vehemence of Emerson's feelings seems odd indeed in a man who the same year in *The American Scholar* had called for wild men "out of unhandselled savage nature; out of terrible Druids and Berserkers" to build an indigenous American culture.25 Despite his protests to the contrary, Emerson's taste for wildness was limited. In his eyes the Southerner was just about as welcome in Cambridge as a polar bear.

Henry Adams, writing long after the Civil War, drew a vivid portrait of the Southerners, among them a son of Robert E. Lee, whom he had known at Harvard in the eighteen fifties. The Southerner, Adams recalled, was characterized by the "habit of command and took leadership as his natural habit." He was "ignorant," "childlike," "simple beyond analysis." "Strictly," he concluded, "the Southerner had no mind; he had temperament." Adams, too, was impressed by the Southerner's essential wildness. The Virginian, he discovered, drank excessively and was apt to become "quarrelsome and dangerous. When a Virginian had brooded a few days over an imaginary grief and substantial whiskey, none of his Northern friends could be sure that he might not be waiting round the corner, with a knife or pistol, to revenge insult by the dry light of *delirium tremens.*" Not only was he "weak in vice itself," but "every quality in which he was strong, made him weaker." He was a type "as little fit to succeed in the struggle of modern life," Adams concluded, as his caveman ancestors, whom he in many ways resembled.[26]

Such a regional stereotype of the South, Paulding discovered, was very inaccurate. The cause of such a misunderstanding lay, he felt, with the tales brought north by Yankee peddlers and the gossipy accounts of plantation life by American travelers who were as irresponsible and uninformed as the British travelers who wrote about America. "One of the first things," he observed, "that strikes a Northern man, who flounders into Virginia, or either of the more southern states, loaded with a pack of prejudices as large as a pedlar's, is, that he has, all life long, been under a very mistaken notion of the state of their manners." The South was not all "gouging" and "julep" drinking. "Before I had been long in this part of the world," he wrote, "I discovered, to my great surprise, that the people were very much like other folks, only a little more hospitable."[27]

Even among the Virginians there was a range of variety which Paulding's narrator professed to find surprising. He found two more or less distinct societies, one of which lay east, and one of which lay west, of the Blue Ridge. "Old Virginia" to the east was the land where the aristocratic planter, the "Tuckahoe," supposedly lived on his baronial estate like a lord of manor. About the Tuckahoe Paulding said little, except to note that the old image of a horse-racing, cock-fighting, julep-drinking gentry seemed hardly any longer to apply to Virginia. The prosperity of the eastern counties of Virginia, Paulding noted, had declined considerably since the end of the Revolution. The soil had been exhausted by repeated, speculative planting and the old Tidewater plantations had been divided or abandoned as a result of new laws that prohibited the entailing of large estates. The proud old houses along the rivers flowing into Chesapeake Bay were in bad repair and were occupied by elderly matrons who lived on memories of the past. The tobacco fields had been permitted to grow to bush. Paulding much preferred the western counties, the so-called "New Virginia," which were occupied by the vigorous and republican "Cohee."

Westward Ho!

West of the Blue Ridge the landscape brightened, the "ruins" disappeared and even the rivers flowed clear and cool like "the fount of Parnassus." Here, he found, a traveler entered a society of virtuous yeomen who lived amply and unpretentiously on their farms; here, in other words, was a version of the pastoral which represented the best possibilities of American life. "The fields are greener, and the people that cultivate them are white men, whose labours being voluntary, seems to make the landscape smile." In 1816 Paulding held a very different view of slavery from the one he was to propound twenty years later. In the Shenandoah Valley, he noted, "you see but few slaves, and every thing is the more gay for not being darkened by them—at least to my eyes." "The cultivators of the land," Paulding felt, "are those who constitute the real wholesome strength and virtue of every civilized country." In every way the American yeoman measured up. At one of the spas he visited, Paulding watched with admiration while a group of local "country people" moved among the idle and fashionable Tuckahoes without a trace of self-consciousness. The country people were born aristocrats, proud and independent. The real slaves, Paulding concluded, were the parvenus, those who had made their money quickly on lucky speculations and attempted to play the aristocrat by imitating English fashions and cultivating English idleness.[28]

Paulding's distrust of fashion, progress—the whole complex of modern life—is never more evident than in the curious and revealing fantasy which he inserted in *Letters from the South*. The narrator has a dream in which he visits a strange land of the future, the "Isles of Engines." In the Engine Isles human life has been largely mechanized and all work formerly done by hand is now done by machines. The narrator encounters toothpick-making machines, steam corkscrews, steam grave diggers and steam washers. Not only have machines replaced manual labor, but machine-made men are rapidly replacing "anatomical men." Anatomical men are being taught to starve scientifically and to give technical explanations for their weakened condition. So desperate have things become that the machines, no longer content with eliminating people, have begun to eliminate each other. Railroads have replaced the canals and steamboats are fast replacing the railroad. Magnetic boats that travel a thousand miles per hour are fast replacing the steamboat. Every trace of intellectual or social life has disappeared. At the nearby Republic of Elsewhere—a thinly disguised England—the dreamer attends a "lecture" in the university town of Oxhorn. The lecture is on the evolution of bottle opening from the fingernails to the steamscrew. A concert of steam instruments terminates abruptly when one of the boilers explodes and nearly demolishes the audience. Those in the audience who survive are completely indifferent to the suffering of those around them. When the dreamer uses the word "courteous," he is told that such expressions have become "obsolete." The dreamer awakens as he is about to have his "boiler" patched.[29]

This little fable about the industrial revolution has all the bleakness of a nineteenth-century *1984* and suggests the dimensions of Paulding's problem. If the European past was corrupt, the shopkeeper's world of tomorrow was for him a utilitarian horror. Paulding hated machines with a vehemence which suggests that his feelings were more than mere affectation. While he was serving as secretary to the navy board, he was very nearly killed by the explosion of a patent carbine. While he was Secretary of the Navy he did everything in his power to retard the inevitable transformation of the navy from sail to steam power. He would humor the thing (steam power) a bit, he wrote to his ordinance-making brother-in-law, Gouverneur Kemble, "but I will never consent to let our old ships perish, and transform our Navy into a fleet of sea monsters." Paulding's son once observed, with what appears to have been considerable restraint, that his father "was not given to novelties." He possessed "the habit of command" which Henry Adams found characteristic of the Virginians at Harvard. Among his navy subordinates he was known as a strict disciplinarian.[30]

Faced with the choice between a future of bewildering and insufferable novelty and a past of courteous corruption, it is not surprising that Paulding, feeling as he did, finally tended by preference to look backward. But first he experimented with another possibility. A part of the United States was still unfallen and might be kept as an idyllic preserve against an industrial future. "We have yet," he remarked in the *Letters*, "an unpeopled world, a blooming, and almost uninhabited Eden in the west."[31] Paulding had himself never traveled in the West, but he had somewhere encountered Timothy Flint's *Recollections of the Last Ten Years*, which had been published in 1826. Flint told in detail of traveling in the Mississippi and Ohio valleys. This was enough for Paulding. He set to work at removing the Southern planter from the noxious and debilitating environment of Old Virginia. The result of Paulding's experiment appeared in 1832 as a two-volume novel entitled *Westward Ho! A Tale*. Perhaps Cuthbert Dangerfield, Paulding's planter hero, could be made to thrive in the garden of the West.

Paulding, it is important to note, chose as his hero a Southerner who combined every trait of the legendary Tidewater aristocrat

whose very existence he had earlier doubted. Cuthbert Dangerfield is described as a "regular Tuckahoe" and a high-mettled
"Cavalier." His plantation on the James River is situated among
"the seats of a great number of the ancient gentry of Old Virginia"—among the Byrds, the Randolphs, the Pages, the Carters
and the Harrisons. He is characterized by his extravagant hospitality, his pride in the Dangerfield genealogy and his addiction
to horses and horse racing. "A Virginian," Paulding comments, "is
all one as a piece of his horse. He realizes the fable of the
centaurs."[32] He is impetuous, proud and unpredictable. When a
Scottish merchant asks for a payment on Dangerfield's long-standing debt to him, Dangerfield challenges him to a duel. He has
exhausted the fertility of his lands by speculative agriculture; his
perennial improvidence and his indifference to money matters in
general give him one of the most essential traits of the legendary
Southerner.

Trouble for Dangerfield begins when he boastfully stakes
£20,000 on a race to be run by one of his horses, in the desperate
hope of recovering his fortune. At the last moment he impetu-
ously doubles his bet. When he loses the race even he is forced
to admit that he is ruined. Yet, when his wife suggests that they
save their money and reduce their expenses by selling the horses
and curtailing their lavish entertainments, Dangerfield is horrified.
" 'Save! impossible,' cried the colonel, in utter astonishment; 'I
never heard of such a thing in the whole course of my life. How
the deuce shall I go about it?' " When the Scottish merchant steps
in and kindly offers to arrange for the payment of Dangerfield's
debts, Dangerfield is unable to tell him even how much he owes.
"I never kept an account in my life," he exclaims proudly.[33]

In exchange for the payment of his debts, Dangerfield signs
over his plantation to the merchant, McTabb, and receives
£5,000 in cash. With this he sets off to begin life anew on the
"dark and bloody ground" of Kentucky. The novel skips over
the period of time during which Dangerfield settles in the West.
A few short years are sufficient, however, to transform both the

colonel and his Kentucky lands. Dangerfield, we are told, has now become an industrious and responsible republican gentleman. Under the tutelage of the Bumppolike woodsman, Ambrose Bushfield, he has learned woodcraft; his settlement has become a model Western community with Dangerfield as its selfless and devoted leader. "From the moment the colonel parted with his estate, his neighbors, and above all with Barebones [his horse], and dashed into the wilderness, his character resumed that native sagacity and vigour which wealth, indulgence, and, above all, idleness, had lulled to sleep with their syren lullabies. His mind rose with the exigences of the occasion."[34] When Paulding came to describe Dangerfield's township, he pulled out all the stops. Dangerfieldville is a utopia as faultless as the Engine Isles were horrible. Here a man might hang his hat, unshoulder his rifle and never want for anything; here was peace and plenty.

The smoke rising above the tall trees, the barking of dogs, the crowing of cocks, the tinkling of bells, the strokes of the woodsman's axe, the crash of the falling tree, and the long echoes of the hunter's gun would announce to him [the traveler] that he was coming to the abodes of civilized men. He would behold a village rising . . . fields of grain. . . . Orchards loaded with fruits, gardens full of vegetables and flowers.[35]

Not a hog nor an ear of corn in sight! In his imaginary West Paulding had discovered a busy society untainted by Yankee business and a present which was the moral equivalent of the past —but without the corruption and effeteness which he associated with the European past. He had found all this, but there were problems.

Paulding long before had observed that "It would puzzle a Philadelphia lawyer to make a romance out of a log-hut."[36] His long, serious poem *The Backwoodsman*, published in 1818, had been an acknowledged failure and the last two thirds of *Westward Ho!* hardly touched on the question which Paulding had raised: how does one go about making a competent and disinterested leader out of an irresponsible, almost childish, Tuckahoe? It would take all the ingenuity of a Philadelphia lawyer to turn John Randolph into George Washington, which, in effect, is what Paulding had attempted to do. Even after two long volumes the character of the Southerner remained as mysterious as before. If John Randolph and George Washington were types of the Southerner, then how in the world was it possible to derive one from the other or to reconcile the two? Could the answer be found in the figure of Andrew Jackson?

There is some suggestion that Paulding had Jackson in mind as he composed some parts of *Westward Ho!* He had met Jackson in Washington at the end of the War of 1812 and had admired him. As *Westward Ho!* was being written, Jackson was completing his first term in the Presidency and had caught the imagination of the country. Paulding, unlike so many of his countrymen, was never in doubt about Jackson. From the first he thought of him as the model of the natural gentleman. A few years after the publication of *Westward Ho!* Paulding visited Jackson for three weeks at the "Hermitage." Jackson, Paulding conceded to Kemble, may have lacked genteel cultivation, but he had something else which Paulding admired: he had dignity and independence. "He was *sui generis*. The power of man is the power over his fellow men."[37]

On the occasion of Jackson's death in 1845, Paulding wrote that he was "the only man I ever saw that excited my admiration to the pitch of wonder. To him knowledge seemed entirely unnecessary. He saw intuitively into everything, and reached a conclusion by a short cut while others were beating the bush for the game. His reasoning was impulse, and his impulse inspiration. His genius and his courage were his guides." Here was a type of American who owed as little to Europe as he did to the machine; here was someone who might bridge the gap between Randolph and Washington. Jackson possessed Washington's simplicity, his military leadership and his devotion to duty; he possessed Randolph's wildness and genius, his "impulse from the vernal wood." He represented for Paulding a kind of success which had nothing to do with commerce and progress. Jackson moved toward his objective with all the directness of a woodsman. "He never sought an object that he did not succeed in attaining; and never fought a battle that he did not win."[38] No wonder Paulding tried to uproot Cuthbert Dangerfield and transplant him to Kentucky!

Unfortunately for Paulding, the roots did not take hold. Paulding recognized that the way to salvage the impecunious and failure-bent Cavalier was to make him into a transcendent Yankee, a gentleman with a supreme object which was not money, a man beholden to no one. Such a solution to the problem of Southern character, in so far as it occurred to Paulding, remained theoretical and was never worked out in practice. Another kind of Westerner, possessing some of the same characteristics, had seized the imagination of the country and forever after seemed to typify the West. David Crockett of Tennessee, with his dependence on "natural-born sense instead of law learning" seemed almost a parody of Andrew Jackson. Crockett had served in Congress from 1827 to 1831. He soon aligned himself with the Whig opposition to Jackson and fictitious versions of Crockett's life and character were later used to satirize Jackson and Jackson's administration.

In *Westward Ho!* Paulding seems to have shared the existing confusion about the Westerner. Although he assured his readers that Dangerfield resumed "his native sagacity and vigour" once he had been removed from the Tidewater and all it stood for, Dangerfield's transformation is insisted upon rather than explained. In the last volume, Paulding gives him only walk-on parts, and even these roles he plays woodenly and unconvincingly. The Westerner who pre-empts the last parts of the story is the comic woodsman, Ambrose Bushfield. Although Bushfield is called "Squire," lives in a log "Hermitage" with a Negro slave and is described as a man whose "feelings, by some strange freak of nature . . . partook of the character of gentleman in more ways than one,"[39] he is even less a gentleman than Harvey Birch or Natty Bumppo. He is all whoop and holler. He is characterized by his outspokenness and by his disregard of all decorum. He breaks in upon the Dangerfields without ceremony and occasionally in arguments threatens to "tree" them like so many squirrels.

"Whoop!" exclaimed a voice without which they all recognized as that of Bushfield.
"Come in, come in," cried the colonel.
"Come in! why, ain't I in?" exclaimed he, as he entered in a great flurry, and seated himself.

Other members of Dangerfield's community refer to Virginia, Dangerfield's daughter, as "Miss Virginia." Bushfield is more direct. "You neat little varmint," he called out to her, "have you got any thing for supper? for may I be lost in a cane-brake . . . if I ain't transcendently hungry. I could eat like all wrath." Bushfield's natural manner, Paulding comments tolerantly, "though odd and extravagant, had nothing in it partaking of vulgarity."[40]

The traits of gentility which Paulding appears to have had in mind when he called Bushfield a kind of "gentleman" are nonetheless worth noting. Bushfield's know-how and his physical endurance make him the superior, in fact the tutor, of all the characters who must encounter the forest. His main function is to tease and humiliate the Easterners and make them see the artificiality of what he calls "civilization." In his pride and independence he sees himself the inferior of no man. Furthermore, Bushfield possesses one other very important genteel qualification: he is a man of leisure. With his gun on his shoulder and the whole book of nature open before him, he is thought to possess a kind of leisure which is unfettered by European fashion or by Yankee acquisitiveness. Unfortunately for Paulding, there existed no way of accommodating Bushfield's gentility to society, even to the society of a frontier town. At the end of the novel Bushfield runs afoul of the law and, like Natty Bumppo before him, he "cuts dirt," goes west, and dies with his gun in his lap and his dog at his feet. Bushfield is as little Andrew Jackson as he is Cuthbert Dangerfield. Similarly, Cuthbert Dangerfield was no more at home in leather breeches than Bushfield was at home in the drawing room. In attempting to create a natural gentleman out of a "mettled cavalier," Paulding had ended by suggesting his inability to become one. He had taken Andrew Jackson's character, split it down the middle and come out with a cagey and outspoken woodsman and a genteel cipher. John Randolph and General Washington, Paulding must have sensed, were still poles apart.

From Jackson to Randolph

For Paulding the mid-thirties was a period of renewed literary activity. Within a period of two years he published two new books and made extensive revisions of his earlier writings for a uniform edition of his works published by Harper & Brothers in 1835. He prepared for Harper a two-volume *Life of Washington*, written especially for schoolchildren. The following year, in 1836, Harper also published his *Slavery in the United States*. Both in his revision and in the Washington and slavery volumes, Paulding manifested a mounting and unmistakable concern with the problem of Southern character. In particular, he gave expression to a long-standing fascination with the characters of two famous Southerners, George Washington and John Randolph. When the new edition of *Letters from the South* appeared in 1835, it contained, along with the Engine Isles, two other important additions, a long sketch of Randolph at the beginning and a lengthy section at the very end on Washington and Mount Vernon.

On the face of it, it seems indeed very strange that Paulding in a single year should have undertaken to write a life of George Washington, a eulogy of John Randolph, and a detailed and virtually unqualified defense of Negro slavery. Yet Paulding, it would appear, did not think of himself as reconciling irreconcilables. One task seemed to lead logically enough to the next and the materials of argument even overlapped. Washington and Randolph were examples of humane and compassionate masters of slaves, and the slave master, like Washington and Randolph—in contrast to the hypocritical abolitionist-Yankee—was a disinterested man who placed duty before private ambition or pleasure. For Paulding, Washington, Randolph and the slave master were types of the natural gentleman, as independent of European fashion as of self-interest. All three were patriots who could be relied upon to place the interest of their country above their own. Notwithstanding the very evident differences that existed between them, Paulding seems to have concluded that the three made common cause against the Yankee North and its handmaiden, "the Progress." They were independent of time, money or place.

The Washington biography was undertaken at the request of Harper & Brothers for its new Common School Library. An act of the New York legislature had recently provided for the establishment of a library in each school district in the state. Harper had contracted to provide two series of suitable texts, one for younger readers and one for more advanced readers. Paulding's *Washington* led off the second series.

In the course of retelling the story of Washington's life, Paulding paused at frequent intervals to dwell on the traits of character which had made Washington what he was. The most important of these and in all ways the most remarkable, Paulding felt, was Washington's complete independence of all outside forces. As a young surveyor in the wilderness, as an officer of militia, as a Revolutionary general and as President, Washington lived *from within* and regulated his life and conduct by moral laws which no difficult circumstance or temptation could alter or transform.

The good man carries his happiness with him wheresoever he goes, for it is the inmate of his bosom. Its source is in the consciousness of virtue and the approval of Heaven. This is the only sure basis of independence, for it places us above the world and all its accidents, which are otherwise beyond our control.

The "serenity" of Washington's life thus placed him "far above the influence of all this world can give or take away."[41] In almost every way, Washington met the requirements of the transcendent Yankee. Paulding, like Sarah Hale, placed great emphasis on Washington's temperance and self-control. The regimen of his daily life was never altered in the slightest detail, even when there were guests present. Every activity was scheduled and given a place in the day, from the letter writing by candlelight before dawn to the glass of Madeira and the two cracked walnuts which followed dinner.

With him idleness was an object of contempt, and prodigality of aversion. He never murdered an hour in wilful indolence, or wasted a dollar in worthless enjoyment. He was as free from extravagance as from meanness or parsimony, and never in the whole course of his life did he turn his back on a friend, or trifle with a creditor.[42]

Take away from Washington his horse, his slaves and his military skill and you have Benjamin Franklin.

But Washington was not Benjamin Franklin, any more than he was Harvey Birch. The singularity of Washington lay in the fact that he combined the best qualities of Yankee and Cavalier, and thus he was the one man who could be a national, rather than a regional, hero. He was characterized by tenderness and compassion rather than ambition. Paulding stresses Washington's courage in battle and his ability to inspire confidence as a leader fully as much as he stresses his self-control and regularity of character. Washington possessed two further Cavalier traits of great importance. He lived on his horse and he idolized his mother and his wife. He cannot be thought of apart from his profound sense of family and social responsibility and the influence he exercised over the lives of other men. He became a leader while still a schoolboy and his career of leadership ended only with his death. His last words were a command.[43]

Whether his subjects were Continental soldiers, members of cabinet or plantation slaves, his authority was derived from the same source. He was the moral superior of every man around him. He was better than other Americans because he was morally perfect.

In discussing Washington's character, the words that spring most readily to Paulding's lips are "symmetry" and "harmony." In Paulding's scheme of things—and in that of his contemporaries—the American was threatened as much by civilization as by wildness. The city threatened to make him into a dandy or a predatory Yankee; life on the edge of a wilderness might make him into something completely idiosyncratic and willful, an admirable but useless social type like Ambrose Bushfield. Washington's life represented the Golden Mean. Washington brought civilization to the wilderness and he brought his autonomous and natural virtue to the city. "The gold was too pure to become rusted by any vicissitudes." He was neither ambitious like the Yankee—he served during the Revolution without pay—nor spendthrift like the planter. Unlike Cuthbert Dangerfield, Washington kept elaborate and detailed accounts. Even in battle he was controlled. As a warrior, Paulding remarks, he established a reputation for "temperate ardor." He was an aristocrat whose superiority all Americans were willing to acknowledge because his aristocracy was characterized not by leisure or by personal cultivation but by a "dignified simplicity of usefulness."[11]

Still and all, one senses in Paulding's account of Washington the absence of some remarkable or eccentric trait. Perfection is never interesting to write about and Paulding clearly experienced difficulty in finding anecdotal materials which would bring the paragon to life. A man without weakness or fault and not subject to temptation must have stretched the credibility as well as the patience of the most responsive schoolboy. Paulding had known enough interesting men to know what distinguished a man and made him interesting. He seems to have sensed the limitations of his present subject. Washington was a man of character who lacked a distinctive character. Andrew Jackson, on the other hand, was a man of distinctive character who seemed a native of the place and who breathed through lungs. So was John Randolph.

If Washington in his ability to transcend local circumstances tended to lose his American distinctiveness, John Randolph's distinctiveness was thought to be the direct product of American experience. He was proud of being a direct descendant of Pocahontas. In the minds of a great many of his contemporaries he was thought to be the very personification of local Southern consciousness. His independence, unlike Washington's, was defiantly personal, and his ardor was never temperate, never moderated.

Paulding met Randolph in Washington shortly after he arrived there in 1816. Paulding appears to have admired him from the first and to have become one of Randolph's few intimates. Randolph was an insomniac and Paulding wrote to friends in New York of sitting up the night with him, talking, drinking and jesting. When he revised his *Letters from the South* in 1835, two years after Randolph's death, Paulding added a long character sketch of his eccentric friend. He described him as a man of savage and defiant independence and incorruptible disinterestedness, a curious blend of wildness and courtliness. "Mr. Randolph," he wrote, "is, beyond comparison, the most singular and striking person I have ever seen." When engaged in debate on the floor of the House, he noted, "he cuts with a two-edged sword, and makes war like his Indian ancestors, sparing neither sex nor age."

That he is irritable, capricious, and careless of wounding the feelings of those for whom he has no particular regard, no one will deny. That he is impatient in argument, and intolerant of opposition, is equally certain; and the whole world knows, that he is little solicitous to disguise his contempt or dislike.[45]

Although Paulding made some effort to temper his admiration and at one point observed that Randolph's fate indicated "the necessity of toleration in politics as well as religion,"[46] he was only halfhearted in his criticism. What impressed Paulding most was Randolph's "lofty independence of mind," his "unsullied integrity as a public agent or a private gentleman."

He has never abandoned his principles to suit any political crisis. . . . His word and his bond are equally to be relied on—and as his country can never accuse him of sacrificing her interests to his own ambition, so no man can justly charge him with the breach of any private obligation.[47]

Paulding found in Randolph's ill health and failing strength a vivid testimony to his friend's disinterestedness. He had nothing to gain from this world and thus devoted himself to winning a place in the next. In other words, Randolph was that obsolescent thing, "an honest man," a valiant warrior in a hostile and corrupt world. Other people might call him irresponsible, arbitrary or mad, but for Paulding these would always be irrelevant charges. "Would to Heaven," he exclaimed, by way of peroration, "there were more such madmen among our rulers and legislators, to make folly silent and wickedness ashamed; to assert and defend the principles of our revolution; to detect quack politicians, quack lawyers, and quack divines."[48] In Randolph the Yankee had found his legitimate adversary.

The Route to Insurgency

For Paulding the search for independence and integrity in American character had taken him in two different directions. One way led to Washington, to Union and to selflessness. Moderation, tolerance and compromise were the means of conveyance. This was the National Road and the route of the Whig party. The other way was finally for Paulding the preferred route. It led to John Randolph and particularism and idiosyncrasy. It proceeded by militant assault and untempered defiance. It recruited its followers from the ranks of would-be martyrs rather than from the ranks of statesmen. It presupposed a world gone wrong and past the retrieving. It was a desperate course.

In the two remaining books which discussed the South, the volume on slavery and his last publication, *The Puritan and His Daughter*, Paulding tried to maintain a precarious balance between these two opposing postures, defiant independence and compliant independence. The scales had nonetheless begun to tilt. *Slavery in the United States*, in its outward form, was an argument for tolerance and for Union. Negro slavery, according to Paulding, was not "an evil of such surpassing enormity as to demand the sacrifice of the harmony and consequent union of the states." He advised his fellow Americans to put aside party views, individual prejudice and look at the problem of slavery dispassionately. Any attempt on the part of the North would necessarily bring on "civil contention and servile war." Abolitionists and those sympathetic to their aims must face the question of "whether THE UNION SHALL LAST ANY LONGER."[49] The choice to be faced was not one between slavery and freedom but rather between social harmony and anarchy.

Those who opposed slavery, he asserted, were not "sincere." Despite their pretensions to virtue and their so-called religious scruples, abolitionists acted out of self-interest, not out of moral conviction. The Yankee reformer was by trade a hypocrite. If he was not, why did he seem indifferent to the industrial servitude and misery which surrounded him in Northern cities? He took as his example a Congressman from Vermont who had recently proposed to abolish slavery in the District of Columbia. How sincerely concerned with the welfare of the slave was such a Northerner? Was it not likely that his *real* concern was to reduce the number of Congressmen from Southern states and to reduce the dominant role which the South played, and had always played, in American politics? Was his real concern humanity, or was it power? He left no doubt of his answer. "Indeed," he remarked, "the most distinguishing characteristic of almost all the champions of the blacks, is an utter disregard to the rights of the white men."[50] The North was in fact waging war on the Southern states. "A ferocious, unrelenting, unbrotherly warfare has been, still is, waging against a large portion of the good citizens of the United States." How long was the South to stand idly by and watch its domestic arrangements being tampered with by prying and curious outsiders? The best thing the North could do was to do nothing at all, to mind its own business and let the South mind hers.[51]

Paulding's attitude toward the North, and toward the American people in general, hardened perceptibly as he advanced in years. By the last decade of his life his alienation from the culture of the North, from American culture as a whole, was virtually complete. For *The Puritan and His Daughter*, published in 1849, he wrote a long and bitterly satirical dedication, addressed to THE MOST HIGH AND MIGHTY SOVEREIGN OF SOVEREIGNS, KING PEOPLE, as though to a ruling monarch. This sovereign, he went on to say, held "the purse-strings of inspiration" and ruled arbitrarily over the reputations of all men who fell under his sway. He was no less a despot than George III. He made one think of revolution. "Not only is your power without limits," he continued, "but your judgment infallible in the selection of favorites, and the bestowal of honors. If you call a pigmy a giant, a giant he becomes; if you dub a man a fool, the wisdom of Solomon cannot save him from the Hospital of Incurables." Paulding professed himself "deplorably behind the spirit of this luminous age." He asked for indulgence and promised to try to please, but his remarks were edged. "I hereby offer at the footstool of your royal clemency a work, which, though it contains a great many truths, I flatter myself they are so dextrously disguised that Your Majesty will not be a whit the wiser for them."[52]

The disguise which Paulding adopted in this last novel is not altogether transparent, even today. He seems on the surface to be pleading for sectional reconciliation. The story concerns two families, one Cavalier and one Puritan, that settle Virginia in the seventeenth century. The family of Hugh Tyringham, "a very ancient and noble family" of Norman descent, had taken refuge in Virginia during the Protectorship of Oliver Cromwell. The family of Harold Habingdon, of Saxon descent, had been persecuted under Laud, freed by Cromwell and had come to America at the time of the Restoration. The original destination of the Habingdons had been New England, but they had been stranded in Virginia by mistake. The two families occupy adjacent plantations on the James River. Both Cavalier and Roundhead conform to type. Tyringham is warm, spontaneous and pleasure-loving. He is (anachronistically) addicted to mint juleps, fighting Indians and fits of wrath. When Tyringham learns of a romance between his son Langley and Miriam Habingdon, there is "a tremendous explosion of wrath, levelled at Crop-ears,[53] Roundheads, Rebels and Republicans, not forgetting Oliver Cromwell and the Rump Parliament."[54] Habingdon is an ascetic and joyless figure who neither drinks nor smokes and who always acts "on principle."

The Habingdons have a difficult time of it in Virginia. They are mocked and persecuted as "crop-ears" and are finally forced to flee to New England. Miriam's mother and father die and Miriam, left alone, is almost hanged as a witch. The plot is devoted to getting Langley to New England, where he can rescue Miriam from the hands of the scheming Yankee villain, Tobias Harpsfield, who has "framed" Miriam by securing false testimony that she is a witch. Langley arrives at the last moment, secures the confession of Harpsfield and carries Miriam back to "the sunny South" as his wife. On the level of plot, the novel thus has a happy ending. Both children have exorcised the bigotry of their parents. "Those feelings of religious and political antipathy which had alienated their fathers, and caused so much suffering to their children, did not take root in the soil of mutual love." Miriam, like Sarah Hale, becomes an Episcopalian. The triumph of tolerance and benevolence, Paulding states a little later, "is the moral of our tale." Thus, it is implied, the New

World soon eliminates the narrow bigotry of the old. The novel ends with the statement that the children of Miriam and Langley, Cavalier and Roundhead, "still flourish in the ANCIENT DOMINION."[55]

Thus, on the most obvious level, Paulding has subscribed to the legend of the dual origin of American national character. A mixture of the Cavalier and the Yankee, he appears to say, has produced a sturdy and tolerant race of men without the weaknesses of the former and the narrowness and bigotry of the latter. Beneath the sugar coating of reconciliation and optimism, however, certain other assertions of a contrary sort are made again and again. All along there is the suppressed premise that there had been an unmistakable declension in the Puritan character since the period of original settlement. Harold Habingdon, Miriam's father, for all his narrowness, is portrayed as a man not without generous impulses. He is sincerely devoted to his religion. The immediate occasion for his flight from Virginia was the furor caused by his sheltering a refugee Quaker family. He is a firm but kindly father and, once he has experienced the hostility of the Indians, a courageous fighter. He dies as a result of wounds received in a battle with the Indians. The difficulty which develops in New England is not the fault of the original Puritan stock. New England, according to Paulding, is suffering from second-generation trouble.

When the Habingdons flee from Virginia they settle in a small community on the western frontier of New England. The land around them is lovely and fertile. Off in the distance can be seen the Southern slopes of Mount Monadnock. "The landscape wanted nothing but flocks, and herds, and piping shepherds, to recall to mind those scenes of the golden age. . . . All around was peace, repose and silence." The minister and spiritual leader of the community is a model of Christian virtue. "He was zealous without bigotry; loved his own faith without hating that of others; and set an example of all that his precepts enforced. He preached the doctrine of love, not that of fear."[56] The people grew wealthy and there was no crime or civil disorder. The Habingdons find themselves in an Eden as harmonious and bountiful as Sarah Hale's Northwood. Suddenly events conspire to bring this golden age to an end. The old minister dies, the old magistrate returns east and a new set of officials accompanied by new parishioners arrive in the settlement. The new minister and his flock are fanatic believers in witchcraft. The witch-hunt begins. Panic and intolerance follow. In a matter of months a harmonious and happy community is transformed into an insufferable tyranny in which every man sits self-righteously in judgment over his neighbor and neglects the beam in his own eye. Public opinion becomes a despot. Paulding leaves no doubt about the historical parallel he has in mind. "At this moment," he observed, "there exists among a large portion of mankind, the latent seeds of that same delusion."[57] Abolitionism is the nineteenth century's witchcraft. Fanaticism is fanaticism. Miriam and Langley go South to sunshine and to tolerance. Paulding for a moment had dropped his disguise.

In 1849 Paulding was an old man of seventy-one with but a decade of expiring life remaining to him. He published no more. For a number of years he had worked halfheartedly on a book which he left unpublished at his death. To judge from the excerpts printed by his son, this book, entitled *The Mother and Daughter; or, The United States and the United Kingdom*, treated the familiar theme of the Old and the New World—only there had been a shift in emphasis, as the title itself suggests. It was no longer John Bull and Brother Jonathan but mother and daughter. Paulding was still the defiant and defensive provincial. England was still decayed and corrupt and America was still "the poor man's inheritance."[58] There was still hope, but America was the world's *last* hope. America would decide forever the question "whether man in his fallen state is fitted to be other than a slave." There were now long shadows falling across the land. The descendants of the heroic settlers and pioneers "have not altogether degenerated," but the process of degeneration had begun. Intolerance and Yankee avarice had already begun to subdue large parts of the nation.

When the love of self becomes the ruling passion, and the golden calf the only divinity; when money is made the standard by which men are estimated, and held as the sole agent in the attainment of that happiness which is the common pursuit of all mankind: then will this majestic fabric of Freedom . . . crumble to pieces, and from its ruins will arise a hideous monster with Liberty in his mouth and Despotism in his heart.[59]

It was no longer a question of which way the cat would jump. James Kirke Paulding was now ready to address the citizens of Charleston on the urgency of secession. Perhaps one southerly corner of the uncontaminated Eden might be preserved against time and progress.

CHAPTER VIII

Revolution in South Carolina

Tell your Virginia Gentlemen that they have lost all right
to counsel S.C. They have put us into the market! Your
old genuine stock seems fairly to have died out. You are
crossed by Yankeedom!

WILLIAM GILMORE SIMMS, *Letters*[1]

THE PART OF the story which follows, while it pertains to the
whole South in ways that will become clear, has mostly to do
with South Carolinians and their struggle to see themselves in
history. The ever-narrowing parochialism of South Carolina in
the thirties and forties is revealed in their reflections on the
idea of revolution—in their attempts to reckon with contempor
ary revolutionary movements abroad and with revolutionary
change, both threatened and actual, at home. The growing isolationism of the state, like that of the South at large, was not the
result of parochial ignorance or indifference to what was occurring
elsewhere any more than it resulted from an absence of men
of universal spirit. There were South Carolinians enough who
were characterized by sophistication, a broad acquaintance with
politics and a knowledge of history. The parochial outlook
which such men finally adopted was forced upon them by their
growing awareness of the singularity of their historical situation,

by the necessity which they felt to cut themselves off from the threatening implications of contemporary social ideals and moral values. One by one they abandoned the ideas of revolution which were stirring others, until at last they had withdrawn into an eccentric posture of rebellion without larger significance.

Nowhere is this retreat more apparent than in the writings which attempted to find in the American Revolution a larger meaning for the South. The fictional Revolutionary became a rebel without a cause and the insurgent Cavalier became a man of doubt. The passing of time has obscured the emotions, the sense of urgency, with which South Carolinians returned to the Revolution for guidance. Time has certainly obscured the troubled answer which the past rendered up. This search for a usable past has a history which is in some ways as interesting in what it reveals about the South as the Civil War itself.

The Spirit of '76

During the eighteen twenties a depression of such severity struck South Carolina that Virginia by comparison seemed to be enjoying flush times. The expansion of cotton culture into the more fertile soils of the Southwest brought a decline in cotton prices and for Charleston merchants heavy competition from Savannah and the river ports of Alabama and Mississippi. The depression in turn caused a major exodus of population from the coastal areas and produced evidences of desolation of the kind that had been haunting Virginians for almost twenty years. With some exaggeration, Robert Y. Hayne complained in the Senate that Charleston's commerce had virtually disappeared, her ships had been sold and her shipyards were rotting away in disuse. In the cities he found "grass growing in our streets, and houses falling into ruins." In the rural areas along the seaboard others noted that the desolation was even greater. The spectacle of deserted plantations, rice fields that had reverted to swamps, and great houses dismantled by time and weather stirred many a South Carolinian to lyric evocations of the past. "On the very hearthstones where hospitality once kindled the most genial fires," one recalled, "the fox may lie down in security and peace, and from the mouldering casement . . . the owl sends forth to the listening solitude of the surrounding wastes her melancholy discant to mark the spot where desolation has come."[2]

In their attempts to determine what had gone wrong, South Carolinians were quick to associate their economic decline with the growth of the federal government, and some with equal swiftness located the source of their trouble in the noxious protective tariff. Still others pursued the cause of disaster further into history. The bountiful days had come, they knew, before the Revolution, when South Carolina was still a semi-independent colony doing its own business and making its own decisions. A depression of equal severity had laid waste the state at the close of the Revolution. The break with England had ended the bounties on indigo and naval stores and destroyed many of the markets for rice.[3] The fact that the state had enjoyed a period of wealth and splendor prior to the Revolution and hard times afterward encouraged a number of South Carolinians to begin to wonder whether they had won or lost their revolution. As they looked about them in the twenties they began to wonder, furthermore, whether the burden of British or federal tyranny were greater. As in '76 they began, once again, to look to neighboring states for redress.

It was clear from the very first that if the South were to agree upon any program of collective action it would have to find more than negative reasons—a hatred of the Yankee, the abolitionist—to cover its historical nakedness. It needed an overarching historical legend which would forge from the anarchic temper and cumbersome institutions of the South an instrument of sectional belligerency. South Carolina, in turn, needed some sense of itself as playing a historical role within the South; it needed at least the historical sanction of a precedent, a model for its insurgency. Such a model was not easy to find. Contemporary revolutionary movements in Europe provided slender comfort for Southerners, who saw in them the fulfillment of their worst fears about the drift of the modern world and the price exacted by progress. The American Revolution, on the other hand, seemed to belong to the whole Union and especially to New England.

Whatever differences Northerners and Southerners saw in their colonial experience, they were in substantial agreement on the meaning which they assigned to their Revolution. At this one moment in their past the corridors of history converged and Cavalier and Yankee had stood and fought shoulder to shoulder. The growth of a distinctly regional interpretation of the Revolution had thus to take place in the face of a vigorous national legend which found support almost everywhere in the South up until the very eve of the Civil War. It had to contend with the image of a war which had come to stand for mutual sacrifice and which had been fought, so many believed, to establish the very Union which Southerners wished to destroy.

Ironically, it was the role of gadfly of the rebellion, a part played by Massachusetts during the Revolution, which South Carolinians—and fire-eaters generally—coveted most. Robert Barnwell Rhett called for another Boston Tea Party to incite the federal government to a repressive action which would unite the South. "In our Revolution," he wrote in 1844, "no assemblage of the colonies was held until the tea was thrown overboard in Boston harbor; and the British Government, by annulling the charter of Massachusetts, and passing the Port Bill and other coercive measures, made up the issue—and so it can be again."[4] He once referred to his own Colleton District as "the Faneuil Hall where the cradle of Southern sovereignty is constantly rocked."[5] Thus the Carolina-born secessionist William Lowndes Yancey in 1858 called on his fellow Southerners to show enough partisan spirit "to call forth a Lexington, to fight a Bunker's Hill, to drive the foe from the city of our rights."[6] An appeal to the "Spirit of '76" became a characteristic part of South Carolina's response to every crisis with the federal government. This response came so spontaneously, almost mechanically, that it seems more a cry of pain than an articulate political idea. Beneath the all too apparent stridency it is possible, nonetheless, to detect a constant and meaningful core of assertion. For South Carolina the Revolution came to mean the revolt of the local against the general government, a war fought to preserve the individuality of Southern domestic institutions. "The same sense of mental independence," Rhett observed in 1844, "which prompted our ancestors to enter the field in 1776, with the British oppressor, will make us warm now, and watchful, to resent every assault upon the province of our local government, from whatever quarter it may come."[7]

This same idea can be found early imbedded in the rhetoric and nomenclature of the nullification crisis, the first important counter-revolution back to the idea of a confederation. The use by the nullifiers of the Revolutionary blue cockade suggests the localism and provincialism in the spirit of the revolt. "Revolution" was the key term. It was left to men like Rhett, the so-called "father of secession," to spell out the full significance of South Carolina's resistance to the tariff. He chose as his occasion a patriotic celebration in St. Bartholomew's parish. The time was July 4, 1832, just after word reached South Carolina that the tariff bill was nearing completion. The tariff, according to Rhett, represented a form of tyranny which must be resisted by every available means, whether the means happened to be Constitutional or not.

... if the worst comes to the worst, it is but naked resistance without legal authority, —it is at last but Revolution—Revolution! ... What, sir, has the people ever gained, but by Revolution? ... What, sir, has Carolina ever obtained great or free, but by Revolution? ... Revolution! Sir, it is the dearest and the holiest word, to the brave and free. But let it not be said, that because we do not fear, that we seek Revolution. We seek our rights, and we will maintain them. ...

[And if] in the madness of tyranny drunk with domination, here on the free soil of Carolina, the fire and the sword of war are to be brought to our dwellings, why then, Sir, I say, let them come! . . . The spirit of '76 is not dead in Carolina.[8]

The loving repetition of "revolution," the almost liturgic cast of the language, suggest the ordered nature of the transformation it was meant to signify. Revolution was a "dear" and "holy" word, which stood for that struggle for the safety of the home which had kept "the fire and sword" from "our dwellings." Despite the efforts of Unionists to pin the label of "Jacobin" upon the nullifiers and to suggest that the Spirit of '89 rather than '76 was abroad, Rhett continued to hold out for the essential similarity between Massachusetts in '76 and South Carolina in '32. Others saw historical parallels between '76 and '44, '76 and '50, and '76 and '60.

What "revolution" finally meant for Rhett and other extremists became clear when they presented their program for a provisional government at the convention held in Montgomery early in 1861. Written large across the concrete proposals he submitted was a clear acceptance of a need for further rebellion, a chain reaction of secession. He predicted a process of social disintegration that must continue until men of like mind finally composed each of the divisions of society. He wished to have written into the Constitution a statement of the right of secession and of the rights of states to demand the withdrawal of Confederate troops from any fort within their borders. He also wished to deny the Confederate Supreme Court appellate jurisdiction over state courts. When these measures—and practically all the others he proposed—went down to defeat and the convention adopted the United States Constitution almost unaltered, Rhett ruefully commented that the revolution had been lost, as it had been lost at Philadelphia in 1787. The instrument which was to govern the Confederacy contained the hated three-fifths clause, a prohibition of the slave trade and the tariff of 1857![9] From Rhett came the cry of counter-revolution. "For what," asked the Charleston

Mercury's Montgomery correspondent, "have we cast off the North as a rotten incubus, if we are to reenact all their swindles, outrages and insolences upon ourselves." From this moment on, Rhett was never at peace with any civil polity. In 1862 two laws for preventing the "mongrelization" of the South which Rhett had vigorously supported were vetoed by Jefferson Davis as "out of harmony with the civilization of the age."[10]

Between the intellectual world of the political orator and constitutional theorist and the situation of those like the novelists who were primarily concerned with Southern life on a domestic scale, yawned a gulf which few Southerners attempted to bridge. The utilitarian needs of the defense lawyer preoccupied with making his case in the public forum drove politicians to table-thumping simplifications of Southern history and denied them the leisure for reflection and the intellectual latitude for quali-fication. "Take my word for it," Simms wrote to Governor James H. Hammond in 1841, "conservatism, in name at least, will not do for a pressing, impetuous people like our own. It must be *ultraism, in profession at least,* if not altogether in practice."[11] The requirements and expectations of a genteel provincial read-ing audience, on the other hand, restricted the novelists to a very cautious and conventional role as interpreters of the past.

Among Southern writers only William Gilmore Simms pos-sessed the experience, the range of interest and the capacity for reflection to undertake a consideration of the Revolution in the broadest sense. He was in almost every way an ideal spokesman. His many talents, as novelist, historian, essayist, orator, politician, editor and correspondent mark him as a man of unusual versa-tility and gargantuan energy. His mercurial temperament made him alternate moods of passionate Southern loyalty with fits of bitter alienation and deep and articulate pessimism. He was all in his own person a militant fire-eater, a trenchant critic both of Southern provincialism and of aristocratic pretensions, and a most informed and objective analyst of Southern character.[12] Simms was at home alike in the literary society of New York

City, which he visited almost annually, and in the world of Southern politics. He was for years a close friend and regular correspondent of Beverley Tucker's, yet he remained on friendly, almost intimate, terms with William Cullen Bryant long after the two had gone their divergent ways over politics and slavery. Probably his two closest friends were James Lawson, a New York financier and gifted dabbler in literature, and James Henry Hammond, governor of South Carolina and later a United States Senator. Most important of all, Simms was one of the most prolific and most versatile of Southern writers. Poe called him an American Lope de Vega.[13] He published within his lifetime some twenty-five novels, three plays, a work of criticism, a collection of his short fiction, and many volumes of speeches and addresses. In addition he edited, or helped to edit, nine magazines, for all of which he contributed much of the content. Five printed volumes of correspondence account for the remaining hours which he spent at his writing desk, where he regularly filled thirty or forty pages of letter sheet each day before turning to his midnight "recreation" of writing to his friends.

The mixture of emotions which Simms brought to his reflections on his native state probably owes a great deal to the circumstances of his childhood and young manhood. Although he was born in Charleston to a family of more than moderate means, married well and for many years lived comfortably as a cotton planter on the Edisto, he was hounded by misfortune, real and imagined, all of his life. Left an orphan by the death of his mother and the desertion of his father, he was forced for the most part to make his own way unaided by social advantages of any kind. Self-taught and independent, he poured his youthful energies into the kind of autodidactic stint which was characteristic of American writers. Despite the recognition which he eventually received, he never entirely ceased to look upon himself as an outsider. He fretted continually over the limitations imposed on a writer in the South, and scarcely a year went by without a barrage of bitter complaints, accompanied by threats to remove permanently to the North or to Europe. Much of the bitterness which he felt toward the established families was the result of his conviction that he was never fully accepted by Charleston society. His letters are punctuated by accounts of imagined rebuffs and by blanket protests against fate and fortune. "All that I can claim is this," he once confided—with more than a touch of self-pity,

that what I am I am in *spite of friends*, of fortune, and all the usual aids of the ambitious. I have worked in the face of fortune and many foes. I have never known what was cordial sympathy, in any of my pursuits among men. I have been an exile from my birth, and have learned nothing but to drudge with little hope, and to think and feel and act for myself. Through painful necessities I have come to the acquisition of an Independent Mind.[14]

Ill health and the tragic loss of nine of his fourteen children caused many of his bitterest protests; and his insatiable ambition and outlandishly unrealistic expectations of life explain many others.

Contrary to the impression which he himself gave, Simms finally enjoyed a prominence and success throughout the South which few other Southerners attained. More than anyone else, Simms became the historical consciousness of the South. In 1860 *De Bow's Review* described him as the leading spokesman for Southern culture. "He reflects . . . the spirit and temper of Southern civilization; announces its opinions, illustrates its ideas, embodies its passions and prejudices, and betrays those delicate shades of thought, feeling, and conduct, that go to form the character, and stamp the individuality of a people."[15] Apart from his literary reputation, which gave him national importance, he received many honors from South Carolina. While still a young man, he served for two years in the South Carolina house of representatives and was a member of the Board of Visitors of the Citadel during the Civil War. In 1846 he ran for lieutenant governor and missed election by only a narrow margin. While he was the editor of the *Southern Quarterly Review*, from 1849 until 1853, he made it one of the most influential political and cultural organs in the South. He declined being nominated for Congress in 1850, and in 1858 actively resisted a move on the part of friends to put him in the United States Senate.

Toward Insurgency

Simms exceeded all others save possibly Calhoun in the time and thought which he gave to the study of the Revolution. In his huge library at "Woodlands" he collected over a period of thirty years some twelve thousand volumes of printed and manuscript materials on the Revolutionary history of the state. It was from this rich source that he drew as he commenced to piece together his own remembrance of things past. "I summon to my aid," he wrote in 1851, "the muse of local History—the traditions of our own home—the chronicles of our own section—the deeds of our native heroes—the recollections of our own noble ancestry."[16] Certainly at the beginning his object in writing about the Revolution in South Carolina was not in any sense invidious. He simply wished to see to it that his native state received its share of kudos and was not forgotten by future historians. He wanted to give such events as the defense of Charleston and the Battle of King's Mountain a place alongside Bunker Hill and Lexington and Concord in American imaginations, and to add such names as Marion, Moultrie and Rutledge to the Revolutionary Hall of Fame. "My own notion," Simms wrote to Benjamin Perry in 1847, "is that we should write as much as possible about home—gather up our own gems & jewels—look about us and within us—what we are, what we have been & what we may be."[17]

A mere listing of his writings on the Revolution suggests how systematically he went about his task. Four of his historical works are particularly devoted to South Carolina in this period.

The History of South Carolina From its First European Discovery to its Erection Into a Republic appeared in 1840. His *Life of Francis Marion* was published in 1845, his *Life of Nathanael Greene* in 1849. In 1853 he brought out his angry defense of South Carolina's patriotism: *South Carolina in the Revolutionary War: Being a Reply to Certain Misrepresentations and Mistakes of Recent Writers in Relation to the Course and Conduct of This State.* During 1846 he composed short sketches of Greene, Charles Lee, Moultrie, Sumter, Gadsden, Huger, Pinckney and Kosciusko for Rufus Griswold's *Washington and the Generals of the American Revolution.* Most important of all were the seven Revolutionary novels which Simms published between 1835 and 1856: *The Partisan*, 1835; *Mellichampe*, 1836; *Katherine Walton*, 1851; *The Sword and the Distaff* (later retitled *Woodcraft*), 1852; *The Forayers*, 1855; *Eutaw*, 1856. Simms was also concerned with the Revolution in many of his speeches and addresses, as for example in "The Sources of Independence" (1843) and in *The Social Principle* (1843).

The word "revolution," in the face of practical political circumstances, underwent radical redefinition for Simms during the period from 1847 to 1852. The fact that his political activities overlapped his energetic researches into Revolutionary sources greatly influenced his conclusions in both areas. There was a fundamental contradiction in the thinking of extremists like Rhett who employed the American Revolution as a model. They saw the Revolution as an outburst of particularism, as a revolt of the local against the general government and, at the same time, as a blow struck for liberty in the most abstract sense. As they conceived of the Revolution, it was both a war fought out of an attachment to the blood and soil of their ancestors and a part of the struggle of the human spirit everywhere for the ideal of liberty.

Two ideas could scarcely have been further apart. One idea was closely identified with the romantic nationalism of the nineteenth century; the other belonged to the Enlightenment and to the Founding Fathers. The growing prominence of the slavery issue and the corresponding isolation of the South finally led the extremists to play down the fervor with which they had once advanced the idea of liberty. Meanwhile, events in Europe during 1848 only confirmed suspicions already felt and caused them to dissociate themselves entirely from the nationalist movements on the Continent. Though there were attempts to dress it up prettily, the feeling grew that South Carolina faced the prospect of a revolt which seemed devoid of any historical significance, a vendetta, a pointless show of anger and defiance. Simms, however, was at first very loath to settle for the obtuse parochialism to which men like Rhett were soon driven. Eighteen forty-eight proved to be a key year both for his re-evaluation of Democratic politics and for his interpretation of the Revolution. Meanwhile, in a spirit of buoyant optimism, he proselytized his friends to join him in carrying forward both tasks—in bringing on a revolution in state politics and in rendering the old Revolution meaningful. In September he was writing to his friend Hammond in an effort to bring him out of a political retirement into which he had been forced by a personal scandal.[18] "Be assured," he announced, "a revolution is in progress which renders necessary, here, on the scene of action, a leader like yourself."[19]

For many years the center of political power in South Carolina had been the state bank, which, through "loans" and other favors, had consolidated the support of a substantial bloc within the Democratic party. The leader of the bank group was a skillful and intelligent tactician, Franklin H. Elmore, next to Calhoun the most influential man in the state. Robert Barnwell Rhett was for many years a close associate of Elmore, and Calhoun himself had accepted Elmore's favors. The opposition to the bank group which developed during the forties does not seem to have been organized along strictly ideological lines. It included men of different political persuasions—Unionists, fire-eaters, moderates and National Democrats—as did the bank group itself. The issues raised and aired by the opposition were those characteristically raised against entrenched power by reform coalitions—corruption, favoritism, stockjobbery and boondoggling in general. It was a movement of political amateurs directed against the professionals, the "politicians."[20]

The insurgent group in South Carolina loosely allied itself in the late forties with the movement in the Democratic party known as "Young America." This movement, to quote Stephen Douglas, its titular leader, professed to find Europe "antiquated, decrepit, tottering on the verge of dissolution," and gave its support to the democratic revolutions which broke out in Europe after 1848. The South Carolina group, calling itself by turns "Young Charleston" and "Young Carolina," shared with "Young America" the drive to reinvigorate American politics through an appeal to the youth of the country and through the creation of a political ethos which stressed the ideas of service and duty. It also shared "Young America's" belief in the dynamic growth of the United States and advocated the extension of its civilizing institutions to Mexico and Cuba. "You must not dilate against military glory," Simms warned Hammond in 1848. "War is the greatest element of modern civilization, and our destiny is conquest. Indeed the moment a nation ceases to extend its sway it falls a prey to an inferior but more energetic neighbor."[21]

Since the early thirties, Simms, through his friendship with literary Democrats like Bryant and the Duyckincks, had been closely informed on the political situation in New York. He knew the ins and outs of Tammany Hall almost as well as he knew the conspiratorial world of the Elmore bank. Thus, when Simms came to conceptualize what he thought he saw occurring in South Carolina, he drew extensively on his knowledge of the political divisions of New York Democracy. In 1841 he had called himself a "loco-foco"; by 1846 he had discarded this term in favor of a more up-to-date political nomenclature. By the late forties the significant split in New York Democrats was between the conservative Hunkers—so called because they were thought to hanker after power, spoils and office—and the radical Barnburners—from the story of the Dutchman who burned his barn to get rid of the rats. The Hunkers stood for internal improvements, the liberal chartering of state banks and smooth operation of the political machinery through the awarding of patronage— in other words, for Tammany Hall. The Barnburners opposed banks, roads and spoils. They further opposed the extension of slavery into the territories, and united with the Free-Soil party in 1848 in a move which helped elect Zachary Taylor.

By 1846 Simms had already begun to belabor "ancient Hunkerism" in the name of the new radical Democracy. Writing from New York to the *Southern Patriot* in August, 1848, he stressed the asceticism and sense of duty of the revolutionary movement and commented that "the old Hunkers, always opposed to any progress which tends to lessen the offices and the spoils, will be more apt to side with Whiggism [for Simms this meant banks and internal improvements], or even Abolitionism, rather than with those among their own avowed associates, who require them to make a patriotic surrender of their fleshpots." The term "Hunker" was immediately picked up by the insurgent press and became a synonym for the political establishment. The following December the *Patriot*, taking a slap at Calhoun, called for new blood in the party.

New names are necessary to every political party. When will ancient Hunkerism learn this truth, as old as the days of Aristides? He was voted into banishment, because people were tired of the same name constantly sounded in their ears. The masses get vexed with and jealous of the assumed superiority of one great person. . . . The same old politician keeps in place the same old parasites, and the great majority have nothing to hope at his hands . . . and old Hunkerism must be taught that it can only live and maintain itself, by an annual infusion of *young* blood into the old veins. The old must absorb the young.[22]

The movement to rally the youth of the state, the disfranchised and disaffected, went on under the banner of "Young Carolina" through 1847.[23] Finally, during the approach of the election campaign of 1848, Simms and the insurgents felt they saw the long-awaited opportunity to overturn party leadership in the state. "There is confusion in the Wigwam," Simms wrote to Hammond in July, "and, as you say, good will come of the uproar." Rhett and Francis Pickens appeared to support Lewis Cass, the Democratic candidate. So, with one exception, did the South Carolina delegation in Congress. On the other hand, Calhoun and Elmore were said to be opposed to Cass, at least publicly. Neither had any use for Taylor. The powerful Charleston *Mercury*, while committing itself early against Cass, continued to emphasize anti-Taylor news stories. Elmore had followed much the same policy. "The game," Simms commented, "is, to keep back the Taylorites, and suffer the Cassites to go ahead."[24] These complicated maneuverings and the absence of positive leadership among the Hunkers had left the electorate puzzled and paralyzed and, so Simms believed, hungry for a revolutionary change. "We are all in an uproar," Simms wrote to Lawson in August. "For the first time for 15 years, the State is loose from her moorings & public opinion divided. This is a great gain for the independence of the people."[25]

There was from the beginning no question about Simms's support of Taylor, whose early protestations of independence from the Whig party he took at face value. A Taylor victory, he believed, would bring a Southern President uncommitted to the White House. In South Carolina the establishment, and along with it the hated bank, would be toppled and the insurgents would at long last rise, as Simms said, like a "strong man from his sleep." At least once during July Simms was a featured speaker at one of the Taylor rallies which were held through the summer. On this occasion he poked fun at the bank party and again lashed out at "Hunkerism."

Simms had thus, by the summer of 1848, accepted a theory of democratic insurgency which saw the political changes about to take place in America and in Europe as a unitary thing, a vast democratic tide flying the banner of Young This or Young That which would sweep away the ancient Hunkerism of the world and push a vigorous Young America into the forefront of democratic change. How was it possible to regard the Calhoun-Elmore axis as anything but an *ancien régime* living corruptly upon the people's wealth? Lewis Cass, the Democratic nominee, stood for the party in power and was hence no friend of the revolution. Taylor, a soldier, a Southerner, a slaveholder and an expansionist, on the other hand, Simms regarded as an ideal candidate, despite his nominal ties to the Whig party.

Thermidor

A few months were sufficient to blast forever the cheery and optimistic expectations which Simms held in 1848. The world solidarity of the democratic and nationalist movements had begun to crumble before Simms had placed the finishing touches on his own theory of political insurgency. Between the fall of the July Monarchy of Louis Philippe in February and the "Bloody June Days" in Paris a few months later, political order in Europe appeared to have disintegrated from the Carpathian Mountains to the English Channel. By summer the democratic and nationalist movement appeared to be anything but unitary. Simms, along with most Americans, drew back in horror at the prospect of a revolution which could fill the gutters of Paris with blood and disrupt the political life of almost every European nation. Beverley Tucker openly embraced the forces of reaction and looked to Czar Nicholas, who had quelled the revolution in Hungary, as the hope of civilization.[26] Calhoun saw Europe as a laboratory in which the principles of his theory of government were being tested. Writing to his daughter in Paris, he commented that Americans might see in French politics, which had not progressed beyond "Dorrism," the consequences of majority rule. He feared, he said, "a great retrograde movement in the most advanced and civilized portion of the world" unless the flow of blood could be stanched and real political order restored.[27] Simms, writing to Hammond in May, expressed relief that the Chartist demonstrations had failed, and felt that as a result England may have "acquired a new lease of life & security . . . but," he concluded, "I am very doubtful." If order were to be restored, a man would have to appear strong enough to put faction to flight and weld together a political alliance capable of governing. "As for France & the Continent, all will depend upon the advent of the proper man. France does not so much require a ruler, as a leader."[28]

Simms's hopes for a national Democratic movement at home dissolved at about the same time. His support of Taylor suggests how far he had already drifted from a formal alliance with the national Democratic party by the mid-forties. As early as June of 1847 he had written to Hammond that the party under Benton's leadership had been pursuing a suicidal policy which would destroy it, at least as a national movement. "As for the Demo. Party," he told Hammond, "it has been doing its best . . . to commit felo de se. Salt cannot save it,—and the simple object now for us . . . is . . . to elect a Southern president."[29] For Simms, then, Taylor's candidacy offered a perfect solution for "Young Carolina." As the campaign advanced through the summer of 1848, Taylor came to seem a political godsend, General Cavaignac and a Louis Napoleon rolled into one.

The reality of Taylor's election, however, blasted forever Simms's dream of a sympathetic national administration serving Southern interests. The man whom Simms had described as "a Southerner—a slaveholder—a man who has good sense" proved to be still another political traitor to the South. Taylor's Whig cabinet, his concurrence in the admission of California as a free state and his reputed submission to Seward's "abolitionist" policies, effectively demolished the myth of a Southern President. The anticipated revolution in South Carolina which was to have turned out the Hunkers and issued in a new democratic "movement party" proved to be equally without substance. To make matters worse, the prototypical New York Barnburners—Simms's model insurgents—revealed abolitionist proclivities by declaring themselves for the new Free-Soil party and for Van Buren. Simms was also personally disappointed in his cherished hope of receiving from Taylor a consular appointment somewhere in Europe, and Europe itself was still in a state of grave political unrest. The foundations of fortress "Young Carolina" thus crumbled and disappeared almost overnight, leaving Simms to reckon with the scattered remains of his hopes and dreams. His reaction was immediate. After 1849 Simms dropped the word "young" from his political vocabulary and ceased to think about democracy in national or international terms. Instead, he operated thereafter on the assumption that the South was fundamentally different from all other contemporary societies and had best be left to solve its own problems and to work out its own destiny without alliances and without interference.

Simms himself was so disheartened and confused by the succession of events which overtook him in 1849 that he never again engaged in politics. Instead, he contented himself with the role of political theorist and counselor to his friends. In his comments on politics he became something of a cynic and a crank. Meanwhile, he undertook a new and extremely significant phase of his career. In February he accepted the editorship of the *Southern Quarterly Review*, a periodical to which he had now and then contributed, and remained its editor until 1853. He also returned with renewed vigor to the writing of history and historical fiction. During the four years which followed he produced in a burst of creative energy his most important novels about the American Revolution and his most incisive historical essays. He meanwhile made the *Quarterly* the instrument of his examination of the Southern past and Southern character, as well as the most vigorous intellectual journal published in the lower South.

The first new emphasis on the subject of the Revolution to appear in the pages of the *Quarterly* was in an article by Simms himself which appeared in September, 1850. In this article, which was designed to discourage travel in the North, Simms associated the radical Democrat with the European revolutionary—the Barnburner with the Chartist—and condemned them both by associating them with the French Revolution. Both were part of "this universal disorder in laws and morals,—this confusion of society, worse confounded every day,—in its general aspects so wonderfully like those which, in France, preceded, and properly paved the way for, a purging reign of terror." Both were responsible for opening the floodgates to the rising tide of social reform and the natural-rights philosophy which lay behind it.

Society in the North was in revolution. Old things were about to pass away; all things were to become new. Property was to undergo general distribution in equal shares. Every man, it was argued, had a natural right to a farmstead, and a poultry-yard, as every woman, not wholly past bearing, had a right to a husband. . . . Debtors liquidated their bonds in the blood of their creditors. The law of divorce gave every sort of liberty to wife and husband.[30]

Simms's attitude toward the civilization of the North underwent a drastic change in the course of the forties. Simms had edited a Unionist newspaper during the nullification crisis. During the late thirties and early forties he consistently took the posture of a cultural nationalist, now calling for an indigenous American literature, now ridiculing derivative writing which slavishly followed English models. In *The Social Principle*, he had concluded that "the difference in moral respects [between the sections], was, perhaps, not very substantial or great."[31] By the end of the decade, however, his uneasiness over the revolutionary tendencies of Northern reform had led him to conclude that the home and family were to be the first victims of Northern progress. Like Paulding, Simms had always viewed industrialism as a serious threat to social stability. In a passage in some ways reminiscent of Thoreau, he had early concluded that "all the steam power in the world can [never] bring happiness to one poor human heart. Still less do I believe that all the railroads in the world can carry one poor soul to heaven." By 1850, the specter of social chaos was firmly associated in Simms's mind with the North, and especially with New England.[32]

Simms's disillusionment was so extreme that he was forced to abandon the idea of insurgency in any meaningful sense. No longer did he speak hopefully of revolution in the sense of over-turning an established order. His horror of reform in the North, meanwhile, led him to disparage the role of the North during the Revolution. By 1848 he had convinced himself that true patriotism during the war had existed only in the South. In 1847 a New England antiquarian named Lorenzo Sabine had published a study of American Loyalists in which he had noted the high number of Tory sympathizers in South Carolina. Simms, in a hostile review of Sabine written for the July *Quarterly*, defended Carolina by impugning the motivation of New England. New England had been unanimous for the Revolution only because it had been profitable to break with England. In South Carolina the patriots, though fewer in number, had been more disinterested, since they had actually acted against their own best interests. The two sec-tions thus represented two different kinds of insurrection in Simms's typology of revolution.[33] New England had engaged in a "modern" revolution, in the sense that it had fought to acquire property; South Carolina had fought the kind of struggle char-acteristic of the "Anglo-Norman race," a war fought in the name of liberty to vindicate the rights of property. "Certainly," Simms concluded, "there were none of those pecuniary considerations, prompting the revolution in Carolina, which prevailed to unite the people of New England in a cause which struck directly at their common interests." New England in '76 was, in other words, simply being her old Yankee self, hypocritically talking of liberty and the rights of man as she stuffed her pocketbooks with good English gold. In Carolina the Cavalier spirit burned brighter than ever before in history.

We contend that purer patriots were never found; that hands cleaner of offense, freer from the stain of base and selfish motives, never grasped the sword of war.[34]

Simms was widely applauded for turning the tables so neatly on Sabine and putting New England, instead of South Carolina, on the defensive. He himself spoke of the review as an invasion of "Yankeedom." Hammond and Tucker were ecstatic. "I read your article," Hammond wrote to Simms. "It is overwhelming. I don't think the North has ever received such a mauling since Bunker Hill."[35]

The Vanishing Patriot

On the strength of his renewed interest in the Revolution, Simms returned the next year to a fictional idea which he had taken up and then promptly dropped thirteen years before. The Revolutionary novels which he published during the next few years were meant to be further skirmishes in the same literary war on Yankeedom which he had opened with his inflammatory review and continued to wage in one form or another until his death. In the novels, however, the historian was betrayed by the artist. It was one thing to talk abstractly about "pure patriots" and quite another to create believable exemplars of chivalry in a work of fiction. Simms, working with the requirements of the novel in mind, was thus led to quite a different emphasis.

Simms appears to have begun the first of these novels late in 1849. *Katherine Walton; or, The Rebel of Dorchester* appeared serially in *Godey's* during the following year and was published in book form in 1851. The story, supposedly part of a trilogy, is a continuation of the events which Simms had first treated in *The Partisan* in 1835. *The Partisan* had been concerned with the fortunes and misfortunes of a beleaguered patriot family in the dark days following the collapse of resistance to the British. Despite essentially superficial similarities of plot and historical setting, the two novels are thematically very different and were clearly written in different phases of Simms's thinking about the Revolution. *The Partisan* is a war novel which, like the biography of Marion, was only incidentally concerned with the political objectives of the Revolution. It is almost exclusively devoted to retailing the experiences of a troop of Marion's men under the command of a Captain Singleton, and its events transpire on the Carolina back roads or in swamp recesses far from the British headquarters in Charleston. The enemy appears only over the sights of the partisans' muskets. Although the novel depicts a bleak moment in the general course of the Revolution, its mood is almost gay and lighthearted. Singleton's strategies are successful, and the partisans, it is implied, are the vanguard of a successful insurgent movement which will bring victory to the Whigs. The novel ends on a note of confidence. *Katherine Walton*, on the other hand, is essentially a political novel in which almost every important character is caught for a time in the crossfire of conflicting allegiances and loyalties.

This time Simms chose for his historical setting the political and social world of Charleston in 1780 during the British occupation, and the events of the novel occur in a swirl of formal balls, soirées and political cabals. Great emphasis is placed on the historical authenticity of the story, even in its details, and the character of Colonel Richard Walton, about whose unsuccessful rescue much of the plot revolves, is closely modeled on the real-life tragedy of Colonel Isaac Hayne, who was executed by the British after attempts to rescue him had failed. In contrast to *The Partisan*, where Walton is successfully rescued, even the most carefully laid plans tend to miscarry in *Katherine Walton*. It soon becomes clear that the ideology of the patriot cause has lost some of its earlier crispness and clarity. The extreme partisans on both sides—the mercenary British officers and the patriot irregulars—are, for the most part, unsympathetically portrayed. Simms obviously takes most interest in those characters who, for one reason or another, are caught in the middle—Walton, who had once been paroled by the British, a young British officer who had been "framed" by his superiors and a former partisan general suspected of Tory sympathies. The focus of the story is upon these doubtful and undecided men who fall between the extremes of loyalty and rebellion.

The most significant of these is General Andrew Williamson,

one of the two important historical figures in the novel. Williamson became a Loyalist after his defeat and capture at the battle at Ninety-Six, but later rejoined the patriots as a spy. Near the end of the novel Williamson is forced by a party of Marion's men to submit to a drumhead court-martial. In the speech which he gives in his own defense Williamson underlines the novel's political tenor when he describes the plight of a revolutionary left without a cause:

As God is my judge . . . I never deserted [the cause] until it had deserted me! My officers recommended the protection—our troops were scattered—we had no army left. Beaufort was cut to pieces—our cavalry dispersed—Congress would, or could, do nothing for us—and, in despair of any success or safety, not knowing where to turn, I signed the accursed instrument which . . . offered us a position of neutrality, when it was no longer possible to offer defence.

"Family and lands," Williamson concluded, "were the thoughts that made me feeble, as it [sic] made others."[36]

Eighteen fifty-one proved to be a black year on Simms's own calendar. Simms had fallen upon hard times. The income from the sale of his books had declined steadily since the thirties and his income from planting had virtually disappeared. A severe drought hit the Carolinas in 1848 and lasted through 1850. The "Woodlands Plantation Book" records a series of misfortunes which must have heightened his despair. March, 1849, contains the entry. "Result of the Crop of 1840 *Dry Year, no Rain, Burns up.*" For May 6: "the drought still continues No rain . . . Prospects gloomy enough every vegetable in the garden burned up, the whole earth a bed of hot sand. . . ." In 1850, the same complaints were summarized on May 30: "This has been a most disastrous Year, no rain of consequence but twice, and those light showers."[37] Politically it was a year of drift and stagnation of spirit—to employ his own recurrent metaphor. "The state is at sea without a pilot," Simms wrote to Tucker in March. Calhoun was dead, and there was no one in sight with the stature to replace him. The purpose and drive of a few years before had entirely disappeared from his letters. Once again, in writing to Hammond, he spoke of putting himself "hors de combat" by leaving South Carolina and settling somewhere in the North. Hammond himself had temporarily withdrawn from active politics some years before. "I . . . regret," he wrote to Simms, "that you return [from New York] as much dissatisfied as usual with So. Ca. I have not a word that I can say in her behalf. It is lamentably true that independence, real spirit, & intellectual endowment & acquirement are no longer appreciated here."[38]

The Nashville conventions of the previous year had made the idea of a united South almost a subject of farce. There seemed to be no prospect of agreeing upon a blockade, Simms confided to Tucker. "Our Patriotism is scarcely equal to such temporary self sacrifice. Meanwhile, there are no attempts made to secure cooperation in the South. Each man paddles his own canoe, up & down stream, at his own pleasure, and without any effort at combination." In the face of this darkened political prospect, Simms became passive and, indeed, almost neutral in his political posture. "Of politics," he confessed to Hammond, "I hear no great deal, & greatly eschew the subject. This is a transition period in which the *scum* must necessarily be uppermost."[39] To Tucker he was hardly less despondent. There seemed to be evident, he wrote, "a downward tendency of political & social moral." "Our sores are every-where running to the surface," he concluded bitterly. He seemed to welcome the idea of a war which he now saw not as a revolution but as an explosion which would clear the air. Only some cataclysmic event, some great purgation, seemed capable of restoring the South to political health. Human agency came more and more to appear pitifully inadequate. "The scum is uppermost," he wrote, "and will remain uppermost until we have the storm."[40]

Even with a state convention coming on which was directed toward taking South Carolina out of the Union, Simms was willing to sit back and let events take their predestined course. He had commented the year before about Rhett and the "bank" party that "nothing but such an outbreak as will shake the State to the centre, can possibly throw off their dominion."[41] Now, with Rhett predicting federal acquiescence in secession, he was willing to watch the federal and state governments battle each other to the death. "I shall withhold myself from any contest," he wrote to Hammond in June, 1851.[42] It was in the wake of feelings such as these that Simms turned to the composition of his last important book. The mood of insurgency had quite passed out of his life, and, overtaken by his incapacity for political combat, the old warrior soon began to exclaim despondently in his letters—"Othello's occupation gone!" His next book caught him in a Falstaffian mood.

The character of Falstaff had always exercised a fascination over Simms's imagination; his letters and books are sprinkled with allusions to this figure of paradox. Partly Simms looked upon Falstaff as an embodiment of his own longings—rarely yielded to—for indolence, self-indulgence and the pleasures of the flesh. It was his constant complaint throughout a friendship of close to forty years that his wealthy New York friend James Lawson had surrendered to the flesh. When letters from Lawson were slow in coming, Simms was given to lecturing and scolding him for his weakness. "I do think," he wrote to him on one occasion, "that you are suffering the flesh to obtain the ascendency. I suspect you are getting fat, and sleep too soon in the evening & too late in the mornings. *Gardez vous*—for such practice is physically evil." Or again, he might complain to a friend, as he did on another occasion to Evert Duyckinck, "Lawson, like Falstaff, grows fat, and forgets his friends."[43]

But, for Simms, the figure of Falstaff posed a problem that was more than personal. Plague Lawson how they would, the pleasures of the flesh came more and more to define for him the problem of the Southern planter. The planter, he believed, was constantly surrounded by temptations of every kind. The very isolated refinement of his life made the fleshpots only the more alluring, and surrender the more debilitating. The planter, contrary to legend, was not a fighter. "You will readily see," he once complained, "that the true conflict of the Planter, is with the flesh & the devil . . . most planters that I know, are Mussulman-like; in disastrous periods, they fold their arms, in stupid despair, & cry 'Allah il Allah! ['] They yield. They submit. Hence they are submissionists."[44] It was an easy step for Simms from these generalized observations about Falstaff, the planter and the flesh to the creation of a Southern warrior-planter modeled rather loosely on the character of Sir John.

Lieutenant Porgy, formerly a rice planter on the Ashpoo, makes his first appearance in *The Partisan* as one of Marion's troopers. He is given the minor, though significant, role of providing comic interludes between the scenes of action. Rather sizable sections of the novel—rather *too sizable*, some reviewers felt—were given over to an exposition of Porgy's "belly philosophy" of life. Like Falstaff, to whom he is specifically compared, Porgy is a figure of contradictions. While his sensuality and animal nature are constantly emphasized and Porgy is described as "a perfect mountain of flesh," he is at the same time the most genteel and cultivated character in the novel, a dilettante and a gourmet, a man at once familiar with Latin poetry and delicacies of food and drink, "a jovial philosopher—one who enjoyed his bottle with his humours."[45]

Porgy's genius lies in his capacity to be the opposite of what he seems. His character tends to be rendered in a series of antithetical statements. Although he is described as a wastrel who "ate and drank and talked everything away," Simms later comments that "Porgy was a man nearly as full of prudence as plethora. He was luxurious, but he was vigilant; fond of good things, but neglectful of no duty in seeking them." Even his eating is done in moderation. "He rather amused himself with a hobby," Simms commented, "when he made food his topic, as Falstaff discoursed of his own cowardice without feeling it." Despite the fact that he adopts the motto, "Never Hurry," and seems to be the most pacific of men, it is said of him that "he rides like the devil, and fights like blazes." Whimsical, witty and benign, he is nonetheless capable of decisive and brutal action i' th' heat, as when he dashes a pot of boiling hominy into the face of a charging British dragoon. For Porgy somehow compounded sensuality and intelligence, reflection and action, imagination and common sense—every quality which the planter appeared to need. He lacked only a certain minimal modesty. "Lord, how he can talk," mutters one character.[46]

Porgy is a very different kettle of flesh from his Shakespearean prototype, even in the qualities that are claimed for him. To begin with, he is a much scrubbed up, almost Victorian, version of the fat knight and not, like Falstaff, a version of low life. In order to create Porgy, Simms had to remove Falstaff from the sack-swilling, lawless tavern life of Eastcheap and make him into a country gentleman. He had to convert his thirst and appetite into taste and discrimination and make Porgy stand for the pleasure principle rather than for the pursuit of pleasure.

It is in this genteel guise that he appears in *The Sword and the Distaff*, a Revolutionary novel set in the ruined, postwar South Carolina of 1782—a South that had already experienced the cataclysm on which his imagination had been dwelling. *The Sword and the Distaff*—which Simms later retitled *Woodcraft*—was conceived and written late in the black year of 1851. In it Simms writes of a South which has won its battles but lost the war. His own mood of pessimism and foreboding hovers over the narrative from beginning to end. If *Katherine Walton* had as its theme the revolutionary deserted by his cause, *Woodcraft* developed the more somber theme of the evil social consequences of war. It was almost as though Simms in his own retirement from politics saw himself in the person of an old Revolutionary partisan returned from the wars. Porgy, as the story opens, has been robbed of everything he once possessed including his youth.

The novel begins as the British, after a final display of venality, are preparing to evacuate Charleston, taking with them their plunder and their stolen slaves. In the early pages of the narrative

Porgy, now mustered out of Marion's brigade, sets off for "Glen-Eberly," his rice plantation on the Ashpoo to begin life anew. As he travels toward home, he moves through a Southern waste land of ruined plantations and blighted forests—a desolate country-side stripped of every living thing. A passage which Simms quotes from General Moultrie's memoirs suggests the extremity to which the state had been reduced by war. Moultrie had found his journey home "the most dull, melancholy, dreary ride that any one could possibly take." The cataclysm of war had everywhere exacted its terrible price, and only evidence of death and exploitation was to be seen—a few turkey buzzards here and there picking at the carcasses of the unburied dead.[47]

It is against such a historical backdrop as this that the tragi-comedy of Porgy's rehabilitation from soldier to planter is played out. More than Porgy's individual lot, it is made clear, is to be decided by the events of the novel. Porgy early introduces him-self confessionally as a symbol of the Cavalier South. "I was always one of that large class of planters," he tells his overseer, "who reap thistles from their planting. I sowed wheat only to reap tares. I never had luck in planting."[48] Before the war had even begun he had fallen victim to high living. "He had never been taught the pains of acquisition," Simms comments, and as a result the war had found him on the verge of ruin, with the "paternal house and hearth . . . transmitted to him through three or more careful generations" covered with debt. For a brief time during the actual fighting Porgy had served as a useful social type. Now with the war ended, Porgy confronts the question of his survival in the new and altered social world which has been introduced by the war. In his confrontation he speaks not only for himself as an individual but for a whole system of values.

The questions "what is to be done?"—"whither am I to turn?" . . . "where is my resource?" to be asked of himself, for the first time, and by the man who has already passed middle age, are well calculated to fling a pall over the prospect, and make the heart to shrink at the entrance upon the unknown void of life which yet spreads before it.[49]

The "unknown void of life" which Porgy encounters would have been sufficiently terrifying to shrink the heart of Simm's earlier and more conventionally heroic types. In the face of it Porgy is reduced to playing the role of a loquacious clown, who is unacceptable to the two women he courts and is virtually the prisoner of his overseer.

The social world surrounding "Glen-Eberly," in which the values of Porgy contend for survival, is in a state of lawlessness which interestingly anticipates the ruined South after Appomattox and during Reconstruction. From his unfavorable perch on the bare and rotting piazza of his plantation house, "swept clean" by pillaging British soldiers, Porgy is harried forth alternately by anarchy and by debt. The war has fostered outlawry and there exists a kind of restless and pointless hostility among the poor whites which derives from their very sense of rootlessness. The social pre-eminence of the planters meanwhile is being challenged in another way by a new moneyed class made up of former war profiteers and Loyalists like the merchant-moneylender M'Kewn who hold them in bondage. The aristocratic ethos is thus being ground away between the opposing millstones of nihilism and opportunism. At one pole is the amoral squatter Bostwick, with his shady past and his squalid anti-Home, which is situated in a corner of an adjacent plantation. The possibility of a different kind of revolution appears as a haunting specter, a revolution which will bring scum like Bostwick to the top. When Bostwick finds his daughter reading from the Book of Acts, he soliloquizes on the meaninglessness of the social order, the senselessness of subordination to either man or God. Every man who wishes to survive, he theorizes, must look out only for himself:

"Acts of the Apostles," quoth he. . . . "They sarved for their time. There's no Apostles now, I reckon, to do any more acts for poor people. . . . No! the days for Apostles is at an *eend*, and men does jest what act suits 'em best. So I does mine."[50]

At the other extreme is the rank materialism and opportunism of Porgy's new overseer, the suitably named Mr. Millhouse. Mill-

house, who had served as a sergeant under Marion, accompanies
Porgy home and agrees to stay on and teach him how to run his
plantation profitably. From the beginning he presumes on his new
position, criticizes Porgy's style of living and even attempts to
select a rich wife for him. As Porgy's "sense-keeper," Millhouse
takes it upon himself to train the Old Cavalier away from his
extravagant habits. Millhouse believes that Porgy has been ruined
because he planted "agin nater," drained his rice fields to catch
perch, and took Negroes from their work in the field to find him
bait and to beat for game. Under Millhouse's austere regime
Porgy is cautioned against acts of generosity, denied house guests,
and allowed a single horse for riding and a single beagle (but no
pointer) for hunting. Partridge, Millhouse tells him, are best
shot on the ground, not on the wing.

Look you, cappin, them's all notions; and when a man's wanting
flesh for the pot, and meal for the hoe-cake, it's not resonable that
he should be a sportsman and a gentleman. That's a sort of extravagance that's not becoming to a free white man, when he's under bonds
to a sheriff.[51]

The central debate of the novel takes place in the two chapters,
"Porgy's Notions of the Useful," and "Millhouse on the Utilitarian
Philosophy," which occur about midway through the story. Here
Porgy is battled to a standstill and everything which follows is a
kind of denouement. There is something peculiarly pathetic
about this scene, in which the shabbily genteel Porgy argues with
his illiterate overseer over the value of polite learning and the
arts, yet argue he does—and not very well. The basis of his
argument is that man, like nature, is a complex being with
complex needs, among them song and art. To this view of life
Millhouse eventually renders a reply which, given Porgy's situation, is unanswerable:

You don't know what's useful in the world. You only know what's
pleasant, and amusing, and ridickilous, and what belongs to music,
and poetry, and the soul; and not about the wisdom that makes crops

grow, and drives a keen bargain, and swells the money-box, and keeps the kiver down. Now, I reckon, you'd always git the worst of it at a horse-swap. You'd be cheated with a blind horse, or a spavin'd, and you'd go off on three legs, though you come on four. Now, ef there's wisdom in this world—that is *raal* wisdom—it is in making a crop, driving a bargain, gitting the whip hand in a trade, and always falling, like a cat, on one's legs. As for music and po'try and them things, it's all flummery. They don't make the pot bile.[52]

Too weak and ineffective to do without Millhouse and too discriminating to wholly approve of him, Porgy is left to handle him with captious irony and pious sermonizing. Assuming the posture of a preacher, Porgy has the last word: "The true man, Millhouse, does not live by money, nor by that which money will always buy—bread and meat. There is still better food than that for which I more hunger."[53] But the Snopeses had moved into the South to stay—and long before William Faulkner.

From Falstaff to Hamlet

The problem which Simms confronted with the Southerner was to preoccupy him almost obsessively toward the close of his life. The fact that he persisted in construing cultural problems as literary problems should not mislead us into thinking that he looked upon these problems as in any sense trivial. For Simms, literature, and especially the literature of the Elizabethan stage, was the Book of Life itself, and to some extent he drew upon his literary experience as we today draw from the literature of sociology and psychoanalysis the terms and examples for interpreting and conceptualizing society. But to say this is not enough. There was an urgency to his exploration of Southern character which is not so easily expressed or explained by contemporary analogies. Once he had discarded his programmatic democracy and divorced himself from the tide of revolution which he saw sweeping America and Europe, he came to look upon his own personal lot and that of the South as essentially tragic. The

South in his newly awakened consciousness was seen as necessarily at war both with itself and with the larger American society of which Simms continued to feel himself a part. The problem for Simms was not simply one of representing his convictions truthfully and faithfully. When he attempted to do this—in his pamphlet literature, his political speeches, his journalistic excursions and his lectures—he indulged in propaganda hardly distinguishable from that written by other Southerners. Something else, the need to see the predicament of the South in all its complex and tragic dignity, drove him toward a larger view, toward myth rather than toward propaganda.

Simms had always intended to carry the character of Porgy through yet another novel, into the post-Revolutionary world and to make him into a "legislator." It is significant that he never did so. As late as 1859 he wrote to John Esten Cooke that he was "not yet *matured* enough" for such a venture. "It will require three years more of life in solitude & in the growth of my own soul, to make the work what I design." Of Porgy he commented, "I must prepare him & myself together to drape our sunsets with dignity."⁵⁴ As he grew to accept the idea of a separate Southern destiny and as he came to feel that an impending doom was settling over his world, his imagination turned compellingly toward the great figures of tragic literature—to Othello, to Macbeth and especially to Hamlet.

Simms, as a self-made man who had enjoyed few of the advantages of gentility, had always looked upon the figure of the Southern gentleman more or less from the outside and with considerable ambivalence. He had admired the refinement, the aristocratic elevation of mind and the reflective gifts which Southern life at its best seemed to make possible. On the other hand, he had criticized from the first the Southern tendency to self-indulgence, indolence and idle fantasy. In Porgy he had attempted to draw together these conflicting characteristics of the Southerner and to create a character who would somehow combine these opposing strains. He did not fully succeed, yet he did do something. If it is impossible to take Porgy's cultural pretensions seriously, he is nonetheless the most believable Southern gentleman to appear in this writing and he is at moments magnificently funny in his almost heroic ineptitude—a prefiguring of Twain's Colonel Beriah Sellers, incapable of decisions of any kind, lovable but hopelessly unrealistic about his own situation and that of the South. A legislator, for all Simms's wishes, Porgy could never have been, any more than Falstaff except in fancy— could have occupied a throne.

As the sectional crisis increased its intensity and Simms became more aware of his own political apathy and lack of political purpose or direction, the problem of Southern indecisiveness more and more preoccupied his thoughts. It is not surprising that in moments of self-torment over his own irresoluteness and on those occasions when a friend had to be goaded into action, the figure of Hamlet should have sprung to his mind. *Hamlet* was without any question the work of tragic literature which Simms knew best. His letters from 1830 on are strewn with references to it and quotations from it. "Remember Hamlet—'Whose native hue of resolution / Was sicklied o'er by the pale cast of thought,' " Simms cautioned Hammond in 1849. "As the augur said to the Emperor—Cut boldly." Again, in 1861 he sent his son Gilmore off to the Confederate army with a letter of advice warning him against "that lack of firmness, that overcaution, always trembling at consequences, & calculating chances, which was the infirmity of Hamlet, and which is fatal to all heroism."[55] By the end of the eighteen fifties it seems clear that *Hamlet* had become for Simms a kind of parable for the South. In his lectures and criticism of the play he had made the indecisive prince into an apotheosis of the Southern planter. He was Porgy grown anxious and confronted by a destiny he could neither understand nor control.

Simms's detailed concern with the play dates from 1844, when he composed four articles on "The Moral Character of Hamlet" for an obscure Southern magazine.[56] Late in 1853, with the prospect of a Northern lecture tour facing him, Simms exhumed these articles, recast them as lectures and made them his *pièce de résistance* when he went north early the next year. The lectures were delivered for the first time at the Smithsonian in Washington —only a few days after Stephen Douglas had reported a bill in the Senate which he had baited with the fateful concept of popular sovereignty. Simms had then journeyed on to deliver the same lectures in Philadelphia, in Richmond and, finally, in Petersburg, Virginia, before he returned home early in February.

It seems clear that high among Simms's objectives on this tour was that of explaining to Northern contemporaries something about the moral temper of the Southerner. He began by claiming Hamlet for the South. Hamlet, he found, was not at all a remote literary fiction. He was "a character in every way natural," of a kind frequently found in all "*old communities*—in which rank and wealth assert the influence they are always likely to obtain." He was "the perfect gentleman." Hamlets, he felt, were most apt to appear in societies where there was no progress and where life is accordingly consumed in trying to meet the requirements of an elaborate social code. Under such circumstances, "the energies of individual manhood . . . become impaired." He expected one would find no Hamlets, for example, in Texas, where qualities of enterprise and decisiveness are demanded by the conditions of frontier life. In Charleston, on the other hand, he had known "several Hamlets," men who encounter hesitation and doubt whenever they are forced to contemplate a bold course of action.[57]

The character of Hamlet, as Simms interprets it, is that of a man whose intellectual training, whose wit and charm, and whose penchant for speculation equip him to move easily and gracefully in society. When faced with a crisis—with treachery in his own household or with a national emergency—he is undone by the very qualities which give him stature. "It is contemplation, specu-lation, thought," he commented, "by which the energies of Hamlet are enfeebled."[58] The essence of Hamlet's character is his capacity to elaborate his own personal feelings into generalizations about the human predicament—"Thus conscience does make cowards of us all." Fat and lymphatic, he is given to "thinking too precisely upon the event," to magnifying his own doubts and hesitations into intellectual and theological positions. Confronted with the necessity of action, he explores all possible routes of escape, especially madness and suicide. In contrast to the manly figure of Fortinbras, he speaks as one born to defeat. He becomes the eloquent spokesman of a doomed world. "He is the child of destiny," Simms concluded. "He is singled out for a conflict—for a trial—an ordeal to which he is unequal—and he perishes because of it."[59] Action, when it comes, comes too late and unaccompanied by sufficient coherent reflection. Hamlet is finally goaded to act almost as a matter of pride. His tragedy lies in the fact that, conscious of all the springs of human action, Hamlet nonetheless acts heedlessly, almost suicidally.

The impulse of desperation prevails. There is no time for thought. All things concur to the catastrophe. Hamlet is too much excited for thought. He is now beyond deliberation.[60]

There is a very significant difference between Simms's evocation of Prince Hamlet and the brisk and fustian military heroes of his earlier novels and plays, men like Robert Singleton in *The Partisan*, or Michael Bonham, his hero of the Texas revolution. These earlier heroes act with decision and purpose; they fight for a cause and they are in large measure the masters of their own destinies. In some sense they may all be described as heroes of the Revolution. They act—and if they die, they die—for the future that is unfolding. Simms's conception of the Southerner, beginning in 1849, seems to follow almost directly from his own political disenchantment. More and more it became difficult for him to counsel action; more and more, his counsel became unrealistic, the mutterings of a crank or a crackpot, as when during the war he urged Beauregard to dress Confederate soldiers as Indians in order to frighten Yankee troops. If he found Hamlets in every Southern closet, it was because he sensed the Hamlet too keenly within his own breast. It was almost as though to himself that Simms late in 1853 addressed his friend, Hammond—his favorite "Hamlet"—on the dangers of melancholy and introspection:

I long since felt satisfied that a mind such as yours, teeming with overfulness, and ranging wide over boundless fields of speculation, must be hurtfully restless, having no adequate human or social exercise. . . . Reverie itself, though, perhaps, the most grateful of mental exercises, is for this very reason dangerous; since it induces a corresponding inertness of the animal, and beguiles perpetually into provinces which make it daily more & more ungrateful to return to the earthy.[61]

Weak and sensitive heroes are, of course, numerous enough in the Southern literature which preceded the war. Augustine St. Clare in *Uncle Tom's Cabin* is simply the best-known example of this breed of man. Southern hotheads, too, abound in the fiction of the Revolution and the novels of Beverley Tucker, Edmund Ruffin and others who wrote of the imagined civil war. It was Simms's contribution to the legend to connect the two types and to point out that one followed from the other; that impetuous, precipitant activism grew out of irresolution and indecision and that outbreaks of the kind he anticipated naturally followed when the hesitant were goaded into a course of action out of a conviction that some necessity, some code of honor, demanded it of them.

The relevance of these considerations to what happened in South Carolina after 1853 is difficult to calculate and must therefore be argued with some caution. Too much, for example, should not be made simply of the fact that Simms concerned himself with *Hamlet*, since the figure of Hamlet was grist for everyone's mill in the nineteenth century and Southerners were by no means alone in their fascination with the man of doubt. Simms's contemporaries everywhere detected—to quote Coleridge—"a smack of Hamlet" in themselves. The South, furthermore, contained at least its share of energetic and decisive men who, far from suffering from any consciousness of paralysis, worked effectively and consistently either for Union or for secession, men who would have scoffed at the idea that Hamlet was kin to them. Simms himself repeatedly broke out of his glooms to take a position on this or that issue and chafed to get into action when fighting began. The crippling confusion which developed and which can be detected in his writings and those of other articulate Southerners lay at a deeper level of consciousness—in the growing awareness of the historical dilemma produced by the anachronism of Negro slavery and by the need to defend it in an egalitarian society. Southerners were finally maneuvered into a posture of revolution by their need to protect the slavocracy, and yet it was the need to justify slavery which rendered the existing ideas of revolution meaningless in a South where the ideals of liberty and equality took on a hollower ring with each passing year. It is a saddening experience to trace the tragic retreat of Southerners like Simms into an ever-narrowing parochialism: in his case from the Jacksonian Democrat, Unionist and Young American of the thirties and forties to the alienated and disillusioned crank of the fifties, from the man who had believed in insurgent democracy to the man who had convinced himself that South Carolina had fought the Revolution out of a sense of chivalric honor which she alone possessed. Faced with articulating libertarian ideals he could neither fully believe in nor completely disown, he cut himself off both from his Revolutionary heritage and from romantic nationalism in Europe and took refuge in the memory of a provincial revolt. Finally—and pathetically— he was forced to abandon even the analogue of Carolina in '76, just as he had been compelled successively to despair of a "Southern" President, a "Southern" South and, at last, a "Southern" South Carolina.

CHAPTER IX

Whistling in the Dark

How this book must cut a true-hearted Southerner to the quick!—cut us all, for we verily are all guilty together.

WILLIAM HENRY CHANNING on *Uncle Tom's Cabin*[1]

THE HISTORICAL ISOLATIONISM of the antebellum Southerner, the fact that he felt increasingly cut off and isolated from the historical forces which were reshaping the society of the Western world left him more and more defensive and touchy about his place within the South. The social order which he had imposed on his household and the surrounding county—an order which required the subordination of woman, Negro slave and nonslaveholding white—was submitted to careful and uneasy scrutiny by the novelists, who often stumbled upon social tensions and expressed reservations of a very worrying sort. It was impossible to live in nineteenth-century America without sharing some of its new concerns and obsessions—its sentimental preoccupation with the family, its evangelical benevolence, its endorsement of democratic change and social mobility. And yet it was impossible to share these new civic values without discovering grave inconsistencies in the planter's social code. The novels written by Southerners reflect better than any other source this attempt of the South to wrestle with the nineteenth century and with itself.

Slavery and the Sentimental Revolution

No aspect of the plantation setting finally assumed greater significance than the relationship between master and slave. Southerners were quick to discover that the strongest weapon which they possessed for justifying their peculiar institution to themselves and to others was the argument of plantation paternalism. The image of sunshine and happiness around the old plantation home could, it was felt, win the sympathies of many, especially women, whom the abstract justifiers—Biblical, Constitutional and historical—were unable to touch. This image worked its magic across the nation for close to twenty years, helping to allay the feelings of those who had grown uneasy over slavery. Then, in 1852, a "female scribbler" from the North named Harriet Beecher Stowe demonstrated that paternalism was a sword that cut two ways. *Uncle Tom's Cabin*, it must have seemed to many, exploded like a bombshell in the sentimental fiction of the fifties and left Southerners stunned and enraged by the use to which their favorite literary conventions had been put—and by a Yankee outsider and, to cap it all, a woman.

Most of the literary techniques for representing the slave were developed by the novelists of the thirties. The first crude efforts to render Negro speech—the talk of "laffing" and "luving," "Massa" and "Missus"—were made at this time, and most of the stock characters of the Uncle Tom fiction—the kind but crotchety old mammies, the wise old "aunts" and "uncles," and what Cash has called the "banjo-picking, heel-flinging, hi-yi-ing happy jacks"[2] of minstrelsy—all make their first appearance in this earlier writing. For a time, however, the significance which later attached to these characters remained muted, and the slave was kept in the plantation background as a kind of conversation piece which, sooner or later, most of these writers felt an obligation to take up.

It is scarcely surprising that they did. Everything for a few years had contributed to highlighting the slavery issue. On January 1, 1831, William Lloyd Garrison fired the opening shot in his holy war against slavery in the first issue of the *Liberator*. His stridency and his irreverent attacks on the Constitution startled not only Southerners but moderate and law-abiding men everywhere. Then on August 22 came the chain of events which began when a Negro Baptist exhorter named Nat Turner led a bloody insurrection in Southampton County, Virginia. The rebellion ended forty-eight hours after it began, but not before sixty whites had been brutally butchered in their beds, in many cases by their own slaves. The repercussions of this event—the periodic panics which swept other parts of the South—continued to be felt for close to thirty years. No important uprising ever again occurred in the South, yet the awful nightmare of the Santo Domingo massacres of the seventeen nineties now seemed an American reality, and from this time on the slightest rumor or anecdote of slave intransigeance was often sufficient to kick off a wave of hysteria and repression.[3]

Virginia itself tried to come to terms with these sobering events before the year was out. In the House of Delegates in Richmond, the slavery question was debated over a period of weeks as it was never again to be debated anywhere in the South. With the events in Southampton fresh in mind, Virginians weighed the ills of domestic slavery with candor and precision.[4] The most penetrating and severe criticisms came this time not from Northerners and outsiders but from Virginians, and they were not the criticisms, furthermore, of sentimentalists who pitied the slave but rather of those who feared and despised him. The most articulate of these critics, Charles J. Faulkner from Berkeley County in the Shenandoah Valley, spoke of the "slothful and degraded African" and, at one point, challenged the eastern delegates:

Sir, tax our lands, vilify our country—carry the sword of extermination through our now defenseless villages; but spare us, I implore you, spare us the curse of slavery—that bitterest drop from the chalice of the destroying angel.[5]

Still other delegates went to the length of proposing that a separate western "free" state be established if Virginia refused to act on slavery.[6] The moment was in many ways opportune for some form of emancipation. The effects of the long agricultural depression were still being felt. The price of slaves, furthermore, had been depressed to one of the lowest levels it was to reach before the war. Even in the eastern counties no one arose as an avowed advocate of slavery.[7] In the western counties, meanwhile, resentment was still running high against the east and the memory of the failure to win relief from the odious three-fifths rule two years before was still fresh in the minds of some of the delegates. In a series of votes taken on January 25, the House proved to be almost evenly divided between those who wanted action on slavery and those who did not. The "abolitionists" successfully opposed an initial measure of indefinite postponement by a margin of 71 to 60. The slavery group, however, succeeded in blocking by a vote of 73 to 58 an amendment calling for immediate action on abolition.[8] Virginia thus began 1832 with its ranks divided and many of its individuals deeply troubled over the issue of slavery.

The fiction of the thirties, as much by its reticence as by its declarations, reflects this general uncertainty and uneasiness about slavery. The surprising thing is not that the novelists discussed the question but rather, in view of the publicity which it had been receiving, that they did not concern themselves with it more than they did. There is very little in any of these novels to suggest that any fresh thinking had taken place since the debate on Missouri twelve years before. The pattern for the literary handling of the slave, as a matter of fact, had been partly unfolded as early as 1824 in George Tucker's *The Valley of Shenandoah*, where the stereotype of the childish and dependent slave makes its first important appearance. Tucker's slaves, at the two or three points where they are discussed, are lighthearted, happy in their work, joyous in their play, fond of music and loyal to their master's interest. Their dependence on their master is further emphasized in a scene where young Edward Grayson is forced to tell a grief-stricken family servant, old "Uncle Bristow," that he may have to be sold. Nonetheless, there is the familiar conflict between the subservience of the slave and the horrors which he threatens. When a visiting New Yorker brings up the question of emancipation, Grayson tells him that although slavery is a moral and political "evil," all the remedies which have been proposed promise worse problems still. Until some practical means have been found for transporting former slaves out of the country, he remarks, it seemed dangerous to discuss the question, since there could be no thought of permitting them to remain where they had once been held in bondage. To do so would risk "renewing the scenes which had made Santo Domingo one general scene of waste and butchery."⁰

Throughout these early novels, no point is more emphasized than the dependence and helplessness of the slave—except perhaps his unquenchable happiness. From the very start he was portrayed as the victim of the gentleman's improvidence, even by those most anxious to argue the merits of plantation paternalism. Colonel Grayson's extravagance has forced the sale of his slaves. In *Westward Ho!* Colonel Dangerfield's gambling has necessitated the sale of his plantation, and Paulding includes a brief scene in which Dangerfield is surrounded by his sorrowing Negroes, who clamor to be taken along to "Old Kentuck." When the local minstrel begins to pluck his banjo, however, the sorrow is immediately replaced by joy. These "light-hearted slaves," Paulding comments, are "the very prototypes of children in their joys, their sorrows, their forgetfulness of the past, their indifference to the future. . . ." But to this assurance he appended the very doubt which such portrayals of the slave were meant to allay:

They seemed to be happy, and we hope they were; for it is little consolation to know, or to believe, that a mode of existence of which millions of beings partake is inevitably a state of wretchedness.[10]

Not far beneath the surface of most of these fleeting portrayals of Negro life lurks the uneasy sense that slavery is a wretched, insupportable, human condition. This becomes evident in the quite contrary tendency of these writers to play down the humanity of the Negro and place him in some special category of livestock. Two conflicting impulses seem to be simultaneously at work. The first is concerned with portraying the Negro as a child-dependent, while the other, which has almost exactly the reverse effect, is directed at dehumanizing the Negro by dwelling on his physical characteristics and stressing his animality. The slave most discussed in *Westward Ho!*, for example, is known as "Pompey Ducklegs," and Kennedy, too, for all his Happy Jacks, is inclined to dwell on the peculiarities of Negroes. He points out that they have faces that are chiefly made up of "protuberant lips," "noses that seemed to have run all to nostril" and "feet of the configuration of a mattock." They are "essentially parasitical" and "extravagantly imitative" and they are characterized by "intellectual feebleness."[11]

There is an important confusion at the root of this conflict between the Negro as child and the Negro as animal which was fast setting a trap for plantation novelists. For the purposes of argument, certainly, it would have been much simpler to hold, as some of the theorists did, that the slave was immune to most normal human emotions and hence did not require or deserve— or, indeed, even want—the things which other human beings needed and aspired to. At the same time, because of the fears which the slave inspired, it became necessary to prove to oneself and demonstrate to others that the slave was not after all so different, that he was something other than a monstrous and unpredictable being who could rise up and lay waste a whole county. It was therefore necessary to allow the slave certain "safe" emotions about the condition of servitude. As soon as the justification for slavery became the paternalism of the planter, furthermore, it was important to portray slaves as susceptible to passive feelings, at least—responsive to kindness, loyal, affectionate and co-operative. It became necessary, in other words, to take them into the family and assign them human feelings, however childlike. Once this had occurred—once the camel got his nose properly into the tent—the whole purpose of this kind of portrayal was subject to inversion and it became possible to argue that the planter, not the slave, was the beneficiary of familial love and affection. To attribute to someone the simplicity of a child, furthermore, especially in the middle of the nineteenth century, was a compliment of the first order, and dangerous, too, if the child were to be mistreated and sympathy was not the response sought for

The rapid growth of sentimental modes of expression, particularly those having to do with the home and family, created an immense temptation for those who chose to write about Negro life, whatever their intentions with respect to slavery. Often the sentimental pull proved stronger than ideological convictions, and writers like Kennedy, for example, were betrayed into expressing attitudes toward slavery which run counter to their pronounced views, or at least seriously qualify them. This is notably true of *Swallow Barn*, nine tenths of which is devoted to a whimsical and somewhat patronizing portrayal of country life in Virginia. Toward the end of the book, however, Kennedy included a long chapter which recounts the pathetic efforts of an old slave, Mammy Lucy, to prevent her master from selling her wayward son, and dwells on her stubborn belief in his essential goodness, a belief which is ultimately justified by the child's reform.

In allowing himself to write sentimentally about a Negro's attachment to her children (the chapter is entitled "A Negro Mother"), Kennedy was unknowingly preparing the way for writers like Mrs. Stowe who were bent on showing the inhumanity and injustice of slavery through exploring the Negro consciousness. "My purpose," he announced, "is to bring to the view of my reader an exhibition of the natural forms in which the passions are displayed in those lowest and humblest of the departments of human society, and to represent truly a class of people to whom justice has seldom been done," people who have previously been thought outside the "pale of human sympathy, from mistaken

opinions of their quality, no less than from the unpretending low-
liness of their position." Even the muted irony which Kennedy
employs in this instance suggests the possibilities which later
writers exploited. Mammy Lucy's reluctance to grant the necessity of selling her son provokes Kennedy to comment that "it is
very hard to convince the mind of a mother, of the justice of
the sentence that deprives her of her child."[12] The irony of this
whole incident is further complicated by the fact that the son
Abe is given Caucasian features and some of the enterprise and
intelligence of a white man.

Beverley Tucker was one of the first Virginians to argue that
slavery was a "positive good,"[13] and yet even he, curiously
enough, was unable to restrain himself from occasionally wring-
ing pathos from the sale of a slave. When the narrator of *George
Balcombe* returns to his ancestral plantation in the Tidewater, he
hears the sad plaint of "Old Charles" at the misfortune of being
sold away from "old Massa." Although Tucker denied the Christian doctrine of the unity of the human race and argued that
the slave was a separate species, he was forced in his fiction to
treat the slave as a nominal member of the planter's family and to
attribute to him human feelings and family loyalties which are
scarcely distinguishable from anyone else's. While his object
was clearly to locate the basis of the planter's paternalism in his
long and intimate contact with the slave, the result was to make
the slave virtually the affectional equal of the white man. The
Southern family, as Tucker describes it, binds its members, Negro
and white, with so many ties of affection and loyalty and commits
them so deeply that it is almost impossible to conceive of anyone
ever wishing to elude its bonds. The members of such a family
are not disciplined or restrained by any form of external coercion; only the natural bonds of love and respect for superiority
are needed to keep the plantation household—and, by implication,
Southern society—in order. The Negroes "are one integral part
of the great black family, which, in all its branches, is united
by similar ligaments to the great white family." The Southern

gentleman begins his life at the breast of a Negro mammy, takes as his first playmates the children of plantation slaves and, in later life views the pickaninnies about the place with affectionate regard, asks their names and inquires after their parents. "These are the filaments which the heart puts out to lay hold on what it clings to. Great interests, like large branches, are too stiff to twine. These are the fibres from which the ties that bind man to man are spun. The finer the staple, the stronger the cord." When a visitor asks one of Tucker's planters if he fears that his slaves "taken as a body," might someday rise up against him, the planter calmly replies, "I have not the least apprehension that they would."[14]

Uncle Tom's Cabin; or Life Among the Lowly was clearly a kind of watershed in this early fiction about the plantation. It was both the summation and the destruction of a literary tradition which had begun some twenty years before. It probably did more than any book ever published to alter the American image of the South, and, once it had appeared, no one could hope to write about the plantation and ignore or slight the Negro. On the contrary, the slave rather than the planter tended to become the center of the legend, especially in the rash of fictional answers to *Uncle Tom* written by Southerners. In quick succession books appeared bearing such titles as *Aunt Phillis's Cabin; Uncle Robin in His Cabin in Virginia and Tom Without One in Boston; The Cabin and Parlor; or, Slaves and Masters*, all of which gave the slave fictional equity with the planter. Some of these books do not profit technically from this sudden shift of the Negro from bit parts to starring roles, but the shift in emphasis was evident and sufficiently widespread to affect the stage and music hall as well as the novel. Its implications, furthermore, were still being felt some twenty years later when Joel Chandler Harris, Thomas Nelson Page and Samuel Langhorne Clemens began to write about the South.

All the internal evidence supports Harriet Stowe's claim that she wrote *Uncle Tom* not to incite the North but to persuade the South that slavery was unjust.[15] In February, 1852, when the Southern attack on her was most severe, she wrote to a friend in North Carolina a brief resumé of her attitude toward the South:

It has seemed to me that many who have attacked the system [of slavery] have not understood the Southern character, nor appreciated what is really good in it. I think *I* have; at least I have tried, during this whole investigation, to balance my mind by keeping before it the most agreeable patterns of Southern life and character.[16]

To accomplish this purpose she adopted in *Uncle Tom* and in *Dred* many of the conventions of the plantation novel as it had developed, and even her innovations seem to be mainly extrapolations from practices already scouted out by these novelists. Certainly, she made use of the plantation setting in its classical form. Decayed old houses, kind masters and mistresses, docile and affectionate household "servants" are placed center stage in both of these stories. While her image of Southern society was in some ways less complex and less detailed than that drawn by Southerners like Kennedy and the two Tuckers, the principal features are still there. For the most part, for example, she adopts the familial pattern for portraying the institution of slavery just as she accepts many of the Southern arguments concerning the intellectual and cultural limitations of the slave. Her exceptional slaves like Uncle Tom (whom she calls "a moral miracle") and some of her mulattoes are clearly meant to be regarded as exceptions. In no sense, moreover, is it possible to argue that either of her books is an indictment of the South to the exclusion of the North. Some of her sharpest invective is aimed at the temporizing and hypocrisy of churchmen and politicians in the North, and, as a reviewer in the *Southern Literary Messenger* noted with surprise, almost all of her villains and monsters are of Northern birth.[17] It would be difficult, in fact, anywhere in Southern writing to assemble a stable of degraded Yankee types to match hers. There is, of course, Simon Legree from Vermont, who represents the culmination of half a century of anti-Northern rhetoric, and there is his less sensational blood brother Abijah Skinflint in *Dred* ("For money he would do anything; for money he would have sold his wife, his children, even his own soul. . . ."),[18] but there are many others who strike off such legendary Yankee traits as acquisitiveness, hypocrisy, emotional frigidity, prudishness and Philistinism. She leaves no doubt that she accepts, furthermore, some of the sentimental clichés about the plantation home. When that charming and doomed little child, Eva, is asked to compare family life with her cousins in Vermont with plantation life in the South, this exchange takes place:

> "Oh, of course, our way is the pleasantest," said Eva.
> "Why so?" said St. Clare, stroking her head.
> "Why, it makes so many more round you to love, you know," said Eva, looking up earnestly.[19]

One other consideration about *Uncle Tom's Cabin* places it even more firmly in the center of the plantation tradition, in tenor as well as in form. Harriet Stowe's sharpest barbs are not, finally, aimed at either Northerners or Southerners as such, but at the ruthless masculine world of business enterprise. Plantation fiction from the beginning had celebrated the virtues of country life over city life, agriculture over commerce and business, impracticality over prudence and providence, and, perhaps most important of all, the primacy of home and family over all other values. Most of the villainous figures who penetrate this pastoral world, like the New York merchant's son James Gildon in *The Valley of Shenandoah*, issue from the world of business and finance, but none of these earlier villains was as profitably employed as the "businessmen" in *Uncle Tom's Cabin*, where commerce in slaves is represented as the ultimate in human exploitation. For in the slave trade, as in no other, all human values are converted into pecuniary values, and human beings are quite literally being turned into dollars and cents. Harriet Stowe's most impressive tactical feat was to connect the kindly, impractical master with the brutalities of the slave trade by showing that his boasted immunity from

Yankee acquisitiveness—his carelessness concerning money and his high sense of honor—were often purchased at the expense of the slave's security and welfare, that the Legrees, in other words, battened on the failures and weaknesses of the St. Clares. The sentimental image of the Southern family is again and again projected against the heartless image of business life, never more effectively than in the scenes set at Legree's plantation on the Red River, where Legree as an anti-planter presides over what can only be thought of as an anti-home. Harriet Stowe employs for these scenes the traditional ruined plantation house and all of its appurtenances, but the house is a hollow shell, not a home. Instead of the harmonious family group there is Legree and his mulatto mistresses, and instead of love there is brutal sexual subjection. The building itself has become defiled. Litter is strewn about and the very altar of domesticity, the hearth, is used only to heat water for Legree's toddies and provide embers to light his cigars. Even the bare plaster walls where the paper has fallen away are covered with the arithmetic scribblings of Legree's accounts. The plantation itself is an inversion of the plantation as sketched by the paternalists. The only discipline is fear and brutality; the slaves are made to beat one another, and nothing is done unless it "pays." What we are given in a few pages is an evocative vision of the home become factory, where everything, finally, is weighed in the balance scale at Legree's cotton house. Southerners, who almost universally objected to these scenes, never fully understood that Harriet Stowe had simply imported into the South the factory scenes which Southerners were fond of invoking as a contrast to the paternalism of the plantation.

In most of what she did, Harriet Stowe had only taken the Southerner at his word. Her method, if it can be called this, had not been to deny the Southern defense of slavery but to suggest that it was inadequate, even if its claims were allowed. In instance after instance she had underlined the fact that, so long as the slave was regarded as property, kindness, generosity and affection provided no assurance against cruelty and brutality.

She also attempted to show that a slave could love his master and mistress and still wish to be free. Most subversively of all, she intimated in *Dred*, parts of which were based on the Nat Turner insurrection, that the slave under some circumstances could be goaded into open rebellion against his master. At every opportunity, furthermore, she blurred the color line both by projecting her readers into the feelings of slaves and by employing mulatto slaves without Negro characteristics. In particular, she directed her largest generalizations at the plight of the American family, and for this purpose she chose her examples indiscriminately from the family life of the Negro and the white. "If it were your Harry, mother, or your Willio, that woro going to bo torn from you by a brutal slave trader, tomorrow morning," she asked, what would you do?[20] In touching upon the separation of families, as she constantly did, she was making the strongest possible appeal to Southern women. Similarly, there seems little question that the human qualities attributed to Tom were, many of them, precisely those which had the greatest attraction for women. Tom is sensitive, tender, pious, trusting and totally passive in his response to brutality and oppression. Indeed, he is so completely without aggressive male traits that there may be some truth in Helen Papashvily's startling assertion that he was a kind of cryptofemale who represented the real image of the American woman ac cho caw horcolf.[21]

In retrospect, it seems evident that Harriet Stowe employed the plantation setting because she herself believed in it as a meaningful evocation of American family life and not out of any shrewd and vindictive intent, as Southerners tended to think. What she feared for the plantation was simply a heightened version of the anxiety she felt for modern family life in general. As Charles Foster has shown, many of the incidents in *Uncle Tom*, such as the death of Eva, were drawn from Harriet's own family life[22] and reflect the spiritual crisis she was undergoing. The extraordinary and unexampled appeal of the novel throughout the Western world, furthermore, suggests its capacity to touch upon and illuminate wider themes. Nonetheless, the novel, as it was interpreted, had quite a special meaning for the South and it is hardly surprising that Southerners did not contribute to the general enthusiasm. The novel's sympathetic portrayal of plantation life and its indictment of the North when coupled with its obvious attack on slavery made for a more complicated response. Confusion, consternation, blanket denials and personal attacks on Mrs. Stowe followed its publication as a book—and in just that order. No one, of course, can say with any assurance what Southerners felt as they read this compelling fantasy, but there is evidence to suggest that many were deeply troubled. Everywhere it was discussed, analyzed and criticized. The *Southern Literary Messenger* reviewed it twice in the same three-month period,[23] and Mrs. Chesnut's diary, written almost ten years later, is studded with references both to *Uncle Tom* and to Mrs. Stowe, not one of which is altogether favorable or altogether hostile. Fictional rebuttals appeared in a matter of months, all of them by moderate and well-meaning people, mostly self-declared Southern Whigs—one book is dedicated to Henry Clay—who looked upon *Uncle Tom* as exaggerated and inflammatory and sought to correct the unfair picture of slavery which they felt Harriet Stowe had drawn. They, too, were caught within the sentimental logic of plantation paternalism, however, and the stories which they wrote, with their harmonious patriarchal plantations and their gullible Northern visitors, were often simply crude imitations of the book they set out to answer, with slave-snatching Yankee abolitionists substituted for Harriet's ruthless Yankee slave traders.[24] Since she had made it clear from the beginning that she was examining the moral logic of slavery rather than its sociology, there really was no answer to what she had written, as Southerners began to discover to their intense frustration. As Mrs. Chesnut seemed to say: she was right but *she had no right!*

Here and there bits of evidence turn up which suggest what the pattern of response to this discovery may have been. A young Williams graduate from New England who was living as a tutor on a plantation in Rockingham County, North Carolina, recorded this interesting sequence of events. On October 1, 1852, a Mr. Glenn arrived from New York bringing with him a copy of *Uncle Tom*. The tutor, whose names was Charles Holbrook, began reading it the same night and had finished it three days later. "I believe it to be the most interesting book I ever read," he wrote in his diary. Almost at once he began reading it to the Galloway children, who easily provided him with incidents of cruelty similar to those described in the book. On October 9 the planter, Mr. Galloway, who had finished the book, suddenly changed his mind about selling a slave named Henderson away from his wife and children. A few days later Galloway bitterly reported to Holbrook that he had met a slave trader transporting a "drove" of Negroes which had included some twenty children. The same day Holbrook noted: "Mr. G. likes *Uncle Tom's Cabin* but Mrs. G. is bitter against it." On October 15 the book was the talk of the household. "Mr. G. is honest—he says he admires 'Uncle Tom's Cabin' for its true characters." On the very next day, however, there was a surprising change. "Mr. Galloway says he will burn 'Uncle Tom's Cabin,'" Holbrook noted. "He has changed his mind on it. Mrs. G. thinks Mrs. Stowe is worse than Legree!" This entry of October 16 was the last mention of the book, which was apparently not further discussed.[95]

CHAPTER X

The Rage for Order

As Mildmay concluded, Mr. Moreton absolutely fell into
his chair. Strange ideas had been awakened in his mind,—
thoughts that had slumbered for years, aroused. A sort of
desolate feeling came over him, the future looked gloomy
and uncertain, and for a moment he mentally groped in
darkness,—and then, brushing his hand across his brow, he
said: "Mildmay, if we would happily live in the South, we
must not look so deeply and darkly upon the things
around us."

THOMAS B. THORPE, *The Master's House*[1]

THE SOCIAL PROBLEMS in the South which worried and perplexed
the novelists were not confined to those which concerned slavery
and the status of women, deeply troubling as these were. Other
tensions were building within the society at about the same time,
and there is evidence that these tensions are responsible for certain features of the plantation novel as it developed. During the
twenty years from *Swallow Barn* to *Uncle Tom*, Southerners
betrayed a growing uneasiness over their ability to keep their
house in order. The fear of a divided South and anxiety about
alienation of the West grew more apparent as the sectional crisis
increased in intensity. If these novelists gave assurance that the
woman and the slave would remain subservient to the planter and

loyal to his interest, they made a very similar point about the South's "new" immigration—the Scotch-Irish and the Germans of the valley and the mountain. The debates at the Virginia constitutional convention in 1829-30 and in the house of delegates two years later had underlined the east-west cleavage which had developed in the state and had raised the question of the yeoman's loyalty to Southern institutions. For many the principal issue to emerge from these exchanges was the division of opinion on slavery, but certain broader implications of this split were recognized by still others who would not at this point have undertaken a defense of slavery. The problem for them was the threatened withdrawal of the whole West from the *entente cordiale* which had joined the South and the West since the Revolution. The South had always looked upon the Trans-Allegheny West as part and parcel of itself. Westward settlement at the end of the Revolution had taken place largely in lands which had once belonged to the Southern states, and especially to Virginia. The ideal of the yeoman which gave westward settlement its social meaning had found its most forceful expression in the writings of Jefferson, John Taylor and other agrarian philosophers. A coalition of South and West, furthermore, had supported the Louisiana Purchase against Federalist opposition, fought the War of 1812 and placed Andrew Jackson in the White House. One of the principal things at stake in the Webster-Hayne debate in 1830 had been the allegiance of the West, which both Hayne and Webster had sought with every rhetorical means at their disposal. The Southern pre-emption of the West was so commonly accepted that it was possible as late as 1846 for a Northerner like William Gilpin to give the South entire credit for the westward impulse, as Henry Nash Smith has pointed out. "The progeny of Jamestown," Gilpin told a committee of the Senate, "has given to the Union twelve great agricultural States; has created that mighty production and generating capacity on which are based the grand power and prosperity of the Nation."[2] It is therefore scarcely surprising that these novels should manifest a lively interest in the West and in those parts of the South which lay beyond the Blue Ridge. Every sort of pretext is used to haul the Western yeoman on stage and give him a part to play around the old plantation.

The Virginia Frontiersman

In almost all of the plantation novels there is some evidence of tension between the Cavalier and the yeoman ideals. George Tucker in *The Valley of Shenandoah* sees little hope for the future in the old Tidewater aristocracy, which he portrays as improvident, rash and self-destructive. If Virginia is to have a future, the novel seems to concede with regret, it lies with the German and the Scotch-Irish settlers of the valley. Of these two groups, the Germans are portrayed as the least attractive. They are acquisitive, "painstaking, plodding, frugal people" with simple domestic traits, but they are given to contentious legal wrangling, narrow self-interest in politics and Philistinism in all matters cultural. They are the "dray-horses" of the population, useful but dull. In many respects, in fact, they resemble the legendary Yankee. There is considerable discussion of Germans in general, but the only character in the novel who is explicitly pinpointed as German is a shrewish planter's wife who haggles over money matters and compels her daughter to seek the main chance in choosing a husband. The Scotch-Irish, on the other hand, are portrayed as an exceedingly attractive group. Like the Cavaliers, they are "ardent and impassioned," careless about money, strongly partisan to liberty and given to extremes in all matters, especially religion. Nonetheless, they are seen as more vigorous and more natural than the gentleman planter. The most important Scotch-Irishman in the novel is the mountaineer M'Culloch, who seems to owe something to Wirt's Patrick Henry. He possesses great natural intelligence; yet in his relaxed way he prefers hunting and fishing to everything else, and he disappears into the woods for days while his crops spoil and his fence posts rot. At the end of the novel he goes off to Kentucky, like Paulding's Colonel Dangerfield, in pursuit of better farming and easier living. In politics, however, it is important to note that M'Culloch is an ardent nationalist who suspects William and Mary for its "jacobinical" tendencies and who is as reliable as President Washington, whom he idolizes. The Scotch-Irishman, as Tucker sees him, is still something of a cultural child, but he is imaginative and free-spirited and one is given the impression that over the long haul he will make out.[3]

Kennedy's first Scotch-Irishman, Mike Brown in *Swallow Barn*, is also a social type of somewhat unpredictable value. Despite a heroic record in the Revolution, he has become rather unenterprising in his later years, with trouble at home and no money in the bank. He is described as a "free and easy, swaggering, sociable chap" and "an open-hearted fellow . . . who liked to spend his money when he had it."[4] When Kennedy came to write his second novel, however, he made a Scotch-Irishman his hero and gave the book his name. Galbraith "Horse-Shoe" Robinson is a wholly admirable character who proves in the course of the story that he possesses many of the qualities of a Cavalier—military prowess, horsemanship and a chivalric sense of honor. The various Bumppo-like frontiersmen who appear in these novels are quite similarly portrayed, although many of them are of uncertain national origin. Ambrose Bushfield in *Westward Ho!* and Joe "Red" Jarvis in Caruthers' *Knights of the Horseshoe* are reliable and tractable woodsmen on whom gentlemen may depend.

These characters possess certain qualities in common. Some of them are illiterate but all of them are credited with such qualities as "native energy," "inborn sagacity" and "daring enterprise."[5] Each of these writers, furthermore, takes pains to show that there is nothing to fear from such men. The wildness in them, though perfectly evident, has been disciplined and subdued until there is nothing left of it but an occasional whoop. Sometimes they approach the natural aristocrat in their sensitivity and their natural sense of decorum. Paulding's Ambrose Bushfield, for example, "could neither read nor write, yet he was not ignorant or vulgar;

and his feelings, by some strange freak of nature . . . partook of the character of the gentleman in more ways than one."[6] Beverley Tucker, in the dedication of *The Partisan Leader*, refers to the "simple virtue," the "instinctive patriotism" and the "untaught wisdom" of the Virginia yeomen whose minds are "uncorrupted by artificial systems of education." "A second glance at Christian Witt," he observes a little later, "might have discovered something intellectual in his countenance,"[7] and M'Culloch in *The Valley of Shenandoah* and Beverley Tucker's *George Balcombe* have both been reading Ariosto's *Orlando Furioso*.

At the same time there is no suggestion in any of these novels that the yeoman, whatever his accomplishments, is entirely the social equal of the gentleman, and many of these figures are cast in menial or semi-menial roles. Beverley Tucker casually refers to them as "peasants" and notes that men like Witt and Schwartz are without the "executive" qualities which are required for political and military leadership. Like Horse-Shoe Robinson and some of Simms's noncommissioned officers, they are best suited to be subalterns. Mr. B—— in *The Partisan Leader* even handles Schwartz's money for him, as though he were a child. In particular these men are inclined to take their social and political views from the gentlemen. Schwartz, Mr. B—— observes, "adopts all my views, as far as he can understand them, and beyond that point trusts me implicitly." This quality of subordination in the mountaineer has a particular importance in the novel since the story concerns a projected civil war in which the loyalty of western Virginia with its hardy yeomen and its mountain stronghold is crucial to victory. It was through intermediaries like Schwartz that B—— counted on winning over the yeoman to the Cavalier cause. "It is through his instrumentality," he tells the narrator, "that the minds of the mountaineers . . . are prepared for action at this moment."[8] The loyalty of the western part of the state was obviously a matter of intense concern to Virginians after about 1830, and it is interesting to note that as late as 1860 the only other novel which fought the Civil War in fantasy,

Edmund Ruffin's *Anticipations of the Future*, has the yeoman and the mountaineer fighting on their home ground for slavery and for states' rights. One of the principal fears that lurked behind this cherished fantasy was expressed in the vicious, amoral and anarchic Tory backwoodsmen who appear in the Revolutionary novels of Simms and Kennedy. This concern with the cultural alienation of the West, furthermore, was not limited to the mountain areas of the older South.

All of this fiction exhibits a lively concern with the aristocratic penetration of the West and Southwest. The model plantations in the Uncle Tom fiction of the fifties were characteristically located in the Shenandoah Valley, and one of the fondest dreams, not only of Southerners but of many others, was expressed in the porticoed white mansions that strew the Southwest in the fiction of the same period. Southerners like Beverley Tucker who had lived in the West were anxious to show that the Virginia Cavalier was capable of carrying his distinctive civilization with him westward and imposing it on an undisciplined frontier society. Although Paulding was not himself a Southerner, he obviously expressed a very similar wish in *Westward Ho!* About Tucker there can be no mistake. He wrote *George Balcombe* to make just such a point. Balcombe is one of the many "bastard" heroes of Southern fiction: he is half Virginia gentleman and half frontiersman. In his rugged but anomalous outward manner he belongs very much to the West (the narrator at first takes him to be an uncultivated "clown"), yet he possesses most of the social qualifications of a gentleman. As an orphaned child who had been adopted by the narrator's grandfather and educated at William and Mary, he possesses a formidable knowledge of genealogy and he is a man of cultivation—his dogs have received their names from the *Orlando Furioso*.

He firmly believes in the social hierarchy and the importance of good blood. When Napier seems to scoff at the importance of his own Plantagenet ancestry and states modestly that he is simply his father's son, Balcombe is incredulous. "Is it not a higher honour," he asks, to be sprung from a race of men without fear and without reproach—the ancient cavaliers of Virginia? Men in whom the spirit of freedom was so blended with loyalty as to render them alike incapable of servility and selfishness; and who, when their sovereign tore himself from his place in their hearts, transferred their allegiance to their country, and again poured out their blood like water, and scattered their wealth like chaff.[9]

At the same time, Balcombe is revealed to be a master of his Western environment—a skilled pathfinder, agronomist, meteorologist and student of the law. He has acquired all the arts of survival in tumultuous frontier society, and, more than this, he has become a respected leader of the community. He has succeeded, for example, in reducing to subservience "a black Dutchman from the mountains of Virginia" named John Keizer, who serves him as a kind of handyman-rogue. Keizer is in every respect a man of destructive and subversive bent. In contrast to the tall, slender, blond and blue-eyed Cavaliers in Tucker's novels, Keizer has "a low slight figure . . . with an olive complexion," "long, lank, black hair" and "small, keen, jet-black eyes." The rest of his description speaks for itself. His buckskin clothing was "all glazed with grease and mottled with blood" and his long hair hung down over his face and shoulders. "He carried in his hand a formidable rifle, and wore a butcher knife stuck in a leather case at his belt."[10] The need to believe in the tractability of such a lawless and potentially violent figure was very strong in men like Tucker whose rage for order was so great that it finally transcended any narrow Southern partisanship. For them the gentleman planter was not simply a Southerner, he was the principal civilizing agent in a society where everything tended toward anarchy and disorder. They hungered for the world to come to rest and they yearned for stability with an intensity it is difficult for us to imagine. In their eyes only the Cavalier possessed the heroic force of character which was required to hold back the restless flood of savagery that threatened to overflow the country. Occasionally in these novels there appears a figure that touches like a bare nerve the source of the anxiety which was so prevalent in this period. In

The Valley of Shenandoah it is the "buckskin independence" of the truculent wagoner, Jacob Scryder, who sullenly refuses to let the Grayson carriage pass him on the road. In several of these novels there are similar instances of insubordination. *Swallow Barn* contains a classical Southern bully of the kind that Hundley later discusses in his profile of Southern society, and the Tory backwoodsmen in Simms and Kennedy are often blind to social distinctions and refuse to recognize "the quality." But the most picturesque example of this kind of Western wolf-man is a brutal slob named Thomas Johnson in *George Balcombe*. Every detail of his portrait is etched with loathing and horror:

His features were flushed and bloated by intemperance, his eyes bloodshot, his hair and beard staring and sunburnt, stuck full of bits of straw, and matted with filth; his dress of leather from head to foot, and for blood and dirt, and grease, that in which I had first seen Keizer might in comparison have become a ballroom. . . . The *tout ensemble* of ferocity and beastliness was horrible to look upon. So degraded and hateful a specimen of humanity I had never conceived of.[11]

In *The Partisan Leader* it is not a Westerner but a boorish nouveau planter that slips through the network of censorship imposed by the legend. He makes his appearance in a tavern scene where the narrator singles him out from various other uncivic types who are attempting to make a quick profit by selling their goods to the Confederacy. His "whole appearance," he comments, "showed him to be a substantial planter, ignorant of every thing but corn and tobacco." There is something about his expensive but tasteless clothing and his air of vulgar affluence which makes the narrator recoil from him even more than from the other effluvia that crowd the room, drinking and wrangling. His coarse "bacon-fed look" and his strident voice, which was "entirely devoid of melody and incapable of inflection or modulation," only heightened the sickening spectacle.[12]

The South's consciousness of destructive forces at work

within its own borders is perfectly evident in these novels, despite the fact that their emphasis was of another kind. Quite a similar phenomenon, of course, occurs in the North, where writers like Sarah Hale and Harriet Stowe preserve their sharpest caricatures and harshest words for rapacious Yankee types. In general it has always been men with the ardent but tortured Southern loyalties of a Tucker, or a Simms or a Hundley—or, indeed, a Wilbur Cash or a William Faulkner—who have possessed the vision required to look into the deepest recesses of Southern character and, if only fleetingly, see it in all of its complexity. They, not the critical outsiders, have spied the Snopeses lurking in the plantation portico, and not only spied them, but understood them, feared and respected them, and known they belonged. Their characterizations have accordingly possessed the force and vitality of felt experience. The Southern gentleman, on the other hand, posed for them an almost insurmountable problem. This is scarcely surprising since they were working not so much from any living model as from a construct compounded out of memories, artifacts and other fragments of an evasive social past, and that, too, further transformed by their own wishes and fears into something even more synthetic. How pale and lifeless such figures seem when pitted against the Keizers and the Thomas Johnsons and the "bacon-fed," new rich swells that occasionally appear in the wings bearing a real air of verisimilitude. Take Edward William Sidney, for example, the narrator of *The Partisan Leader;* what could Tucker have been feeling and thinking as he put him together in phrase after phrase—"a native of South Carolina, and the heir of a goodly inheritance," a graduate of the Citadel with a penchant for the military life, a sportsman, "a zealous advocate for the rights of the States"?[13]

It would be difficult to read through this literature without concluding that few, if any, Southerners, no matter what they said, really believed in the Cavalier—only in the need for him. Writing in her diary at the beginning of the war, Mary Chesnut, in one of her many moments of subversion, commented on the diminished vitality of the old English stock. "Of late," she noted, "all of the active-minded men who sprang to the front in our government were the immediate descendants of Scotch or Scotch-Irish; Calhoun, McDuffie, Cheves, Petigru—who Huguenotted his name, but could not tie up his Irish."[14] Toward the end of his life—and long after the Civil War—John Esten Cooke described himself as a Virginian, monarchist and a Cavalier, and yet his first lighthearted romances composed on the eve of the war paint a far from reassuring portrait of the gentleman planter. The scheming Hans Huddleshingle in *Leather Stocking and Silk* and the effete Champ Effingham in *The Virginia Comedians* are placed beside vigorous and enterprising characters of a more plebeian kind like John Hunter and the Patrick Henry figure who appears in a final scene of *The Virginia Comedians* as the mysterious "man in a red cloak." This portrayal of Henry during the Stamp Act crisis with its echoes of William Wirt presents him as the coarse and strident archetype of the fire-eater and leaves little doubt concerning the social class to which Cooke then consigned the future. "The book," Cooke wrote to the editor of the *Messenger*, "is profoundly democratic, and American—the aristocracy whom I don't like, getting the worst of it."[15] And so they did.

EPILOGUE

AND THE WAR CAME

The argument is exhausted, further remonstrance is dis
honorable, hesitation is dangerous, delay is submission, "to
your tents O! Israel" and let the God of battles decide the
issue.

DAVID CLOPTON to SENATOR
CLEMENT C. CLAY[1]

By THE SUMMER of 1861 the subdued, candid and reasonable exchange of views which had taken place between Jefferson and John Adams some forty-five years before seemed to belong to another, faraway age. Early that year, as every schoolboy knows, a separate Southern government had been organized in Montgomery, Alabama. Fort Sumter had fallen in April, a peace conference in Washington had collapsed and by July the United States were at war with themselves. Historians agree that the vast majority of people in the North and the South had not wanted secession, to say nothing of war, but events swept them up in a whirlwind of excitement and precipitant action over which no one, finally, could exercise control.

In the South the move to separate had not at first received massive support. Of those who hung back, some, perhaps most, were genuinely undecided, others confused or indifferent, and still others afraid to acknowledge their secret convictions. Little recourse was left open for moderation. The choice, to use the language of the time, lay between "secession" and "submission." The insurgents, capitalizing on the fears inspired by Lincoln's election and emboldened by their confidence in the invincibility of a united South, had moved ahead, heedless of dissenting views.

One by one the "erring sisters" had departed "in peace"—South Carolina on December 20; Mississippi, Alabama, Georgia and Louisiana during the month of January, and Texas on February 1. Not until late spring or early summer did Tennessee, North Carolina and Arkansas finally secede. Only on April 17, and after Lincoln had called upon her for her militia, did Virginia, the historical leader of Southern opinion, pass an ordinance of secession. Missouri, Maryland and Kentucky, although tragically divided, chose to remain with the Union.

Along this middle tier of states, which separated New England and the Northwest from the lower South, a resolution of conflicting loyalties was arrived at only after agonizing and prolonged reflection and debate. Lincoln correctly gauged the mood which existed in these still uncommitted parts of the South when he inserted into his Inaugural Address, delivered in March of that year, a pointed reference to Hamlet's Third Act soliloquy. Was the South, he asked, contemplating suicide?

Will you hazard so desperate a step while there is any possibility that any portion of the ills you fly from have no real existence? Will you, while the certain ills you fly to are greater than all the real ones you fly from, will you risk the commission of so fearful a mistake?[2]

In state capitals, county seats, in village assemblies and in individual families, anguishing, seldom unanimous, decisions were made, and by midsummer the peoples of the North and the South, sometimes with reluctance and sometimes in a fever of excitement, were beginning to array themselves on opposite sides of the battle lines. In a poem written that year, one of the Union's warmest advocates caught the sense of the moment in a few lines of verse.

Beat! beat! drums!—blow! bugles! blow!
Make no parley—stop for no expostulation,
Mind not the timid—mind not the weeper or prayer. . . .[3]

The most memorable war in American history was about to begin.

Historians have long debated the causes which precipitated this rapid series of events, and doubtless they always will. Much has been learned about the subtle shifts of opinion which occurred within the various Southern states between John Brown's raid on Harpers Ferry in October, 1859, and Lincoln's fateful decision in April, 1861, to send supplies to the beleaguered garrison at Fort Sumter. Careful studies have been made of the parochial political circumstances which heightened the sensitivity of parts of the South to sectional issues and made the election of Abraham Lincoln, as the Northern President backed by a Northern party, a nightmarish prospect. The list of Southern grievances against the federal government, it has been made clear, had been growing since the debates over Missouri in 1819-20; and the Constitutional arguments employed at the time of secession have a history almost as long as the Union itself. The growth of the Southern movement for independence has been traced back to the statements of its earliest proponents in the thirties. It is the importance of this idea of Southern nationality, the popular supposition that Southerners and Northerners were distinct and different peoples, which has prompted the present study. If this idea had not been firmly embedded in the consciousness of extremists on both sides and vaguely present in the thinking of countless others, it seems doubtful that secession and Civil War would have taken place at the time and in the way that they did.

No one, of course, will ever be able to recapture in their totality the elusive feelings of individual Southerners in the face of these bewildering events, but it is clear that a significant shift in attitude took place after 1859. For a time, during the early fifties the threat of open rebellion seemed to have disappeared. Problems there were, and some of them very grave, but concessions had been made. The South was enjoying flush times with cotton and slave prices at an all-time high, and Democrats responsive to Southern opinions were in control of the government in Washington. Then came the brief rehearsal for civil war, between Northerners and Southerners fighting over the corpse of "bleeding Kansas," the appearance on the scene of a sectional party with growing strength, a sudden and disastrous economic depression and Lincoln's highly publicized "House Divided" speech, made during his Senatorial campaign in 1858. Lincoln himself conceded that some kind of crisis lay ahead, and a great many people who saw eye to eye with him on little else were inclined to agree. Then, in quick succession, came two events which shattered what little complacency remained in the South. Miscalculation of the significance of these dramatic moments was in the spirit of the times, rumors consciously launched grew rapidly out of control and genuinely conciliatory gestures on the part of the North slipped by unnoticed.

The first shock was provided by John Brown's Private War, as C. Vann Woodward has called it. This brief but highly publicized skirmish began near Harpers Ferry on the night of October 16, 1859, when Brown and eighteen cohorts captured a federal arsenal. The struggle was of short duration, and it collapsed in a matter of hours. It left in its wake some fifteen dead, a great mass of documents compromising Brown's supporters in the North and one of the most controversial prisoners ever to be arrested and executed by an American state. For many Southerners who took the documents at face value and let their imaginations play over the potential consequences of a massive conspiracy of this kind, John Brown personified Northern predatory intentions which they all along had suspected lurked behind the reasonable and accommodating gestures of Northern statesmen. His name evoked almost everything hateful about the Yankee character: destructiveness, conspiracy and hypocrisy. Upon this one man for a time were focused the emotions which for close to thirty years had been gathering around the figure of the Yankee. Brown's defense by a few New Englanders such as Emerson and Thoreau, who looked upon him as a saint and a martyr, only quickened Southern response. The possibility that he may have been mad was dismissed by his attackers and supporters alike. The fact that certain of his defenders, like the Reverend Theodore Parker of Boston, were actively implicated in his conspiracy led to gross exaggerations of his real support in New England and the magnitude of his enterprise generally. Although not a single slave rose in rebellion and Brown's action was deplored in Washington and by all but a few extremists in the North, the South in a matter of weeks was thrown into a state of panic and one of the worst witch-hunts in American history occurred as eccentrics and "suspicious characters" of all kinds, many of them innocent strangers passing through, were mobbed, beaten, and tarred and feathered in a vigilante effort to root out Yankees and potential Southern subversives. No relaxation of tension followed. Rumors of slave insurrections swept the South during the next year. Finally, the election of Lincoln, who was popularly believed to be the pawn of abolitionists, and the anticipated prominence in his coming administration of William Seward of "Irrepressible Conflict" fame provided the finishing touches to the picture of a Northern conspiracy about to be launched against the South.[4]

The state of feeling that existed in the South during these fateful months can be suggested in a series of brief tableaux. In Washington Southern Congressmen, and in the South, federal judges, began to resign their offices; some like Senator James H. Hammond with hesitation, some with feelings of vindictiveness and triumph. Northerners who happened to be stranded in the South were threatened, mistreated, and even mobbed, and most of them rapidly headed for home. Daniel Hundley, a Southerner living in Chicago, fled the city under cover of night out of fear for his life. There was in fact a general exodus of Southerners from Northern cities. On December 22, 1859, a trainload of students from Philadelphia arrived in Richmond, marched past the stately capitol designed by Jefferson, and assembled before the governor's mansion to hear a speech from Governor John A. Wise on Southern self-sufficiency. "Let Virginia call home her children!" the governor told them, and he went on to advocate self-sacrifice and austerity. "Let us," he said, "dress in the wool raised on our own pastures. Let us eat the flour from our own mills, and if we can't get that, why let us go back to our old accustomed corn bread."[5] Troops of "Minute Men" wearing the blue cockade drilled before admiring Negroes who caught only the holiday spirit of color and display. Everywhere the hated Yankee became a figure of ridicule and contempt. He was a conspirator and a hypocrite, but he was also a coward. He would never fight, and he could certainly never win.

The move to dissociate the South from every contaminating Northern influence had reached almost hysterical proportions by the time of Lincoln's inauguration. The capital was almost empty of its former official occupants. Southern politicians and their ladies, including many of the city's most prominent hostesses, had departed for home, leaving the incoming Northern administration to run the country and—such as it was—Washington society. It was all a little mad, Senator Hammond, himself once an ardent secessionist, frankly conceded—and suicidal too. "It is an epidemic and very foolish," he wrote in December, 1860. "It reminds me of the Japanese who when insulted rip open their own bowels."[6]

By the following summer, then, communications between North and South had broken down—even the mail had stopped moving across the Potomac—and many leading spokesmen of both sections now regarded one another suspiciously and hostilely as symbols of alien cultures. To Mrs. Chesnut, who was inclined to see things somewhat melodramatically and—like Lincoln—in familial terms, it was also a question of a divided household and a marriage gone bad. "We separated," she wrote in her diary, "because of incompatibility of temper; we are divorced, North from South, because we have hated each other so."[7] "And for so long a time," she might have added without greater exaggeration than she had already employed, since the hatred to which she referred had been slowly intensifying for over thirty years, and along with it the awakening sense of a divided culture.

Two English astronomers, Charles Mason and Jeremiah Dixon, in an effort to settle a boundary dispute, had run a line between Pennsylvania and Maryland in the seventeen sixties, but no one had then conceived of such a boundary as dividing a North from a South. Jefferson had seen the danger of such a distinction at the time of the Missouri Compromise, but a popular belief in a precise demarcation between North and South was a development of the decades which followed, and the frontier was still indistinct even after secession. Maryland, immediately south of the line, remined loyal and other so-called slave states like Missouri and Kentucky, both of them in some measure Southern in their traditions and style of life, remained officially in the North. If there was a line, and increasingly Americans agreed that there was, it possessed no geographical definition. It was a psychological, not a physical division, which often cut like a cleaver through the mentality of individual men and women everywhere in the country.

The shift in attitude which occurred during the fifties and the alignment which rapidly appeared during the tense months following Lincoln's election in 1860, much as they owe to particular contemporary events, are deeply rooted in an equally significant but much less easily defined reorientation of American mentality which had been taking place at least since the thirties. If separation as a political and social fact was the immediate result of the political pressures, miscalculations and excited activism of these tumultuous months, the idea of a coherent South, of a distinct and different Southern civilization was not new in 1850, to say nothing of 1859; yet it was an idea which would have startled both Jefferson and Adams in 1816, and did in fact alarm Jefferson when he caught the first intimation of it in 1820.

Neither Jefferson nor Adams, furthermore, had thought of the natural aristocrat—their choice for the republican leader—as possessing any particular regional traits. Neither, certainly, would have localized either lower-class villainy or aristocratic honor and virtue in any North or South which they knew. Adams, with his alertness to the danger of a false aristocracy in New England and with his keen sense of fallibility, saw evil and ambition lurking in every man's heart. He probably would have found the fully developed idea of the Yankee laughable and yet a little appealing, but he scarcely would have looked for better human materials south of the Potomac. Jefferson would have looked upon the full-blown Cavalier ideal with something like loathing and seen in its currency the undoing of much that he had worked to accomplish. Yet some three decades were sufficient to bring about these changes and to usher in a whole new set of assumptions concerning the history, cultural background and racial composition of the two regions from which these two men had sprung— and for which they had made themselves the spokesmen. The nature of these changes is implicit in the preceding chapters, but the pattern of change is a somewhat complicated one and perhaps deserves brief reiteration.

The Southern Cavalier Redivivus

The first quarter of the nineteenth century had not passed before a significant number of Americans in both the North and the South had begun to express decided reservations about the direction progress was taking and about the kind of aggressive, mercenary, self-made man who was rapidly making his way in their society. In everyone's eyes this type of parvenu came to express a worrisome facet of the national character, to symbolize, in fact, both the restless mobility and the strident materialism of new world society. In the face of the threat which seemed to be posed by this new man, Americans—genteel and would-be genteel—began to develop pronounced longings for some form of aristocracy. They longed for a class of men immune to acquisitiveness, indifferent to social ambition and hostile to commercial life, cities and secular progress. They sought, they would frankly have conceded, for something a little old-fashioned.

Writers like Cooper, Sarah Hale and Paulding, themselves representative spokesmen of a much larger group, were particularly attracted by the idea of a conservative country gentry such as England possessed—or, at least, had possessed—only purer and better. The equalitarian character of life in the North provided an unsuitable terrain in which to locate, even in fantasy, an aristocracy of this kind. By the eighteen thirties the legendary Southern planter, despite reservations of one kind or another, began to seem almost perfectly suited to fill the need. His ample estates, his spacious style of life, his Cavalier ancestry and his reputed obliviousness to money matters gained him favor in the eyes of those in search of a native American aristocracy. More and more, he came to be looked upon as *the* characteristic expression of life in the South. Meanwhile, the acquisitive man, the man on the make, became inseparably associated with the North and especially with New England. In the end, the Yankee—for so he became known—was thought to be as much the product of the North as the planter-Cavalier of the South. By 1850 these two types—the Cavalier and the Yankee—expressed in the popular imagination the basic cultural conflict which people felt had grown up between a decorous, agrarian South and the rootless, shifting, money-minded North.

No such absolute division, of course, ever really existed between the North and the South. Southerners engaged in business, speculated on real estate, sought profits, lived in towns and cities, voted for the same national parties and subscribed to many of the same ideals and values as other Americans. What differences they developed, as over the issue of Negro slavery, did not lead many of them to formulate a totally different set of social objectives; these differences simply complicated their response to objectives which they already in large measure had accepted. Thus, in crying out against the Yankee North, Southerners who did so were, in a sense, striking out at a part of themselves. By 1860 they had become self-divided, frustrated in their hopes and wishes, increasingly unrealistic in their social aspirations and ripe for some kind of bloody showdown.

The problem for the self-conscious South finally lay in the need which it felt to isolate—to quarantine—itself from the contaminating influence of the Yankee North, which it both feared and envied—and which, finally, was so much a part of itself. The result was the creation of an exclusively Southern historical, and even racial, heritage. Outvoted or overruled in national affairs, outgrown in population, outproduced and, as many Southerners at least secretly felt, outargued on the justice of slavery, the South in 1860 sought some kind of redemption in separateness, only to set up a Confederate government which was not essentially different, even in its constitutional details, from the federal republic from which it had just seceded.

The "Southern" problem was, then, for these men a condition of paralysis brought on by conflicting loyalties—they finally could not believe in either their own regional ideals or those of the country as a whole. Belief in the one conflicted with belief in the other; the result was confusion, indecision and a kind of gnawing dispiritedness. By the eighteen fifties, certainly, they no longer believed wholeheartedly in the effectiveness of the Cavalier gentleman, since they, too, came to measure achievement by financial success and the gentleman planter was, almost by definition, born to fail. But neither could they worship success, since it was measured in dollars and cents rather than in honor and cultural elevation. The improvident, generous-hearted gentleman planter for them became increasingly a symbol of a Lost Cause—an insurgent, a dueler, a fighter against overwhelming odds —in short, a figment of a utopian social world which was doomed to be submerged under a tide of middle-class materialism.

Without quite acknowledging it, many Southerners during these years had been waging a kind of war with themselves. Increasingly their ideal of a stable social order came into conflict with the social and political realities with which they were confronted. The lowly, whether white or black, gave clear evidence that they did not wish to remain lowly and feudally dependent upon the planter's good will. Even women were beginning to speak out in their own names, and some of the things they said represented a distinct challenge to the patriarchal role which the planter had assumed for himself and to many of the values which he thought of himself as embodying. Meanwhile, in the larger sphere of political events, the planter class in the Southern states, divested of the support of the West and challenged at home by its own yeomanry, found its power threatened both in Washington and in state legislatures. And what was an aristocrat who did not possess the power to order his own home, to say nothing of ruling over the national councils, especially when he was beginning to question some of the sanctions upon which his power had been based?

The Alabaman, Daniel Hundley,[8] for example, expressed his ambivalent attitude toward the force of the Cavalier ideal in his *Social Relations in our Southern States,* the book which he published on the eve of the war. In it he drew an ominous picture of the aristocrat in the South surrounded by predatory, or at least more forceful, social types, who seemed destined to overthrow his cultural and political domination. His book contained chapters devoted to the Southern Yankee, the Southern bully, the poor white, and the enterprising and forward-looking representative of the new middle classes. While he argued for the aristocratic ethos of the Southern gentleman, his confidence in his effectiveness clearly wavered before the vision of a rising Southern bourgeoisie.

Few figures in Southern history exemplify better than Edmund Ruffin the tensions and frustrations felt by those who had long battled for the Lost Cause. Ruffin, for years one of the South's leading agricultural scientists and an advocate of a diversified farm economy, was never reconciled to the defeat of the Cavalier ideal. Toward the end of his life, weary and partly deaf, he became obsessed by the idea of an independent, uncontaminated South and fought every inroad of what he regarded as Yankeeism. Dressed—rather conspicuously—in coarse Southern homespun; or, in 1859, at the age of sixty-three, attending John Brown's hanging clad in the uniform of a VMI cadet; or, as a volunteer in the Palmetto Guards, pulling the lanyard that sent one of the first shells toward Fort Sumter, he became a kind of Lanny Budd of the Old South, his every act a symbolic representation of Southern intransigeance before the Yankee North.

Few men more keenly sensed or more deeply resented the

obstacles with which true Southernism was confronted within the South itself; no one, certainly, lashed out at the Yankee with greater bitterness or, finally, expressed his feelings of frustration and self-defeat more melodramatically. As an agitator he repeatedly faced indifferent Southern audiences and, poor speaker that he was, he constantly reproached himself for his failure to bring the South to a boil. Virginia he early abandoned as reprobate; he was appalled to find the large planters in Kentucky holding strong Unionist views; and even South Carolina constantly disappointed him by her unwillingness, as in 1850, to take deliberate action. On a visit to White Sulphur Springs in August, 1859, he was astonished to find himself virtually alone among some sixteen hundred Southern guests in calling for secession. For a time after John Brown's raid he hoped "the sluggish blood of the South" would be stirred,[9] and he personally sent pikes with which Brown had intended to arm the slaves to the governors of all the Southern states; but once again he was disappointed in his expectations. Even when confronted with the virtual certainty of Lincoln's election, no state except South Carolina expressed a willingness to take the initiative in seceding. The election of 1860, in which the more moderate Bell triumphed over Breckinridge within the South by a majority of 136,875, only confirmed his fear that the South would never act.

Then, as Southern states began to pass ordinances of secession, his hopes soared one final time. After a lifetime of ceaseless struggle, his dream of an independent South seemed about to become a reality. Once the exciting days of Fort Sumter were over, even these hopes were dashed as Jefferson Davis neglected former secessionists and formed a government dominated by moderates and men Ruffin regarded as would-be reunionists. Davis himself, furthermore, seemed slow to move and indecisive, and left Southern extremists generally dissatisfied with his leadership. But for Ruffin—as for most Southerners—the most crushing blow, one which destroyed for all time the myth of Southern invincibility, was the military defeat of the South by the Northern armies that swarmed across his beloved Virginia, destroying his plantation "Beechwood" and leaving obscene graffiti scrawled on the walls of his house. His plantation a shambles, deserted by his slaves, his hearing gone and the alien North on his very doorstep, he had little left to him that he valued save his sense of honor, his bitterness and his pride, to which he regularly gave expression in a diary kept through these trying years.

On June 17, 1865, after he had digested the news from Appomattox, he made this entry in the diary:

I here declare my unmitigated hatred to Yankee rule—to all political, social and business connections with the Yankees and to the Yankee race. Would that I could impress these sentiments, in their full force, on every living Southerner and bequeath them to every one yet to be born! May such sentiments be held universally in the outraged and down-trodden South, though in silence and stillness, until the now far-distant day shall arrive for just retribution for Yankee usurpation, oppression and atrocious outrages, and for deliverance and vengeance for the now ruined, subjugated and enslaved Southern States! . . . And now with my latest writing and utterance, and with what will be near my latest breath, I here repeat and would willingly proclaim my unmitigated hatred to Yankee rule—to all political, social and business connections with Yankees, and the perfidious, malignant and vile Yankee race.[10]

Almost before the ink of this entry had dried the old man performed his most symbolic act. Seating himself erectly in his chair, he propped the butt of his silver-mounted gun against a trunk at his feet, placed the muzzle in his mouth and, as his son reported in a letter to members of the family, "pulled the trigger with a forked stick."[11]

Coda

With Edmund Ruffin's suicide and the collapse of the Confederacy which it symbolized, the Old South as a concrete entity passed beyond history and into legend. One prolonged attempt to establish and sustain an aristocratic ideal in the face of obstacles of the kind invariably thrown up by American circumstances had ended. It was not the first such attempt, as colonial historians have shown,[12] nor was it to be the last, as those familiar with elitist groups at the end of the century can testify;[13] but perhaps, because of its bearing on the course of American history before 1861 and because of its more general consequences for the development of our cultural self-awareness, it has been the most important.

The Cavalier ideal was predestined to fail, as some of its earliest proponents secretly knew. The men who originated it were not aristocrats in any sense which Europeans would have recognized. Often they themselves were self-made men, provincial in their outlook and historically naïve, who possessed no sure sense of any cultural tradition. I have spoken, principally as a matter of convenience, of "the South" and "the planter class" in assigning a specific locus to the kind of thinking which I have been describing; but at no time, I suspect, was the Cavalier ideal as it was defined by Beverley Tucker, for example, widely understood or embraced by Southern planters in general, to say nothing of other people living within the South. Such an ideal was significant because it exemplified an important American cultural problem and because it defined a tendency in Southern thought which ultimately affected political events.

As it moved toward implementation, of course, the ideal was repeatedly and necessarily compromised. The constitution of no Southern state, not even that of South Carolina, provided for anything more than a kind of modified planter oligarchy; most of the older states within the South yielded to democratic pressures before the war; and the newer states of the Southwest were no more exclusive in their political arrangements than comparable states in the North. The Confederate constitution, finally, despite its explicit recognition of slavery, was in no sense meant to set up an aristocracy, and in certain ways it provided more assurance of popular government than the federal Constitution.

The legacy left behind by the Cavalier ideal is a little difficult to define; a careful consideration of it would require a study in itself. The close of the war did not mean, certainly, that some kind of aristocratic ideal ceased to form a part of Southern thinking, nor did it mean, once Reconstruction was over, that some kind of planter class ceased to dominate Southern politics. Quite the contrary. The century had virtually ended before the old dominant groups in the South and their new business allies received any substantial challenge from the majority of Southerners, whose affairs they had historically directed. After the war, as everyone knows, the legend, far from dying away, was given a new lease on life and, in the North, probably enjoyed greater popularity and evoked more interest than at any other time. Its vitality, it seems apparent enough, has not yet exhausted itself today after more than a century of discussion and dramatic re-embodiment. The nostalgia felt by Americans for the antebellum South and for the drama of the Civil War is a phenomenon which continues to startle those unfamiliar with our culture, with our collective anxieties about the kind of civilization we have created, and with our reservations concerning the kind of social conformity which, it appears, it has been our destiny to exemplify before the world. Some of our greatest writers—Henry Adams and Henry James within the nineteenth century—have employed the Cavalier legend as a means of defining and measuring the failures and limitations of our culture at large. It seems scarcely necessary to add that this same concern has characteristically engaged the imagination of William Faulkner. But for the great mass of Americans, even those who take their impression exclusively from popular novels, television plays and Civil War centennials, the Old South has also become an enduring part of our sense of the past. At odd moments probably even the most skeptical of us allow our thoughts to play over this lingering social image, and to concede with mingled pride and wonderment: "Once it was *different* down there."

REFERENCES

References

1. See Charles Grier Sellers, ed., *The Southerner as American* (Chapel Hill, 1960).
2. Article XII, *The North American Review* (hereafter cited as NAR) Vol. XV, (July, 1822), p. 252.

Prologue

1. Thomas Heyward to James Louis Petigru in William J. Grayson, *James Louis Petigru* (New York, 1866), p. 61.
2. Lester J. Cappon, ed., *The Adams-Jefferson Letters* (Chapel Hill, 1959), Vol. II, p. 456.
3. *Ibid.*, pp. 467, 471.
4. *Ibid.*, p. 358.
5. *Ibid.*, p. 357.
6. *Ibid.*, pp. 467, 459.
7. *Ibid.*, p. 348.
8. *Ibid.*, p. 551.
9. *Ibid.*, p. 435.
10. *Ibid.*, p. 484.
11. *Ibid.*, p. 391.
12. *Ibid.*, pp. 370, 370, 388.
13. *Ibid.*, p. 400.
14. *Ibid.*, pp. 371, 372.
15. *Ibid.*, p. 389.
16. *Ibid.*, pp. 401-402.
17. *Ibid.*, p. 352.
18. *Ibid.*, p. 391.
19. *Ibid.*, p. 434.
20. For an outline of his educational proposals see "Bills on Education," drafted by Jefferson and reported to the Virginia Assembly for the Committee of Revisors by T. Jefferson and G. Wythe, June 18, 1779, in Paul L. Ford, *The Writings of Thomas Jefferson* (New York, 1893), Vol. II, pp. 220-237.
21. Charles S. Sydnor, *Gentlemen Freeholders: Political Practices in Washington's Virginia* (Chapel Hill, 1952), p. 9.
22. William Wirt, *Sketches of the Life and Character of Patrick Henry* (Philadelphia, 1817), pp. 33-34.

Chapter I

1. Daniel R. Hundley, *Social Relations in Our Southern States* (New York, 1860), p. 49.
2. Ticknor's travels and study in Europe are recounted in the *Life, Letters and Journals of George Ticknor*, George S. Hilliard, ed. (Boston, 1876), Vol. I, pp. 48-300. For a general discussion of these students see Orie William Long, *Literary Pioneers: Early American Explorers of European Culture* (Cambridge, Mass., 1935).
3. Samuel Eliot Morison, *Three Centuries of Harvard, 1636-1936* (Cambridge, Mass., 1936), p. 230.
4. Richard Beale Davis, *Francis Walker Gilmer: Life and Learning in Jefferson's Virginia* (Richmond, 1939), pp. 109-110.
5. William C. Preston, *The Reminiscences of William C. Preston*, Minnie Clare Yarborough, ed. (Chapel Hill, 1933).
6. Ticknor, *Life*, Vol. I, p. 23.
7. Preston, *Reminiscences*, p. 5.
8. Ticknor, *Life*, Vol. I, pp. 116-118.
9. *Dictionary of American Biography* (hereafter cited as *DAB*) (New York, 1928), Vol. VI, p. 223; Vol. XI, pp. 382, 461; Vol. XVII, p. 160; Vol. I, pp. 564-565.
10. Morison, *Three Centuries*, p. 260.
11. Ticknor, *Life*, Vol. I, pp. 358-359.
12. E. Alfred Jones, *American Members of the Inns of Court* (London, 1924), pp. ix-xxx. Statistics vary from source to source but the proportions remain the same. Charles Warren in his *A History of the American Bar* (Boston, 1911), p. 188, says: "Probably from twenty-five to fifty American-born lawyers had been educated in England prior to 1760. . . . 115 Americans were admitted to the Inns, from 1760 to the close of the Revolution; from South Carolina 47, from Virginia 21, from Maryland 16, from New York 5, and from each of the other colonies 1 or 2." The most generous estimate is given by J. G. de Roulhac Hamilton in "Southern Members of the Inns of Court," *The North Carolina Historical Review*, Vol. X (October, 1933), p. 74. He finds 350 Americans before 1860, 230 of them Southerners—South Carolina 89, Virginia 76, Maryland 37, Georgia 17, North Carolina 11.

There is no way of determining how many Americans pursued mercantile activities in Europe during this period, but the evidence concerning those who studied medicine there seems to suggest a similar kind of distribution among the colonies and states. The Library of Congress has a manuscript list of Americans studying medicine at the University of Edinburgh between 1724 and 1836. Most of these studied abroad in the ten years before and after the

American Revolution. Of the 157 Americans listed, 73 are from Southern colonies or states, only 19 are from the North and 66 are simply designated "American." Virginia with 52 Edinburgh-trained physicians leads all the other states and colonies, Pennsylvania with 13 is second, and South Carolina is third with 10.

13. Hamilton, "Southern Members," p. 282.
14. Ralph Waldo Emerson, *English Traits* (Boston, 1860), p. 35.
15. Washington Irving, *Sketch Book* (New York, 1853), p. 20.
16. Jesse Burton Harrison, letter July 20, 1829, Harrison Collection, Library of Congress.
17. *Ibid.*, Henry Clay to Harrison, January 3, 1830:

> I am not surprised that you should form so unfavorable an opinion of our countrymen whom you met at Paris. I was obliged to adopt a similar opinion of those whom I saw there in 1815. It is to be regretted that so few of them who visit that captivating metropolis are able to resist the temptation to indulgence which it presents.

18. Philip Alexander Bruce, *History of the University of Virginia, 1819-1919* (New York, 1920), Vol. I, p. 149.
19. Ticknor, *Life*, Vol. I, pp. 84-85.
20. Preston, *Reminiscences*, p. 30.
21. For an interesting discussion of the Yankee, see Constance Rourke, "Corn Cobs Twist Your Hair," *American Humor: A Study of the National Character* (New York, 1931), pp. 3-32. See also Merle Curti, *Roots of American Loyalty* (New York, 1946), p. 141.
22. Emerson, *English Traits*, p. 25.
23. "Thus have I committed myself to the great world of Europe," wrote Jesse Harrison as the American coastline drifted from sight, "dubious of the fate that will succeed this step. . . ." Letter June 19, 1829, Harrison Collection.
24. Ticknor, *Life*, Vol. I, p. 23.
25. *Ibid.*, Vol. II, p. 505.
26. Harrison, letter, March 16, 1830.
27. Ticknor, *Life*, Vol. I, p. 72.
28. *Ibid.*, p. 73.
29. Jay B. Hubbell, *The South in American Literature, 1607-1900* (Durham, N.C., 1954), p. 306.
30. Harrison, letter, August, 1829.
31. Hugh Swinton Legaré, *Writings of Hugh Swinton Legaré*, ed. by his sister (Charleston, 1846), Vol. I, p. 236.
32. Linda Rhea, *Hugh Swinton Legaré: A Charleston Intellectual* (Chapel Hill, 1934) is a detailed and, on the whole, objective biography.
33. *Ibid.*, p. 132.
34. Legaré, *Writings*, Vol. I, p. 31.
35. *Ibid.*, p. 215.

36. Rhea, *Legaré*, p. 145.
37. *Ibid.* Compare this sentiment with that of George Ticknor written in 1820 at the Plymouth bicentennial, in Ticknor, *Life*, Vol. I, p. 328:

> I have seldom had more lively feelings from the associations of place than I had when I stood on this blessed rock; and I doubt whether there be a place in the world where a New England man should feel more gratitude, pride, and veneration than when he stands where the first man stood who began the population and glory of his country. The Colosseum, the Alps, and Westminster Abbey have nothing more truly classical, to one who feels as he ought to feel, than this rude and bare rock.

38. Legaré, *Writings*, Vol. I, p. 43.
39. James Petigru Carson, *Life, Letters and Speeches of James Louis Petigru* (Washington, 1920), pp. 84 ff.
40. Legaré, *Writings*, Vol. I, p. 203.
41. *Ibid.*, p. 215.
42. See Richard Hofstadter, *The Age of Reform, From Bryan to F.D.R.* (New York, 1955), pp. 139-140:

> Protestant and Anglo-Saxon for the most part, they were very frequently of New England ancestry; and even when they were not, they tended to look to New England's history for literary, cultural, and political models and for examples of moral idealism. Their conception of state-craft was set by the high example of the Founding Fathers, or by the great debating statesmen of the silver age, Webster, Sumner, Everett, Clay, and Calhoun. Their ideal leader was a well-to-do, well-educated, high-minded citizen, rich enough to be free from motives of what they often called "crass materialism," whose family roots were deep not only in American history but in his local community. Such a person, they thought, would be just the sort to put the national interest, as well as the interests of civic improvement, above personal motives or political opportunism. And such a person was just the sort, as Henry Adams never grew tired of complaining, for whom American political life was least likely to find a place. To be sure, men of the Mugwump type could and did find places in big industry, in the great corporations, and they were sought out to add respectability to many forms of enterprise. But they tended to have positions in which the initiative was not their own, or in which they could not feel themselves acting in harmony with their highest ideals. They no longer called the tune, no longer commanded their old deference. They were expropriated, not so much economically as morally.
>
> They imagined themselves to have been ousted almost entirely by new men of the crudest sort.

For another description of the Mugwump, see James Bryce, *The American Commonwealth* (New York, 1889), Vol. II, pp. 15, 19.
43. Bruce, *History*, Vol. I, p. 157.
44. Charles Fenton Mercer commented in 1856 of his philosophical views at the time he entered college:

. . . I had derived my principles of action and theory from Plutarch, and the then fashionable democratic philosophy of Godwin, whose *Political Justice* and *Inquiries* were among my favorite volumes. —Both had taught me that I was to live not for my country, but in a sense more enlarged, for mankind.

From a letter to Mrs. Maria H. Garnett, London, June 6, 1856, printed in James Mercer Garnett, *Biographical Sketch of Hon. Charles Fenton Mercer, 1778-1858* (Richmond, 1911), p. 89.

45. *Catalogue of the Library of the Hon. Hugh S. Legaré* (Washington, 1843)
46. Hubbell, *The South*, p. 442.
47. *Address*, by the Virginia Agricultural Society (1852), cited by Clement Eaton, *Freedom of Thought in the Old South* (Durham, N.C., 1940), p. 47.
48. William C. Preston, *Eulogy on Hugh Swinton Legaré* (Charleston, 1843), p. 14.
49. William J. Grayson, *James Louis Petigru* (New York, 1866), pp. 89-90.
50. Preston, *Legaré*, p. 14.
51. William J. Grayson, *Autobiography*, cited by Hubbell, *The South*, p. 439.
52. Grayson, *Petigru*, p. 102.
53. Garnett, *Mercer*. I am indebted to Clement Eaton for first calling my attention to Mercer.
54. Charles Fenton Mercer, *An Exposition of the Weakness and Inefficiency of the Government of the United States of North America* (Printed for Author, 1845), pp. 167, 68.
55. Except for a term as Van Buren's Secretary of War.
56. Hubbell, *The South*, pp. 304-313.
57. *DAB*, Vol. XII, p. 539. Hubbell, *The South*, p. 427, quotes Tucker as saying toward the end of his life:

South Carolina alone can act, because she is the only State in which the gentleman retains his place and influence, and in which the statesman has not been degraded from his post.

See also Avery Craven, *Edmund Ruffin, Southerner* (New York, 1932), p. 80.
58. Thomas Govan, "Was the Old South Different?" *Journal of Southern History* (hereafter cited as *JSH*), Vol. XXI (November, 1955), p. 453.
59. *DAB*, Vol. VII, pp. 633-636.
60. Calhoun, in many ways, fits this general type. See Eaton, *Freedom*, pp. 151-152:

From 1835 to his death in 1850 Calhoun was an agitator and an alarmist on the slavery issue. "The great point is to rouse the South and to unite it," he wrote to a Charleston follower. His effectiveness as an agitator was weakened, however, by his devotion to abstract ideas. Supremely confident in the infallibility of his reason, he introduced abstract resolutions in Congress, which seemed to him to be indisputably the truth and destined to triumph. Such an addiction to metaphysics and to pushing logic to extreme limits was a decided drawback to him in politics. None the less, he made few of the usual concessions adopted by politicians to win the fickle favor of the people. He devised no popular slogans; he scorned the florid oratory characteristic of his period. . . . Too much of a philosopher, he could not qualify as a natural agitator, but was forced into this role by a keen realization of the dangerous minority position of the South.

61. Craven, *Ruffin*, pp. 39-46, 80.
62. Henry H. Simms, *The Rise of the Whigs in Virginia, 1824-1840* (Richmond, 1929), p. 83. Jackson's veto in 1832 of a bill to recharter the Second Bank of the United States (whose charter was to expire in 1836) was perhaps the most controversial issue in his first administration. In 1833 interests favoring easy credit policies and the free chartering of state banks, and those who wanted the administration to pursue a hard money policy convinced Jackson of the political expediency of taking the further step of withdrawing federal deposits from "Biddle's monster," as the National Bank was called. Jackson's veto message and this further action stirred up heated controversy in Virginia and divided previously united political groups within the state.
63. Carson, *Petigru*, p. 85.
64. William Campbell Preston, *Speech of the Hon. Mr. Preston on the Abolition Question*, Tuesday, March 1, 1836, p. 2.
65. Eaton, *Freedom*, pp. 89-117.
66. Edwin C. Holland and others, *A Refutation of the Calumnies Circulated Against the Southern and Western States, Respecting the Institution and Existence of Slavery Among Them* (Charleston, 1822), cited by George Dangerfield, *The Era of Good Feeling* (New York, 1952), p. 245.

Chapter II

1. Ralph Waldo Emerson, *The American Scholar* (Ithaca, N.Y., 1955), p. 14.
2. Letter to Thomas Cooper, August 14, 1820, in *The Writings of Thomas Jefferson*, Library Edition (Washington, D. C., 1903), Vol. XV, p. 269.
3. George Ticknor, *Life, Letters and Journals of George Ticknor*, George S. Hilliard, ed. (Boston, 1876), Vol. I, p. 348.
4. George Ticknor Curtis, *Life of Daniel Webster* (New York, 1870), Vol. I, p. 585.

References

5. Bernard Mayo, *Myths and Men* (Athens, Ga., 1959), p. 13.
6. Thomas Jefferson, *Reminiscences of Patrick Henry: in the Letters of Thomas Jefferson to William Wirt*, John Gribbel, ed. (Philadelphia, 1911), p. 3.
7. Curtis, *Webster*, p. 585.
8. Jefferson, *Reminiscences*, p. 6.
9. Jay B. Hubbell, *The South in American Literature, 1607-1900* (Durham, N.C., 1954), p. 240.
10. John P. Kennedy, *Memoirs of the Life of William Wirt* (Philadelphia, 1856), Vol. II, p. 51. Though bowdlerized and incomplete, this is the only form in which Wirt's correspondence is readily available.
11. *Ibid.*, pp. 43-44.
12. *Ibid.*, p. 51.
13. *Ibid.*, pp. 180-181.
14. *Ibid.*, Vol. I, p. 13.
15. *Ibid.*, p. 34.
16. William Wirt, *The Letters of the British Spy* (Richmond, 1803), p. 68.
17. Kennedy, *Wirt*, Vol. II, p. 266.
18. *Ibid.*, p. 67.
19. Repeatedly through these years Wirt discounts his own oratorical skills, his gift for the fanciful by comparing the imagination and literary power unfavorably to the power of analysis, reason. On December 22, 1809, he wrote to Benjamin Edwards:

    This power of analysis, the power of simplifying a complex subject, and showing all its parts clearly and distinctly, is the *forte* of Chief Justice Marshall, and is the great *desideratum* of every man who aims at eminence in the law. Genius, fancy, and taste may fashion the drapery and put it on; but Reason alone is the grand sculptor, that can form the statue itself. (Kennedy, *Wirt*, Vol. I, p. 246.)

    It is ironic that this assertion should be made through the use of a characteristic fanciful metaphor.
20. Kennedy, *Wirt*, Vol. II, p. 356.
21. *Ibid.*, p. 97.
22. *Ibid.*, p. 16.
23. *Ibid.*, p. 84.
24. From the unpublished letters by Wirt to Dabney Carr, which I was able to see through the courtesy of Joseph C. Robert. For the benefit of non-Virginians, a whip syllabub is a frothy whipped dessert.
25. Wirt, *British Spy*, p. 68.
26. Kennedy, *Wirt*, Vol. I, p. 179.
27. *Ibid.*, p. 208.
28. *Ibid.*, p. 307.

29. *Ibid.*, Vol. II, p. 71.
30. *Ibid.*, Vol. I, p. 116.
31. To Benjamin Edwards, Wirt wrote December 22, 1809:

> Alas! poor country! what is to become of it? . . . My apprehensions, therefore, have no reference to them [administration], nor to any event very near at head; And yet, can any man who looks upon the state of public virtue in this country, and then casts his eyes upon what is doing in Europe, believe that this confederated republic is to last for ever? Can he doubt that its probable dissolution is less than a century off? Think of Burr's conspiracy, within thirty-five years of the birth of the republic;—think of the characters implicated with him;—think of the state of political parties and of the presses in this country;—think of the execrable falsehoods, virulent abuse, villainous means by which they strive to carry their points. (Kennedy, *Wirt*, Vol. I, p. 247.)

In a letter to Edwards written July 12, 1808, in the wake of the Franco-Russian alliance, which seemed to sell out the Revolution to Eastern despotism, Wirt expresses disillusionment with Napoleon and the cause of liberty in Europe and at home:

> We have but to look upon nations abroad, and men at home, to see that everything under the sun is uncertain and fluctuating; that prosperity is a cheat, and virtue often but a name.

Napoleon, he felt, had replaced the old monarchies with something much worse:

> Look upon the map of Europe. See what it was fifty or sixty years ago—what it has since been, and what it is likely to become. . . . Yet now see, all at once, the revolution *gone*, like a flash of lightening; France suddenly buried beneath the darkness of despotism, and the voracious tyrant swallowing up kingdom after kingdom. The combining monarchs thought that they were in danger of nothing but the propagation of the doctrines of liberty; but ruin has come upon them from another quarter. The doctrines of liberty are at an end, and so are the monarchies of Europe—all fused and melted down into one great and consolidated despotism. How often have I drunk that Caesar's health, with a kind of religious devotion! How did all America stand on tiptoe, during his brilliant campaigns in Italy at the head of the army of the republic! . . . Yet see in what it has all ended! The total extinction of European liberty, and the too probable prospect of an enslaved world. (Kennedy, *Wirt*, Vol. I, pp. 233-234.)

32. *Ibid.*, Vol. I, p. 251.
33. *Ibid.*, p. 302.
34. *Ibid.*, p. 345.
35. *Ibid.*, p. 344.
36. *Ibid.*, p. 315.
37. *Ibid.*, p. 345.
38. Jefferson, *Reminiscences*, p. 27.

39. Robert Douthat Meade, *Patrick Henry: Patriot in the Making* (Philadelphia, 1957), pp. 49-51.
40. *Ibid.*, pp. 49-50.
41. Wirt's favorite comparison is to the Roman under the republic. Complaining of the quality of the legislature in a letter to Dabney Carr in 1810, he mutters, "How little does it resemble a Roman Senate!" and then continues:

> Can you conceive any pleasure superior to the enjoyment of hearing a debate, on a great public measure, conducted by such men as Cicero, Cato, Caesar, and their compeers;—that pleasure which Sallust so often tasted, and of which he has left us such brilliant specimens? What stores of knowledge had those men; what funds of argument, illustration and ornament; what powers of persuasion, what force of reason, what striking and impressive action, what articulate and melodious elocution! —yet each speaker marked with a character of his own, which distinguished him from all the world,—the sportive amenity of Cicero, the god-like dignity of Cato.
>
> But without going back to Rome, how little does any House that we have had for some years past resemble the House in which Jefferson, Pendleton, Henry, Richard H. Lee, Wythe, Bland and others were members; or the Convention which ratified the Constitution; or the Assembly of 99-1800, in which Madison, Giles, John Taylor of Caroline, Brent, Swann, Tazewell and Taylor of Norfolk were members!
>
> Yet, without any extraordinary prejudice in favour of antiquity, I apprehend that we have never yet, by any of our Houses, matched a Roman Senate *as a whole*. (Kennedy, *Wirt*, Vol. I, p. 261.)

42. Wirt, *Patrick Henry*, p. 408.
43. *Ibid.*, p. 39.
44. Cited by Hubbell, *The South*, p. 90.
45. Wirt, *Patrick Henry*, pp. 49, 107.
46. Like Lincoln of the legend, he makes an almost clownish appearance at the opening of his career:

> His person is represented as having been coarse, his manners uncommonly awkward, his dress slovenly, his conversation very plain, his aversion to study invincible, and his faculties almost entirely benumbed by indolence. (Wirt, *Patrick Henry*, p. 6.)

47. *Ibid.*, p. 25.
48. *Ibid.*, pp. 26, 28.
49. *Ibid.*, p. 252.
50. *Ibid.*, p. 32.
51. *Ibid.*, p. 119.
52. *Ibid.*, p. 50.
53. *Ibid.*, pp. 64-65, 295.
54. *Ibid.*, pp. 425, 427.
55. *Ibid.*, p. 148.

56. *Ibid.*, p. 234.
57. *Ibid.*, p. 377.
58. Wirt, *British Spy*, p. 22.
59. William Wirt, *A Discourse on the Lives and Characters of Thomas Jefferson and John Adams, Who Both Died on the Fourth of July, 1826* (Washington, D.C., 1826), p. 9.
60. *Ibid.*, pp. 15, 26.
61. See above, pp. 32-33.
62. Wirt, *Jefferson and Adams*, p. 26.
63. Kennedy, *Wirt*, Vol. II, pp. 182-183.
64. *Ibid.*, p. 324.
65. *Ibid.*, pp. 366-367.
66. *Ibid.*, pp. 369-370.

Chapter III

1. Erik Erikson, *Childhood and Society* (New York, 1950), p. 244.
2. Howard R. Floan, *The South in Northern Eyes, 1831-1861* (Austin, 1958), pp. 89-107 and *passim*.
3. Daniel R. Hundley, *Social Relations in Our Southern States* (New York, 1860), pp. 14-15.
4. James Fenimore Cooper, *Notions of the Americans: Picked up by a Travelling Bachelor* (Philadelphia, 1836), Vol. II, p. 293.
5. Daniel Webster, *Address Delivered at the Completion of the Bunker Hill Monument, June 17, 1843* (Boston, 1843), p. 3.
6. Louis L. Noble, *The Course of Empire, Voyage of Life, and Other Pictures of Thomas Cole, N.A., With Selections From his Letters and Miscellaneous Writings: Illustrative of his Life, Character, and Genius* (New York, 1853). Perry Miller, "The Romantic Dilemma in American Nationalism and the Concept of Nature," *The Harvard Theological Review*, Vol. XLVIII, No. 4 (October, 1955).
7. Curtis Dahl, "The American School of Catastrophe," *American Quarterly*, Vol. XI (Fall, 1959), pp. 380-390.
8. George Ticknor Curtis, *Life of Daniel Webster* (New York, 1870), Vol. I, p. 249.
9. William Wirt, *An Address Delivered Before the Peithessophian and Philoclean Societies of Rutgers College*, 3rd edition (New Brunswick, 1838), p. 14.
10. Daniel Webster, *Discourse in Commemoration of the Lives and Services of John Adams and Thomas Jefferson* (New York, 1885), p. 44.
11. Daniel Webster, *The Works of Daniel Webster* (Boston, 1851), Vol. I, pp. 196-197.
12. James Fenimore Cooper, *The Spy: A Tale of the Neutral Ground* (London, 1849), p. 25.

13. *Ibid.*, p. 47.
14. *Ibid.*, p. 50.
15. *Ibid.*, p. 327.
16. *Ibid.*, p. 337.
17. *Ibid.*, p. 400.
18. *Ibid.*, p. 125.
19. Susan Fenimore Cooper, "A Glance Backward," *Atlantic Monthly*, Vol. LIX (February, 1887), p. 205.
20. J. Cooper, *The Spy*, pp. 124, 398, 401.
21. For a perceptive discussion of this problem see Henry Nash Smith's chapter "Leatherstocking and the Problem of Social Order," *Virgin Land* (Cambridge, Mass., 1950), pp. 59-70.
22. For an illuminating discussion of American literary culture in this period, see R. W. B. Lewis' *The American Adam. Innocence, Tragedy and Tradition in the Nineteenth Century* (Chicago, 1955). I encountered his excellent discussion of the hero in American romance (Chapter V, "The Hero in Space") only after I had completed my own draft of this chapter.
23. The critic was "a prominent Wall Street merchant" whom Cooper met one morning as he walked up Broadway. He stopped Cooper to express his admiration for *The Spy* and especially for the character of Harvey. Cooper, he felt, had made "one capital mistake" in sketching Harvey's character:

    Why, my dear sir, you have given the man no motive! The character is well drawn in other particulars; but so much the pity that you failed on that point. Just look at the facts: here is a man getting into all kinds of scrapes, running his neck into the noose of his own accord; and where, pray, was his motive? Of course I thought until the last page, that he would be well paid for his services; but just as I expected to see it all settled he refuses the gold. There was your great mistake. You should have given Harvey some motive. (S. Cooper, "Glance," p. 205).

24. Robert Y. Hayne and Daniel Webster, *The Several Speeches Made During the Debate in the Senate of the United States, on Mr. Foot's Resolution, Proposing an Inquiry Into the Expediency of Abolishing the Office of Surveyor General of Public Lands, and to Suspend Further Surveys, &c.* (Charleston, 1830).
25. Webster, *Debate on Public Lands in Senate* (January 20, 1830), pp. 17-18.
26. Hayne, Speech in Senate (January 21, 1830), p. 17.
27. *Ibid.*, pp. 17-36.
28. Curtis, *Webster*, Vol. I, pp. 154-156.
29. Clement Eaton, "Calhoun and State Rights," *A History of the Old South* (New York, 1949), pp. 323-339.
30. Webster, Speech in Senate (January 26, 1830), p. 40.
31. *Ibid.*, p. 69.

32. Richard N. Current, *Daniel Webster and the Rise of National Conservatism* (Boston, 1955), pp. 61-62.
33. *Ibid.,* pp. 62-63.
34. Isabelle Webb Entrikin, *Sarah Josepha Hale and Godey's Lady's Book* (Philadelphia, 1946), p. 132.
35. *Ibid.,* p. 121.
36. *Ibid.,* pp. 1-10.
37. *Idem.*
38. For the details of Sarah Hale's life see Ruth E. Finley, *The Lady of Godey's—Sarah Josepha Hale* (Philadelphia, 1931).
39. Entrikin, *Hale,* pp. 101-102.
40. Sarah Josepha Hale, *Traits of American Life* (Philadelphia, 1835), p. 10.
41. Entrikin, *Hale,* pp. 4, 27.
42. A representative statement of Sarah Hale's view of men versus women is in her *Sketches of American Character* (Boston, 1838), p. 255:

> There is for them [women] but *one* pursuit. Of what use is it for us to deny the fact, that it is in the marriage establishment only, that woman seeks her happiness and expects her importance, when all history and our own observation, confirm it to be the truth. It is not so with men,—they have more than *one* medium through which to seek for fortune, fame and happiness, and that is, in my opinion, the sole reason of their superiority of mind over us. How I do wish women would be sensible of this, and endeavor to find or make an employment, consistent with *propriety.* . . .

43. Entrikin, *Hale,* p. 104.
44. Sarah Josepha Hale, *The Genius of Oblivion; and Other Original Poems* (Concord, N.H., 1823).
45. Entrikin, *Hale,* pp. 44-45.
46. *Ibid.,* p. 11.
47. Sarah Josepha Hale, *Northwood, or Life North and South; Showing the True Character of Both* (New York, 1852), p. 7.
48. *Ibid.,* p. 10.
49. *Ibid.,* p. 7.
50. Hale, *Sketches,* p. 8.
51. *Ibid.,* pp. 52-53.
52. *Ibid.,* pp. 67-68.
53. Hale, *Traits,* p. 110.
54. *Ibid.,* p. 111.
55. *Ibid.,* pp. 99-100.
56. *Ibid.,* pp. 101-102.
57. Hale, *Northwood,* pp. 9-12.
58. Sarah Josepha Hale, *Northwood; a Tale of New England* (Boston, 1827), Vol. II, p. 146.

59. Hale, *Northwood* (1852), p. 180.
60. *Ibid.*, p. 235.
61. *Ibid.*, p. 73.
62. Hale, *Sketches*, p. 193.
63. J. Cooper, *Notions*, Vol. II, pp. 191-192:

> The sword of Washington did not leap from its scabbard with the eagerness of military pride, or with the unbridled haste of one willing to make human life the sacrifice of an unhallowed ambition. It was deliberately drawn at the call of his country, but with a reluctance that came deep from the heart, and with a diffidence that acknowledged the undisputed dominion of his God. He went forth to battle with the meekness of a mortal, the humanity of a Christian, the devotedness of a patriot, and the resolution of a victor. . . . He took the trust his country offered, because it was the pleasure of that country he should do so; and when its duties were excellently performed, he returned it to the hands from whence it had come, with a simplicity which spoke louder than a thousand protestations. . . . It is impossible to look closely into the conduct and motives of this man, and not to feel that his simple rule of morals said, self before dishonour, my country before self, and God, before all.

64. Hale, *Northwood* (1852), p. iv.
65. *Ibid.* These "few additions" are nonetheless very interesting. Many of the small changes she made suggest the years that had elapsed. Steam power and the telegraph had made their appearance (1827, vol. II, pp. 8-10; 1852, p. 219). A reference to Sir Walter Scott was dropped (1827, Vol. I, pp. 3-5); so were the references to the Scotch reviewers (1827, Vol. I, p. 206; 1852, p. 164). An "apprentice" has become a "clerk" (1827, Vol. II, p. 194; 1852, p. 356), and "females" have become "women" (1827, Vol. I, p. 12; 1852, p. 13). Coffee replaced tea in the Romilly household (1827, Vol. I, p. 118; 1852, p. 96) and beer was added to the list of drinks served (1827, Vol. I, p. 155; 1852, p. 124). The Episcopalian Church received some free propaganda in the new edition. Sidney has become an Episcopalian like Sarah Hale herself, and Horace Brainard, it is implied, is about to leave the Catholic Church and join the church of his foster son (1852, p. 170). More significant, a reference to "American Liberty" was changed to "American Liberty and Power" (1827, Vol. I, p. 74; 1852, p. 60). Sidney's father has become an advocate of Manifest Destiny and a promoter of African colonization for Negro slaves (1852, Chap. XIV). The name of a Brainard Negro has been changed from "Cato" to "Tom" (1827, Vol. I, p. 26; 1852, p. 24). The family name, spelled "Romilee" in the first edition, has been changed to "Romilly" and stress was laid on the English ancestry of the family, despite the fact that the name Romilly had the same kind of ambiguous nationality as Sarah Hale's maiden name,

References

Buell. A long discussion of the possible dangers and advantages of the new European immigration is entirely new (1852, Chap. XIV). So is the final chapter of the book, which describes Sidney's plans for operating the Brainard plantation and justifying his gentility (1852, Chap. XXXIV).
66. Hale, *Northwood* (1852), p. 407.
67. *Ibid.*, p. 401.
68. *Ibid.*, p. 389.
69. *Ibid.*, p. 402.

Chapter IV

1. Thomas Nelson Page, *Social Life in Old Virginia Before the War* (New York, 1897), p. 46.
2. Harriet Beecher Stowe, *Dred: A Tale of the Great Dismal Swamp* (Boston, 1856), Vol. I, p. 182.
3. The only attempt to survey the whole field of plantation fiction is Francis Pendleton Gaines, *The Southern Plantation; A Study in the Development and the Accuracy of a Tradition* (New York, 1924).
4. Kenneth S. Lynn, *Mark Twain and Southwestern Humor* (Boston, 1959), pp. 53-54, 113. Sometimes Mr. Lynn, whose analysis of the Southwest humorists is otherwise both subtle and sophisticated, —and from which I have learned much—seems to suggest that these novels were propaganda tracts comparable to Hinton Helper's *The Impending Crisis*, with which he compares them, and that they were explicitly written by "Southern Whigs" to convince "Northern Conservatives" to support Southern interests. See, for example, p. 113:

To maintain their traditional alliance with Northern conservatives was thus one of the chief objectives of Southern Whig propaganda. Plantation novels that conjured up soft-spoken gentlemen and lovely ladies dancing minuets in chandeliered ballrooms; genealogies that traced the bloodlines of Delta cotton farmers back to Cavalier refugees from Cromwell's England; sociologies that proved the South to be the successor to fifth-century Athens; these things were all a part of the process of keeping the moneyed classes of the North persuaded of the virtues of the slavocracy. So was Southwestern humor.

5. Henry Nash Smith, *Virgin Land; The American West as Symbol and Myth* (Cambridge, Mass., 1950), p. 151. Mr. Smith points out that the "myth of the Southern plantation" was "so powerful and persuasive" that it long survived slavery and the plantation system, but the very fact that it survived so long should suggest how little special pleading was built into such a myth and what

slender evidence there is for construing this writing as propaganda.

6. Page, *Social Life*, p. 31:

> Though the plantations were large, so large that one master could not hear his neighbor's dog bark, there was never any loneliness: it was movement and life without bustle; whilst somehow, in the midst of it all, the house seemed to sit enthroned in perpetual tranquility, with outstretched wings under its spreading oaks, sheltering its children like a great gray dove.

7. Daniel R. Hundley, *Social Relations in Our Southern States* (New York, 1860), p. 8.
8. Blanche H. C. Weaver, "D. R. Hundley: Subjective Sociologist," *Georgia Review*, Vol. X (Summer, 1956), pp. 222-234.
9. Hundley, *Social Relations*, pp. 21-22.
10. *Ibid.*, pp. 27-29.
11. George Tucker, *The Valley of Shenandoah* (New York, 1828), Vol. II, p. 292.
12. *Ibid.*, Vol. II, p. 100.
13. John Pendleton Kennedy, *Swallow Barn* (New York, 1851), pp. 27-30; Tucker, *Shenandoah*, Vol. II, pp. 31-32; Stowe, *Dred*, Vol. I, p. 179; William Gilmore Simms, *Woodcraft; or, Hawks About the Dovecote* (New York, 1882), p. 174; John Esten Cooke, *Canolles: The Fortunes of a Partisan* (Detroit, 1887), pp. 3-4.
14. Avery O. Craven, "The Rural Depression, 1800-1832," *The Coming of the Civil War* (New York, 1942), pp. 41-43.
15. *Ibid.*, p. 53.
16. *Annals of the Congress of the United States*, 18th Congress, 1st Session, April, 1824 (Washington, 1856), p. 2371.
17. Page, *Social Life*, pp. 45-46. It was Jefferson who originally used this startlingly apt image to describe the predicament of the Southern slaveholder. Writing to David Holmes during the Missouri controversy in 1820, he intimated that for the moment there was no solution to the slavery question. "But as it is, we have the wolf by the ears, and we can neither hold him, nor safely let him go." Thomas Jefferson to David Holmes, April 22, 1820, *The Works of Thomas Jefferson*, ed. Paul Leicester Ford (New York, 1905), Vol. XII, p. 159.
18. "John Randolph," *DAB*, Vol. XV, p. 364.
19. Henry Adams, *History of the United States of America* (New York, 1889-91), Vol. III, p. 157.
20. William Cabell Bruce, *John Randolph of Roanoke, 1773-1833* (New York, 1922), Vol. II, pp. 203-204.

21. *Ibid.*, Vol. I, pp. 302-379.
22. George Bagby, *The Virginia Gentleman and Other Sketches* (Richmond, 1943), p. 19.
23. John Esten Cooke, *The Virginia Comedians; or, Old Days in the Old Dominion* (New York, 1883), Vol. II, pp. 274-279.
24. Harriet Beecher Stowe, *Uncle Tom's Cabin, or, Life Among the Lowly* (Boston, 1887), pp. 257, 256.
25. Stowe, *Dred*, Vol. I, pp. 18-19.
26. *Ibid.*, pp. 19, 31.
27. Mary Boykin Chesnut, *A Diary From Dixie*, ed. Ben Ames Williams (Boston, 1949), pp. 237-238.
28. Margaret Mitchell, *Gone With the Wind* (New York, 1936), p. 26.
29. Hundley, *Social Relations*, p. 73.
30. Page, *Social Life*, pp. 34-38.
31. Tucker, *Shenandoah*, Vol. II, p. 107.
32. Kennedy, *Swallow Barn*, pp. 38, 40.
33. Stowe, *Dred*, Vol. II, p. 46.
34. Kennedy, *Swallow Barn*, pp. 44-46.
35. Cooke, *Canolles*, p. 61.
36. William Makepeace Thackeray, *The Virginians; A Tale of the Last Century* (New York, 1869), pp. 729-733.
37. Eugene A. Hecker, *A Short History of Women's Rights* (New York, 1914), pp. 156-165.
38. Forrest Wilson, *Crusader in Crinoline; The Life of Harriet Beecher Stowe* (Philadelphia, 1941), p. 196.

   The good people here, you know, are about half Abolitionists. A lady who takes a leading part in the female society in this place, yesterday called and brought Catharine the proceedings of the Female Anti-Slavery Convention.
   I should think them about as ultra as to measures as anything that had been attempted, though I am glad to see a better spirit than marks such proceedings generally.
   Today I read some in Mr. Birney's *Philanthropist*. Abolitionism being the fashion here, it is natural to look at its papers.
   It does seem to me that there needs to be an *intermediate* society. If not, as light increases, all the excesses of the abolition party will not prevent humane and conscientious men from joining it.

39. Kennedy, *Swallow Barn*, pp. 44-45.
40. Helen Waite Papashvily, *All the Happy Endings; A Study of the Domestic Novel in America, the Women who Wrote it, the Women who Read it, in the Nineteenth Century* (New York, 1956), pp. xiii-xvii.
41. Sarah Moore Grimké, *Letters on the Equality of the Sexes, and the Condition of Woman* (Boston, 1838), p. 23.
42. Wilbur J. Cash, *The Mind of the South* (New York, 1941), p. 84.
43. Chesnut, *Diary*, pp. 122, 123, 139, 145, 169.

44. *Southern Literary Messenger* (hereafter cited as SLM), Vol. I, (May, 1835), pp. 493-512; (July, 1835), pp. 621-623; (August, 1835), pp. 672-691.
45. *Ibid.*, p. 495.
46. *Ibid.*, pp. 495-496.
47. *Ibid.*, p. 673.
48. *Ibid.*, p. 498.
49. Nathaniel Beverley Tucker, *George Balcombe* (New York, 1836), Vol. II, p. 165.
50. *Ibid.*, p. 166.
51. *Ibid.*, Vol. I, pp. 275, 274.

Chapter V

1. William J. Grayson, *James Louis Petigru* (New York, 1866), pp. 136-137.
2. Jay B. Hubbell, *The South in American Literature, 1607-1900* (Durham, N.C., 1954), p. 492 n.
3. John Pendleton Kennedy, *Swallow Barn, or A Sojourn in the Old Dominion,* ed. with an introd. by Jay B. Hubbell (New York, 1929), p. 3.
4. *Ibid.*, pp. 5-6.
5. John Pendleton Kennedy, "A Word in Advance, from the Author to the Reader," *Swallow Barn* (New York, 1851), p. 7.
6. Edgar Allan Poe, *SLM,* Vol. I (May, 1835), p. 522.
7. George Ticknor, *Life, Letters and Journals of George Ticknor,* ed. George S. Hilliard (Boston, 1875), Vol I, pp. 268-270.
8. Kennedy, *Swallow Barn* (1851), p. 53.
9. *Ibid.*, p. 86.
10. *Ibid.*, p. 358.
11. *Ibid.*, p. 148.
12. *Ibid.*, p. 497.
13. *Ibid.*, p. 70.
14. *Ibid.*, p. 11.
15. *Ibid.*, pp. 95, 311.
16. John Pendleton Kennedy, *Swallow Barn* (Philadelphia, 1832), pp. 19-20; *Ibid.* (1851), pp. 27-28. The way in which Kennedy altered his description of the plantation house at "Swallow Barn" bears this out. This particular revision, while more extensive than others, is consistent with the less playful tone of the 1851 edition.
17. *Ibid.* (1851), pp. 8-9.
18. *Ibid.* Francis Parkman, in "The Works of James Fenimore Cooper," *NAR,* Vol. LXXIV (January, 1852), p. 159 notes the absence of anything peculiarly native and distinctive among genteel

Americans. The American woodsman like Natty Bumppo seemed to grow out of landscape, he wrote:

> But when we ascend into the educated and polished classes, these peculiarities are smoothed away, until, in many cases, they are invisible. An educated Englishman is an Englishman still; an educated Frenchman is often intensely French; but an educated American is apt to have no national character at all.

19. Kennedy, *Swallow Barn* (1851), p. 10.
20. Edward M. Gwathmey, *John Pendleton Kennedy* (New York, 1931), p. 17.
21. *Ibid.*, p. 21.
22. Henry T. Tuckerman, *The Life of John Pendleton Kennedy* (New York, 1871), pp. 50-51.
23. Gwathmey, *Kennedy*, pp. 20-21.
24. *Ibid.*, p. 31.
25. *Ibid.*, pp. 48-54.
26. *Ibid.*, pp. 39-40.
27. *Ibid.*, pp. 32-35.
28. *Ibid.*, pp. 34-35.
29. *Ibid.*, p. 18.
30. Tuckerman, *Kennedy*, p. 139.
31. Washington Irving was the son of Deacon William Irving (originally Irvine), a Scotch Covenanter from the island of Orkney, off the coast of Scotland. Kennedy jestingly refers in his autobiography to ancient feuds between the Kennedy clan and the Irving clan. Gwathmey, *Kennedy*, pp. 16-17.
32. Preface to the first edition, reprinted in John Pendleton Kennedy, *Horse-Shoe Robinson*, ed. with introduction, chronology, and bibliography by Ernest E. Leisy (New York, 1937), p. 11.
33. *SLM*, Vol. I, (May, 1835), pp. 522-524.
34. *Ibid.*, p. 523.
35. Kennedy, *Horse-Shoe*, p. 74.
36. *Ibid.*, p. 230.
37. *Ibid.*, p. 308.
38. *Ibid.*, p. 309.
39. *Ibid.*, p. 338.
40. *Ibid.*, p. 547.
41. Tuckerman, *Kennedy*, pp. 165-166.
42. Poe, who reviewed *Horse-Shoe Robinson* for the *SLM*, Vol. I, (May, 1835), p. 523, has this to say about the blacksmith-soldier:

> Horse-Shoe Robinson, who derives his nick-name of Horse-Shoe (his proper *praenomen* being Galbraith)—from the two-fold circumstance of being a blacksmith, and of living in a little nook of land hemmed in by a semi-circular bend of water, is fully entitled to the character of "an original." He is the life and soul of the drama—the

bone and sinew of the book—its very breath—its every thing which gives it strength, substance, and vitality. Never was there a rarer fellow —a more laughable blacksmith—a more gallant Sancho. He is a very prince at an ambuscade, and a very devil at a fight. He is a better edition of Robin Hood—quite as sagacious—not half so much of a coxcomb— and infinitely more moral. In short, he is the man of all others we should like to have riding by our side in any very hazardous expedition.

Simms reviewed the revised edition of the novel for the *Southern Quarterly Review* (hereafter cited as SQR), Vol. XXII (July, 1852), pp. 204-205. He found many historical inaccuracies in Kennedy's account of the Revolution in South Carolina, and he found Kennedy a poor raconteur, but his admiration for the character of Horse-Shoe was unqualified. He professed to find him in many ways superior to Cooper's Leather-Stocking. His tribute (in part) reads:

The true attraction of the work lies wholly in the character of "Horse-Shoe Robinson." This is a faithful portrait of a frank, shrewd, generous, high-spirited backwoodsman; rough and untutored, but warm and kindly; unlearned in books, but of admirable mother wit; quick in expedients, fertile in resource; of large experience, and of that buoyant nature which never knows how to succumb to misfortune, and so laughs under the pressure of fate as to take from it most of its sour aspects. . . . He is quite as ready and practical as Cooper's Hunter, but not so poetical. Where the latter indulged in musings, the former dealt in argument. While Natty Bumppo nursed the solitude, Horse-Shoe was eminently social; and while the one inclined to melancholy, the other was the very personification of *bonhommie*. Both are manly, honest, generous; above meanness; self-sacrificing always, and abounding in loyalty. Both are eminently adhesive. The character of Horse-Shoe was one that seizes immediately upon the sympathies of the reader, as well from its truthfulness as its buoyancy. It is just such a character as every man will recognize, who has seen any thing of the world in the region where the scene is laid. . . . You cannot daunt him. You can never take him by surprise. . . . Altogether, a more perfect and perfectly drawn study, of its class, you will hardly find anywhere in American fiction, and the felicity of the portrait was at once established, by the popularity of the character.

43. Peter A. Browne (1782-1862), was an American ethnologist whose most important work—the only one of which there is any record —is *Trichologia Mammalium; or a Treatise on the Organization, Properties, and Uses of Hair and Wool; Together with an Essay Upon the Raising of and Breeding of Sheep* (Philadelphia, 1853).
44. Kennedy received $782.59 from Carey and Lea for the first edition (2,000 copies) of *Swallow Barn*. There is no record of what, if anything, he received from the second edition in 1851. *Horse-Shoe Robinson* quickly went through a first printing of 3,000, for which Kennedy was paid $1,200: "A small sum," he commented, "considering its success." He probably received additional

sums for subsequent printings. His *Life of William Wirt,* on which he worked for two years, brought him less than $600. The success of his earlier writing encouraged Carey and Lea to pay him a lump sum of $1,850 for *Rob of the Bowl.* He probably never received altogether more than $5,000 from the sale of his books. (Gwathmey, *Kennedy,* pp. 105-107, 82, 120.)

45. Tuckerman, *Kennedy,* p. 337.
46. John Pendleton Kennedy, *Rob of the Bowl. A Legend of St. Inigoe's* (Philadelphia, 1860), p. 432.

Chapter VI

1. Said by Alexander Spotswood in William Alexander Caruthers, *The Knights of the Horseshoe: A Traditionary Tale of the Cocked Hat Gentry in the Old Dominion* (New York, 1928), pp. 198-199.
2. John Hope Franklin, *The Militant South; 1800-1861* (Cambridge, Mass., 1956), p. 99.
3. J. D. B. De Bow, "The Belligerents," *SQR,* Vol. XXXI (1861), p. 72.
4. The famous English rogue and escape-artist, Jack Shepherd (1702-1724), who had once escaped from Newgate.
5. Curtis Carroll Davis, *Chronicler of the Cavaliers* (Richmond, Va., 1953), pp. 298-299. Aristocratic names furnished were: Beverley, Blair, Bland, Bray, Byrd, Carter, Chicheley, Corbin, Digges, Fairfax, Fitzhugh, Grymes, Harrison, Hill, Lee, Nelson, Page, Peyton, Randolph and Skipwith. Plebeian names were: Bagewell, Bass, Bullock, Burras, Dodds, Fenwick, Grindon, Grub, Hen, Hite, Hogg, Hunt, Hutchins, Kidd, Laydon, Pace, Pate, Roach, Speed, Spraggins, and Wright (p. 493).
6. The most comprehensive study of Caruthers' life and writings is Curtis Carroll Davis, *Chronicler of the Cavaliers.* References to Caruthers' life, though not my interpretation of it, have been based on Davis. A bibliography of Caruthers' published writings is to be found in Davis, pp. 525-533.
7. Thomas J. Wertenbaker, *The Old South: The Founding of American Civilization* (New York, 1942), p. 2. Cited in Davis, *Chronicler,* p. 4.
8. Davis, *Chronicler,* p. 13.
9. *Ibid.,* p. 81.
10. *Ibid.,* pp. 64-67.
11. Paulding's play, *The Lion of the West* (later retitled *The Kentuckian; or, A Trip to New York*) opened at the Park Theatre in New York in April, 1831, with James H. Hackett, "The American Falstaff," in the principal role of Colonel Nimrod Wildfire. Caruthers almost certainly saw the play and there are striking

similarities between Wildfire and Caruthers' Montgomery Damon. See James Kirke Paulding, *The Lion of the West*, ed. and with an introduction by James N. Tidewell (Stanford, 1954), pp. 8-14.

12. Davis, *Chronicler*, pp. 284-290.
13. William Alexander Caruthers, *The Kentuckian in New York* (New York, 1834), Vol. I, p. 13.
14. *Ibid.*, Vol. I, pp. 50-51. "You cannot conceive of any more thoroughly disgusting feeling than that produced upon the mind of a young man bred up in the country, upon this first exhibition of the detestable forms which vice and dissipation assume in every large city,—young females with bloated countenances,—boys with *black* eyes and bruised faces, with their disgusting slang and familiar nicknames." (*Ibid.*, Vol. I, p. 154).
15. *Ibid.*, Vol. I, p. 78.
16. Davis, *Chronicler*, pp. 143-162.
17. *Ibid.*, p. 189.
18. William Alexander Caruthers, *The Cavaliers of Virginia* (New York, 1834), Vol. I, p. 33.
19. *Ibid.*, Vol. I, p. 4.
20. *Ibid.*, Vol. I, p. 3.
21. Ezra Stiles, *A History of Three of the Judges of Charles I* (Hartford, 1794). See Davis, *Chronicler*, pp. 156-162.
22. Caruthers, *Cavaliers*, Vol. I, pp. 71, 12.
23. *Ibid.*, Vol. I, p. 118.
24. *Ibid.*, Vol. II, pp. 50-51, 179.
25. *Ibid.*, Vol. II, pp. 75-76.
26. See Albert K. Weinberg, *Manifest Destiny, A Study of Nationalist Expansion in American History* (Baltimore, 1935), Chs. IV-VII.
27. *Ibid.*, "The Destined Use of the Soil," pp. 72-99.
28. Ollinger Crenshaw, "The Knights of the Golden Circle. The Career of George Bickley," *American Historical Review*, Vol. XLVII (October, 1941), pp. 23-50.
29. Davis, *Chronicler*, p. 308.
30. Caruthers, *Knights*, p. 174.
31. *The Knights*, like the earlier novels, is in part a temperance and antidueling tract and Caruthers himself lectured before the Georgia Temperance Society and on at least one occasion intervened to prevent a duel.
32. William Alexander Caruthers, "Daniel Boone," *The National Portrait Gallery of Distinguished Americans*, conducted by James B. Longacre and James Herring (Philadelphia, 1835), Vol. II, pp. 2, 13, 4, 1.
33. Caruthers, *Knights*, pp. 335-336.
34. *Ibid.*, p. 312.
35. *Ibid.*, pp. 199, 266-267.
36. *Ibid.*, p. 156.

37. Davis, *Chronicler*, p. 317.
38. William Alexander Caruthers, "Love and Consumption," *The Magnolia* (July, 1842), pp. 35-38; (August, 1842), pp. 103-108; (September, 1842), pp. 177-182.

Chapter VII

1. John Bunyan, *The Pilgrim's Progress from This World to That Which is to Come* (New York, 1910), p. 63.
2. James Kirke Paulding, "Letter from Hon. James K. Paulding," *1860 Association, Tract No. 2* (Charleston, S.C., 1860), p. 25.
3. *Ibid.*, pp. 28-29.
4. William I. Paulding, *Literary Life of James K. Paulding* (New York, 1867), p. 24.
5. *Ibid.*, pp. 27-28.
6. *Ibid.*, p. 19.
7. *Ibid.*, p. 20.
8. *Ibid.*, pp. 22, 25.
9. *Ibid.*, pp. 24-25.
10. *Ibid.*, pp. 26-27.
11. *Ibid.*, p. 26.
12. *Ibid.*, p. 29.
13. *Ibid.*, pp. 29-41.
14. *Ibid.*, pp. 29-30.
15. *Ibid.*, p. 30.
16. William Irving, James Kirke Paulding and Washington Irving, *Salmagundi: or, the Whim-Whams and Opinions of Launcelot Langstaff, Esq., and Others* (New York, 1835).
17. W. Paulding, *Life*, pp. 68-69, 182, 270.
18. *Ibid.*, p. 70.
19. *Ibid.*, p. 183.
20. *Ibid.*, p. 78.
21. Percival Reniers, *The Springs of Virginia* (Chapel Hill, 1941), Ch. II.
22. Jay B. Hubbell, *The South in American Literature, 1607-1900* (Durham, N.C., 1954), pp. 376-377.
23. Ralph Waldo Emerson, *Journals of Ralph Waldo Emerson*, ed. Edward Waldo Emerson and Waldo Emerson Forbes (Boston, 1910), p. 275.
24. Hubbell, *The South*, p. 377.
25. Ralph Waldo Emerson, *The American Scholar* (New York, 1901), p. 33.
26. Henry Adams, *The Education of Henry Adams* (New York, 1930), pp. 57-59.
27. James Kirke Paulding, *Letters from the South* (New York, 1835), Vol. I, p. 33.

28. *Ibid.*, Vol. I, pp. 92, 91, 140.
29. *Ibid.*, Vol. II, pp. 18-35.
30. W. Paulding, *Life*, p. 278.
31. J. Paulding, *Letters*, Vol. II, p. 79.
32. James Kirke Paulding, *Westward Ho! A Tale* (New York, 1832), Vol. I, pp. 11, 47.
33. *Ibid.*, pp. 18-19, 43.
34. *Ibid.*, Vol II, p. 39.
35. *Ibid.*, Vol. I, pp. 86-87.
36. J. Paulding, *Letters*, Vol. II, p. 39.
37. W. Paulding, *Life*, p. 287.
38. *Ibid.*, pp. 287-288.
39. J. Paulding, *Westward Ho!*, Vol. I, p. 68.
40. *Ibid.*, pp. 177, 173-174.
41. James Kirke Paulding, *A Life of Washington* (New York, 1839), Vol. II, pp. 145-146.
42. *Ibid.*, Vol. I, p. 111.
43. *Ibid.*, Vol. II, p. 204.
44. *Ibid.*, Vol. II, p. 229; Vol. I, pp. 60, 112.
45. J. Paulding, *Letters*, Vol. I, pp. 18, 14, 16.
46. *Ibid.*, p. 15.
47. W. Paulding, *Life*, pp. 239-240.
48. *Ibid.*, p. 243.
49. James Kirke Paulding, *Slavery in the United States* (New York, 1836), pp. 9, 7.
50. *Ibid.*, p. 88.
51. *Ibid.*, pp. 6, 126.
52. James Kirke Paulding, *The Puritan and his Daughter* (New York, 1849), Vol. I, pp. 1-6.
53. A derogatory term for Puritan.
54. J. Paulding, *Puritan*, Vol. II, p. 86.
55. *Ibid.*, Vol. II, pp. 267-270.
56. *Ibid.*, Vol. II, pp. 139, 141.
57. *Ibid.*, Vol. II, pp. 186-187.
58. W. Paulding, *Life*, p. 338.
59. *Ibid.*, pp. 340, 347.

Chapter VIII

1. William Gilmore Simms, *The Letters of William Gilmore Simms*, ed. Mary C. Simms Oliphant, Alfred Taylor Odell and T. C. Duncan Eaves (Columbia, S.C., 1954), Vol. III, p. 108.
2. Avery Craven, "The Rural Depression, 1800-1832," *The Coming of the Civil War* (New York, 1942), p. 59.
3. *Ibid.*, p. 58.

4. Laura A. White, *Robert Barnwell Rhett: Father of Secession* (New York, 1931), p. 80.
5. *Ibid.*, p. 18.
6. John Witherspoon Du Bose, *The Life and Times of William Lowndes Yancey* (New York, 1942), Vol. I, p. 362.
7. Robert Barnwell Rhett, Charleston *Mercury*, August 1, 1844.
8. White, *Rhett*, p. 24.
9. *Ibid.*, pp. 197-198.
10. *Ibid.*, p. 222.
11. Simms, *Letters*, Vol. I, p. 294.
12. No satisfactory biography of Simms exists. I have relied entirely on the published volumes of his letters. See footnote 1 above.
13. Edgar Allan Poe, *The Broadway Journal*, Vol. II (October 4, 1845), pp. 190-191.
14. Simms, *Letters*, Vol. II, p. 65.
15. *De Bow's Review*, Vol. XXIX (1860), p. 708. Cited by John W. Higham, "The Changing Loyalties of William Gilmore Simms," *JSH*, Vol. IX (May, 1943), p. 210.
16. William Gilmore Simms, *Katherine Walton; or, the Rebel of Dorchester* (New York, 1882), p. 2.
17. Simms, *Letters*, Vol. II, p. 32.
18. *Ibid.*, p. 235 n.
19. *Ibid.*, p. 444.
20. A letter to Hammond, October 20, 1847, contains charges against the Bank of South Carolina and the power it exercised over politicians, including Calhoun, through loans made. Simms, *Letters*, Vol. II, pp. 354-355.

Hammond wrote a series of twenty-one essays signed "Anti' debt" on the railroad mania for the *Mercury* (October 21, 1847—January 5, 1848). These essays were later published as a book, James H. Hammond, *The Railroad Mania: And Review of the Bank of the State of South Carolina* (Charleston, S.C., 1848).

Simms warned Hammond *not* to attack all banks, since his stanchest allies were now those bankers who opposed the Bank of South Carolina. Simms, *Letters*, Vol. II, p. 428.
21. Allen Johnson, *Stephen A. Douglas: A Study in American Politics* (New York, 1908), p. 216; Simms, *Letters*, Vol. II, p. 322.
22. *Ibid.*, 206 n.
23. The main political alignment in South Carolina was between the machine (Calhoun and the bank) and a group of younger insurgents (Simms, in one letter asks: "Do you know Orr of Anderson?"). The alliance which formed—Aldrich was an extreme fire-eater—had much less to do with sectional ideology than opposition to the bank axis. "The Bank is tottering. I dread her

recuperative powers, & wish there were some strong arms to give her blows thick & heavy. . . . As it is their whole influence is centered in Columbia where Preston rules omnipotent." Hammond, January 11, 1847, cited in Simms, *Letters*, Vol. II, pp. 255-256 n.

24. Simms, *Letters*, Vol. II, pp. 418-419.
25. *Ibid.*, pp. 430-431.
26. In a letter to Simms, February 14, 1851, Tucker said that he feared the tyranny of "numbers" and that if he were twenty years younger he would go to Russia and claim protection of "the Emperor Nicholas." William P. Trent, *William Gilmore Simms* (Boston, 1892), pp. 183-184.

    Simms by 1851 had taken his attention away from state domination of the Hunkers and focused squarely on the Union as the foe; Rhett became an ally, rather than an enemy. "Rhett is not a wise man, but, in the great struggle before us, if rash, he is perhaps right." Written to Tucker, March 2, 1851, in Simms, *Letters*, Vol. III, p. 94.
27. John C. Calhoun, *Annual Report of the American Historical Association for the Year 1899* (Washington, 1900), pp. 752-753.
28. Simms, *Letters*, Vol. II, p. 411.
29. *Ibid.*, pp. 321-322.
30. William Gilmore Simms, "Summer Travel in the South," *SQR*, Vol. XVIII, New Series II (September, 1850), pp. 27, 26.
31. William Gilmore Simms, *The Social Principle: The True Source of National Permanence* (Tuscaloosa, Ala., 1843), p. 39.
32. The one serious attempt to explain the change in Simms's political orientation [Higham, "Simms," *JSH*, Vol IX (May, 1943), p. 233] places too exclusive emphasis on Simms's second marriage into the Roach family and into the planter class. Higham is correct in placing the switch sometime early in 1849, but he does not give sufficient weight to the effect on Simms of the political situation in South Carolina and in Europe. Simms did not, furthermore, become more intensely secessionist during the fifties, as Higham implies. After 1852 Simms went through a long period of political apathy, from which he was roused only by the outbreak of war.
33. This typology which originated in the need to distinguish between the American and French revolutions became a familiar characteristic of Southern conservative thought. In an article for the *SQR* entitled, "The Present State of Europe," which appeared in the January, 1850, issue, Beverley Tucker made the same distinction between contemporary revolutions and those of the past. Liberty, he felt, was a principle too abstract to stir up the masses and to incite rebellion. *SQR*, Vol. XVI, No. XXXII (January, 1850), pp. 277-323.

34. William Gilmore Simms, "South Carolina in the Revolution," *SQR*, Vol. XIV (July, 1848), pp. 49-50.
35. Simms, *Letters*, Vol. II, pp. 465, 465 n.
36. Simms, *Katherine Walton*, p. 163.
37. William Gilmore Simms, "Woodlands Plantation Book, 1845-1850," *Letters*, Vol. II, pp. 594, 595, 597.
38. Simms, *Letters*, Vol. III, pp. 99, 142 n.
39. *Ibid.*, pp. 100, 128.
40. *Ibid.*, pp. 98-99.
41. *Ibid.*, p. 40.
42. *Ibid.*, p. 128.
43. *Ibid.*, Vol. I, p. 277; Vol. III, p. 62.
44. *Ibid.*, Vol. IV, p. 226.
45. William Gilmore Simms, *The Partisan, A Romance of the Revolution* (New York, 1882), p. 110.
46. Simms, *The Partisan*, pp. 98-99, 110; *Katherine Walton*, p. 364.
47. William Gilmore Simms, *Woodcraft; or, Hawks About the Dovecot* (New York, 1882), p. 174.
48. *Ibid.*, p. 189.
49. *Ibid.*, pp. 101-102.
50. *Ibid.*, p. 225.
51. *Ibid.*, p. 191.
52. *Ibid.*, pp. 290-291.
53. *Ibid.*, p. 360.
54. Simms, *Letters*, Vol. IV, p. 168.
55. *Ibid.*, Vol. II, p. 488; Vol. IV, p. 379.
56. *The Orion, A Monthly Magazine of Literature and Art*, ed. William C. Richards, Vol. IV (March, 1844), pp. 41-51; (April, 1844), pp. 76-89; (May, 1844), pp. 105-119; (June, 1844), pp. 179-194.
57. Simms, "Hamlet," *The Orion*, Vol. IV (March, 1844), pp. 44-45. No text for the lectures has survived, and I have been forced to rely in what follows upon the article version published in 1844 but apparently extensively revised by Simms in 1853.
58. Simms, "Hamlet," *Orion*, Vol. IV (May, 1844), p. 113.
59. *Ibid.* (April, 1844), p. 46.
60. *Ibid.* (June, 1844), p. 193.
61. Simms, *Letters*, Vol. III, pp. 253-254.

Chapter IX

1. Octavius Brooks Frothingham, *Memoir of William Henry Channing* (Boston, 1886) p. 259.
2. Wilbur J. Cash, *The Mind of the South* (New York, 1954), p. 95.
3. Kenneth M. Stampp, *The Peculiar Institution* (New York, 1956), pp. 132-140. The story of the Turner insurrection has been told

a number of times. See Thomas R. Gray, *The Confessions of Nat Turner* (Baltimore, 1831); William S. Drewry, *The Southampton Insurrection* (Washington, D.C., 1900).

4. William Summer Jenkins, *Pro-Slavery Thought in the Old South* (Chapel Hill, 1935), pp. 81-89.
5. *Ibid.*, p. 83.
6. Joseph C. Robert, "The Road from Monticello. A Study of the Virginia Slavery Debate of 1832," *Historical Papers of the Trinity College Historical Society*, Series XXIV (Durham, N.C., 1941), p. 28.
7. Jenkins, *Pro-Slavery Thought*, p. 87 n. This fact was noted by Faulkner in a speech January 31, 1832.
8. Robert, "The Road From Monticello," pp. 29-35.
9. George Tucker, *The Valley of Shenandoah* (New York, 1828), Vol. I, pp. 61-62.
10. James Kirke Paulding, *Westward Ho! A Tale* (New York, 1832), Vol. I, pp. 57-58.
11. John Pendleton Kennedy, *Swallow Barn*, ed. with introd. by Jay B. Hubbell (New York, 1929), pp. 18, 375, 377-378.
12. *Ibid.*, pp. 392-393
13. Nathaniel Beverley Tucker, "Note to Blackstone's Commentaries," *SLM*, Vol. I, p. 230.
14. Nathaniel Beverley Tucker, *The Partisan Leader; A Tale of the Future* (Washington, 1856), Vol. II, pp. 6-7.
15. Forrest Wilson, *Crusader in Crinoline. The Life of Harriet Beecher Stowe* (Philadelphia, 1941), p. 276.
16. *Ibid.*, p. 336. The letter, dated February 9, is addressed to Daniel Reeves Goodloe.
17. *SLM*, Vol. XVIII (October, 1852), pp. 635-636.
18. Harriet Beecher Stowe, *Dred: A Tale of the Great Dismal Swamp* (Boston, 1856), Vol. I, p. 282.
19. Harriet Beecher Stowe, *Uncle Tom's Cabin* (Boston, 1887), p. 205.
20. *Ibid.*, p. 56.
21. Helen Waite Papashvily, *All the Happy Endings* (New York), 1956), pp. 73-74.
22. Charles H. Foster, *The Rungless Ladder; Harriet Beecher Stowe and New England Puritanism* (Durham, N.C., 1954), pp. 13-63.
23. *SLM*, Vol. XVIII (October, 1852), pp. 630-638; (December, 1852), pp. 721-731.
24. John W. Page, *Uncle Robin in his Cabin in Virginia and Tom Without One in Boston* (Richmond, 1853); Robert Criswell, *"Uncle Tom's Cabin" Contrasted with Buckingham Hall, The Planter's Home; or A Fair View of Both Sides of the Slavery Question* (New York, 1852); Mrs. Mary H. Eastman, *Aunt Phillis's Cabin; or, Southern Life as It Is* (Philadelphia, 1852); Charles Jacobs Peterson (pseud. J. Thornton Randolph), *The*

Cabin and Parlor; or, Slaves and Masters (Philadelphia, c. 1852); Rev. Baynard Rush Hall, *Frank Freeman's Barber Shop: A Tale* (New York, 1852); Martha Haines Butt, *Anti-Fanaticism: A Tale of the South* (Philadelphia, 1853).

25. D.D. Hall, "A Yankee Tutor in the Old South," *The New England Quarterly*, Vol. XXXIII (March, 1960), pp. 89-90.

Chapter X

1. Thomas B. Thorpe, *The Master's House; or, Scenes Descriptive of Southern Life* (New York, 1854), p. 152.
2. 29 Cong., 1 Sess. Senate Report No. 306. Committee on the Post office and Post Roads (April 20, 1846), pp. 28-29, as cited by Henry Nash Smith, *Virgin Land; The American West as Symbol and Myth* (Cambridge, Mass., 1950), p. 146. For most of the preceding I am indebted to Professor Smith's perceptive chapter, "The South and the Myth of the Garden," pp. 145-154.
3. George Tucker, *The Valley of Shenandoah* (New York, 1828), Vol. I, pp. 49-59.
4. John Pendleton Kennedy, *Swallow Barn* (New York, 1851), pp. 268, 272.
5. Nathaniel Beverley Tucker, *The Partisan Leader* (Washington, 1856), Vol. II, p. 59. James Kirke Paulding, *Westward Ho!* (New York, 1832), Vol. I, p. 68.
6. Paulding, *Westward Ho!*, Vol. I, p. 68.
7. N. B. Tucker, *The Partisan Leader*, Vol. I, pp. iv, 6.
8. *Ibid.*, Vol. II, p. 59.
9. Nathaniel Beverley Tucker, *George Balcombe* (New York, 1836), Vol. I, p. 22.
10. *Ibid.*, p. 77.
11. *Ibid.*, p. 237.
12. N. B. Tucker, *The Partisan Leader*, Vol. II, pp. 31-32.
13. *Ibid.*, p. 145.
14. Mary Boykin Chesnut, *A Diary From Dixie* (Boston, 1949), p. 238.
15. Jay B. Hubbell, *The South in American Literature, 1607-1900* (Durham, N.C., 1954), p. 514.

Epilogue

1. Representative David Clopton of Alabama to Senator Clement C. Clay, December 13, 1860, in Clement Eaton, *A History of the Southern Confederacy* (New York, 1954), p. 12.
2. Richard Hofstadter, ed., *Great Issues in American History: A Documentary Record* (New York, 1958), p. 392.

3. Walt Whitman, "Beat! Beat! Drums!" *Complete Poetry and Selected Prose and Letters*, ed. Emory Holloway (London, n.d.), p. 260.
4. C. Vann Woodward, "John Brown's Private War," *The Burden of Southern History* (Baton Rouge, 1960), pp. 41-68.
5. Eaton, *Confederacy*, p. 1.
6. *Ibid.*, pp. 9-10.
7. Mary Boykin Chesnut, *A Diary From Dixie* (Boston, 1949), p. 20; cited by Eaton, *Confederacy*, p. 17.
8. See above pages 151-153.
9. Avery Craven, *Edmund Ruffin Southerner: A Study in Secession* (New York, 1932), p. 171.
10. *Ibid.*, p. 259. The information about Ruffin, except for the details of his death, derives entirely from Professor Craven's biography.
11. Edmund Ruffin, Jr. in his diary, June 20, 1861, in "Death of Edmund Ruffin," *Tyler's Quarterly Historical and Genealogical Magazine*, Vol. V (January, 1924), p. 193.
12. Bernard Bailyn, "Politics and Social Structure in Virginia," *Seventeenth-Century America: Essays in Colonial History*, ed. James Morton Smith (Chapel Hill, 1959), pp. 90-115.
13. Barbara Miller Solomon, *Ancestors and Immigrants: A Changing New England Tradition* (Cambridge, Mass., 1956); Arthur Mann, *Yankee Reformers in the Urban Age* (Cambridge, Mass., 1954).

Index

Abolition, 277
Adams, Henry, 59, 157, 242, 341;
    on Southern gentlemen, 238-
    239
Adams, John, 19, 23, 32, 71, 72, 81,
    100, 119, 327, 333; as Yankee,
    91; on American Revolution,
    69, 70; on Patrick Henry, 69,
    70; on natural aristocracy,
    27-30; on progress, 25-27; on
    Wirt, 90, 91
Adams, John Quincy, 65, 94, 199
Addison, Joseph, 56
Alexander, Archibald, 207
American, the, distinct character-
    istics of, 10, 11
American Colonization Society,
    the, 139-140
Antimasonic party, the, 71, 94
Aristocracy, 96; Northern, 96, 97;
    see also Cavalier, the; gentil-
    ity; Southern gentleman, the
Atlantic, The, 139

Bacon, Nathaniel, Caruthers on,
    212-216
Bagby, George, 159
Bancroft, George, 19, 42, 43
Beard, Charles A., 15
Benton, Thomas Hart, 110
Berlin, University of, 41

Blackstone, Sir William, 72
Blennerhassett, Harman, 76
Bloomer, Amelia Jenks, 166
Bonaparte, Napoleon, 78, 84
Boone, Daniel, popular image of,
    220
"Boston Brahmins," 43, 44
Bowdoin College, 42
Brooks, Peter, 43
Brown, John, as Yankee, 330
Bryant, William Cullen, 273
Burk, John Daly, 212
    History of Virginia, 212
Burr, Aaron, 25, 76, 78, 80, 84
Byrd, William, 44
Byron, George Gordon, Lord, 48

Cabell, Joseph Carrington, 47, 56
Calhoun, John C., 94, 110-113,
    272, 274-276, 283, 324
Carr, Dabney, 74, 75, 78
Caruthers, William Alexander,
    151, 205-224; sketch of, 205-
    209
    The Kentuckian in New York,
    149, 209-211
    The Knights of the Horseshoe,
    149, 205, 217-223
    Love and Consumption, 223-
    224

The Cavaliers of Virginia, 149, 211-217
Cash, Wilbur J., 300, 323; on Southern chivalry, 168
Cass, Lewis, 275, 276
Cavalier, the, 15, 111, 183, 189, 210, 248, 250, 264, 265; characteristics of, 104, 105, 110, 132, 134, 147, 148, 196, 199, 200, 201, 203, 205, 208, 212, 217, 222, 246, 254, 258, 262, 280, 317; ideal evaluated, 340; legacy of, 341; Cooke, on, 324; N. B. Tucker on, 320, 321; *see also* Southern gentleman, gentility, aristocracy
Channing, William Ellery, 56
Channing, William Henry, quoted on *Uncle Tom's Cabin,* 299
Charleston *Mercury,* 275
Chateaubriand, François, Vicomte de, 38
Chesnut, Mary Boykin, on secession, 332; on Southern gentleman, 323-324; on Southern Hothead and Hamlet types, 161; on Southern women, 168, 169; on *Uncle Tom's Cabin,* 312
Cheves, Langdon, 111, 324
Child, Lydia Maria, 165
Civilization, 198, 251; Wirt on, 90-94
Clay, Clement C., 326
Clay, Henry, 94, 140, 312
Clopton, David, quoted on Civil War, 326
Cogswell, Joseph, 43
Cole, Thomas, 99
Coleridge, Samuel Taylor, 57, 296

Coles, Edward, 61
Compromise of 1850, 226
Cooke, John Esten, 150, 165, 292
Leather Stocking and Silk, 324
The Virginia Comedians, 159, 324
Cooper, James Fenimore, 19, 20, 97, 101-103, 105, 107, 109, 195, 199, 233, 334; Harvey Birch, as Yankee, 102-104; as transcendent Yankee, 105-106
The Spy, 19, 20, 101-106, 109, 196
Country life, American image of, 186-187
Country squire, 180-181
Crockett, David, 20, 86, 246

Dartmouth College, 118
Davis, Jefferson, 338
De Bow's Review, 52
Democratic party, 216, 239, 277; Barnburners, 273, 274, 277, 278, 279; Hunkers, 273-275, 277; divisions in South Carolina, 272, 273
Dew, Thomas R., influence on N. B. Tucker, 172; on women, 170-172
Dickinson, John, 45
Dixon, Jeremiah, 332
Douglas, Stephen, 273, 294
Drayton, William, 60
Duyckinck, Evert, 285

Edwards, Ninian, 74
Eliot, Samuel, 43
Elliott, William, 55, 60, 63, 65
Elmore, Franklin H., 272, 273, 275, 276

Emerson, Ralph Waldo, 30, 31, 43, 46, 52, 330; "American Scholar," quoted, 67; on Southerners, 237-238

English Emancipation Act, 64

Erikson, Erik, 95
Childhood and Society, quoted, 95

Essex Junto, 114

Europe, impact on American travelers, 38-50; New England image of, 51; Southern image of, 51, 52, 62, 64

Everett, Edward, 42-44, 94

Family, 146-148; Sarah Hale on, 119, 120, 164; Harriet Beecher Stowe on, 164, 309-311

Faulkner, Charles J., 301

Faulkner, William, 148, 291, 323, 341

Feudalism, 183-186

Filson, John, 220
Discovery, Settlement and Present State of Kentucke, 220

Flint, Timothy, 242

Foster, Charles, on *Uncle Tom's Cabin,* 311

Franklin, Benjamin, compared with Wirt, 71, 75; type of Yankee, 250

Free-Soil Party, 278; and Barnburners, 274

French Revolution, 26

Garrison, William Lloyd, 62, 301

Gayarré, Charles, 8

Gentility, 207, 219-220, 247-248; and usefulness, 136; and

emergent Yankee, 136; and transcendent Yankee, 136

Gilmer, Francis Walker, 74, 77, 78

Gilpin, William, on South, 316

Glasgow, Ellen, 148

Godey, Louis Antoine, 115

Godey's Lady's Book, 20, 115, 117, 121, 139

Goethe, Johann Wolfgang von, 38, 57, 72

Goldsmith, Oliver, 56

Gore, Christopher, 111

Gottingen, University of, 38, 42

Grayson, William, 57, 58, 60, 65

Grimké, Angelina Emily, 62, 63, 165, 166, 167

Grimké, Frederick, 62

Grimké, John Faucheraud, 61

Grimké, Sarah Moore, 62, 63, 165, 167; on women, 168

Grimké, Thomas Smith, 62

Grund, Francis J., 96
Aristocracy in America, 96

Hale, David, 117, 120, 121

Hale, Frances Ann, 117

Hale, Horatio, 117, 118

Hale, Josepha, 117

Hale, Sarah Josepha, 20, 115, 186, 189, 227, 228, 231, 234, 235, 250, 256, 258, 323, 334; compared with Webster, 116-118; becomes Episcopalian, 133; early literary career, 121; on family, 119, 120; on self-improvement, 126; on South, 123; on Southern family, 164; on Union, 138; on women, 119, 166; Sidney Romilly, 131-135; Horace Brainard, 132-135, 160

Northwood, 121-123, 131-135, 139-141

Sketches of American Character, 20, 124

Traits of American Life, 20, 124

"The Lloyds," 130

"The Lottery Ticket," 128

"The Poor Scholar," 129

"The Silver Mine," 127

"A Winter in the Country," 129

"Walter Wilson," 129

Hale, William, 117

Hamilton, Alexander, 25

Hammond, James H., 267, 268, 272, 273, 275, 276, 277, 281, 284, 293, 331, 332

Harper's Magazine, 139

Harris, Joel Chandler, 307

Harrison, Jesse Burton, 50

Hartford Convention, 26, 78, 112, 114

Harvard College, 38, 41, 44, 50

Hawthorne, Nathaniel, 20, 31

Hayne, John, 110

Hayne, Robert Y., 101, 109, 110, 112-114, 262, 316; *see also* Webster-Hayne debate

Henry, Patrick, 68, 69, 70, 75, 78, 79, 80-89, 90; as prototype of the Southern Hothead and Hamlet, 159-160; *see also* William Wirt

Herder, Johann Gottfried von, 57

Heyward, Thomas, quoted, 23

Holmes, Oliver Wendell, 43

Home, image of, 147; woman and, 148

Huckleberry Finn, 84

Hundley, Daniel R., quoted, 37; 97, 151, 152; on Southern women, 162-163, 331, 337; on Southern gentlemen, 152-153

Inns of Court, 44, 45

Irving, Washington, 20, 39, 46, 193, 199, 229, 230, 231, 232, 235, 236

Bracebridge Hall, 180, 233

The Sketch Book, 233

Jackson, Andrew, 57, 60, 86, 94, 244-248, 252, 316

"Jacobin," as applied to nullifiers, 55, 266; Negro slave as, 64

James, Henry, 341

James, William, 49

Jay, John, 71

Jefferson, Thomas, 19, 25, 27, 55, 61, 71-73, 77-81, 83, 84, 100, 119, 327, 331-333; on natural aristocracy, 23, 27-32, 52; on New England, 26; on Patrick Henry, 68, 69; on progress, 25-27; Wirt on, 90-92; on yeomen, 316

John Brown's raid, 329, 338

Johnson, Samuel, 78

The Lives of the Poets, 78

Keats, John, 57

Kemble, Gouverneur, 231, 242

Kemble, Peter, 236

Kennedy, John Pendleton, 151, 154, 165, 206, 308, 320; sketch of, 188-193; on self-improvement, 190; on slavery, 305-306; on Southern bully, 322;

on William Wirt, 71; on women, 164-165

Horse-Shoe Robinson, 318

Rob of the Bowl, 200, 201

Swallow Barn, 149, 164-165, 167, 178-188, 199, 318, 322

Knights of the Golden Circle, 217

Lawrence, Amos, 115

Lawson, James, 268, 285

Lee, Richard Henry, 83

Lee, Robert E., 238

Legaré, Hugh Swinton, as a mugwump, 53-55; 55-57, 59, 60, 63, 235

Lincoln, Abraham, 226, 327; on Border States, 328; 329, 332, 333, 338

Longfellow, Henry Wadsworth, 42, 43

Louis Philippe, quoted, 8, 276

Lowell, James Russell, 42

McDuffie, George, 324

Madison, James, 61, 77, 115, 234

Maistre, Joseph de, 55

Manifest Destiny, 218

Marion, Francis, 114, 281

Marshall, John, 71, 74, 76, 94

Mason, Charles, 332

Melville, Herman, 31, 120, 233

Mercer, Charles Fenton, 59

Miller, Perry, 99

Missouri Compromise, 64

Mitchell, Margaret, 162

Gone With the Wind, 162

Monroe, James, 70, 77, 89

Moore, Thomas, 57

Moultrie, Gen. William, 288

Mugwumps, Southern, 55-65, 78, 82, 204

Myth, democratic, 77

National character, interest in definition of, 19, 20; Webster on need for, 101; *see also* Yankee, Cavalier and *individual listings*

Nationalism, Southern, idea of, 329

Nat Turner insurrection, 301

Natural aristocracy, Adams and Jefferson on, 27-31; Jefferson's view of, 52; Patrick Henry as embodiment of, 83, 87; Wirt's ideal as compared with Jefferson's, 86; *see also* aristocracy, gentility, national character

Natural genius, and Patrick Henry, 85, 86, 87; William Wirt on, 90, 92, 93; Andrew Jackson as, 244-248

North American Review, 20, 70

Northwood, 115

Nullification, 53, 57, 60, 101, 111, 113

Nullifiers, 265, 266

Old Dominion, 150, 182, 206, 213

Old South, 151, 201, 203; image of, 211; 341

Page, Thomas Nelson, 307; quoted, 145; on Southern women, 162, 163; on Southern gentleman, 157, 159

Papashvily, Helen, 167; on *Uncle Tom*, 311

Parker, Theodore, 330

Parochialism, American, in contact with Europe, 50; *see also* provincialism

Parson's Cause, 84

Paulding, James Kirke, 20, 165, 180, 182, 188, 199, 209, 226-259, 279, 318, 320, 334; Cavalier as Roundhead, 254-258; on England, 233, 234; on Jackson, 245-248; on Randolph, 248-249, 252-253; on South, 236-240; on Southern gentleman, 242, 243; on Southern women, 164; on slavery, 303-304; on Westerners, 244-248; on Washington, 249-253

Letters from the South, 237-242

Westward Ho!, 149, 154, 165, 242-248, 318

The Puritan and his Daughter, 254-258

Slavery in the United States, 254-255

Petigru, James Louis, 23, 55, 59, 61, 63, 324

Pinckney, Charles Cotesworth, 45, 114

Pinkney, William, 74

Plantation legend, 208; origins of, 76, 77, 177-188; William Wirt on, 82-83, 91; definition of, 146; *see also* country life, country squire, Southern gentleman, Cavalier, Southern planter

Poe, Edgar Allan, 160, 199, 233, 268

Poinsett, Joel R., 60

Pope, Alexander, 57

Porter, Jane, 69

Scottish Chiefs, 69

Prescott, W. H., 43

Preston, William Campbell, 39, 40, 47, 64

Reminiscences, 41

Princeton College, 41, 59

Pringle, John Julian, 44

Progress, 200, 249; John Adams on, 25-27; Paulding on, 241-242; Thomas Jefferson on, 25-27

Provincialism, 46, 47; Southern, 37, 46, 47; in Paulding, 230-232; in Simms, 297; in nullification crisis, 265; in South Carolina, 261; *see also* parochialism

Randolph, John, 21, 55, 63, 69, 111, 112, 114, 156-158, 245, 248-249; as prototype of Southern Hothead and Hamlet, 159-160; type of Southern gentleman, 252-253; *cf.* Washington, 253-254

Rhett, Robert Barnwell, 55, 65, 86, 264-266, 271, 275, 284

Roundhead, 210, 222; *cf.* Cavalier, 211-216, 254-258

Ruffin, Edmund, 60, 61, 62, 65, 114, 296

Anticipations of the Future, 159, 320

on Southern yeomen, 320; exemplification of Old South idea, 339; attitude toward Yankee North, 331-339; suicide, 339

Rutledge, Edward, 114

Rutledge, John, 45

Sabine, Lorenzo, 280
Savagery, 198
Schiller, Johann Christoph Fried-
rich von, 57
Schlegel, August von, 38
Scotch-Irish, 149, 154, 178, 197,
198, 205, 206, 316, 324; yeoman in fiction, 317-318
Scott, Sir Walter, 38, 69, 105, 115
Secession, 115
Seward, William, 331
Shelley, Percy Bysshe, 57
Silliman, Benjamin, 42
Simms, William Gilmore, 19, 149,
150, 151, 166, 199, 273, 320,
323; sketch of life, 268-270;
on Southern provincialism
and aristocracy, 261, 267; on
revolution in South Carolina,
270; writings on revolution,
271; as Loco-Foco, 273; on
Hunkers, 274, 275; on European upheaval of 1848, 276,
277; on theory of world
democratic movement, 275,
276; disappointment in results of 1848 election, 277,
278; on French Revolution,
279; on industrialism, 279;
on New England and South
Carolina in the Revolution,
280, 281; Revolutionary novels, shift in attitude, 282-297
Katherine Walton, 281, 282,
287
The Partisan, 281, 282, 286, 297
The Sword and the Distaff,
287
Woodcraft, 287

Slavery, 33, 227, 248, 254-255,
335; in fiction, 299-313;
George Tucker on, 302-303;
Paulding on, 303-304; Ken-
nedy on, 305-306; Beverley
Tucker on, 306-307; H. B.
Stowe on, 307-311; in *North-
wood*, 139, 140
Smith, Henry Nash, 150, 316
*Virgin Land: The American
West as Symbol and Myth*,
16
Social structure, in colonial society, 29, 31, 33, 91, 97; and
legendary Yankee, 115-131;
and plantation legend, 131-
141, 146-176, 299-327; Hundley on, 337; Wirt on, 81-89;
see also aristocracy, Cavalier,
Yankee, yeomanry
*South Carolina Exposition and
Protest*, 112
Southern bully, N. B. Tucker on,
324; Kennedy on, 322;
George Tucker on, 322
Southern chivalry, 164, 165, 168,
183-186, 196-197, 201; Cash
on, 168; cause of, 147-148
Southern gentleman, the, 21, 96,
146, 198, 207, 239; types of,
112, 134, 159, 160, 161, 324,
334-335, 336; problem of in
fiction, 323; in Southern fiction, 153-162; Hundley on,
152, 153; Page on, 157;
Paulding on, 242, 243; Randolph on, 156, 157; Simms on,
261, 282-297; N. B. Tucker
on, 320-321; see also aristocracy, Cavalier, gentility, social structure

Southern Literary Messenger, 149, 170, 172, 194; on *Uncle Tom's Cabin,* 308, 312
Southern nationalism, *see* nationalism, Southern
Southern Patriot, 274
Southern planter, legend of, 92; *see also* Southern gentleman, plantation legend
Southern provincialism, *see* provincialism, Southern
Southern Quarterly Review, 205, 278, 280; Simms as editor of, 270
Southern Review, 53
Spectator and Lady's Album, 121
Spotswood, Alexander, 206; fictional image of, 218-222
Stanton, Elizabeth Cady, 166, 167
Stowe, Harriet Beecher, 132, 133, 145, 166, 167, 323; on Yankee, 308-310; quoted on Southern character, 308; and plantation legend, 308-310; on masculine world of business, 309-310; on American family, 309, 312; on Southern family, 164
  Dred, 161, 308, 309, 311
  Uncle Tom's Cabin, 138, 149, 160, 161, 296, 300, 307-311; Southern response to, 307, 311-313
Success, new men, 67, 73, 92; types of, 152; and Wirt, 70-80
Sumter, Thomas, 114

Taney, Roger B., 94
Taylor, John, of Caroline, 69, 316
Taylor, Zachary, 275, 276, 277

Thackeray, William Makepeace, 165
Thoreau, Henry, 108, 279, 330
Thorpe, Thomas B., 315
  The Master's House, quoted, 315
Ticknor, George, 38, 40-43, 47, 49, 50, 51, 53, 68, 69, 129, 235
Tocqueville, Alexis de, 33
Trollope, Mrs. Frances, 19
  Domestic Manners of the Americans, 19
Tucker, George, 154, 165, 308; on Southern bully, 322; on Southern women, 163; on yeoman, 317-318
  The Valley of Shenandoah, 149, 153, 302, 303, 309, 317, 322
Tucker, Nathaniel Beverley, 61, 63, 65, 154, 165, 169, 268, 276, 281, 283, 284, 296, 308, 320; on slavery, 306-307; on Southern bully, 322; on Southern yeoman, 318-320; on women, 174, 175; reliance on Dew, 173
  George Balcombe, 149, 154, 173, 320-321
  The Partisan Leader, 149, 322, 323
Tucker, St. George, 63, 77, 79, 83, 165
Tyler, John, 53

Van Buren, Martin, 94, 235, 278
Virginia and Kentucky Resolutions, 113

Waddell, James, 85

Washington, George, 56, 81, 100, 102-106, 108, 114, 123, 196-197, 245, 318; as transcendent Yankee, 137; as type of Southern gentleman, 249-253; cf. Randolph, 253-254

Weber, Max, 29

Webster, Daniel, 68, 69, 71, 82, 94, 98, 99, 101, 109, 111, 112-115, 123, 124, 126, 129-131, 140, 141, 186, 196, 227, 231, 235, 316; as transcendent Yankee, 110, 119, 120, 137; as Black Dan, 138; on American family, 119; on hero worship, 119; compared with Sarah Hale, 116, 117, 118, 119, 120

Webster, Thomas, 110

Webster-Hayne Debate, 109-115, 316

Weems, Mason Locke, 81, 137

Weld, Theodore, 62

West, the, 21, 210; and South, 316; *see also* yeoman

Westerner, the, Andrew Jackson, type of, 245-246, 248, David Crockett, type of, 246-248

Whig party, 140, 200, 210, 253, 275; Southern, 150; *see also* Webster, Webster-Hayne Debate

Wilde, Richard Henry, 51, 60

Wirt, Laura, 74

Wirt, William, 68, 69, 70, 98, 99, 182, 186, 188, 193, 206, 324; sketch of life, 70, 71; runs for President, 71; compared with Franklin, 71; legend of, 71; estimate of, 72; as Attorney General, 74; on lawyers, 74; on Patrick Henry, 78-89; and mugwumps, 78; on Virginia

society, 91, 92; on natural genius, 90, 92, 93; on civilization, 90-94; compared with Webster on heroes, 119; on *Swallow Barn*, 178-180

Patrick Henry, 76, 81, 82, 89, 90, 91, 178-180

Letters of the British Spy, 73, 75, 76, 77, 85, 90, 178-180

The Old Bachelor, 178-180

Wise, Gov. John A., 331

Women, in Southern fiction, 315; and Southern home, 140, 141; and Southern plantation, 162-165; Dew on, 170, 171, 172; Hundley on, 162, 163; Sarah Grimké on, 168; G. Tucker on, 163; N. B. Tucker on, 174, 175

Woodward, C. Vann, 330

Wordsworth, William, 38, 86

Wright, Fanny, 166

Yale College, 41

Yancey, William Lowndes, 65, 66, 137, 264

Yankee, the, 111, 147, 210, 239, 244, 247, 249, 250, 253-254, 259, 312, 331, 335; and Cavalier, 225; in Revolution, 264; characteristics of, 15, 21, 48; and Puritan, 91; and Protestant ethic, 133; problem of, 95, 96; and yeoman, 195-199; types of: Southern, 152; predatory, 108, 109, 146, 251, 330; emergent, 135, 136, 138, 158, 235; transcendent, 102-110, 112, 213, 246, 250

Yeoman, *see* social structure; cf. Yankee, transcendent, 195-

199; *cf.* Cavalier, Southern, 154, 195, 209, 306, 324; Western, 240, and *individual listings*

"Young America," 273
"Young Carolina," 273, 274, 277, 278
"Young Charleston," 273